14-50
Reduced To
10-90

משנה

ArtScroll Mishnah Series®
A rabbinic commentary to the Six Orders of the Mishnah

Rabbis Nosson Scherman / Meir Zlotowitz

General Editors

the mishnah

ARTSCROLL MISHNAH SERIES / A NEW
TRANSLATION WITH A COMMENTARY **YAD
AVRAHAM** ANTHOLOGIZED FROM TALMUDIC
SOURCES AND CLASSIC COMMENTATORS.

Published by

Mesorah Publications, ltd

ששה סדרי מ**שנה**

FIRST EDITION
First Impression ... January, 1987

Published and Distributed by
MESORAH PUBLICATIONS, Ltd.
1969 Coney Island Avenue
Brooklyn, New York 11223

Distributed in Israel by
MESORAH MAFITZIM / J. GROSSMAN
Rechov Harav Uziel 117
Jerusalem, Israel

Distributed in Europe by
J. LEHMANN HEBREW BOOKSELLERS
20 Cambridge Terrace
Gateshead
TYNE AND WEAR
England NE8 1RP

THE ARTSCROLL MISHNAH SERIES®
SEDER NEZIKIN Vol. I(b): *BAVA METZIA*
© *Copyright 1987*
by MESORAH PUBLICATIONS, Ltd.
1969 Coney Island Avenue / Brooklyn, N.Y. 11223 / (718) 339-1700

ISBN
0-89906-291-1 (hard cover)
0-89906-292-X (paperback)

Typography by CompuScribe at ArtScroll Studios, Ltd.
1969 Coney Island Avenue / Brooklyn, N.Y. 11223 / (718) 339-1700

Printed in the United States of America by Moriah Offset
Bound at Sefercraft, Brooklyn, NY

◆§ Seder Nezikin Vol. I(b):
מסכת בבא מציעא
Tractate Bava Metzia

Translation and anthologized commentary by
Rabbi Avrohom Yoseif Rosenberg

Edited by:
Rabbi Tzvi Zev Arem

The Publishers are grateful to
TORAH UMESORAH
and
YAD AVRAHAM INSTITUTE
for their efforts in the publication of the
ARTSCROLL MISHNAH SERIES

הסכמה

Rabbi Moshe Feinstein
455 F. D. R. Drive
New York, N. Y. 10002

משה פיינשטיין
ר"מ תפארת ירושלים

בע"ה

[מכתב הסכמה בכתב יד]

משה פיינשטיין

בע"ה

הנני מברך בזה את ידידי הרב הנכבד מהר"ר מאיר יעקב בן ידידי הרב הגאון ר' אהרן שליט"א זלאטאוויץ ואת ידידי הרב הנכבד מהר"ר נתן שערמאן שליט"א שעמדו בראש הנהלת **חברת ארטסקרול**, אשר הוציאו כבר הרבה חבורים חשובים בשפת אנגלית לזכות את הרבים, וגם הוציאו על משניות כרך אחד ועכשיו מוציאים לאור עוד כרך שני, ויש בו לקוטים מספרי רבותינו מפרשי משניות על כל משנה ומשנה, מלוקטים בטוב טעם ע"י תלמידי חכמים חשובים ומומחים לרבים, והוא לתועלת גדול להרבה אינשי ממדינה זו שלא התרגלו מילדותם במשניות, וגם יש הרבה שבעזהשי"ת התקרבו לתורה ויראת שמים כשכבר נתגדלו ורוצים ללמוד, שיוכלו ללמוד משניות בנקל בשפה המורגלת להם, שלכן הם ממזכי הרבים שזכותם גדול ואני מברככם שיצליחם השי"ת בחבור זה ובעוד כרכים.

וגם אני מברך בזה את ידידי הרב הנכבד מאד עסקן ותומך גדול לתורה ולתעודה מוהר"ר אלעזר גליק שליט"א אשר עזר הרבה להדפסת משניות אלו לזכר נשמת בנו המנוח החשוב מאד מר **אברהם יוסף** ז"ל ונקרא הפירוש **יד אברהם** על שמו והוא זכות גדול לעילוי נשמתו בלמוד הרבים. יהי זכרו ברוך. וע"ז באתי על החתום בער"ח אלול תש"מ.

משה פיינשטיין

מכתב ברכה

יעקב קמנצקי

RABBI J. KAMENECKI
38 SADDLE RIVER ROAD
MONSEY, NEW YORK 10952

בע"ה

יום ה' ערב חג השבועות תשל"ס, פה מאנסי.

כבוד הרבני איש החסד שוע ונדיב מוקיר רבנן מר אלעזר נ"י גליק
שלו' וברכת כל טוב.

מה מאד שמחתי בהודעי כי כבודו רכש לעצמו הזכות שייקרא ע"ש
בנו המנוח הפירוש מבואר על כל ששת סדרי משנה ע"י "ארטסקראל"
והנה חברה זו יצאה לה מוניטין בפירושה על תנ"ך, והבה נקוה שכשם
שהצליחה בתורה שבכתב כן תצליח בתורה שבע"פ. ובהיות שאותיות
"משנה" הן כאותיות "נשמה" לפיכך טוב עשה בכוונתו לעשות זאת לעילוי
נשמת בנו המנוח אברהם יוסף ע"ה, ומאד מתאים השם "יד אברהם" לזה
הפירוש, כדמצינו במקרא (ש"ב י"ח) כי אמר אין לי בן בעבור הזכיר
שמי וגו'. ואין לך דבר גדול מזה להפיץ ידיעת תורה שבע"פ בקרב
אחינו שאינם רגילים בלשון הקדש. וד' הטוב יהי' בעזרו ויוכל לברך
על המוגמר. וירוה רוב נחת מכל אשר אתו כנפש מברכו.

יעקב קמנצקי

[ix]   *Approbation*/מכתב ברכה

מכתב ברכה

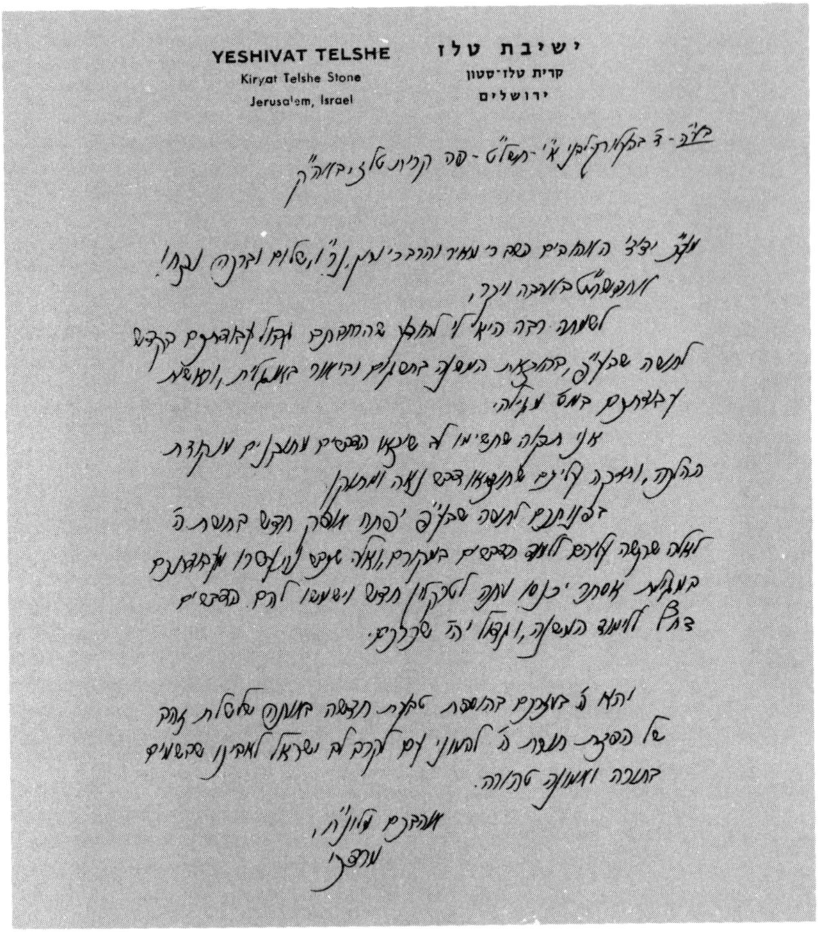

ישיבת טלז
קרית טלז-סטון
ירושלים

YESHIVAT TELSHE
Kiryat Telshe Stone
Jerusalem, Israel

[כתב יד — handwritten text]

בע״ה — ד׳ בהעלותך — לבני א״י, תשל״ט — פה קרית טלז, באה״ק

מע״כ ידידי האהובים הרב ר׳ מאיר והרב ר׳ נתן, נר״ו, שלום וברכה נצח!

אחדשה״ט באהבה ויקר,

לשמחה רבה היא לי להודע שהרחבתם גדול עבודתכם בקודש לתורה שבע״פ, בהוצאת המשנה בתרגום וביאור באנגלית, וראשית עבודתכם במס׳ מגילה.

אני תקוה שתשימו לב שיצאו הדברים מתוקנים מנקודת ההלכה, וחזקה עליכם שתוציאו דבר נאה ומתוקן.

בפנותכם לתורה שבע״פ יפתח אופק חדש בתורת ה׳ לאלה שקשה עליהם ללמוד הדברים במקורם, ואלה שכבר נתעשרו מעבודתכם במגילת אסתר יכנסו עתה לטרקלין חדש וישמשו להם הדברים דחף ללימוד המשנה, וגדול יהי׳ שכרכם.

יהא ה׳ בעזרכם בהוספת טבעת חדשה באותה שלשלת זהב של הפצת תורת ה׳ להמוני עם לקרב לב ישראל לאבינו שבשמים בתורה ואמונה טהורה.

אוהבכם מלונ״ח,
מרדכי

מכתב ברכה

RABBI SHNEUR KOTLER   בס״ה   שניאור קוטלר
BETH MEDRASH GOVOHA   בית מדרש גבוה׳
LAKEWOOD, N. J.   לייקוואוד, נ. דז.

בשורת התרחבות עבודתם הגדולה של סגל חבורת ,,ארטסקרול״, המעתיקים ומפרשים, לתחומי התושבע״פ, לשים אלה המשפטים לפני הציבור ערוך ומוכן לאכול לפני האדם [ל׳ רש״י], ולשימה בפיהם — לפתוח אוצרות בשנות בצורת ולהשמיעם בכל לשון שהם שומעים — מבשרת צבא רב לתורה ולימודה [ע׳ תהלים ס״ח י״ב בתרגום יונתן], והיא מאותות ההתעוררות ללימוד התורה, וזאת התעודה על התנוצצות קיום ההבטחה ,,כי לא תשכח מפי זרעו״. אשרי הזוכים להיות בין שלוחי ההשגחה לקיומה וביצועה.

יה״ר כי תצליח מלאכת שמים בידם, ויזכו ללמוד וללמד ולשמור מסורת הקבלה כי בהרקת המים החיים מכלי אל כלי תשתמר חיותם, יעמוד טעמם בם וריחם לא נמר. [וע' משאחז״ל בכ״מ ושמרתם זו משנה — וע׳ חי׳ מרן רי״ז הלוי עה״ת בפ׳ ואתחנן] תהי׳ משנתם שלמה וברורה, ישמחו בעוזרדם חברים ותלמידים, ,,ישוטטו רבים ותרבה הדעת״, עד יקוים ,,אז אהפוך אל העמים שפה ברורה וגו׳ [צפני׳ ג׳ ט, עי׳ פי׳ אבן עזרא ומצודת דוד שם].

ונזכה כולנו לראות בהתכנסות הגליות בזכות המשניות כל׳ חז״ל עפ״י הכתוב ,,גם כי יתנו בגוים עתה אקבצם״, בגאולה השלמה בב״א.

הכו״ח לכבוד התורה, יום ו׳ עש״ק לס׳ ,,ויוצא פרח ויצץ ציץ ויגמל שקדים״, ד׳ תמוז התשל״ט

יוסף חיים שניאור קוטלר
בלאאמו״ר הגר״א זצוק״ל

מכתב ברכה

בס"ד
לכבוד ידידי וידיד ישיבתנו, מהראשונים לכל דבר שבקדושה
הרבני הנגיד המפורסם ר' אליעזר הכהן גליק נ"י
אחדש"ה באהבה,

בשורה טובה שמעתי שכב' מצא את המקום המתאים לעשות יד ושם להנציח זכרו של **בנו אברהם יוסף ע"ה** שנקטף בעודו באיביו. "ונתתי להם בביתי ובחומתי יד ושם". אין לו להקב"ה אלא ד' אמות של הלכה בלבד. א"כ זהו בית ד' לימוד תורה שבע"פ וזהו המקום לעשות יד ושם לנשמת בנו ע"ה.

נר ד' נשמת אדם אמר הקב"ה נרי בידך ונרך בידי. נר מצוה ותורה אור, תורה זהו הנר של הקב"ה וכשמשמרים נר של הקב"ה שעל ידי הפירוש, "יד אברהם" בשפה הלעוזית יתרבה וויתפסה לימוד ושקיעת התורה בבתי ישראל. ד' ישמור נשמת אדם.

בנו אברהם יוסף ע"ה נתברך בהמדה שבו נכללות כל המדות, לב טוב והיה אהוב לחבריו. בלמדו בישיבתנו היה לו הרצון לעלות במעלות התורה וכשעלה לארצנו הקדושה היתה מבוקשו להמשיך בלמודיו. ביקוש זה ימצא מלואו על ידי הרבים המבקשים דרך ד', שהפירוש "יד אברהם" הוא מפתח להם לים התלמוד.

התורה נקראת ,,אש דת'' ונמשלה לאש יש לה הכח לפעפע ברזל לפצוע כוחות האדם, הניצוץ שהאיר ע רבנו הרב שרגא פייוועל מנדלוויץ זצ"ל שמרת עליו, ועשה חיל. עכשיו אתה מסיע להאיר נצוצות בנשמות בני ישראל שיעשה חיל ויהא לאור גדול.

תקותי עזה שכל התלמידי חכמים שנדבה רוחם להוציא לפועל מלאכה ענקית זו לפרש המשניות כולה, יצא עבודם ברוח פאר והדר וויכוונו לאמיתת של תורה ויתקדש שם שמים ויתרבה נחת רוח מצאצאיו.

הכו"ח לכבוד התורה ותומכיה עש"ק במדבר תשל"ט

אלי' שווי

דוד קאהן   ביהמ"ד גבול יעבץ   ברוקלין, נוא יארק

בס"ד   כ"ה למטמונים תשל"ט

כבוד רחימא דנפשאי, עושה ומעשה
ר' אלעזר הכהן גליק נטריה רחמנא ופרקיה

שמוע שמעתי שכבר תקעת כפיך לתמוך במפעל האדיר של חברת ארטסקרול — הידוע בכל קצווי תבל ע"י עבודתה הכבירה בהפצת תורה — לתרגם ולבאר ששה סדרי משנה באנגלית. כוונתך להנציח זכר בנך הנחמד אברהם יוסף ז"ל שנקטף באבו בזמן שעלה לארץ הקודש בתקופת התרוממות הנפש ושאיפה לקדושה, ולמטרה זו יכונה הפירוש בשם, "יד אברהם"; וגם האיר ה' רוחך לגרום לנשמתו הטהורה שעי"ז יתרבה לימוד התורה שניתנה בשבעים בשבעים לשון, על ידי כלי מפואר זה.

מכיוון שהנני מכיר היטב שני הצדדים, אוכל לומר לדבק טוב, והנני תקוה שיצליח המפעל הלזה לתת יד ושם וזכות לנשמת אברהם יוסף ז"ל. חזקה על חברת ארטסקרול שתוציא דבר נאה מתוקן ומתקבל מתחת ידה להגדיל תורה ולהאדירה.

והנני מברך אותך שתמצא נחם לנפשך, שהאבא זוכה לברא, ותשבע נחת — אתה עם רעיתך תחיה — מכל צאצאיכם היקרים אכי"ר

ידידך עז
דוד קאהן

Preface

אָמַר ר׳ יוֹחָנָן: לֹא כָּרַת הקב״ה בְּרִית עִם יִשְׂרָאֵל אֶלָּא עַל־תּוֹרָה שֶׁבְּעַל
פֶּה שֶׁנֶּאֱמַר: ,,כִּי עַל־פִּי הַדְּבָרִים הָאֵלֶּה כָּרַתִּי אִתְּךָ בְּרִית ...״
R' Yochanan said: The Holy One, Blessed is He, sealed a
covenant with Israel only because of the Oral Torah, as it is
said [Exodus 34:27]: For according to these words have I
sealed a covenant with you ... (Gittin 60b).

With gratitude to Hashem Yisborach we present the Jewish public
with Bava Metzia, the second tractate of Seder Nezikin. The
ArtScroll Mishnah Series now includes all of Moed and Nashim,
portions of Zeraim and Nezikin, and work is in progress on Kodashim
and Taharos. All of this is thanks to the vision and commitment of MR.
AND MRS. LOUIS GLICK. The concept of a complete Mishnah series with a
serious, comprehensive English commentary was once only a glimmer in
their eyes; now it is on the road to completion. In their quiet, self-
effacing way, the Glicks have been a major force for the propagation of
Torah knowledge and the enhancement of Jewish life for a generation.
The commentary to the mishnayos bears the name YAD AVRAHAM, in
memory of their son AVRAHAM YOSEF GLICK ה״ע. An appreciation of the
niftar will appear in Tractate Berachos. May this dissemination of the
Mishnah in his memory be a source of merit for his soul. תנצב״ה.

By dedicating the ArtScroll Mishnah Series, the Glicks have added a
new dimension to their tradition of service. The many study groups in
synagogues, schools and offices throughout the English-speaking world
are the most eloquent testimony to the fact that thousands of people
thirst for Torah learning presented in a challenging, comprehensive, and
comprehensible manner.

We are proud and grateful that such venerable luminaries as MARAN
HAGAON HARAV YAAKOV KAMINETZKI זצ״ל and להבל״ח MARAN HAGAON
HARAV MORDECHAI GIFTER שליט״א have declared that this series should
be translated into Hebrew. Boruch Hashem, it has stimulated readers to
echo the words of King David: גַּל־עֵינַי וְאַבִּיטָה נִפְלָאוֹת מִתּוֹרָתֶךָ, Uncover
my eyes that I may see wonders of Your Torah (Psalms 119:18).

May we inject two words of caution:

First, although the Mishnah, by definition, is a compendium of laws,
the final halachah does not necessarily follow the Mishnah. The
development of halachah proceeds through the Gemara, commentators,
codifiers, responsa, and the acknowledged poskim. Even when our

commentary cites the Shulchan Aruch, the intention is to sharpen the reader's understanding of the Mishnah, but not to be a basis for actual practice. In short, this work is meant as a first step in the study of our recorded Oral Law — no more.

Second, as we have stressed in our other books, the ArtScroll commentary is not meant as a substitute for the study of the sources. While this commentary, like others in the various series, will be immensely useful even to accomplished scholars and will often bring to light ideas and sources they may have overlooked, we strongly urge those who can, to study the classic seforim in the original. It has been said that every droplet of ink coming from Rashi's pen is worthy of seven days' contemplation. Despite the exceptional caliber of our authors, none of us pretends to replace the study of the greatest minds in Jewish history.

The author of this volume, RABBI AVROHOM YOSEIF ROSENBERG, is familiar to ArtScroll Mishnah readers; he has written several earlier volumes including the very first in the Series. His manuscript was edited by RABBI TZVI ZEV AREM, whose work is well known from earlier volumes of the Mishnah Series. On several chapters, he was assisted by RABBI YEHEZKEL DANZIGER.

We are also grateful to the staff of Mesorah Publications: RABBI HERSH GOLDWURM, whose encyclopedic knowledge is always available; REB ELI KROEN whose very fine graphics production of this volume, carries on the tradition of REB SHEAH BRANDER who remains a leader in bringing beauty of presentation to Torah literature; RABBI AVIE GOLD, SHIMON GOLDING, YOSEIF TIMINSKY, YEHUDAH NEUGARTEN, LEA FREIER, MRS. ESTHER FEIERSTEIN, MRS. SIMIE KORN, MRS. FAIGIE WEINBAUM, MRS. JUDI DICK, ESTIE ZLOTOWITZ, and MENUCHAH MARCUS.

Finally, our gratitude goes to RABBI DAVID FEINSTEIN א״טילש and RABBI DAVID COHEN א״טילש, whose concern, interest, and guidance throughout the history of the ArtScroll Series have been essential to its success.

Rabbi Nosson Scherman / Rabbi Meir Zlotowitz

י״א טבת תשמ״ז / January 12, 1987
Brooklyn, New York

מסכת בבא מציעא ‎

Tractate Bava Metzia

General Introduction to Bava Metzia

◆§ The Tractate

The first tractate of *Seder Nezikin* is the tractate *Nezikin*, which is divided into three parts: *Bava Kamma* (the first gate), *Bava Metzia* (the middle gate), and *Bava Basra* (the last gate). [It was a common practice among classical authors to divide their work into sections called 'gates'; see e.g., *Shaarei Teshuvah, Chovos Halevavos*]. The term 'gate' is certainly a most appropriate description of the Mishnah in general, because it is a gateway to the understanding of the laws of the Torah *(Tos. Yom Tov,* Introduction to *Seder Nezikin).*

In reckoning the number of tractates comprising the Mishnah, some count these three *Bavos* as three tractates; others, as one. *Ri Migash* and *Ritva* consider the entire *Seder Nezikin* as one long tractate (see first *Tosafos* to *Bava Basra; Yad Malachi,* p. 80).

Together these tractates define the bulk of the Torah's civil law — damages, litigations, personal liabilities and responsibilities, and property rights and transactions. *Bava Metzia* deals primarily with laws relating to the finding of lost items, sales, rentals, deposits, and other monetary matters.

In connection with these topics, there are two concepts which underlie many of the mishnah's rulings. These are: the concept of קִנְיָן [*kinyan*], *a formal act of acquisition*, and the judicial principle of הַמּוֹצִיא מֵחֲבֵרוֹ עָלָיו הָרְאָיָה, *The burden of proof lies upon the one who seeks to exact something from the other.*

◆§ קִנְיָן [kinyan] — Act of Acquisition

Torah law stipulates that a transfer of property from one owner to another can be effected only through a *kinyan*. Mere agreement — whether written or oral — and in some instances even payment, are insufficient to effect a transfer. This can only be accomplished through one of these legally defined formal acts. In the absence of such an act, the property does not change hands, the agreement is not binding, and either party can renege. This applies whether the transfer is a sale or a gift. Similarly, property and monetary agreements of any kind (e.g., easements, waivers) are finalized only with an appropriate *kinyan*. The *kinyan* is performed by the person acquiring the property, at the behest of the one giving it up.

Different types of acts are mandated for different types of property. For example, real estate is acquired through כֶּסֶף, *payment;* שְׁטָר, (handing over) *a bill of sale;* and חֲזָקָה [*chazakah*], *an act of possession* (see *Kiddushin* 1:5 and *ArtScroll* commentary there). Chattel, on the other hand, cannot be acquired through any of these methods — even payment — but only through one of several acts which at least symbolically indicate taking physical possession of the object being acquired. These are: הַגְבָּהָה [hagbahah], lifting the object being acquired; מְשִׁיכָה [meshichah], drawing or pulling it; and מְסִירָה [mesirah], grasping hold of it (Kiddushin 1:4,5; see ArtScroll commentary there). Hagbahah may be used in any situation in which it is practical. Meshichah and mesirah are valid as methods of acquisition only if the object is too heavy or unwieldly to be lifted readily.

The operative theory for the act of meshichah is that the new owner draws the object into his sphere by pulling it into an area which either belongs to him or which he has the right to use. For this reason, in order for an article to be acquired by meshichah, the act must take place in a property which is at least partially owned by the buyer or in a simta — a recess off the side of a public thoroughfare in which people do not generally walk but in which they may put down their objects. If the article is in a public thoroughfare or the property of the seller, where the buyer's pulling the object does not indicate ownership, meshichah is not valid unless he pulls it completely out of that area and into his property or a simta (see commentary to Kiddushin 1:4).

In addition to the direct acts of acquisition described above, chattel may be formally acquired through real property in two ways. The first is simply by being in the receiver's land or utensil at the time of transaction. This is known as קִנְיַן חָצֵר, lit., acquisition by courtyard. The second way is by the mechanism of אַגַב, agav [lit., along with] — the rule that if a transaction involves both chattel and real property, formal acquisition of the land by any method appropriate to it brings with it formal acquisition of the chattel as well.

ᵛᵉ§ ... הַמוֹצִיא מֵחֲבֵרוֹ — The Burden of Proof ...

A basic principle of Torah law regarding monetary litigations is הַמוֹצִיא מֵחֲבֵרוֹ עָלָיו הָרְאָיָה, the burden of proof lies upon the one who seeks to exact something from the other (Bava Kamma 3:11). That is, if one person is in possession of property and another claims it as his, the court assumes that it belongs to the one presently in possession of it, and it is the claimant's responsibility to prove otherwise. Though the holder's possession of the property does not prove his ownership of it, it establishes a presumption of ownership which the claimant must refute.[1] [The modern-day equivalent of this is the dictum, 'Possession is nine-tenths of the law.']

---

1. Physical possession — holding the object in question on one's person or in one's property — establishes a presumption of ownership only in the case of chattel. The law concerning real property, however, is different. Here simple presence in a field or house is not sufficient, since it is impossible to prevent people from ever entering one's property. Rather, presumption of ownership is assigned to the last person known to have owned the property (מָרָא קַמָּא). For an occupant to supersede the last known owner and achieve presumptive ownership [thereby removing the necessity for him to prove that the land is his], he must occupy the property for three consecutive years. This rule is discussed at length in Bava Basra, chapter 3.

As was just explained, the Torah requires a claimant seeking to collect something from someone to prove his claim in order to collect. Therefore, if he supplies no proof, the defendant need only deny it to exempt himself from paying.[1]

This is the general rule. However, there are instances in which the Torah requires the defendant to support his denial with an oath. The two instances of oaths discussed in this tractate are: שְׁבוּעַת הַשּׁוֹמְרִים, *the oath of the shomerim* (guardians), and שְׁבוּעַת מוֹדֶה בְּמִקְצָת, *the oath of one who admits to part of a claim*.

A *shomer* (guardian) is one who takes upon himself to safeguard someone else's property. There are four classes of *shomerim* and they have varying degrees of liability for the damage or loss of any property entrusted to them for safekeeping. These will be discussed at length in the preface to chapter 3 and throughout that chapter. However, there is one feature that all share, viz., that if the *shomer* should claim that the article entrusted to him was lost due to some cause for which he is *not* liable, he must swear a Biblical oath to that effect in order to exempt himself. If he refuses, he must pay for the article even though the owner of the article has offered no proof to the contrary. For example, a שׁוֹמֵר חִנָּם, *unpaid shomer*, is liable only if the article entrusted to him was lost through his negligence, but not if it was lost or stolen through no fault of his (see preface to ch. 3). Should the *shomer* claim that the article was in fact stolen and he was not at fault, he must swear a Biblical oath — the oath of the *shomerim* — that this is indeed what happened. If he refuses to do so, he must pay for the lost article despite the fact that the owner offers no evidence of the *shomer's* negligence.

The second instance of oath with which this tractate frequently deals is the *oath of one who admits to part of a claim*. Although one who denies a claim totally is exempt from paying unless the claimant can prove otherwise, the Torah decrees that if he admits owing *part* of the claim, he is required to swear a Biblical oath that he does not also owe the remainder of the claim which he denies. For example, if Reuven claims that Shimon owes him one hundred *zuz* and Shimon admits owing fifty but denies owing the other fifty, Shimon must swear a Biblical oath that he does not owe the fifty *zuz* he denies. If he refuses, he must pay all one hundred *zuz*. The *Gemara* (3a) sees the basis for this Torah law to be the natural reluctance of a person who owes someone else money, to deny entirely the other's claim, even

---

1. If the defendant should claim that he *does not know* if he is liable or not, there is a dispute between *Amoraim* whether the claimant's definite claim is sufficient to exact payment from the uncertain defendant. This will be discussed in the commentary to mishnah 8:2. See also comm. to ArtScroll *Bava Kamma* 10:7. All opinions agree, however, that if it is clear that the money was once owed and the uncertainty is only whether it has already been repaid, the defendant's uncertainty is an insufficient response to the claimant's definite claim, and he must therefore pay (*Bava Kamma* 10:7).

though he cannot at the moment meet his obligation. Since the other did him a favor by lending him money or extending him credit, it would be the height of ingratitude for him to deny the claim. In reality, therefore, he would like to admit the full amount, but, since he feels that he cannot pay at the moment, he eases his conscience by admitting part of the claim and denying the rest — with the intention of repaying that part, too, when he can afford it. To force him to admit the truth, if he is indeed lying, the Torah obligated him to swear that he does not owe the part of the claim he denies.

⋅§ Summary of Chapters

Chapter 1 (שְׁנַיִם אוֹחֲזִין) discusses laws pertaining to the finding of lost items.

Chapter 2 (אֵלּוּ מְצִיאוֹת) continues the discussion of laws concerning lost articles, and also touches upon the obligation of helping to load and unload another person's animal.

Chapter 3 (הַמַּפְקִיד) deals with the laws regarding a פִּקָּדוֹן, *deposit,* and the four types of שׁוֹמְרִים, *shomerim* (guardians).

Chapter 4 (הַזָּהָב) discusses transactions of buying and selling, concentrating mainly on the laws of אוֹנָאָה, *fraud.*

Chapter 5 (אֵיזֶהוּ נֶשֶׁךְ) deals with the prohibition of taking and giving interest on loans or as part of business transactions.

Chapter 6 (הַשּׂוֹכֵר אֶת־הָאֻמָּנִין) is devoted primarily to the laws of hiring craftsmen, laborers, and animals. It also includes several mishnayos concerning *shomerim.*

Chapter 7 (הַשּׂוֹכֵר אֶת־הַפּוֹעֲלִים) deals with the obligation of an employer to his workers and vice versa, and continues with the laws of *shomerim.*

Chapter 8 (הַשּׁוֹאֵל) discusses laws pertaining to loans, sales, and rentals of houses and other things.

Chapter 9 (הַמְקַבֵּל) treats the obligation of sharecroppers and tenant farmers, the requirement to pay workers on time, and the prohibition of entering a debtor's house to take security.

Chapter 10 (הַבַּיִת וְהָעֲלִיָּה) deals with the respective rights and obligations of the holders of a two-story house; worker's wages; the temporary use of the public domain in conjunction with the needs of a private domain; and the ownership of vegetation growing between two gardens, one above the other.

[א] **שְׁנַיִם** אוֹחֲזִין בְּטַלִּית, זֶה אוֹמֵר: "אֲנִי
מְצָאתִיהָ," וְזֶה אוֹמֵר: "אֲנִי
מְצָאתִיהָ," זֶה אוֹמֵר: "כֻּלָּהּ שֶׁלִּי," וְזֶה אוֹמֵר:
"כֻּלָּהּ שֶׁלִּי" — זֶה יִשָּׁבַע שֶׁאֵין לוֹ בָהּ פָּחוֹת
מֵחֶצְיָהּ, וְזֶה יִשָּׁבַע שֶׁאֵין לוֹ בָהּ פָּחוֹת מֵחֶצְיָהּ,
וְיַחֲלֹקוּ.

יד אברהם

Chapter One

1.

שְׁנַיִם אוֹחֲזִין בְּטַלִּית, — [If] two [persons]
are holding a cloak,

[They appear in court grasping a
cloak.]

The mishnah's law applies equally to
any item which one can hold by the
edges without taking any substantial
amount in his hands. In the mishnah's
example, the two litigants are holding
on to the cloak by its fringes (*Tif. Yis.*
from *Gem.* 7a).

[The significance of how the item is
being held is discussed at length below.]

Should one person hold the item
itself, and the other is [wrestling with
him (*Rambam, Hil. To'en Venitan* 9:11)
and] clinging to the edge of it, the item is
considered as being in the former's
possession, and if the latter wishes to
exact it from him, he must bring proof
that it is his, as dictated by the principle
of ... הַמּוֹצִיא מֵחֲבֵרוֹ, *the burden of proof
... [see General Introduction] (Gem.* 6a).

זֶה אוֹמֵר: "אֲנִי מְצָאתִיהָ," וְזֶה אוֹמֵר: "אֲנִי
מְצָאתִיהָ," — [and] one says: 'I found it,'
and the other says: 'I found it,'

Each one claims that he picked up the
item first and only then did the other
person grasp it as well (*Rashi* 2b; *Tos.*
3a). It is possible that both of them
picked up the item simultaneously, and
yet each one truly believes that he was
the first to do so (*Gem.* 2b). It is
necessary for the *Gemara* to tell us this,
for in a case in which it is impossible
that both of them believe they are telling

the truth — such as one in which each
one claims that a cloak is his, and that he
had woven it himself — the halachah
would be different, as discussed below.

Obviously, the mishnah is dealing
with one of the following three cases, in
which the item need not be returned to
its original owner, and therefore, the
one who picks it up first acquires it
[through הַגְבָּהָה, *lifting,* a legal means of
acquisition (see General Introduction)]:

(1) The object was known to be
ownerless.

(2) It was found in a city inhabited
mostly by gentiles, and consequently, is
assumed to have been lost by one of
them. The Torah (*Deut.* 22:3) requires
only the return of אֲבֵדַת אָחִיךָ, *a lost
article belonging to your brother,* not
one belonging to a gentile (*Bava Kamma*
113b). *Tosafos* (24a, s.v. כי) add that
even if it is certain that the item found
in such a city had been lost by a Jew, the
finder may return it, because the owner
has surely despaired of recovering the
item, expecting that it would be found
by either a gentile or a Jew who would
not announce it, since he presumes that
it was lost by a gentile.

(3) It was found in a public place; we
therefore assume that its owner
despaired of retrieving it.

In any other instance, the one who
found the item would be obligated to
announce his find so that its owner
should claim it, as discussed in the next
chapter (*Meiri*).

1.

[I**f] two [persons] are holding a cloak, [and] one says: 'I found it,' and the other says: 'I found it,' [or] one says: 'It is all mine,' and the other says: 'It is all mine' — this one must swear that he owns no less of it than half, and that one must swear that he owns no less of it than half, and they divide [it].**

YAD AVRAHAM

זֶה אוֹמֵר: „בֻּלָּהּ שֶׁלִּי," וְזֶה אוֹמֵר: „בֻּלָּהּ שֶׁלִּי" — — [or] one says: 'It is all mine,' and the other says: 'It is all mine' —

In this instance, the item in question had been purchased from a certain person who had accepted money for it from both litigants — one to whom he had intended to sell the article, and the other who threw the money for it to him. The seller does not know to whom he had intended to sell the item (*Gem.* 2b). If he does know, he would be considered a witness corroborating that person's claim, in which case [the court would award that person his share without exacting an oath from him, because just as one witness imposes an oath on the party against whom he testifies, so can he exempt the one whose testimony he corroborates (*Tos.* ad loc.), while] the other litigant would have to swear a Biblically ordained oath refuting the witness' testimony in order to receive his share (*Rav; Tos.*).[1]

Rashi, however, maintains that since the article is out of the seller's hands, even if he claims that he knows to whom he intended to sell it, he is not believed. Apparently, *Rashi* does not subscribe to *Tosafos'* view that a litigant whose testimony is supported by one witness is exempt from taking an oath. *Rif* agrees with *Rashi* in this regard, but qualifies the mishnah as dealing with a case in which the seller is still in possession of the article. Therefore, he is believed in stating to whom he had intended to sell it (*Rosh*).

This segment of the mishnah could not possibly mean that each one claimed he had woven the garment himself, since, in that case, the halachah would be different, although what it would be

is a subject of controversy among the authorities. According to *Tosafos* (2b, s.v. אי), since one of them knows that he is lying, it is obvious that the court would require them to take an oath, confident that the liar will retract his claim rather than commit perjury, as explained below. According to *Rashi* (2a, s.v. במקח), the garment would be put away until Elijah the Prophet comes to herald the Messiah, at which time he will reveal the identity of the rightful owner.

In the case that they both claim they bought it, however, it is possible that each one truly believes that the seller intended to sell it to him, similar to the mishnah's first case, in which each litigant actually believes that he picked up the item first, as explained above (*Rashi; Tos.; Tif. Yis.*).

זֶה יִשָּׁבַע שֶׁאֵין לוֹ בָה פָּחוֹת מֵחֶצְיָה, וְזֶה יִשָּׁבַע שֶׁאֵין לוֹ בָה פָּחוֹת מֵחֶצְיָה, וְיַחֲלֹקוּ. — *this one must swear that he owns no less of it than half, and that one must swear that he owns no less of it than half, and they divide [it].*

[Each of the litigants must take an oath that at least half of the item in question is rightfully his.]

He does not swear that the entire item is his, although that is his claim, since he will nevertheless not be awarded the entire item, and it would be disgraceful for the court to impose an oath upon a litigant to the effect that something is entirely his, and then give only half of it to him. He does not swear that half the item is his, since that would imply that

1. [In order for one of the litigants to win possession of the entire garment, he would need the testimony of *two* valid witnesses, as is usually the rule in Jewish law (see *Deuteronomy* 19:15).]

only half is his — a contradiction to his claim. Rather, he swears that not less than half of the item is his, implying that he is actually claiming the entire item, but is swearing regarding only half of it, because the court does not believe him with regard to the other half (*Rav* from *Gem.* 5b, *Rashi* ad loc.).

According to the apparent meaning of the *Gemara* (ibid.), the formula of the oath required by the mishnah of each litigant contains two parts: (1) he has a share in the item; (2) his share is not less than half the item. Indeed, *Ran*, cited by *Nimmukei Yosef*, rules that the first part of the formula is necessary lest the litigant mean, 'My share is not less than half — it is nothing!'; i.e., he has no share in it. *Rambam (Hil. To'en Venitan* 9:7) and *Rif*, however, maintain that the second half of the formula is sufficient, as implied by the mishnah. *Beis Yosef* (138) explains that by declaring that one's share in the item is not less than half, it is understood that he does have some share in the article (*Tos. Yom Tov*).

The Rabbis innovated this oath lest a person, upon seeing another acquiring a lost item by picking it up, seize the item and claim that he picked it up first (*Rav* from *Gem.* 5b). Although he is suspected of theft, he is not suspected of perjury (*Gem.* ibid.). *Tosafos* explain that this is because of the gravity of the latter sin, as the Rabbis taught (*Shevuos* 39a): The entire world shook when God declared at Sinai לֹא תִשָּׂא, *You shall not take the Name of HASHEM, your God, in a vain oath* (*Tos. Yom Tov*).

The *Gemara* (2b) explains that it was necessary for the mishnah to state this law both in regard to found articles and in regard to buying and selling, since we would not have been able to derive it from one case to the other. Had the *Tanna* taught us the ruling only with regard to finding a lost article, we would

think that the oath was imposed in that case, because the litigant who is lying may justify his grabbing of the article by reasoning that the one who found the item suffers no real loss if someone else grabs hold of it and is awarded half of it by the court, since he neither paid nor worked for it. To discourage such actions, the Rabbis imposed an oath on both litigants in this case. In the case of buying and selling, however, a lying litigant could not justify his act by reasoning that the true buyer suffers no real loss; it is obvious that the latter has a genuine need for the item because, otherwise, he would not have sought to purchase it. Rather, each litigant in this case actually believes that the seller intended to sell it to him, and we would therefore think that imposing an oath would be unnecessary. Consequently, the *Tanna* states specifically that the ruling applies to cases of buying and selling as well.

On the other hand, should he have stated the ruling only with regard to buying and selling, we may think that the oath is imposed in that case because the one who forced the money on the seller may justify his action by reasoning that he, too, is paying for an article that he needs, and the other person can always go elsewhere to purchase another one like it. In the case of the found article, however, the lying litigant cannot reason that the other person can go elsewhere to find another such item. Rather, the case must be that each litigant truly believes that he found the article before the other person. It would therefore seem that requiring them to swear would not accomplish anything. Consequently, the *Tanna* states that the oath applies to the case of finding an article as well (*Rav; Tos. Yom Tov* from *Gem.*; *Rashi; Tos.* 2b).

[As explained above] the *Gemara* (7a) qualifies the mishnah as referring to a case in which each of the litigants is holding the item by its fringes at one end of it. Should they be holding the item itself, rather than its fringes, each one is awarded the part of the item extending from the edge on the side where he is standing until the place where his hand is, and the remainder is divided equally between them, provided they take the oath prescribed by the mishnah *(Rav)*.

According to *Tosafos* (ad loc.), the litigants in the latter case must swear regarding the part of the item they grasp, as well. Since the purpose of this oath is to serve as a deterrent against seizing another person's item and claiming it as one's own, it applies just as well to the part that is being held.

Rosh deduces this from the fact that the *Gemara* deems it necessary to tell us that if both litigants are holding the item itself, they must swear. He maintains that the *Gemara* must be referring to the oath regarding the parts they are holding, for it is obvious that they must swear regarding the remainder of the item, which neither of them is holding, just as the two litigants in the mishnah's case must take an oath regarding the entire item, because neither of them is holding on to any part of it but its fringes.

Ravad, Ramban, and *Rashba* concur with this view.

Rambam (Hil. To'en 9:9) disagrees, contending that if the two litigants are holding the item itself, they must swear only with regard to the remaining part. However, each litigant may, if he wishes, exact an additional oath from his opponent to the effect that whatever he was awarded by the court was indeed his. [This is an instance of גִּלְגוּל שְׁבוּעָה, *attaching an oath* — a principle which dictates that if the defendant in a case is required by the court to take an oath, the plaintiff can attach certain additional oaths to it, which the defendant could not otherwise have been compelled to swear (see commentary to ArtScroll *Sotah* 2:5).]

Tos. Yom Tov explains *Rambam's* reasoning: The oath mentioned in the mishnah certainly does not apply to that which the litigants hold in their hands, for if it did, it would be applicable to any case in which one claims ownership of something in

another's possession, and we do not find such an oath discussed anywhere in the Mishnah. The שְׁבֻעַת הֶיסֵּת, *hesses oath*, which is taken in such instances, was instituted many generations later [in the times of the *Amoraim*] *(Tif. Yis.*, Introduction to *Shevuos* ch. 6).

A practical difference between the two views would occur in the event that both litigants are holding the complete item in their hands. According to the view of *Tosafos* and *Rosh*, they would have to swear that what they are holding is theirs. According to *Rambam*, however, since there is no remaining part regarding which the oath of the mishnah is imposed, there can be no other oaths attached to it *(Meiri)* — i.e., they divide the item without swearing at all.

The intention of the mishnah in prescribing that the item be divided is that the court sell it and divide the money between the litigants *(Tos. Yom Tov* from *Gem.* 7b, 8a). Should the article be of the type that loses no value by severing it, it is indeed severed *(Choshen Mishpat* 138:4). *Sma* (ad loc. 12) asserts that even if it would not lose all its value by being severed, as long as it would depreciate somewhat thereby, it is not to be severed. *Terumas Hadeshen* (ch. 336), quoted by *Rama* (loc. cit. 171:5), contends that this applies only if the item depreciates by a fifth or more of its original value. *Maharshach*, however, differs *(Baer Hetev* ibid. 138:10; *Nesivos Hamishpat* ibid. §6).

[The following segment of the mishnah deals only with the case of an article that had been found, and both litigants are holding it by its fringes.]

זֶה אוֹמֵר: "כֻּלָּהּ שֶׁלִּי," — *[If] one says: 'It is all mine,'*

He claims to have picked up the item first *(Meiri)*.

וְזֶה אוֹמֵר: "חֶצְיָהּ שֶׁלִּי," — *and the other says: 'Half of it is mine'* —

He claims that they both picked it up simultaneously (ibid.).

הָאוֹמֵר: „כֻּלָּהּ שֶׁלִּי'' יִשָּׁבַע שֶׁאֵין לוֹ בָהּ פָּחוֹת
מִשְּׁלֹשָׁה חֲלָקִים, וְהָאוֹמֵר: „חֶצְיָהּ שֶׁלִּי'' יִשָּׁבַע
שֶׁאֵין לוֹ בָהּ פָּחוֹת מֵרְבִיעַ, זֶה נוֹטֵל שְׁלֹשָׁה
חֲלָקִים, וְזֶה נוֹטֵל רְבִיעַ.

[ב] הָיוּ שְׁנַיִם רוֹכְבִין עַל גַּבֵּי-בְהֵמָה, אוֹ

יד אברהם

הָאוֹמֵר: „כֻּלָּהּ שֶׁלִּי'' יִשָּׁבַע שֶׁאֵין לוֹ בָהּ פָּחוֹת
מִשְּׁלֹשָׁה חֲלָקִים, — *he who says: 'It is all
mine' must swear that he owns no less
of it than three quarters,*

Since both litigants agree that half of
the item belongs to the one who claims it
entirely as his, it should be sufficient for
the latter to swear only with regard to
half of what is being disputed [as in the
first part of the mishnah] — i.e., one
quarter of the item. Nevertheless, we
fear that when he swears that he owns at
least one quarter of the item, he may be
referring to the part which both of them
agree is his. Although an oath administered by the court is construed to mean
what the judges understand it to be — in
our case, that he is referring to the part
of the item whose ownership is being
disputed — and one who swears
knowing that the truth is not as the
court interprets his oath is guilty of
perjury, the Rabbis sought to formulate
languages for oaths which preclude any
ambiguities or possibilities of deceit.
This is because a person is more
reluctant to specifically make a false
statement under oath than to perjure
according to the court's interpretation
of his statement (*Tos. Yom Tov* from
Nimmukei Yosef, Rosh).

וְהָאוֹמֵר: „חֶצְיָהּ שֶׁלִּי'' יִשָּׁבַע שֶׁאֵין לוֹ בָהּ פָּחוֹת
מֵרְבִיעַ, — *and he who says: 'Half of it is
mine' must swear that he owns no less
of it than one quarter,*

Since he claims only half the item,
admitting that the other half is not his,
he must swear only with regard to half
of the half he claims (*Rashi*).

זֶה נוֹטֵל שְׁלֹשָׁה חֲלָקִים, וְזֶה נוֹטֵל רְבִיעַ. —
[*and*] *this one takes three quarters, and*

that one takes one quarter.

Since the controversy involves only
half the item, they divide that part of it
(*Meiri*).

The commentators ask why the one who
claims half the item does not benefit from a
מִגּוֹ [*miggo*] (lit., *because*) — the principle that
if a claimant, had he wished to lie, could have
invented a statement more advantageous to
him, the fact that he instead says a less
advantageous statement indicates that he is
telling the truth. In our case, had the one who
claims half the item been lying, he could have
claimed that the entire thing belongs to him,
in which case he would have received half.
Therefore, now that he claims that only half
belongs to him, he should be believed, and
awarded that half.

Tosafos, quoting *Rivam*, answer that a
miggo would not apply in this case, since it is
effective only in supporting the claim of one
who seeks an item that is in his possession,
but not to exact something from another, for
which witnesses are required. Since, in our
case, both litigants are holding on to the item
by its fringes, they are both considered to be
equally in possession of the entire item —
including the disputed half. Consequently, a
miggo cannot help either of them exact any
part of it from the other.

Nimmukei Yosef suggests three answers to
this question:

(1) The principle of *miggo* applies only if
the litigant could have claimed the more
advantageous statement just as easily as the
claim he is now making. If, however, it is
more difficult for him to make the other plea,
there is obviously no indication that he is
telling the truth. In our case, more audacity is
required to claim the entire cloak than to
claim half.

(2) The principle of *miggo* applies only if
the more advantageous statement that the
litigant could have made concerns the same
thing as the claim he actually makes. If,
however, it concerns something else — even if

1
2
'Half of it is mine' — he who says: 'It is all mine' must swear that he owns no less of it than three quarters, and he who says: 'Half of it is mine' must swear that he owns no less of it than one quarter, [and] this one takes three quarters, and that one takes one quarter.

2. **[**If**]** two were riding an animal, or [if] one was

YAD AVRAHAM

the latter is equivalent to that about which he is now claiming — it does not demonstrate that what he now says is true, because — for whatever reason — he may not be audacious enough to claim more than he is claiming now. In our case, he cannot use the fact that he could have claimed the other half of the item as a *miggo*.

(3) A person would rather make a claim for less and be awarded all of it, than a claim for more and receive only part of it. Thus, in our case, were one to be awarded half the item whether he claims all of it or half of it, he would rather claim half of it and receive it. Hence, there is no *miggo* that he could have claimed all of it.

2.

◄§ מְשִׁיכָה, *Meshichah* / **Causing Something to Move**

As mentioned in the General Introduction, *meshichah* (lit., 'pulling') is a legal means of acquiring movable property. If one wishes to acquire an animal in this manner, he need not actually drag it; causing the animal to move merely by hitting it or calling to it is sufficient (*Bava Basra* 75b). It is apparent from the following mishnah that riding the animal, too, is a valid means of acquiring it. However, the exact details concerning this method is a subject of controversy, as discussed below.

הָיוּ שְׁנַיִם רוֹכְבִין עַל־גַּבֵּי בְהֵמָה, — [If] two were riding an animal,

That is, an ownerless animal (*Meiri*) [or one that fits into the other categories discussed above with regard to the cases in mishnah 1 (see commentary ad loc., s.v. "...זֶה אוֹמֵר: „אֲנִי].

Some authorities (*Rif; Rambam, Hil. Gezeilah Va'aveidah* 17:7, according to *Maggid Mishneh* ad loc.) construe the mishnah as teaching us that riding an animal is a valid means of acquiring it (see *Ketzos HaChoshen* 197:2, *Nesivos Hamishpat* ibid. §2). *Rav* goes so far as to say that this includes merely sitting on the animal in a riding position, although it does not move. [Since, by riding the animal, he does not cause it to move, it is immaterial whether it actually moves or stands still.] *Beis Yosef* (*Choshen Mishpat* 197),

however, interprets *Rambam* to mean that the animal must walk at least to the extent of picking up its forefoot and hind foot.

Others (*Rosh; Rambam Commentary*) qualify the mishnah as referring to cases in which the ones riding on the animal also prodded it with their feet, causing it to move. They contend that only in such a manner is riding a valid form of *meshichah*.[1]

The interpretations of the mishnah advanced by *Rav* and *Rif* are based on the *Gemara* (8a), which states that the *Tanna* is teaching us that riding — even without prodding (*Rashi* ad loc.) — is a method of acquisition.

The interpretation propounded by *Rosh* and *Rambam Commentary* is based on a statement of Shmuel (8b), who qualifies the mishnah as referring

1. [It is not uncommon for *Rambam's Mishnah Commentary* to contradict a ruling in his *Mishneh Torah*. The latter was written many years later, and we assume that *Rambam* reversed his ruling in these cases. Therefore, the later work is considered more authoritative.]

בבא
מציעא
א/ג שֶׁהָיָה אֶחָד רוֹכֵב וְאֶחָד מַנְהִיג, זֶה אוֹמֵר: „כֻּלָּהּ
שֶׁלִּי,‟ וְזֶה אוֹמֵר: „כֻּלָּהּ שֶׁלִּי‟ — זֶה יִשָּׁבַע שֶׁאֵין
לוֹ בָהּ פָּחוֹת מֵחֶצְיָהּ, וְזֶה יִשָּׁבַע שֶׁאֵין לוֹ בָהּ
פָּחוֹת מֵחֶצְיָהּ, וְיַחֲלֹקוּ.
בִּזְמַן שֶׁהֵם מוֹדִים אוֹ שֶׁיֵּשׁ לָהֶן עֵדִים, חוֹלְקִים
בְּלֹא שְׁבוּעָה.

[ג] הָיָה רוֹכֵב עַל־גַּבֵּי בְהֵמָה, וְרָאָה אֶת־
הַמְּצִיאָה, וְאָמַר לַחֲבֵרוֹ:

יד אברהם

to riders who prodded the animal with their feet; otherwise, they would not have acquired it. *Rosh* explains that according to Shmuel, the point of the mishnah is that not only does the one riding in front acquire rights to the animal, but also the one riding behind him. We might think that the one in the back does not acquire any part of the animal, since it is customary for slaves to sit behind their masters to rest while they are riding, and hence, doing so would not be a sign of ownership, which must be demonstrated in order to acquire the animal in this manner. The mishnah also comes to teach us that in the second case — in which one person is riding and prodding the animal and the other is leading it — both acquire it equally (*Tos. Yom Tov*).

אוֹ שֶׁהָיָה אֶחָד רוֹכֵב — *or [if] one was riding*
As in the above case, some commentators qualify this as meaning that he prods the animal with his feet, while others construe it as referring simply to riding (ibid.).

וְאֶחָד מַנְהִיג, — *and the other was leading,*
He was holding the reins and drawing the animal (*Rambam, Hil. Gezeilah* 17:6), or coaxing it along with a rod (*Meiri*). [This is certainly a valid form of *meshichah* according to all opinions, as discussed in the preface.]
Although, as explained above, *Rav* interprets the term *riding* in the mishnah's

first case as referring to merely sitting in a riding position, he qualifies the same term in the second case as including prodding with the feet. *Tos. Yom Tov* is at a loss to reconcile *Rav*'s conflicting interpretations.

Shoshanim LeDavid explains that since — as mentioned above — there are two views in the *Gemara* as to whether riding an animal is in itself a sufficient means of acquiring it, *Rav* rules that as long as another person does not perform a better act of acquisition, the riding suffices to acquire the animal. Thus, if, as in the first case, two are riding the animal, it is divided between them. In the second case, however, in which one is riding the animal and the other is leading it, the latter — who performs a superior act of acquisition — acquires the entire animal if the other person merely rides it. Only if the rider also prods the animal with his feet is he considered to have done an act of acquisition strong enough to match that of the one who leads. *Rav* therefore qualifies the second case as one in which the rider also prodded the animal with his feet.

זֶה אוֹמֵר: „כֻּלָּהּ שֶׁלִּי,‟ וְזֶה אוֹמֵר: „כֻּלָּהּ שֶׁלִּי‟ — — *[and] one says: 'It is all mine,' and the other says, 'It is all mine' —*
Each one claims that only after he had already acquired the animal by riding it or leading it does the other person come along and do one of these acts (*Meiri*).

זֶה יִשָּׁבַע שֶׁאֵין לוֹ בָהּ פָּחוֹת מֵחֶצְיָהּ, וְזֶה יִשָּׁבַע שֶׁאֵין לוֹ בָהּ פָּחוֹת מֵחֶצְיָהּ, וְיַחֲלֹקוּ. — *this one must swear that he owns no less of it than half, and that one must swear that he owns no less of it than half, and they*

משניות / בבא מציעא — פרק א: שנים אוחזין [12]

riding and the other was leading, [and] one says: 'It is all mine,' and the other says, 'It is all mine' — this one must swear that he owns no less of it than half, and that one must swear that he owns no less of it than half, and they divide [it].

Whenever they admit or they have witnesses, they divide without an oath.

3. [If] one, [while] riding an animal, saw an acquirable object, and said to another: 'Give it to

YAD AVRAHAM

divide [it].

[See commentary to mishnah 1, s.v. זֶה יִשָּׁבַע, regarding the method of division.]

בִּזְמַן שֶׁהֵם מוֹדִים — *Whenever they admit*

The two of them admit that they acquired it simultaneously *(Meiri).*

אוֹ שֶׁיֵּשׁ לָהֶן עֵדִים, — *or they have witnesses,*

There are witnesses to that effect (ibid.).

חוֹלְקִים בְּלֹא שְׁבוּעָה. — *they divide without an oath.*

According to *Rav* and *Rambam (Commentary)*, this teaches us that even if the court had already handed down a verdict that the two litigants must swear in order to divide the item, if they subsequently admit that they picked up the item together, they need not take an oath.

Tos. Yom Tov remarks that this is obvious, and there is no need for the mishnah to tell it to us. Rather, he and *Meiri* cite the *Gemara* (8a), which explains that this final statement in the mishnah refers back to the case of the previous mishnah dealing with a lost item, and teaches us that if one picks up an acquirable item on behalf of another

person, the latter acquires it. This is implied by the last statement in our mishnah, since — otherwise — their having picked up the item simultaneously would not acquire it for them, because in order to acquire an item through הַגְבָּהָה, *lifting*, it must be lifted completely. In our case, however, with regard to each of the two who picked it up, the part of the item being held by the other person should be considered as if it were lying on the ground or a table, in which case neither of them would acquire it, and if a third person came along and seized it from them, he would acquire it. Since the mishnah rules that the first two who picked up the item do indeed acquire it, the *Gemara* deduces that the *Tanna* must be dealing with a case in which each one claims that he picked up half the item for himself and half for the other person holding it. [Because each one of them picked up half of the item, and the other person picked up the second half for him, it is considered as if each one picked up the entire item.] Were it not for the ruling that one can acquire an item on behalf of another person by lifting it, neither of them would acquire it in this case, as explained above.

3.

הָיָה רוֹכֵב עַל־גַּבֵּי בְהֵמָה, וְרָאָה אֶת־הַמְּצִיאָה, — *[If] one, [while] riding an animal, saw an acquirable object* [lit., *a find*],

[He was riding an animal and spotted an object lying before him on the ground, that was ownerless, or had been

„תְּנֶהָ לִי" — נְטָלָהּ וְאָמַר: „אֲנִי זָכִיתִי בָהּ," זָכָה
בָהּ. אִם, מִשֶּׁנְּתָנָהּ לוֹ, אָמַר: „אֲנִי זָכִיתִי בָהּ
תְּחִלָּה," לֹא אָמַר כְּלוּם.

[ד] **רָאָה** אֶת־הַמְּצִיאָה וְנָפַל עָלֶיהָ, וּבָא אַחֵר

יד אברהם

lost and need not be returned to its original owner (see commentary to mishnah 1, s.v. ... אני אומר זה).]

וְאָמַר לַחֲבֵרוֹ: „תְּנֶהָ לִי" — *and said to another: 'Give it to me'* —

The rider asked the other person merely to give the object to him, not to acquire it for him (*Rav, Tos. Yom Tov* from *Gem.* 10a).

The *Tanna* chooses the example in which the person is riding on an animal, because in any other situation, he would probably pick up the item himself. Since he was riding on an animal, however, he found it difficult to dismount, and therefore asked another person to pick up the article he spotted and give it to him (*Rav; Tif. Yis.*).

נְטָלָהּ וְאָמַר: — *[if the latter] took it and said:*

[The one whom the rider has asked to pick up the item did so, and then said:]

„אֲנִי זָכִיתִי בָהּ," — *'I have acquired it [for myself],'*

'I intended to acquire it for myself, not for you' (*Tos. Yom Tov*).

זָכָה בָהּ. — *he has [indeed] acquired it.*

Since the one riding the animal requested merely that the other person give him the article — meaning that he should acquire it only when it is given to him — and not that the other person should acquire it for him upon picking it up, we assume that the latter did not do more than the rider had asked of him — i.e., he did not intend to acquire it for the rider when he picked it up. Consequently, when he then decides to acquire it for himself, he may do so, since the rider has not yet acquired it. However, should the rider have re-quested of the other person to acquire the article for him by picking it up, then if the latter complies, he may no longer acquire it for himself. This is based on the ruling discussed in the commentary to the end of the previous mishnah — that if one picks up an acquirable object on behalf of another, the latter acquires it.

The above explanation follows the apparent meaning of the *Gemara. Tur* (*Choshen Mishpat* 269), however, rules that the rider acquires the item only if, when the other person picks it up, the latter announces that he is thereby acquiring it for the rider. Otherwise, the one who picked it up may acquire it for himself as long as he has not yet given it to the rider. Accordingly, *Tur* explains the mishnah to mean that the one who picks it up says: 'Although I originally picked up the item with the intention of acquiring it for you, I now wish to acquire it for myself' (*Rav, Tos. Yom Tov*).

אִם, מִשֶּׁנְּתָנָהּ לוֹ, אָמַר: „אֲנִי זָכִיתִי בָהּ תְּחִלָּה," — *If, after he gave it to him, he said: 'I acquired it first,'*

After the one who picked up the item gave it to the rider, he claims that upon picking it up, he intended to acquire it for himself, and that he gave it to the rider only to show it to him, or so that he should hold it for him (*Meiri*).

לֹא אָמַר כְּלוּם. — *[it is as though] he said nothing.*

Although he claims that his intention had been to acquire it for himself, his giving it to the rider proves that he actually intended to acquire it for the latter when he picked it up (*Rashi*).

1
4
me' — [if the latter] took it and said: 'I have acquired it [for myself],' he has [indeed] acquired it. If, after he gave it to him, he said: 'I acquired it first,' [it is as though] he said nothing.

4. [I]f] one saw an acquirable object and fell upon

YAD AVRAHAM

The *Gemara* discusses the significance of the word תְּחִלָּה, *first*. Obviously, the one who picked it up and gave it to the rider cannot acquire it anymore, since it is no longer in his hands; rather, his claim must be that he acquired it before he gave it. Indeed, the *Gemara* (10a) explains that the word תְּחִלָּה, *first*, is superfluous — even if not mentioned in the statement, it would be understood (*Rashi*). It is included only to indicate that in the previous case of this mishnah, too, the one who picked it up claims that he had intended to acquire it for himself before giving it to the rider,

as explained above.

Rav comments that the item in this case is ownerless until the rider takes it from the one who picked it up. [*Rav*'s statement is difficult to understand, for — regardless of the intentions of the one who picked it up — the item should not remain ownerless. If he picked it up to acquire it for himself, it becomes his; if he did so to acquire for the rider, it becomes the latter's. Although *Rashi* (9b), too, states that it is possible that the item would be ownerless, he says this only according to the opinion that one cannot acquire an item for another person by picking it up, a view that is rejected by the Halachah.]

4.

The previous mishnayos have discussed the *kinyanim* (acts of acquisition) known as הַגְבָּהָה, *lifting*, and מְשִׁיכָה, *pulling*. The following mishnah introduces קִנְיַן יָד, *acquisition by the hand* — i.e., if one grasps an article in his hand, even without picking it up or pulling it, he acquires it. We find this method of acquisition alluded to in the Torah (*Ex.* 22:3) with regard to the thief who becomes liable for כֶּפֶל, *the twofold payment*, if the article is found in his hand (*Gem.* 10b). It is also alluded to in the verse (*Deut.* 24:1) which states that a man wishing to divorce his wife must give the *get* (bill of divorcement) into his wife's hand (loc. cit.). This *kinyan* includes acquiring an object by it being in one's property — even if he is unaware of it — provided that the property is sufficiently guarded (*Gem.* 11a). This is known as קִנְיַן חָצֵר, *acquisition by a courtyard*.

Based on this method of acquisition, the Rabbis innovated the *kinyan* of אַרְבַּע אַמוֹת, *four cubits* — i.e., the four cubits of ground next to a person can legally acquire chattels for him. Hence, if an acquirable article is within that distance from him, he acquires it. This *kinyan* was enacted to prevent quarrels over such items (ibid. 10a) — this way, as soon as it is seen to be within four cubits of a person, no one else will attempt to acquire it (*Meiri*). The *kinyan* applies only in an alleyway or at the sides of a public domain, where there is no heavy pedestrian traffic, or in an ownerless field (*Rambam, Hil. Gezeilah* 17:8,9).

רָאָה אֶת־הַמְּצִיאָה — [If] one saw an acquirable object
[As in the previous mishnah, this term refers to an ownerless object or one that had been lost and need not be returned to its original owner (see

commentary to mishnah 1, s.v. זֶה אוֹמֵר: ",אֲנִי... "].]

וְנָפַל עָלֶיהָ, — and fell upon it,
He fell upon the item with the intention of acquiring it through that

וְהֶחֱזִיק בָּה, זֶה שֶׁהֶחֱזִיק בָּה זָכָה בָּה.
רָאָה אוֹתָן רָצִין אַחַר מְצִיאָה — אַחַר צְבִי
שָׁבוּר, אַחַר גּוֹזָלוֹת שֶׁלֹּא פָרְחוּ — וְאָמַר: "זָכְתָה
לִי שָׂדִי," זָכְתָה לוֹ.

יד אברהם

act (Meiri from Gem. 10a).

וּבָא אַחֵר וְהֶחֱזִיק בָּה, — and another came
and seized it,

He seized it, and then — when the one
who had fallen upon it stood up — he
picked it up (Shitah Mekubetzes).

זֶה שֶׁהֶחֱזִיק בָּה זָכָה בָּה. — the one who
seized it acquired it.

The Gemara (10a) qualifies the
mishnah as referring to a public domain.
Since such places are crowded with
people, no one person is considered as
having four cubits for himself (Rashi),
and the kinyan of four cubits does not
apply. Therefore, in our case, the one
who fell on the article does not acquire
it. The kinyan applies only in a narrow
street, which is not frequented by
crowds, on the sides of the public
domain near the houses, where there are
posts designed to protect the houses
from the wagons, or in corners or
recesses of the public domain — away
from the mainstream of traffic — where
a person can have his own space of four
cubits square, undisturbed by others. In
such places, the one who falls on an
acquirable object acquires it, and no one
may seize it from him. As stated above,
this kinyan was enacted to prevent
quarrels between finders (Rav, Tos.
Yom Tov). Were it to apply in a public
domain, it would only lead to more
quarrels, since — most likely — more
than one person would be within four
cubits of each acquirable item (Meiri).

The Gemara (10b) states also that
there is no kinyan of four cubits in
private property. Indeed, it would be
illogical to think that the Rabbis allowed
such an acquisition on another person's
property (Tos. Yom Tov).

Another explanation for the mish-

nah's ruling is offered by the Gemara
(10a): By falling upon the object, the
person indicated that he wished to
acquire it by falling upon it, and not
with the kinyan of four cubits.
Therefore, since falling upon something
is not a valid manner of acquisition, he
does not acquire it.

[Although several authorities (Ran;
Rashba; Maggid Mishneh, Hil. Gezeilah
17:1) maintain that the latter explanation is accepted by the halachah, the
consensus is that it is not. See Choshen
Mishpat 268:1.]

Rav cites this explanation in his
commentary to Peah 4:3, but omits it
here, intimating that he originally
believed it to be the prevailing view, but
later reversed his opinion (Tos. Yom
Tov).

רָאָה אוֹתָן רָצִין אַחַר מְצִיאָה — [If] one
saw people running after an acquirable
object —

[He saw people running through his
field in order to acquire something.]

אַחַר צְבִי שָׁבוּר, אַחַר גּוֹזָלוֹת שֶׁלֹּא פָרְחוּ —
after a lame [lit., broken] deer [or] after
young birds that cannot [yet] fly —

These cannot run or fly away, and are
therefore secure for him in his field if
others do not take it (Rav; Rashi).

Tos. Yom Tov (citing Rambam, Hil.
Gezeilah 17:11) and Meiri explain that
the mishnah lists the deer and birds as
examples of an acquirable object. [Of
course, the same would apply to any
inanimate item that is acquirable; the
Tanna mentions these only in order to
contrast them with the next part of the
mishnah, which states that if the deer or
birds can run or fly, the ruling is the
opposite.]

וְאָמַר: "זָכְתָה לִי שָׂדִי," זָכְתָה לוֹ. — and he

it, and another came and seized it, the one who seized it acquired it.

[If] one saw people running after an acquirable object — after a lame deer [or] after young birds that cannot [yet] fly — and he said: 'My field has acquired [it] for me,' it has [indeed] acquired [it] for him.

YAD AVRAHAM

said: 'My field has acquired [it] for me,' it has [indeed] acquired [it] for him.

[As explained in the preface, a person can acquire an item by the fact that it is in his property, if the property is sufficiently guarded. Accordingly, in our case] the ruling applies only if the owner of the field is standing beside it and is able to catch the deer or the birds before they leave the field (Rav from Gem. 11a). Should the field be guarded in some other manner [e.g., there is a fence around it], the owner need not stand beside it (Gem.).

[In the preface it is explained that one's property can acquire objects for him as an extension of the concept of יָד, a hand. For example, although — as mentioned there — the Torah requires that in order to divorce a woman, her husband must give the get into her hand, it is sufficient that he put it into her property — e.g., her field, yard, etc. However, in order that the property be considered like her hand, the wife must be standing next to the property, just as one's hand is next to him.]

The Gemara adds that one's property can sometimes serve as a שָׁלִיחַ, agent, for him — e.g., in the case of a gift, the giver can designate the property as an agent to receive the item on behalf of the recipient. In the case of an ownerless object or a lost object that need not be returned, however, no one can designate the property in which it lies as an agent, since only the owner of the object is empowered to do so (Yerushalmi to Maaser Sheni 4:4). Consequently, it is difficult to understand the Gemara's statement, cited above, that one can acquire such an object lying in his field even if he is not standing beside the field. Although it may be a guarded field, the fact that he is not standing there prevents it from being like his hand, and the fact that he is not the owner of the object precludes the field serving as his agent.

Nimmukei Yosef, quoting Ran, explains that since a person who receives something in his hand which he wants to acquire usually places it in a property of his that is properly guarded, such a property is considered an 'extension' of his hand, and can acquire the item for him even if it is not put into his hand, and even if he is not standing beside it. This is true in our mishnah's case, since the owner of the field wants to acquire the item. An item that one does not wish to acquire, however, is not placed by him in his property, and is therefore not considered like his hand. Hence, in such cases — e.g., that of a divorce — the recipient must stand beside his property in order for this method to be effective (Tos. Yom Tov).

Although it appears from the mishnah that if one wishes his property to acquire an object for him, he must express his intention vocally, he need not do so in order to acquire an object through the kinyan of four cubits. The difference is that the efficacy of the latter kinyan is superior to that of the former, since — if an article is within his four cubits — he can easily bend over and take it (Maggid Mishneh, Hil. Gezeilah 17:11). Alternatively, since the Sages instituted this kinyan in order to avoid quarrels, they did not differentiate whether the person in question had expressed his intention or not, since such a differentiation would also lead to quarreling between the persons involved (Beis Yosef 268). Tosafos and Rosh, however, contend that in no case is it necessary for one who wants his property to acquire something for him to announce his intention. The person in our case did so merely to discourage strangers from taking the ownerless item for themselves (Tos. Yom Tov).

הָיָה צְבִי רָץ כְּדַרְכּוֹ אוֹ שֶׁהָיוּ גוֹזָלוֹת מַפְרִיחִין,
וְאָמַר: ,,זָכְתָה לִי שָׂדִי,'' לֹא אָמַר כְּלוּם.

[ה] מְצִיאַת בְּנוֹ וּבִתּוֹ הַקְּטַנִּים, מְצִיאַת עַבְדּוֹ

יד אברהם

הָיָה צְבִי רָץ כְּדַרְכּוֹ אוֹ שֶׁהָיוּ גוֹזָלוֹת מַפְרִיחִין, —
[If] the deer was running normally or if
the young birds were flying,

The same applies even if the deer is
lame or the birds cannot yet fly, but the
owner of the field cannot overtake them
before they go out of his property (ibid.
from *Rambam, Hil. Gezeilah* 17:3).

The *Tanna's* choice of the plural
birds, as opposed to the singular *deer*,
and the causative מַפְרִיחִין — rather than
פּוֹרְחִין, *were flying* — is puzzling. *Tos.
Yom Tov* explains that birds usually fly
in groups, each one attempting to fly
ahead of the others. Thus, the birds
cause each other to fly.

Lechem Shamayim explains that the
young birds, who are just beginning to
learn to fly, exert themselves to practice
flying. Hence, the causative form is
used, since they force themselves to fly.

וְאָמַר: ,,זָכְתָה לִי שָׂדִי,'' — *and he said: 'My
field has acquired [it] for me,'*

[That is, *even* if he made this
statement.]

לֹא אָמַר כְּלוּם. — [*it is as though*] he said
nothing.

His words are of no avail, since the
field cannot acquire a running deer or
flying birds, which will not stay in it.

Although, as mentioned above, this
ruling includes young birds that cannot
fly and a lame deer if they cannot be
caught before leaving the field, these do
differ from the healthy, mature animals
in one respect: should one give them to
the owner of the field as a gift or sell
them to him and they are in the field, he
cannot subsequently rescind the gift or
sale, since the owner of the field has
already acquired them, even if he cannot
catch them before they leave the field.
[Although one would not acquire an
ownerless animal under such circumstances, a gift or sale has the added
advantage of the giver's or seller's desire
that the recipient acquire the item (*Gem.*
11b).] In a similar case involving a
running deer or flying birds, however,
the field does not acquire them for its
owner (*Tif. Yis.; Rambam* loc. cit. §11;
Meiri; Choshen Mishpat 268:4).

The reason for this distinction is not clear.
R' Nissan Alpert, in his glosses to *Meiri*,
concludes that a running deer or flying birds
are considered as if they were not in the field
at all. [This seems to disagree with the
explanation of *Lechem Shamayim*,
mentioned above, since — according to him —
the birds are not yet proficient in flying and,
if so, why would they be regarded as not
being in the field at all?]

5.

The preceding mishnayos have discussed how a person acquires an article
through an act of his own or through the agency of his field. This mishnah
delineates how one may acquire an item through an act of acquisition performed by
members of his household.

מְצִיאַת בְּנוֹ וּבִתּוֹ הַקְּטַנִּים, — *The finding of
one's minor son or daughter,*

[That is, an acquirable object found
by one's minor child.] Although the
term קְטַנִּים, *minors*, usually refers to
boys under the age of thirteen and girls

under twelve, here it includes even those
above these ages if they are still
supported by their father. The Rabbis
awarded their findings to the father,
fearing that if the child would retain his
findings for himself, it would create ill

[If] the deer was running normally or if the young birds were flying, and he said: 'My field has acquired [it] for me,' [it is as though] he said nothing.

5. **T**he finding of one's minor son or daughter, the

YAD AVRAHAM

will between him and his father, and the latter might discontinue his support [since supporting a child is voluntary, not obligatory (*Rashi* to *Kesubos* 47a; see *Kesubos* 4:6 and commentary there] (*Rav* from *Gem.* 12b, following the view of R' Yochanan). Accordingly, children who are self-supporting — even those below the ages mentioned above — may retain their own findings (*Gem.* ibid.).

This applies only to a father, because if he does not support his children, no one else will. However, it does not appear that the Rabbis awarded the findings of an orphan or any other needy person to the one who supports him [because it is likely that if he chooses to discontinue his support, some other charitable person will do it instead]. Certainly, the findings of Jewish bondmen and bondwomen are not awarded to their masters, as the mishnah states below, since they are being supported only in return for their services. [Hence, we do not fear that any ill will would result by their keeping the findings (*Tos. Yom Tov* from *Tos.* 12b).]

The term *minor daughter* in the mishnah applies also to a נַעֲרָה, *naarah* (loosely, *maiden*; generally, a girl between the ages of twelve and twelve and a half)[1] — her findings, too, belong to the father, even if he does not support her. However, once she becomes a *bogeres* (see footnote), she may retain her findings. *Rav*, following *Rashi* and *Rambam* (*Commentary*), explains that this is derived from a phrase in the section dealing with the absolution of vows — בִּנְעֻרֶיהָ בֵּית אָבִיהָ, *in*

her maidenhood, in her father's house (*Num.* 30:17), which implies that as long as she is a *naarah* [and certainly when she is a minor], she is under her father's authority, and all her benefits belong to him, regardless of whether or not he supports her.

Tosafos (12b) strongly question this assertion on the grounds that the *Gemara* itself (*Kesubos* 46b) refutes this derivation because of the principle that laws concerning monetary matters cannot be derived from those related to prohibitory matters — in this case, vows. Instead, they explain that the findings of a *naarah* and a minor daughter are awarded to her father even if he does not support her, because we fear that otherwise ill will would result, and he may marry her off to an ugly man or one afflicted with leprosy. A *bogeres*, on the other hand, cannot be married off by her father against her will. Therefore, he is entitled to her findings only if he supports her (*Tos. Yom Tov*).

In order to reconcile the comments of *Rashi* and *Rambam* with the *Gemara*, some of the later commentators explain that once we have sources for other privileges enjoyed by the father (see *Kesubos* 4:4), we find that the Torah gives him authority over his daughter in both pecuniary and prohibitory matters. This leads us to interpret the above-cited verse as teaching us that during these stages, *all* her benefits belong to him, including her findings (*Beis Aharon, Birkas Avraham* to 87a; *Pnei Yehoshua* to *Kesubos* 46b).

Meiri (*Kesubos* 4:4) states that a man is entitled to his daughter's findings even if she is betrothed — i.e., אֵירוּסִין, *the first stage of*

---

1. [Actually, only a girl of this age who has already grown two pubic hairs — as is usually the case — is in the category of a *naarah*. Six months later, she is known as a בּוֹגֶרֶת, *bogeres* (mature girl). See footnote to ArtScroll *Kesubos* 3:1, p. 49.]

וְשִׁפְחָתוֹ הַכְּנַעֲנִים, מְצִיאַת אִשְׁתּוֹ הֲרֵי אֵלּוּ שֶׁלּוֹ.
מְצִיאַת בְּנוֹ וּבִתּוֹ הַגְּדוֹלִים, מְצִיאַת עַבְדּוֹ
וְשִׁפְחָתוֹ הָעִבְרִים, מְצִיאַת אִשְׁתּוֹ שֶׁגֵּרְשָׁהּ —
אַף־עַל־פִּי שֶׁלֹּא נָתַן כְּתֻבָּתָהּ — הֲרֵי אֵלּוּ שֶׁלָּהֶן.

[ו] **מָצָא** שְׁטָרֵי חוֹב, אִם יֵשׁ בָּהֶן אַחֲרָיוּת
נְכָסִים, לֹא יַחֲזִיר, שֶׁבֵּית דִּין נִפְרָעִין

יד אברהם

marriage, has been performed (see General Introduction to ArtScroll *Kiddushin*). [This conforms with his commentary here, in which he concurs with the explanation of *Rashi* and *Rambam*, and obviously disagrees with *Tosafos*, since their reason that the father may marry her off to an ugly man does not apply once she is betrothed.]

מְצִיאַת עַבְדּוֹ וְשִׁפְחָתוֹ הַכְּנַעֲנִים, — *the finding of one's gentile* [lit. *Canaanite*] *slave — male or female —*

Gentile slaves are totally owned by their masters and are even inherited by their children, as stated in *Leviticus* 25:46 (*Rav; Rashi*). [Therefore, their findings belong to the master.]

מְצִיאַת אִשְׁתּוֹ — [and] the finding of one's wife

The Rabbis enacted that the wife's findings belong to the husband lest it cause ill will between them (ibid. from *Gem.* 12b).

הֲרֵי אֵלּוּ שֶׁלּוֹ. — *belong to him.*
[The findings of all of the above individuals belong to the father/master/husband for the reason mentioned in each case.]

מְצִיאַת בְּנוֹ וּבִתּוֹ הַגְּדוֹלִים, — *The finding of one's son or daughter who is of age,*

As explained above, if children — regardless of their age — are self-supporting, their findings belong to them. In this respect, they are regarded as being of age (*Tif. Yis.* from *Gem.* ibid.). [As discussed previously, an exception to this rule is the *naarah* whose findings belong to her father, even if she supports herself.]

מְצִיאַת עַבְדּוֹ וְשִׁפְחָתוֹ הָעִבְרִים — *the finding of one's Jewish bondman or bondwoman,*

[In contrast to a gentile slave, who is his master's chattel, a Jew can never be owned by anyone; only his labor can belong to his master. To reflect this difference, when the terms עֶבֶד and שִׁפְחָה are used with reference to a Jew — as in our mishnah — we translate them as *bondman* and *bondwoman* respectively, rather than the usual *slave*.]

מְצִיאַת אִשְׁתּוֹ שֶׁגֵּרְשָׁהּ — אַף־עַל־פִּי שֶׁלֹּא נָתַן כְּתֻבָּתָהּ — *the finding of one's wife whom he divorced — although he has not [yet] paid her kesubah —*

[The כְּתוּבָה, *kesubah*, is the marriage contract that a man gives his wife upon their marriage. It briefly describes the obligations of the husband — such as supporting her — but its main feature is the dower awarded the wife in the event of their divorce or the husband's death.]

Should a man have divorced his wife, it is obvious that her findings do not belong to him. The mishnah refers to a case in which the validity of the divorce was doubtful, such as the one described in *Gittin* 8:2, in which the husband threw the *get* into the public domain where his wife was standing, in a place where both of them could watch it. Since, in such instances, the husband must still support the wife — which is what the mishnah is alluding to by its reference to the *kesubah* — we might think that her findings belong to him.

finding of one's gentile slave — male or female —
[and] the finding of one's wife belong to him.

The finding of one's son or daughter who is of age,
the finding of one's Jewish bondman or bondwoman,
the finding of one's wife whom he divorced —
although he has not [yet] paid her *kesubah* — belong
to them.

6. [If] one finds loan contracts [and] there is a lien
on property in them, he should not return
[them], since the court would exact payment with

YAD AVRAHAM

The *Tanna* therefore tells us that because the entire purpose of awarding a woman's findings to her husband is to avoid ill will between them, it is not applicable in this case, since he has tried to divorce her, and there is obviously much ill will between them already (*Tos. Yom Tov*).

Lechem Shamayim and *Shoshannim LeDavid* explain the mishnah literally: Although the husband has not paid the wife for the *kesubah*, and is still bound to her in this respect, her findings nevertheless belong to her.

Alternatively: Although the time has not arrived for him to pay her *kesubah*, since she is not definitely divorced, her findings belong to her (*Tos. Chachmei Anglia; Tos. Rabbeinu Peretz; Tos. HaRosh*).

הֲרֵי אֵלּוּ שֶׁלָּהֶן. — *belong to them.*

[In these cases, the findings belong to the finders.]

6.

The remaining mishnayos in this chapter deal with findings that do not benefit the finder in any way, such as a contract for a loan. By returning it, one person will benefit, while the other will lose. The *Tanna* delineates the circumstances under which such items should be returned (*Meiri*).

מָצָא שְׁטָרֵי חוֹב, — *[If] one finds loan contracts*

[For example, he finds a contract for a loan which states that Reuven borrowed money from Shimon.]

The word שְׁטָר, *contract*, denotes any written document which one gives to another person, granting the latter some kind of dominion over him. We find it used in *Job* 38:33 to mean *dominion* and in *Targum* to *Jeremiah* 32:10 as meaning a document (*Tos. Yom Tov* quoting *Tishbi*).

Aruch Hashalem etymologizes the word to an Arabic term meaning an engraving tool; hence, any written document, engraved or written, came to be called שְׁטָר.

Although the singular form of the word is שְׁטָר, and the plural, שְׁטָרוֹת, *Tishbi* insists that

the plural possessive form is שְׁטָרֵי. He bases this on *Targum* to *Job* 9:9; 38:32,33 (*Tos. Yom Tov*). The traditional vowelization, however, is שְׁטָרֵי, the accuracy of which is defended by *Iyun Tefillah* (in *Siddur Otzar Hatefillos*) in his commentary to the *Avinu Malkeinu* prayer, which — according to him — reads: שְׁטָרֵי חוֹבוֹתֵינוּ.

אִם יֵשׁ בָּהֶן אַחֲרָיוּת נְכָסִים, — *[and] there is a lien on property in them,*

The contract which he found states explicitly that the borrower's real property is pledged toward payment of the loan (*Rav; Rashi*).

לֹא יַחֲזִיר, — *he should not return [them],*

Even if the borrower admits that he

מֶהֶן. אֵין בָּהֶן אַחֲרָיוּת נְכָסִים, יַחֲזִיר, שֶׁאֵין בֵּית
דִּין נִפְרָעִין מֵהֶן. דִּבְרֵי רַבִּי מֵאִיר. וַחֲכָמִים
אוֹמְרִים: בֵּין כָּךְ וּבֵין כָּךְ לֹא יַחֲזִיר, מִפְּנֵי שֶׁבֵּית
דִּין נִפְרָעִין מֵהֶן.

[ז] **מָצָא** גִּטֵּי נָשִׁים, וְשִׁחְרוּרֵי עֲבָדִים, דְּיַתֵּיקֵי,

has not yet paid the debt, the finder may not return the contract to the lender (*Rav* from *Gemara*, following the view of Abaye).

שֶׁבֵּית דִּין נִפְרָעִין מֵהֶן. — *since the court would exact payment with them.*

Since the court exacts payment from the borrower's real estate even after he has sold it to someone else, we fear that although the borrower has already paid his debt, he may be claiming that he has not, as part of a fraudulent scheme contrived together with the lender: the latter will collect his debt a second time from mortgaged properties that had been bought from the borrower without a guarantee that they would not be seized by creditors. The borrower and the lender would then share the property that had been unjustly taken from the purchasers *(Rav).*

We suspect that the contract had been lost by the borrower, who — having already paid the loan — was not careful to watch it properly. If the lender is holding the contract, however, we have no reason to suspect that it had already been paid *(Tos. Yom Tov* from *Gem.* 13a).

The lost contract may also not be returned to the borrower, since it may be true that the debt has not been paid *(Tif. Yis.).*

אֵין בָּהֶן אַחֲרָיוּת נְכָסִים, — *[If] there is no lien on property in them,*

[No mention is made in the loan contract that there is a lien on the borrower's property.]

יַחֲזִיר, — *he should return [them],*

[He must return the contract to the lender.]

שֶׁאֵין בֵּית דִּין נִפְרָעִין מֵהֶן. דִּבְרֵי רַבִּי מֵאִיר. — *since the court would not exact payment with them. [These are] the words of R' Meir.*

R' Meir maintains that since the court would not exact payment from the purchasers of the borrower's properties, there is no reason to suspect a collusion between the borrower and the lender *(Tif. Yis.).*

וַחֲכָמִים אוֹמְרִים: בֵּין כָּךְ וּבֵין כָּךְ לֹא יַחֲזִיר, — *The Sages, however, say: In either case he should not return [them],*

[Whether or not the contract includes a lien on the borrower's property, the finder should not return it to the lender.]

מִפְּנֵי שֶׁבֵּית דִּין נִפְרָעִין מֵהֶן. — *since the court would exact payment with them.*

Even with a contract that does not include a lien on the borrower's property, the court exacts payment from the purchasers of the property, since the omission of the clause regarding the lien is assumed as being merely an oversight on the part of the scribe who wrote up the contract. Therefore, in this case, too, we suspect a fraudulent scheme between the borrower and the lender to wrest the mortgaged properties from the purchasers *(Rav* from *Gem.* 14a).

The intention is that even if a lender and a borrower do not specifically men-

1
7
them. [If] there is no lien on property in them, he should return [them], since the court would not exact payment with them. [These are] the words of R' Meir. The Sages, however, say: In either case he should not return [them], since the court would exact payment with them.

7. [If] one finds documents of divorce, [deeds of] emancipation of slaves, testaments, gifts, or

YAD AVRAHAM

tion that there is a lien on the property, the witnesses should nevertheless record it in the contract. If a contract not including such a lien was found, it is merely because of the scribe's oversight (*Tos. Yom Tov* from *Nimmukei Yosef; Chiddushei HaRan*). [It is unclear what these commentators mean by saying that the witnesses should record it in the contract. Perhaps it means that the witnesses should see to it that the lien should be written in.]

Meiri words the explanation somewhat differently: even if witnesses attest that no lien was mentioned at the time of the loan, the Sages contend that it is not necessary to be mentioned, and the scribe should have included it nevertheless.

The reason for the Sages' view is that one does not give away his money recklessly and would obviously not lend

it without a guarantee that he will be able to collect the debt from all of the borrower's real properties, even if they are subsequently sold (*Gem.* 14a).

The halachah is in accordance with the Sages with regard to loan contracts as well as sale contracts. Therefore, if one finds either type of contract he shall not return it — even if the lender or buyer proves that it is his by giving an identifying sign — since we fear a fraudulent scheme. Should it be stated explicitly in the contract that there is no lien on the property, or if the borrower presently possesses sufficient properties to pay the debt, or if the contract was found on the day it had been written — leading us to assume that it had not been paid — even if the debtor is not present, the finder must return the contract to the lender (*Tif. Yis.* from *Choshen Mishpat* 65:6,7).

7.

מָצָא גִטֵּי נָשִׁים, — [*If*] *one finds documents of divorce* [lit., *of women*],

[That is, *gittin* (sing., *get*), documents by which a man divorces his wife according to Jewish law.]

וְשִׁחְרוּרֵי עֲבָדִים, — [*deeds of*] *emancipation of slaves,*

[I.e., documents by which Jews free their gentile slaves.]

דְּיַתֵיקִי, — *testaments,*

Originating from the Greek, this term was incorporated into the Talmudic language because it serves as a contraction of the words דָּא תְּהֵא לְמֵיקַם וְלִהְיוֹת, *this shall be established and executed,* referring to the principle that the statements — even oral ones — of a critically ill person have the legal validity of a document that is written and delivered, as long as he does not retract them before his death (*Tif. Yis.* from *Gem.* 19a).

מַתָּנָה, וְשׁוֹבְרִים, הֲרֵי זֶה לֹא יַחֲזִיר, שֶׁאֲנִי אוֹמֵר:
כְּתוּבִים הָיוּ, וְנִמְלַךְ עֲלֵיהֶם שֶׁלֹּא לִתְּנָם.

[ח] **מָצָא** אִגְּרוֹת שׁוּם, וְאִגְּרוֹת מָזוֹן, שְׁטָרֵי
חֲלִיצָה, וּמֵאוּנִין, וּשְׁטָרֵי בֵרוּרִין,

יד אברהם

מַתָּנָה, — gifts,

[That is, deeds regarding gifts given by healthy persons.]

וְשׁוֹבְרִים, — or receipts,

This is a writ given by a creditor to the debtor, stating that the latter has paid his debt. The word שׁוֹבֵר, stemming from the root שבר, to break, is used, because this document breaks the power of the loan contract (Tif. Yis.).

Such receipts may be used for any kind of debts, and also if a creditor wishes to relinquish his debt as though the debtor had paid him (Rambam Commentary).

The change in the list of the various types of documents from the plural to the singular, and back to the plural, is in accordance with the frequency of these documents — those used more frequently are written in the plural, those less frequently are in the singular (Tif. Yis.).

הֲרֵי זֶה לֹא יַחֲזִיר, — he should not return

them,

[The finder of any of these documents should not return it to the one for whom it was written — i.e., the bill of divorce to the wife, the deed of emancipation to the slave, the testament or the deed of gift to the recipient, or the receipt to the debtor.]

שֶׁאֲנִי אוֹמֵר: כְּתוּבִים הָיוּ, וְנִמְלַךְ עֲלֵיהֶם שֶׁלֹּא לִתְּנָם. — for I say that [after] they were written, he reconsidered, [deciding] not to give them.

[Perhaps after writing this document, the one who wrote it decided not to give it, and subsequently lost it.]

However, if the one who wrote it instructs the finder to give it to the one for whom it was written, he should do so. The only exception would be a bill of divorce, in which case it must be ascertained that it had not been written for another couple with the same names [see Gittin 3:3] (Tos. Yom Tov from Gem. 18a).

8.

מָצָא אִגְּרוֹת שׁוּם, — [If] one finds evaluation documents,

This refers to a document, given by the court to a creditor, stating that the debtor's property has been evaluated and turned over to the creditor in payment of his debt (Rav; Rashi). This is issued after the court announces that the property is for sale in payment of the debt, and prospective customers bid for it. If the creditor is willing to accept it for the price offered, he is awarded the field in payment (Rambam Commentary).

These documents are returned to the creditor, since the court would not have written them without actually issuing

them to the creditor. Had the debtor paid after the field had been awarded to the creditor, he should have demanded that the evaluation document be returned to him or that a new deed of sale be drawn up, stating that the field had been sold back to him. Should he fail to do so, and the creditor repossesses the field by dint of this evaluation document, the debtor himself is at fault (Tos. Yom Tov from Gem. 16b).

The certificate also enables the creditor to transfer the assigned property to someone else, since it serves as proof of title (Talmido shel Rabbeinu Yechiel MiParis to Moed Katan 18b). Alternatively, the document was

receipts, he should not return them, for I say that [after] they were written, he reconsidered, [deciding] not to give them.

8. [I]f] one finds evaluation documents, support documents, *chalitzah* certificates, refusals,

YAD AVRAHAM

written by a court when it divided an estate, as evidence of the value of property which was awarded to one heir, while other properties of equal value were awarded to the others *(Rashi to Moed Katan* ad loc.).

וְאִגְּרוֹת מָזוֹן, — *support documents,*

[At every marriage, the bride receives from the groom a כְּתֻבָּה, *marriage contract*, which provides, among other things, that she and their daughters will receive support from the estate in case of the husband's death. If, in such an event, there is no money at hand,] the court sells a part of the estate to raise funds for their support. [In order to prevent the heirs from contesting the sale] the courts would write a support document *(Rambam Commentary*, see *Kesubos* 4:11,12; 11:2).

Alternatively, if a man obligates himself to support his stepdaughter for a given period, a document is written to that effect. See *Kesubos* 12:1 *(Rashi).*

Rav cites both of the above explanations.

Others explain אִגְּרוֹת שׁוּם וְאִגְּרוֹת מָזוֹן as one phrase meaning *documents of evaluation for support.* This refers to a case in which one undertakes to support his stepdaughter for a certain amount of time, but is delinquent in doing so. At the end of the specified period, the stepdaughter sues him, and the court evaluates the cost of supporting her for that amount of time and grants her real estate worth that sum *(Meiri; Maggid Mishneh to Hil. Gezeilah* 18:13, quoting *Rabbeinu Yehonasan; Chiddushei HaRitva Hachadashim).*

It is interesting that these first two documents listed in the mishnah are described as אִגְּרוֹת [lit., *letters*], whereas

all other documents are referred to as שְׁטָרוֹת [poss. שְׁטָרֵי], *contracts* or *certificates. Rabbeinu Tam* explains that the former are letters that a court in one city sends to a court in another city to evaluate the debtor's property or the amount due for support *(Tos.* to *Kesubos* 100b). According to *Rashi* — who interprets *support documents* as dealing with the support of a step-daughter — they are referred to as אִגְּרוֹת, because they publicize the generosity of the stepfather, who undertakes to support his stepdaughter for an extended period of time *(Tos. Yom Tov).* [Perhaps this is also the reason that evaluating documents are called אִגְּרוֹת, since the sale of the property to pay the debt thereby becomes publicized.]

שְׁטָרֵי חֲלִיצָה, — *chalitzah certificates,*

If a married man dies childless and is survived by one or more brothers, the Torah commands that one of the brothers marry his widow. This marriage is known as יִבּוּם, *levirate marriage* [a practice that has since been prohibited by the Rabbis]. In case the brothers refuse to marry her or vice versa [or — since the Rabbinical prohibition — in all such instances], חֲלִיצָה, *chalitzah* [lit., *removal* (of the shoe)] is performed. This is a rite which releases the widow from her obligation to her brothers-in-law and permits her to marry whomever she pleases *(Deut.* 25:5-10; see General Introduction to ArtScroll *Yevamos).*

[The certificate mentioned here attests to the fact that *chalitzah* has been performed.]

וּמְאוּנִין, — *refusals,*

וְכָל־מַעֲשֵׂה בֵית־דִּין, הֲרֵי זֶה יַחֲזִיר. מָצָא בַחֲפִיסָה אוֹ בִדְלֶסְקְמָא, תַּכְרִיךְ שֶׁל־ שְׁטָרוֹת, אוֹ אֲגֻדָּה שֶׁל־שְׁטָרוֹת, הֲרֵי זֶה יַחֲזִיר. וְכַמָּה אֲגֻדָּה שֶׁל־שְׁטָרוֹת? שְׁלֹשָׁה קְשׁוּרִין זֶה בָזֶה.

יד אברהם

Though the Torah grants a father the exclusive right to marry off his minor daughter, if such a girl is fatherless, the Rabbis assigned this right to her mother or brothers. In the latter event, however, the girl has the option of retroactively invalidating the marriage as long as she has not yet attained majority (see *Yevamos* 13:1). This מֵאוּן, *refusal* [to continue the marriage], was certified by the court to enable her to marry another man. The document reads: 'So-and-so refused to continue her marriage with So-and-so, her husband' (*Rav* here and to *Moed Katan* 3:3).

וּשְׁטָרֵי בְרוּרִין, — *selection certificates*,

Each of the two litigants in a suit has the right to select one of the three judges who hear the case. This selection is documented to prevent the litigants from changing their choices (*Rav; Rashi* to *Gem.* 20a).

Another explanation given in the *Gemara*, which is quoted by *Rambam* (*Hil. Gezeilah* 18:13), is that this term refers to documents recording the pleas of the litigants. This is done lest they change their pleas for more profitable ones.

Alternatively, these are documents evidencing the division of the property of an estate. The court selects the various properties to be given to each heir. Without this document, the division may be contested, thereby resulting in a loss for one of the heirs (*Rashi, Ran* to *Moed Katan* 18b).

וְכָל־מַעֲשֵׂה בֵית־דִּין, — *or any act of court*,

The *Gemara* (16b) interprets this as referring to documents containing decrees of the court which confirm the creditor's right to belongings appropriated from the debtor, and those authorizing a creditor to search for the debtor's belongings and to seize them wherever they may be found. Since there is no fear that the debts in these documents have been paid — for the same reason stated above with regard to evaluation documents — they are returned to the creditor. *Sma* (65:36) explains that the difference between evaluation documents and this type of document is that the former term refers to a case in which the creditor and the debtor are both present, and the court evaluates the property, announces the sale, and issues the proper document. This term, however, is referring to an instance in which the debtor is absent, in which case a different formula is written in the document (*Tos. Yom Tov*).

הֲרֵי זֶה יַחֲזִיר. — *he should return* [them].

[As explained above, the court does not issue any of these documents before the deed stated in it has been done. There is also no fear that the debt stated in any of these documents has already been paid.]

מָצָא בַחֲפִיסָה — [*If*] one finds [any document] *in a leather bag*

That is, even if one of the documents mentioned in mishnah 6, that should not be returned, is found in a leather bag or the other items enumerated below, he should return them (*Meiri*).

חֲפִיסָה is a small bag used for keeping wine (*Rashi* 20b).

אוֹ בִדְלֶסְקְמָא, — *or in a case*,

That is, a leather case in which old men keep their utensils so that they should not have to search for them (*Rav; Rashi* loc. cit.).

The finder must return these to the one who claims that he lost documents in a leather bag or case, since this is a valid means of identification [see

selection certificates, or any act of court, he should return [them].

[If] one finds [any document] in a leather bag or in a case, a roll of documents, or a bundle of documents, he should return [them]. Now, how many [constitute] a bundle of documents? Three fastened one to the other.

YAD AVRAHAM

preface to chapter 2] *(Rav; Rashi).*

According to *Rav* and *Rashi,* it is unusual to keep documents in such items; otherwise, this would not be sufficient identification. *Tosafos,* however, claim that it is customary to keep documents in such leather bags or cases. Accordingly, the mishnah must mean that he identified it by stating something about the bag or case itself *(Tos. Yom Tov).*

Pointing out some distinguishing characteristic of the document itself is not acceptable, since both the debtor and the creditor are familiar with it (ibid. from *Nimmukei Yosef).*

תַּכְרִיךְ שֶׁל־שְׁטָרוֹת, — *a roll of documents,*

That is, three or more documents [see below, s.v. וְכַמָּה] rolled one within the other *(Rav).* One document is rolled up by itself, then another is rolled around it, then the third one is rolled around both of them. Hence, they are not so tightly together, and one can be separated from the others without unrolling them *(Tos. Yom Tov* from *Gem.* 21b).

אוֹ אֲגֻדָה שֶׁל־שְׁטָרוֹת, — *or a bundle of documents,*

In this case, the documents are laid one upon the other, the length of one corresponding to the length of the other *(Rav* from *Gemara),* and are then rolled up. Thus, it is impossible to take out any one of them without unrolling it *(Tos. Yom Tov).*

הֲרֵי זֶה יַחֲזִיר. — *he should return [them].*

[Since the one who claims the documents identifies them by stating what type of receptacle they were in,

how they were rolled, or — as discussed below — how many there were, the finder must return them to him.] In such cases, we do not suspect a fraudulent scheme between the lender and the borrower to seize mortgaged properties from those who bought them from the borrower. This suspicion is applicable only if it seems that the documents had been carelessly lost because they were invalid. In this case, however, since the owner rolled the documents in such a way that they could be identified, or put them into a bag or case by which they could be identified, there is no reason to believe that they are invalid *(Shoshannim LeDavid).*

Alternatively, since it is obvious that the one who lost the documents had been careful to place them in a bag or case, or to roll them securely, we do not suspect that he had thrown them away because of their worthlessness. Moreover, since the identifying marks prove who the owner is, we have no reason to believe there had been a fraudulent scheme. This is feared only when the document would be returned to the creditor because of the debtor's admission, such as in the case of mishnah 6 *(Tos. HaRosh).*

וְכַמָּה אֲגֻדָה שֶׁל־שְׁטָרוֹת? שְׁלֹשָׁה קְשׁוּרִין זֶה בָּזֶה. — *Now, how many [constitute] a bundle of documents? Three fastened one to the other.*

As explained above, the three documents are rolled together, one lying on the other. Accordingly, the word קְשׁוּרִין does not literally mean *tied,* as we find in several places in the Talmud *(Tos. HaRosh).*

רַבָּן שִׁמְעוֹן בֶּן־גַּמְלִיאֵל אוֹמֵר: אֶחָד הַלֹּוֶה
מִשְּׁלֹשָׁה, יַחֲזִיר לַלֹּוֶה; שְׁלֹשָׁה הַלֹּוִין מֵאֶחָד,
יַחֲזִיר לַמַּלְוֶה.

מָצָא שְׁטָר בֵּין שְׁטָרוֹתָיו, וְאֵינוֹ יוֹדֵעַ מַה־טִּיבוֹ,
יְהֵא מֻנָּח עַד שֶׁיָּבֹא אֵלִיָּהוּ.
אִם יֵשׁ עִמָּהֶן סִמְפוֹנוֹת, יַעֲשֶׂה מַה־
שֶּׁבַּסִּמְפוֹנוֹת.

יד אברהם

The *Gemara* explains that only if there are three or more documents can the number be considered a means of identification. If there are two, however, since the finder announces, 'I have found documents,' it is likely that one who wishes to guess will choose that amount, because it is the minimum number that takes the plural form.

According to *Rashi* (20b) the one who lost the documents must produce both distinguishing features — the number and the manner in which they are rolled — in order to claim them. This view coincides with that of *Ramah*, quoted by *Tur Choshen Mishpat* 65:11 (see *Beis Yosef, Bach* ad loc.).

Rosh maintains that the number of the documents is the sole means of identifying them. The reason the mishnah states that the documents must be in a roll or a bundle is that otherwise, they may scatter, and the one who lost them cannot be sure that there are still as many as there had been originally. Because he can no longer use their number as a means of identification, he despairs of recovering them, and the finder would be permitted to keep them for himself. *Nimmukei Yosef* adds that this would be analogous to the case of scattered money mentioned in the following mishnah. Our case is referring to an instance in which the documents were rolled together very securely to be sure they do not separate (*Tos. Yom Tov*).

According to the view of *Rosh*, the documents need not be rolled exactly in the manners mentioned in the mishnah.

As long as they are tied or fastened together [e.g., stapled] so that they will not separate, it is sufficient (*Nimmukei Yosef*).

The halachah follows the opinion of *Rosh* (*Choshen Mishpat* 65:10).

רַבָּן שִׁמְעוֹן בֶּן־גַּמְלִיאֵל אוֹמֵר: אֶחָד הַלֹּוֶה מִשְּׁלֹשָׁה, — *Rabban Shimon ben Gamliel says: [If they are of] one who borrows from three,*

The three loan contracts that were found record three loans that one person borrowed from three different people (*Rav; Rashi*).

יַחֲזִיר לַלֹּוֶה; — *he must return [them] to the debtor;*

The fact that all three are together proves that they were already paid and returned to the debtor. Should they have been unpaid and still in the possession of the creditors, there is no way of explaining how they happened to be all together. This applies only if the documents were confirmed by the court. If they were not confirmed, however, it is possible that the three creditors brought them to the court for confirmation, and the scribe lost them before they could be confirmed. Once they are already confirmed, we need not fear that the scribe lost them after recording the confirmation, since people do not leave their documents in the possession of the scribe, but take them back immediately (*Rav from Gem.* 20b).

שְׁלֹשָׁה הַלֹּוִין מֵאֶחָד, — *[if of] three who borrow from one,*

[One found three loan contracts

1
8
Rabban Shimon ben Gamliel says: [If they are of] one who borrows from three, he must return [them] to the debtor; [if of] three who borrow from one, he should return [them] to the creditor.

[If] one found a document among his documents, and he does not know who gave it to him, it must remain until Elijah comes.

If there are receipts among them, he should do what is [written] in the receipts.

recording that three different people borrowed from the same creditor.]

יַחֲזִיר לַמַּלְוֶה. — *he should return [them] to the creditor.*

The finder must return them to the creditor, since he was obviously the one who lost them (ibid.).

In this case, we cannot say that perhaps the three debtors took the documents to the court to have them confirmed, and that the scribe lost them, since only creditors confirm loan contracts, not debtors (*Tos. Yom Tov* from *Gem.* ibid.).

The *Gemara* states also that the loan contracts are returned to the creditor only if they were written by three different scribes. Should the handwriting be identical, however, perhaps the same scribe wrote the three loan contracts for three prospective borrowers and lost them before the loans took place. Therefore, he should not return them (*Rav*) unless either the creditor or the debtor properly identifies them (*Tos. Yom Tov*).

Should the contracts be confirmed, however, leaving no doubt that the loans took place, they must be returned to the creditor even if they were written by the same scribe (*Tos. R' Akiva*).

מָצָא שְׁטָר בֵּין שְׁטָרוֹתָיו, וְאֵינוֹ יוֹדֵעַ מַה-טִּיבוֹ, — [*If*] *one found a document among his documents, and he does not know who gave it to him* [lit., *what its nature is*],

He found a loan contract and does not know whether the creditor or the debtor gave it to him, or perhaps the loan was

partly paid, and he was designated by both to keep the contract (*Rav; Rashi*). If it was the debtor who had given the contract to this third party, he had done so before the loan was finalized, and had asked the latter to hold it for him until the loan would actually take place (*Ritva*, quoted in *Shitah Mekubetzes*).

יְהֵא מֻנָּח עַד שֶׁיָּבֹא אֵלִיָּהוּ. — *it must remain until Elijah comes.*

The loan contract shall remain in his possession and be returned neither to the creditor nor to the debtor (*Rav; Rashi*).

Even if the debtor admits that he did not pay his debt, the contract may not be returned, since we fear a fraudulent scheme between the debtor and the creditor, as explained in the commentary to mishnah 6 (*Meiri*).

[The allusion is to the coming of Elijah the Prophet as the herald of the Messiah. At that time, he will clarify all doubtful cases.]

Should the one holding the contract subsequently remind himself who gave it to him, he is believed (*Nesivos Hamishpat* 65:1).

אִם יֵשׁ עִמָּהֶן סִמְפּוֹנוֹת, — *If there are receipts among them,*

This final segment of the mishnah is not a continuation of the previous sentence. The intention is that a creditor finds among his contracts a receipt recording that one of his loan contracts has been paid (*Rav; Rashi*).

יַעֲשֶׂה מַה-שֶּׁבַּסִּמְפּוֹנוֹת. — *he should do*

[א] **אֵלוּ** מְצִיאוֹת שֶׁלוֹ, וְאֵלוּ חַיָּב לְהַכְרִיז. אֵלוּ

יד אברהם

what is [written] in the receipts.

He must regard the contract as paid. Although a receipt of a paid loan should be in the possession of the debtor, rather than the creditor, we assume that the debtor entrusted it to him and then forgot to take it back. This applies only if the contract for which this receipt was written is among his torn contracts, although it itself is not torn. The facts

that it is among the torn contracts and that a receipt was written for it indicate that it was indeed paid *(Rav; Rashi 20b)*. *Rashi* states also that the receipt, too, was found among the torn contracts. This indicates that it had already been given to the debtor and was no longer needed by the creditor. He therefore put it among his torn contracts.

Chapter 2

◄§ Returning Lost Articles

The following chapter is based on the section of the Torah *(Deut.* 22:1-3) dealing with returning lost articles:

לֹא־תִרְאֶה אֶת־שׁוֹר אָחִיךָ אוֹ אֶת־שֵׂיוֹ נִדָּחִים וְהִתְעַלַּמְתָּ מֵהֶם הָשֵׁב תְּשִׁיבֵם לְאָחִיךָ. וְאִם־לֹא קָרוֹב אָחִיךָ אֵלֶיךָ וְלֹא יְדַעְתּוֹ וַאֲסַפְתּוֹ אֶל־תּוֹךְ בֵּיתֶךָ וְהָיָה עִמְּךָ עַד דְּרֹשׁ אָחִיךָ אֹתוֹ וַהֲשֵׁבֹתוֹ לוֹ. וְכֵן תַּעֲשֶׂה לַחֲמֹרוֹ וְכֵן תַּעֲשֶׂה לְשִׂמְלָתוֹ וְכֵן תַּעֲשֶׂה לְכָל־אֲבֵדַת אָחִיךָ אֲשֶׁר־תֹּאבַד מִמֶּנּוּ וּמְצָאתָהּ לֹא תוּכַל לְהִתְעַלֵּם.

You shall not see your brother's ox or his lamb straying, and hide yourself from them; you shall surely return them to your brother. But if your brother is not near you, and you do not know him, you shall take it into your house, and it shall be with you until your brother seeks it, and you shall return it to him. And so shall you do with his donkey, and so shall you do with his garment, and so shall you do with any lost article belonging to your brother, which he loses and you find; you shall not hide yourself.

From here we derive that if one finds an object that has been lost, he is obligated to return it to its owner. If the identity of the owner is not known, it must be announced in public that such an article has been found. When someone comes and identifies the item by stating a סִימָן, *distinguishing feature,* of it, it is given to him.

◄§ יֵאוּשׁ / Despair

If the object has no distinguishing features, it is assumed that the owner has despaired of ever recovering it, because he knows that he will never be able to prove that it is his, and the finder may keep it.

According to *Rashi* (21a), when an owner despairs of recovering an item, it is deemed ownerless, and may be acquired by anyone who picks it up. According to *Tosafos (Bava Kamma* 66a), it is not deemed ownerless; it still belongs to the owner until someone else picks it up, at which time the latter acquires it.

This rule applies only if the article is found after the owner discovers his loss and — because there are no distinguishing features by which to claim it — despairs of ever recovering it. Should the article be picked up prior to the owner's knowledge of its loss, this is known as יֵאוּשׁ שֶׁלֹּא מִדַּעַת, *despair without knowledge.* Whether the finder may keep the item in such a situation is the topic of a controversy in the *Gemara* (21b-22b). Abaye maintains that it is not deemed as if the owner had despaired, since he, in fact, is unaware of the loss. Rava contends that it is considered as if the owner had despaired, since he would have done so had he known of the loss. The halachah follows the view of Abaye. Consequently, one may keep a lost article for himself only if it has no distinguishing features, and only if it

YAD AVRAHAM

is something which the owner would surely realize is missing immediately after it is lost.

Should the owner despair of retrieving the article only after the finder has picked it up, the latter is not permitted to retain it. Since he picked up the item when it still belonged to the original owner, he becomes a שׁוֹמֵר, *guardian,* over it, and it is considered as if it were lying in the owner's domain. Despairing of an article lying in one's own domain does not allow someone else to acquire it *(Ramban* in *Milchamos Hashem,* quoted by *Tos. R' Akiva).*

◄§ סִימָנִים / Distinguishing Features

The *Gemara* (27a,b) discusses whether the practice of identifying a lost article by stating a distinguishing feature is Biblically valid, or whether it is a Rabbinical innovation, while the Torah, in fact, requires witnesses in order for one to claim an item as his own. According to the latter theory, the Rabbis enacted this institution as a benefit to those who have lost items and have no witnesses to prove that they are the owners. Such people do not fear that this will allow others to come along and claim the items, since they believe that no one knows the distinguishing features as well as they do. Although mishnah 5 seems to state that this institution is of Biblical origin, it is possible that the *Tanna* did not intend that literally, and was merely referring to the Rabbinical innovation (see comm. there). The question whether the distinguishing-feature institution is Biblical or Rabbinical in origin would determine the halachah in the case in which one finds a *get,* a bill of divorce, and the agent who is to deliver it to the woman (see first *Rashi* to 27b, *Ketzos HaChoshen* 259:2) claims it by stating its distinguishing features. If the institution is Biblical, the *get* is returned to him; if Rabbinical, the institution would apply only to monetary matters, not to items like a *get* which involves the prohibitory matters of marriage and divorce.

◄§ Types of Distinguishing Features

Maggid Mishneh (Hil. Gezeilah 13:3) classifies distinguishing features into three categories:

(1) Those that are totally unmistakable: This includes such marks as a hole next to a certain letter in a document. These are acceptable according to Biblical law without a doubt, and even a *get* is returned on such evidence, since they are equivalent to witnesses.

(2) Those that are superior: These are the normal means of identification accepted in all cases in the Mishnah and the *Gemara,* such as the weight, length, or width of an article. It is concerning this type of distinguishing features that the *Gemara* questions whether or not they are accepted by the Torah as proper identification.

(3) Those that are inferior: This category includes such means of identification as the color of the item, or stating that it is long or short, without giving the measurements. These are of no value whatsoever. The second group is sometimes referred to as *unmistakable features* in contrast with the third category.

1.

אֵלוּ מְצִיאוֹת שֶׁלּוֹ, וְאֵלוּ חַיָּב לְהַכְרִיז. — *Some finds* [lit., *these*] *belong to him, and some he must announce.*

[Some translate: *Which finds are his,*

and which must he announce? This does not appear to be correct, however, since the word אֵלּוּ is spelled without a *yud;* were the sentence a question, it would

בבא
מציעא
ב/א

מְצִיאוֹת שֶׁלּוֹ: מָצָא פֵּרוֹת מְפֻזָּרִין, מָעוֹת מְפֻזָּרוֹת,
כְּרִיכוֹת בִּרְשׁוּת הָרַבִּים, וְעִגּוּלֵי דְבֵלָה, כִּכָּרוֹת

יד אברהם

be אֵילוּ.[1] Moreover, the repetition of the phrase אֵלּוּ מְצִיאוֹת שֶׁלּוֹ indicates that it is a statement, rather than a question, because when the *Tanna* employs the question-and-answer form, he uses slightly different expressions in the two parts, as in *Shabbos* 2:1, 4:1, 5:1, 6:1.]

The *Tanna* does not word the first phrase, *Some finds need not be announced*, to parallelize it with the next phrase, since — were he to do so — we would think that in such cases, if one brings witnesses that the object is his, the finder would be required to return it to him. To prevent such a misinterpretation, the *Tanna* states: *Some finds are his*, implying that the finder may retain these items even if someone proves that they originally belonged to him [see below] *(Shitah Mekubetzes quoting Ritva; Chiddushei HaRitva Hachadashim).*

אֵלּוּ מְצִיאוֹת שֶׁלּוֹ: — *These finds belong to him:*

[If a person finds the following items, he may keep them, since they have no distinguishing features, and the owner is assumed to have despaired of them, as explained in the preface.]

This is one instance in which the *Tanna* commences to expound on the first of the categories mentioned. Other times, he begins by discussing the last category mentioned. See *Nedarim* 1:1 [and ArtScroll comm. ad loc., p. 8] *(Tos. Yom Tov).*

מָצָא פֵּרוֹת מְפֻזָּרִין, — *[If] he found scattered produce,*

We assume that the owner has despaired of them, and they are therefore ownerless *(Rav; Rashi).* [As explained in the preface, *Rashi* equates יֵאוּשׁ, *despair*, with הֶפְקֵר, *abandonment*; he therefore states that the lost produce

is ownerless. According to *Tosafos* (*Bava Kamma* 66a), however, they are two distinct laws: that of abandonment, which renders an article ownerless; and that of despair, which merely permits the public to take possession of something belonging to someone.]

Although the halachah is in accordance with the view of Abaye, who maintains that 'despair without knowledge' [see preface] is not deemed despair, one who finds scattered produce may take it for himself. This is because produce is weighty, and it is therefore assumed that the owner realized his loss immediately and despaired of recovering it. Also, since the produce is expensive, he periodically taps his pack to check it, and it is therefore assumed that he is aware of the loss by now *(Tos. Yom Tov from Ramban, Nimmukei Yosef; Rif; Rashba; Rambam, Hil. Gezeilah* 15:8). Should the fruit be lying in a way that indicates that it had been placed there intentionally, it may not be touched *(Rambam* ibid. from *Gem.* 21a).

Alternatively, the *Gemara* explains that this segment of the mishnah is dealing with a case in which produce had been gathered from the threshing floors. [In other words, rather than an instance of the owner having lost produce, the case is one in which he merely left over some of the produce that had been threshed.] If there is a *kav* [a certain measure] of produce scattered four or more cubits square, it belongs to the finder, since the owner will not bother to come back and gather it. If, however, it is scattered within less than four cubits square, the finder may not touch it, since it is possible that the owner left it there intentionally *(Rambam* loc. cit. §12), and because it is

---

1. [See, for example, *Pesikta Rabbasi* (ed. Friedman, p. 138b): ... לְאֵילוּ נַאֲמִין, *which ones shall we believe ...?*]

nounce. These finds belong to him: [If] he found
scattered produce, scattered money, small sheaves in
a public domain, round cakes of pressed figs, loaves

YAD AVRAHAM

not that great of a bother to gather it, he will return and do so.

The *Gemara* qualifies the mishnah as referring to such an instance, rather than to the case mentioned above — that the produce was found in a manner indicating that it fell, in which case the quantity of the produce and the space that it occupied are irrelevant. This is because, as opposed to this instance of the produce being scattered, the following mishnah states that if it is found in piles, it must be announced. The *Gemara* must therefore explain the cases in a way that would differentiate between produce that is scattered and that which is in piles. That is why our mishnah is qualified as referring to produce left over from that which is gathered from the threshing floors, so that there is a difference between a *kav* within four cubits square, which is regarded as scattered, and a *kav* within a smaller area, which is regarded as piled (*Nachalas David*).

מָעוֹת מְפֻזָּרוֹת, — *scattered money,*

Since the money has no distinguishing feature, the owner despairs of it, and it becomes ownerless. This is the reason that all the items listed in this mishnah may be retained by the finder (*Rav; Rashi*).

Concerning this item, too, even Abaye agrees that the finder may keep it, because people usually tap their pockets from time to time, and the loser is surely aware of his loss (*Tos. Yom Tov* from *Gem.* 21b).

בְּרִיכוֹת בִּרְשׁוּת הָרַבִּים, — *small sheaves in a public domain,*

In the *Gemara*, there is a controversy between Rabbah and Rava concerning the explanation of this ruling. Rabbah maintains that the mishnah permits taking the sheaves even if they have a

distinguishing feature. Since they are apt to be trodden upon, the owner believes that the distinguishing feature has been obliterated and despairs of recovering the sheaves. This is applicable only if they are found in a public domain, where people and beasts usually walk. In a private domain, however, where there usually is little or no traffic, the distinguishing feature will remain. Likewise, large sheaves — which are too high for people and beasts to trample upon — must be announced, since the owner expects the distinguishing feature to remain.

Rava, however, contends that the ruling of the mishnah applies only if the sheaves have no distinguishing features; if they do, the finder would be obligated to announce them. Rava maintains that a distinguishing feature that is apt to be trodden upon is nevertheless valid as long as it still exists. He rules also that the location of a lost article is deemed a distinguishing feature. Consequently, if small sheaves were left in a public place, the owner despairs of recovering them, since they are likely to be kicked away from the place where they were left. In a private domain, on the other hand, he expects them to be found where he left them. Likewise, if one finds large sheaves, he must announce them, since they are too heavy to be kicked away from their original place (*Rav, Tos. Yom Tov* from *Gem.* 22b, 23a).

The halachah is in accordance with Rava's view (*Gem.* ibid.). *Tos. R' Akiva* is therefore puzzled why *Rav* explains the mishnah according to Rabbah.

וְעִגּוּלֵי דְבֵלָה, — *round cakes of pressed figs,*

That is, dried figs pressed together in a round form like a loaf of bread (*Tif. Yis.*).

שֶׁל־נַחְתּוֹם, מַחֲרוֹזוֹת שֶׁל־דָּגִים, וַחֲתִיכוֹת שֶׁל־
בָּשָׂר, וְגִזֵּי צֶמֶר הַבָּאוֹת מִמְּדִינָתָן, וַאֲנִיצֵי פִשְׁתָּן,
וּלְשׁוֹנוֹת שֶׁל־אַרְגָּמָן — הֲרֵי אֵלּוּ שֶׁלּוֹ. דִּבְרֵי רַבִּי
מֵאִיר. רַבִּי יְהוּדָה אוֹמֵר: כָּל־שֶׁיֶּשׁ־בּוֹ שִׁנּוּי חַיָּב

יד אברהם

כִּכָּרוֹת שֶׁל־נַחְתּוֹם, — *loaves of a baker's
bread,*

Since all his loaves are uniform, and
many people purchase from him, no
loaf has a distinguishing feature.
Homemade loaves of bread, however,
can be identified, since everyone who
makes them does so in a different shape
(*Rav; Rashi*).

מַחֲרוֹזוֹת שֶׁל־דָּגִים, — *strings of fish,*

That is, fish attached to a string.
These have no distinguishing feature,
since everyone strings them in the same
manner (*Tif. Yis.*).

וַחֲתִיכוֹת שֶׁל־בָּשָׂר, — *pieces of meat,*

This applies only if the pieces are of
the uniform weight and shape into
which butchers usually cut their meat
(ibid.). Should the meat be in an
unusual shape, such as a triangle,
however, it is indeed a distinguishing
feature, and it must be announced. On
the other hand, the part of the animal
from where the piece was taken is not a
valid means of identification (*Gem.*
23b).

[The loss of any of the foodstuffs
listed in the mishnah is readily realized,
since they are heavy. Therefore, there is
no fear that the owner was unaware that
he had lost them when the finder picked
them up. Although the *Gemara* (21b)
states this only with regard to two of the
items listed, it seems to apply to all of
them.] *Rosh* states that since all
foodstuffs are important, those carrying
them tap their packs often to ascertain
whether they are still there. [To
reconcile *Rosh* with the *Gemara*, see
*Hagahos HaGra, Pilpula Charifta, Tos.
HaRosh, Tos. Rabbeinu Peretz.*]

וְגִזֵּי צֶמֶר הַבָּאוֹת מִמְּדִינָתָן, — *fleeces of wool
brought from their country,*

That is, wool that has not been
changed since its shearing. It is therefore identical to all the wool brought
from that country. On the other hand,
once the wool is in the shop of the
craftsman, he makes an identifying
mark on each fleece in order to prevent
it from being switched with wool
belonging to someone else (*Tos. Yom
Tov* from *Rashi; Meiri*).

The expression הַבָּאוֹת מִמְּדִינָתָן,
brought from their country, is unusual.
Rosh renders: *brought from their ties,*
meaning: from their original status,
when they are tied together after the
shearing. A similar word is found in
Shabbos 33b: מְדָנֵי אָסָא, *bundles of
myrtle* [מדני, מדינות = *bundles, ties*].

וַאֲנִיצֵי פִשְׁתָּן, — *bundles of flax,*

This refers to flax that has been
beaten and carded, and is ready for
spinning (*Tif. Yis., Aruch,* from *Succah*
12b).

וּלְשׁוֹנוֹת שֶׁל־אַרְגָּמָן — — *or tongues of
purple wool —*

That is, wool died purple and drawn
out in the shape of a tongue (*Rav;
Rashi*). *Rashi* adds that they are
common.

[Since the above three items are
expensive, one carrying them will often
tap his load to make sure that he has not
lost them. Consequently, he will soon be
aware of their loss, and despair of
recovering them. Here, too, although
the *Gemara* (21b) states this only with
regard to tongues of purple wool, it
seems to apply to the other two items as
well.]

הֲרֵי אֵלּוּ שֶׁלּוֹ. — *these belong to him.*

As explained above, one who loses
any of the aforementioned items,
knowing that it has no distinguishing

of a baker's bread, strings of fish, pieces of meat, fleeces of wool brought from their country, bundles of flax, or tongues of purple wool — these belong to him. [These are] the words of R' Meir. R' Yehudah says: Anything containing something unusual must

feature, despairs of retrieving it. It is therefore permissible for the finder to keep it (Rav).

The Tanna lists all of the above items because we learn a different halachah from each one, as follows: Scattered produce and scattered money: since they are heavy or expensive, the owner becomes aware of the loss soon after it occurred, and despairs of recovering them. According to Rava — who contends that the owner will not realize the loss — these two cases teach us that despair without knowledge is considered despair. Small sheaves in a public domain: since they will be kicked about, their location is not deemed a distinguishing feature. Round cakes of pressed figs: even if the finder announces merely that he found pressed figs, the fact that they were pressed into a round cake is not considered a valid means of identification. Loaves of a baker's bread: since the shapes are mostly the same, they are not distinguishing features. Pieces of meat: the part of the animal's body from where the piece was cut is not sufficient to properly identify it. Fleeces of wool: the manner in which they are rolled or tied is not a distinguishing feature. Bundles of flax: even if the finder announces merely that he found flax, the fact that it was in bundles is not sufficient identification. Tongues of purple wool: the color is not a distinguishing feature (Ritva, quoted by Shitah Mekubetzes; Chiddushei HaRitva Hachadashim).

[Although Ritva does not mention strings of fish, the halachah apparently derived from it is that — as stated above — they have no distinguishing feature, since everyone strings them in the same

manner.]

דִּבְרֵי רַבִּי מֵאִיר. — [These are] the words of R' Meir.

[R' Meir rules that all the above articles are not considered as having distinguishing features, even if something unusual is inside them, as discussed below.]

In many editions, this attribution is omitted; accordingly, this first view in the mishnah is that of an anonymous Tanna. Rambam, whose reading is like ours, rules in accordance with the opinion of R' Yehudah, mentioned below, since the halachah always follows his view when he differs with R' Meir (Beis Yosef 265). Rosh, however, whose version omits the attribution to R' Meir, rules in accordance with the first, anonymous view (Tos. Yom Tov).

רַבִּי יְהוּדָה אוֹמֵר: כָּל־שֶׁיֶּש־בּוֹ שִׁנּוּי — R' Yehudah says: Anything containing something unusual

That is, containing something not usually placed in it (Tif. Yis.). [Examples are given below.]

חַיָּב לְהַכְרִיז. — must be announced.

Rashi (23a) explains that although these unusual things normally fall into the articles by accident, we nevertheless consider the possibility that the owner inserted them in order to identify them. Therefore, they must be announced.

Tosafos (ad loc.), however, reject Rashi's interpretation, and explain instead that although this unusual thing obviously fell into the article by accident, the owner may have been aware of it and can use it as a means of identification. The first Tanna, on the other hand, does not consider that possibility, maintaining that since it fell

לְהַכְרִיז. כֵּיצַד? מָצָא עָגוֹל, וּבְתוֹכוֹ חֶרֶס; כִּכָּר,
וּבְתוֹכוֹ מָעוֹת.

רַבִּי שִׁמְעוֹן בֶּן־אֶלְעָזָר אוֹמֵר: כָּל־כְּלֵי אַנְפּוֹרְיָא
אֵין חַיָּב לְהַכְרִיז.

[ב] **וְאֵלּוּ** חַיָּב לְהַכְרִיז: מָצָא פֵּרוֹת בִּכְלִי, אוֹ
כְּלִי כְּמוֹת שֶׁהוּא, מָעוֹת בְּכִיס, אוֹ

יד אברהם

in by accident, the owner was certainly unaware of it.

כֵּיצַד? — *How?*
[What is an example of an item with something unusual inside it?]

מָצָא עָגוֹל, וּבְתוֹכוֹ חֶרֶס; — *He found a round cake, and a potsherd was inside it;*

The reference is to a round cake of pressed figs (Rav).

כִּכָּר, וּבְתוֹכוֹ מָעוֹת. — [or] *a loaf, and money was inside it.*
[This refers to a loaf of baker's bread; a loaf of homemade bread must be announced in any case, as stated in the following mishnah.]

⋙ Items without Distinguishing Features / Recognition by a Torah Scholar

The following segment of the mishnah deals with utensils that have no distinguishing features. Should a Torah scholar, noted for his truthfulness, claim to recognize them as his own, he is believed. Therefore, if one finds such an object in a place frequented by scholars, such as a study hall, he is required to announce it (Tos. 24a). Every Torah scholar is assumed to be truthful unless the finder proves that he is not (Choshen Mishpat 262:21; Rama ad loc.). [See Tos. to Chullin 96a and Ritva ibid.]

רַבִּי שִׁמְעוֹן בֶּן־אֶלְעָזָר אוֹמֵר: כָּל־כְּלֵי אַנְפּוֹרְיָא — *R' Shimon ben Elazar says: All new utensils*

That is, new vessels that have not yet been used, and whose owner is not yet familiar with them (Rav from Gem. 23b, 24a).

Rashi defines אַנְפּוֹרְיָא as an abbreviation of אֵין פֹּה רְאִיָּה, *there is no seeing here,* meaning that the owner has not yet become accustomed to seeing the utensils.

Others derive it from the Greek or Latin, meaning *merchandise* — i.e., newly acquired goods from the store (Mussaf He'Aruch). Aruch Hashalem derives it from a Greek word meaning *no knowledge,* and attributes this definition to Rambam Commentary and Tos. Yom Tov.

The Gemara (24a) gives examples of

new utensils whose owner is not yet familiar with them: poles of needles, poles of knitting needles, strings of hatchets. Since they are still hanging on the poles or strings, it is apparent that the owner did not use them yet (Toras Chaim).

אֵין חַיָּב לְהַכְרִיז. — *need not be announced.*

Since the owner is not expected to recognize them, there is no need to announce them. Tosafos (loc. cit.) add that even if a Torah scholar claims to recognize a new vessel, R' Shimon ben Elazar rules that he is not believed. Only according to the *Tanna* alluded to in the *baraisa* quoted by the *Gemara* — who does not differentiate between new and old utensils — is a Torah scholar believed to identify a new object with no distinguishing feature.

be announced. How? He found a round cake, and a potsherd was inside it; [or] a loaf, and money was inside it.

R' Shimon ben Elazar says: All new utensils need not be announced.

2. These must be announced: [If] he found produce in a vessel, or a vessel just as it is,

YAD AVRAHAM

Tos. R' Akiva maintains that there is no proof for this assertion, and that the difference between the anonymous *Tanna's* view and that of R' Shimon ben Elazar may be that according to the anonymous *Tanna*, new utensils must be announced, since the owner is possibly a Torah scholar, who might recognize them. R' Shimon ben Elazar rules that we need not announce them, since it is unlikely that the owner will recognize them. Should it happen that a Torah scholar claims to recognize them, however, even R' Shimon ben Elazar agrees that they must be returned to him.

In the case of the poles of needles and the like, the finder is exempt from announcing them only if he found one pole. If he finds two or more, however, he is obligated to announce them, since the number is a distinguishing feature. The owner will state that they are hanging on poles and how many there are (*Rosh*).

In 1:8 it is stated that if one finds a roll or bundle of documents, he must announce it only if there are at least three documents. If there are only two, he is not required to announce it, since if one were to guess how many documents there were, he might very well choose the number two, that being the minimum amount that would take the plural

form. In our case, however, the finder must announce the needles even if he finds only two poles. The difference is that in the case above, it is announced that documents have been found, whereas here needles are announced, not poles of needles [so that no hint is given as to whether there are one or more poles] (*Tos. HaRosh; Pilpula Charifta; see Tos. Yom Tov*).

Should one find something on a highway or a large marketplace, and it has a distinguishing feature — if it is in a city inhabited primarily by gentiles, he is not obligated to announce it [see commentary to 1:1, s.v. "...אֲנִי, ,,זֶה אוֹמֵר]; if in a city inhabited primarily by Jews, he is obligated to announce it (*Rav, Rambam Commentary* from Gem. 24a). In the former case, even if the finder knows that a Jew lost the item, he need not return it to him. This is because we assume that the owner despaired of recovering the item, expecting that it would be found by either a gentile or a Jew who would not announce it, since he presumes that it was lost by a gentile (*Tos.* ad loc., s.v. כי). If the finder wishes to go beyond the demands of the halachah, he should return even such an item (*Gem.* 24b).

2.

וְאֵלוּ חַיָּב לְהַכְרִיז: — *These must be announced:*

[If one finds the following items, he must announce them, since they have distinguishing features, and the owner therefore has not despaired of recovering them.]

מָצָא פֵרוֹת בִּכְלִי, — *[If] he found produce in a vessel,*

A vessel usually has distinguishing features (*Rav; Rashi*).

אוֹ כְלִי כְּמוֹת שֶׁהוּא, — *or a vessel just as it is,*

That is, an empty basket or the like (ibid.).

מָעוֹת בְּכִיס, — *money in a purse,*

A purse, too, has a distinguishing

בבא
מציעא
ב/ג

כִּיס כְּמוֹת שֶׁהוּא, צְבוּרֵי פֵרוֹת, צְבוּרֵי מָעוֹת,
שְׁלֹשָׁה מַטְבְּעוֹת זֶה עַל־גַּב זֶה, כְּרִיכוֹת בִּרְשׁוּת
הַיָּחִיד, וְכִכָּרוֹת שֶׁל־בַּעַל הַבַּיִת, וְגִזֵּי צֶמֶר
הַלְּקוּחוֹת מִבֵּית הָאֻמָּן, כַּדֵּי יַיִן, וְכַדֵּי שֶׁמֶן — הֲרֵי
אֵלּוּ חַיָּב לְהַכְרִיז.

[ג] **מָצָא** אַחַר הַגַּפָּה אוֹ אַחַר הַגָּדֵר גּוֹזָלוֹת

יד אברהם

feature, and can therefore be identified by its owner (*Rashi*).

אוֹ כִּיס כְּמוֹת שֶׁהוּא, — *or a purse just as it is,*

[That is, an empty purse.]

צְבוּרֵי פֵרוֹת, — *piles of produce,*

The Gemara (25a) is in doubt whether the distinguishing feature is the number of piles or the place where they were found (*Rav; Rashi*).

צְבוּרֵי מָעוֹת, — *piles of money,*

In this case, too, either the number or the place is the distinguishing feature (*Tif. Yis.* from *Gem.*).

שְׁלֹשָׁה מַטְבְּעוֹת זֶה עַל־גַּב זֶה, — *three coins one upon the other,*

The finder announces, 'I have found coins,' and the one who claims them replies, 'There were three of them, and they were lying one upon the other' (*Rav* from *Nimmukei Yosef*).

The announcement specifies *coins* — indicating that there are more than one — since the finder must describe the articles as accurately as possible [omitting only a distinguishing feature with which the owner can claim it] (*Ran; Nimmukei Yosef*).

Rosh — consistent with his view cited above in the commentary to 1:8, s.v. וְכַמָּה — disagrees, maintaining that it is sufficient to identify the coins merely by stating how many there were. The mishnah specifies that they were lying on top of each other only because this demonstrates that the owner had deliberately placed them there and,

hence, would know how many coins there were. If, however, they are not lying so, he would not know how many fell together. Consequently, he would despair of recovering them, and there would be no obligation for the finder to announce them.

If two coins were found, they need not be announced, since — as explained above — stating the number of items when there are only two of them is not a sufficient means of identification, because — being the minimum amount that takes a plural form — it is too easily guessed (*Gem., Rashi* ad loc.). Apparently, two coins can happen to fall on top of each other; otherwise they could be identified by the place where they were found, and the finder would be obligated to announce it (*Rosh*).

Ravad, however, contends that with regard to small things like coins, one will not remember exactly where he placed them (*Tos. Yom Tov*).

כְּרִיכוֹת בִּרְשׁוּת הַיָּחִיד, — *small sheaves in a private domain,*

That is, in a sown field, where few people walk (*Tos. Yom Tov* from *Rashi* 22b).

[In the commentary to mishnah 1, s.v. כְּרִיכוֹת, it is explained that the place where the sheaves are lying is the distinguishing feature.] Since they are in a private domain, they will not be kicked away from where the owner left them (*Gem.* 23a).

וְכִכָּרוֹת שֶׁל־בַּעַל הַבַּיִת, — *loaves of homemade bread,* money in a purse, or a purse just as it is, piles of produce, piles of money, three coins one upon the other, small sheaves in a private domain, loaves of homemade bread, fleeces of wool taken from the craftsman's workshop, jugs of wine, or jugs of oil — these must be announced.

3. **[**I**f]** behind a fence or behind a wall he found

YAD AVRAHAM

Since every person who bakes bread privately does so with his own distinctive shape, his loaves have a distinguishing feature (*Rav* to mishnah 1; *Rashi*).

וְגִזֵּי צֶמֶר הַלְקוּחוֹת מִבֵּית הָאֻמָּן, — *fleeces of wool taken from the craftsman's workshop,*

When a craftsman is given wool for dyeing, he knots it in order to recognize each customer's fleece. Thus, it has a distinguishing feature (*Meiri*).

בַּדֵּי יַיִן, וְכַדֵּי שֶׁמֶן — — *jugs of wine, or jugs of oil —*

The size of the jug cannot be used as a means of identification, since all jugs are usually the same size. However, if the jug is not full, the amount of wine or oil in it is considered a distinguishing feature. Another method of identification is the seal with which the owner closed the jug, since each person makes his own seal different from those of others. After the wine cellars are open, however, this method is no longer valid, since the wine is sold to many retailers, and the same seal is found on jugs of wine owned by various retailers (*Tos.* 23b).

Even if the wine is deposited on the river bank after being transported by ship, the place where it is left is not a distinguishing feature, since many sailors deposit their cargo on the river bank and carry off the jugs one by one, sometimes forgetting some. Consequently, the fact that one of them names the place the jug was found does not prove that it is his; it may have been lost by one of the many others who left their jugs there (*Tos. Yom Tov* from *Gem., Rashi* 23b).

הֲרֵי אֵלּוּ חַיָּב לְהַכְרִיז. — *these must be announced.*

[As explained, each of these items has a distinguishing feature.]

3.

The following mishnah teaches us that if an item was found, and it seems that its owner deliberately put it in that place with the intention that it remain there, as long as it is a place in which it is relatively safe — so that the owner could not be considered to have knowingly allowed it to get lost or destroyed — the item should not be touched. For if someone does take it away, the owner may return, and upon not finding the item — if it is one without a distinguishing feature — will despair of recovering it. Hence, the finder will have caused him a loss (*Meiri*).

If the item has a distinguishing feature, the finder should not take it — even for the purpose of announcing it — since he is needlessly troubling the owner to search for the article and identify it (*Rambam, Hil. Gezeilah* 15:1).

מָצָא אַחַר הַגַּפָּה אוֹ אַחַר הַגָּדֵר — *[If] behind a fence or behind a wall he found*
גַּפָּה is a fence made of wood or reeds;

גָּדֵר is a stone fence (*Rav; Rashi*).

These places afford some degree of safety. Should it not, the owner surely

מְקֻשָּׁרִין — אוֹ בַּשְׁבִילִין שֶׁבַּשָּׂדוֹת — הֲרֵי זֶה לֹא **בבא**
יִגַּע בָּהֶן. **מציעא**
ב/ג
מָצָא כְלִי בָּאַשְׁפָּה, אִם מְכֻסֶּה, לֹא יִגַּע בּוֹ; אִם
מְגֻלֶּה, נוֹטֵל וּמַכְרִיז.
מָצָא בְגַל וּבְכֹתֶל יָשָׁן, הֲרֵי אֵלּוּ שֶׁלּוֹ. מָצָא

יד אברהם

despairs of recovering an item that he left there if it has no distinguishing feature. In a place that affords adequate safety, even if the item has a distinguishing feature, one who finds it should not touch it. This can be deduced from the next statement in the mishnah — [If] he found a utensil in a heap of garbage, [and] it is covered [i.e., completely, so that it is safe], he should not touch it. The Tanna is surely dealing with a utensil bearing a distinguishing feature, since the mishnah continues: if it is uncovered, he must take [it] and announce [it] (Tos. Yom Tov from Tos. 25b).

גוֹזָלוֹת מְקֻשָּׁרִין — young birds with their wings tied —

The wings were tied with an ordinary knot, which does not serve as a distinguishing feature (Rav from Gem. ibid.).

אוֹ בַּשְׁבִילִין שֶׁבַּשָּׂדוֹת — or in the paths of the fields —

[There he found young birds with their wings tied. See below for an explanation of the mishnah's peculiar sentence structure.]

הֲרֵי זֶה לֹא יִגַּע בָּהֶן. — he should not touch them.

It is assumed that someone hid the birds there, but since they have no distinguishing feature, he will be unable to identify them. Therefore, if the one who finds them picks them up, the owner will not be able to claim them. To be sure, should the birds be standing still, the owner would be able to identify them by stating where he left them. However, the mishnah deals with birds that are hopping, and hence, there is no

way of telling where they had originally been left.

It is also possible that these birds were not hidden there, but were lost by a traveler passing by. In that case, since they have no distinguishing feature, the owner despairs of them, and they may be taken. Consequently, it is uncertain whether the article had been lost or placed here, and the halachah in such a case is that it may not be touched (Rav, Tos. Yom Tov from Gem.).

In view of this qualification of the mishnah, we can understand the peculiar sentence structure of this segment. It may be understood to mean that he found the young birds behind a fence or behind a wall, and then found the same birds in the paths of the fields. This is the sign that they were hopping. For this reason, the phrase or in the paths of the fields is placed at the end of this segment of the mishnah (Shoshannim LeDavid).

Sma (260:45) qualifies the mishnah's case as one in which the birds were found at least fifty cubits away from another birdhouse. Should they be found closer to one, they belong to the owner of the birdhouse, in accordance with Bava Basra 2:6 [see commentary there], since young birds that hop rather than fly do not wander more than fifty cubits away from their dwelling (Tos. Yom Tov ad loc.).

Shach (loc. cit. §28) disagrees and differentiates between the two cases. He qualifies the mishnah in Bava Basra as referring to an instance in which the birds' wings are not tied. Hence, since they are within fifty cubits of a birdhouse, it is assumed that they came from there and belong to its owner. In our case, however, the wings are tied, which may be an indication that someone hid them there and will come

2
3
young birds with their wings tied — or in the paths of
the fields — he should not touch them.

[If] he found a utensil in a heap of garbage, [and] it
is covered, he should not touch it; if it is uncovered,
he must take [it] and announce [it].

[If] he found [objects] in a heap [of stones] or in an
old wall, they belong to him. [If] he found [objects] in

YAD AVRAHAM

back for them. Therefore, although the birds
are within fifty cubits of a birdhouse, since it
is possible that they had been put in this
place by someone other than the owner of the
birdhouse, the halachah in such instances is
that they should not be touched, as discussed
above.

Shoshannim LeDavid, citing *Kol
HaRemez,* contends that birds in a birdhouse
are never tied. Consequently, since the birds
in our case were tied, even if they were found
within fifty cubits of a birdhouse, it is
unlikely that they came from there.

מָצָא כְלִי בָאַשְׁפָּה, אם מְכֻסֶּה, — *[If] he found
a utensil in a heap of garbage, [and] it is
covered,*
[The utensil is covered completely so
that it is safe.]

לֹא יִגַּע בּוֹ; — *he should not touch it;*
Since it is hidden in a safe place, the
precept of returning a lost article does
not apply *(Rav; Rashi).* On the
contrary, he should not pick it up,
because — as explained above — he
would thereby be putting the owner to
the trouble of searching for the article
and identifying it *(Rambam, Hil.
Gezeilah* 15:1).

Although the item was found among
garbage, we do not assume that it was
lost and that it therefore must be
announced *(Tif. Yis.).*

This ruling applies only to a heap of
garbage that is not usually cleared.
Should it usually be cleared, however,
one who places a utensil there is considered as if he knowingly allowed it to
get lost, in which case some authorities
maintain that it is considered ownerless
and anyone can take it for themselves
(ibid. from *Gem., Rama* 261:4).

The ruling is applicable only to large
vessels, such as pitchers and cups —
which could not have been inadvertently thrown away with the garbage — but
not to small utensils, such as knives and
forks. If the latter have a distinguishing
feature, they must be announced *(Gem.*
25b).

אם מְגֻלֶּה, — *if it is uncovered,*
[Hence, it is not safe.]

נוֹטֵל וּמַכְרִיז. — *he must take [it] and
announce [it].*
Since the mishnah is dealing with a
garbage heap that is not usually cleared,
one who leaves his utensil there is not
considered to have knowingly allowed it
to get lost. Although it was found uncovered, we assume that it had originally been covered, and subsequently
became uncovered *(Meiri).*

Others, however, maintain that the
utensil being uncovered indicates that it
had fallen into the heap. Consequently,
the finder must pick it up and announce
it *(Ritva,* quoted in *Shitah Mekubetzes;
Chiddushei HaRitva Hachadashim).*

מָצָא בְגַל — *[If] he found [objects] in a
heap [of stones]*
That is, a heap of stones from a wall
that fell *(Tif. Yis.; Rashi; Meiri).*

וּבְכֹתֶל יָשָׁן, — *or in an old wall,*
This refers to a wall whose origin no
one remembers, and which was not
always in the possession of its present
owner or his ancestors *(Tos. Yom Tov*
from *Tur Choshen Mishpat* 260).

הֲרֵי אֵלּוּ שֶׁלּוֹ. — *they belong to him.*
The mishnah is dealing with a case in

בְּכֹתֶל חָדָשׁ — מֶחֶצְיוֹ וְלַחוּץ, שֶׁלּוֹ; מֶחֶצְיוֹ
וְלִפְנִים, שֶׁל־בַּעַל הַבַּיִת. אִם הָיָה מַשְׂכִּירוֹ

יד אברהם

which the article is rusty, indicating its extreme antiquity. The finder can therefore claim that it had belonged to the people who inhabited the land prior to those living there now. Hence, it is not the property of the owner of the wall or heap and may be acquired by anyone. In *Eretz Yisrael*, for example, he can claim that it had belonged to the Amorites who inhabited the Holy Land prior to the Jewish people's conquest of it in the time of Joshua *(Rav from Gem.* 25b, 26a, as explained by *Tos. Yom Tov, Sma* loc. cit. §1).

Rambam (Hil. Gezeilah 16:7), based on a variant reading, comments that the item was found deep down in the ground, as ancient treasures usually are. *Sma* (§3) explains that although the item had originally been placed in a hole in the wall, the wall subsequently sunk, and the earth around it piled up above it over the years, which is why the item was buried so deeply in the ground.

Although it is possible that the owner of the wall or heap or his ancestors had put the item there, the fact that it was rusty and buried deeply seems to indicate that its placement there predates their ownership of the wall or heap. Accordingly, the finder may keep the item unless the owner proves otherwise (ibid. §1).

Should it seem that the item had been put there recently, even though this is uncertain, the finder may not touch it, since it may have been hidden there *(Tos. Yom Tov* from *Rambam,* loc. cit.).

Many commentators ask why the item does not belong to the owner of the wall or heap, since it is lying in his property and is analogous to an ownerless article lying in his courtyard, which becomes his even if he is unaware of it (see preface to 1:4).

Tosafos explain that one's courtyard acquires property for him only if it is certain that he will eventually become aware of its presence. In our case, however, it is likely that the owner will never even realize that the

item exists.

Rosh suggests that since the spoils of the Amorites did not belong to the owner of the property in which they were found, but were shared among the entire Jewish nation, the owner of the wall at the time of the conquest was tantamount to one who picks up a lost article prior to its owner's despairing of it. In such a case, even if the owner subsequently despairs of recovering the item, the one who picked it up does not gain ownership of it, since it came into his possession when it was prohibited to him (see preface to this chapter, s.v. ויאוש). Here, too, since the hidden item was the property of the entire Jewish people, the owner of the wall had no right to it. Since he was in possession of it in its prohibited state, neither he nor his heirs have any right to it.

Rambam (Hil. Gezeilah 17:8) advances yet another answer. He reasons that this hidden object is considered lost to everyone, and is analogous to an article washed away by a river, which — since it is lost to everyone — becomes ownerless. How much more should this apply to our case in which the article never belonged to the owner of the wall or heap! [Although *Tos. Yom Tov* identifies *Rambam's* explanation with that of *Tosafos, Smag* (Essin 74) states that they are two distinct views.]

Another answer is that this wall is analogous to a yard which is not safe. [Since anyone can come and take it, the item is not secure for the owner of the wall or heap] *(Ravad* ad loc.).

Smag quotes *Rabbeinu Yonah ben R' Nassan,* who asserts that a courtyard does not acquire property for its owner if it was put there before the courtyard became his. In our case, we assume that the item was in the wall prior to the Jewish conquest.

מָצָא בְּכֹתֶל חָדָשׁ — — *[If] he found [objects] in a new wall —*

That is, a wall known to have been built by the ancestors of the present owner, and one that was always owned by that family, who were always living there *(Tos. Yom Tov* from *Rosh).*

מֶחֶצְיוֹ וְלַחוּץ, — *from the middle toward the outside,*

2
3

a new wall—from the middle toward the outside, they
belong to him; from the middle toward the inside,
they belong to the owner of the house. If he rent-

YAD AVRAHAM

That is, the objects were found in a hole in the wall opening to the street, between the middle of the depth of the wall and the outside (Rav; Rashi).

שֶׁלּוֹ; — they belong to him;

We presume that one of the passersby had hidden it there and then forgotten it. [Had the owner of the wall put it there, he would not have placed it toward the outside.] This ruling applies only if the article is very rusty, indicating that its owner had left it there a long time ago, and probably, after looking for it unsuccessfully, despaired of recovering it (ibid.; Tos.).

Ravad, quoted by Shitah Mekubetzes, suggests that the owner of the item probably forgot about it, and when he reminded himself, he despaired of it, since he assumes that either the passersby or the owner of the wall had already taken it.

Since the hole is open to the public domain, enabling passersby to take the item out, it is analogous to a courtyard which is insecure, so that the owner of the wall does not acquire the item by dint of it being in his property (Rashba).

Although the item may have a distinguishing feature, the finder may keep it and need not announce it, since we assume that the one who hid it there despaired of recovering it. Others qualify the mishnah as referring to a city populated mainly by gentiles. Therefore, the one who hid the object assumes that a gentile will take it, and he despairs of recovering it (Maggid Mishneh, Hil. Gezeilah 17:9).

Others consider placing anything in a hole in the wall to which all passersby have access as deliberately abandoning it (Hashlamah; Shitah Mekubetzes).

מֶחֶצְיוֹ וְלִפְנִים, — from the middle toward the inside,

[That is, if the item was found in the inside half of the hole in the wall.]

שֶׁל־בַּעַל הַבָּיִת. — they belong to the owner of the house.

This ruling applies only if the householder claims that the item is his, or if he had inherited the wall, since we advance on his behalf the plea that it may have belonged to his father. But if he admits that he has no claim to the item, it belongs to the finder (Rambam loc. cit.).

Maggid Mishneh (ad loc.) explains that in the latter instance, the owner of the wall does not acquire the item by virtue of it being in his property, because the hole in the wall is not secure, being open to passersby. Otherwise, the item would become his, even if it were in the outside half of the wall, as explained above. Tos. Yom Tov disagrees, contending that since the item was in the wall before its owner despaired of it, the owner of the wall does not acquire it. Moreover, the fact that the hole is not secure would not prevent the owner of the wall from acquiring the item, since he resides there, and hence is equivalent to one standing beside his property, which allows him to acquire an ownerless item in it, even if it is not secure.

The ruling of the mishnah applies only to items such as tongues of gold and silver, which have not been formed into vessels. However, should the item be a vessel containing coins, for example, if its opening is pointing to the outside, it belongs to the finder; if to the inside, it belongs to the householder (Rav from Gem. 26a). Similarly, should the item be a knife, the decision is based on which direction its handle is pointing to (Gem. ad loc.).

אִם הָיָה מַשְׂכִּירוֹ לַאֲחֵרִים — If he rented it to others —

[The owner of the house rented it to

לַאֲחֵרִים — אֲפִלּוּ בְּתוֹךְ הַבַּיִת, הֲרֵי אֵלּוּ שֶׁלּוֹ.

[ד] מָצָא בְּחָנוּת, הֲרֵי אֵלּוּ שֶׁלּוֹ; בֵּין הַתֵּבָה
וְלַחֶנְוָנִי, שֶׁל-חֶנְוָנִי. לִפְנֵי הַשֻּׁלְחָנִי,
הֲרֵי אֵלּוּ שֶׁלּוֹ; בֵּין הַכִּסֵּא וְלַשֻּׁלְחָנִי, הֲרֵי אֵלּוּ

יד אברהם

others.]

אֲפִלּוּ בְּתוֹךְ הַבַּיִת, — *even within the house,*

That is, even if in the house itself one found articles that had obviously been lost (*Tos. Yom Tov* from *Tos.* 26a).

הֲרֵי אֵלּוּ שֶׁלּוֹ. — *they belong to him.*

[The finder may keep them.]

The *Gemara* cites two views regarding the interpretation of this case. The first qualifies it as one in which the house had been rented to three gentiles. According to *Rashi*, the *Gemara* does not mean that there were necessarily three; it uses that number merely because the previous interpretation that had been advanced involved three people. Rather, the intention is that the most recent occupant had been a gentile. Since it is obvious that the article had been lost by him, the finder may keep it (see commentary to 1:1, s.v. זה אומר ... אני). *Tosafos*, however, presume that the owner, too, resides in the house together with the tenants. They construe this interpretation of the *Gemara* as meaning that three gentiles currently share the house with the owner. [Consequently, one who finds a lost item in the house may retain it, since we assume it had been lost by one of the majority — a gentile. Even if it is certain that it had been lost by the landlord, he has surely despaired of recovering it, expecting it to be found first by the gentiles, since they are in the majority. See *Maharsha*, who explains

why *Tosafos* deem it necessary to have three gentiles in order to constitute a majority in this instance.]

The second view maintains that the mishnah can be referring also to a house that had been rented to three Jews. The one among them who lost the item has despaired of retrieving it for the following reason: No one other than the three of them had been in the house; hence, he is certain that one of them had taken it. Since he already mentioned his loss to them several times, and none of them responded, he is convinced that the one who took the item did so with the intention of stealing it, and will never return it. Therefore, a person who subsequently finds the item may keep it.

Most authorities (*Rif; Rambam, Hil. Gezeilah* 16:10; *Rosh; Shulchan Aruch* 260:3) rule in accordance with the first view in the *Gemara*. *Ravad*, however, follows the second view. [It appears that *Rav* and *Rashi* do too.]

The *Gemara* explains that it is necessary to qualify the mishnah in one of these manners, because otherwise, the halachah would be that any object found in the house cannot be kept by the finder, and must be returned to the most recent occupant. According to *Rashi*, this means the last tenant — it is returned to him if he is Jewish. *Tosafos*, however, consistent with their opinion that the owner, too, generally resides in the house, interpret this as referring to the owner himself, who remains there after the tenants move out.

4.

מָצָא בְּחָנוּת, — *[If] he found [things] in a store,*

And they did not have any distinguishing features (*Rav; Rashi*).

2
4

ed it to others — even within the house, they belong to him.

4. **[**I**f]** he found [things] in a store, they belong to him; between the counter and the storekeeper, they belong to the storekeeper. [If he found money] in front of a moneychanger, they belong to him; between the stool and the moneychanger, they

YAD AVRAHAM

הֲרֵי אֵלּוּ שֶׁלּוֹ; — *they belong to him;*

This applies to articles found in front of the counter separating the storekeeper from the public (*Tif. Yis.*). [These were surely lost by one of the customers, who despaired of recovering them, as explained below.]

Rambam (*Hil. Gezeilah* 16:4) rules that even those articles found on the counter [which appear to have been lost] belong to the finder. Other authorities (*Tur* 260:5; *Nimmukei Yosef*) maintain that anything found on the counter belongs to the storekeeper. [Although the article is in the premises of the storekeeper, his premises do not acquire it for him for the reasons discussed in the commentary to the preceding mishnah, s.v. שֶׁל.]

Tosafos explain that the mishnah deals with a place frequented mostly by gentiles. Therefore, even an object having a distinguishing feature may be kept by the finder.

Rosh contends that because the storekeeper lives in the store, the one who lost the item reasons that since the storekeeper did not return the lost article after being asked for it, but instead claimed that one of the customers had probably picked it up, he surely has it, and there is no chance of recovering it. Hence, it may be kept by the finder although it bears a distinguishing feature (see *Nimmukei Yosef*).

בֵּין הַתֵּבָה וְלַחֶנְוָנִי, — *between the counter and the storekeeper,*

The storekeeper would sit behind this counter or box, sell merchandise from it,

and deposit money into it (*Rav; Rashi*).

שֶׁל־חֶנְוָנִי. — *they belong to the storekeeper.*

Anything behind the counter was surely lost by the storekeeper (ibid.).

לִפְנֵי הַשֻּׁלְחָנִי, — *[If he found money] in front of a moneychanger,*

Both the moneychanger and his customers place their monies on the table in front of the moneychanger (*Rashi*) [which apparently consisted of a flat surface on top of a stool].

הֲרֵי אֵלּוּ שֶׁלּוֹ; — *they belong to him;*

It is presumed that the money had been lost by the customers, because had the moneychanger lost it, it would have been found between him and his table (*Rav; Rashi*). [Since money has no distinguishing features, its owner has surely despaired of retrieving it, and the finder may therefore keep it.] The *Gemara* (26b) explains that even if the money is found on the table, it belongs to the finder, since the customers place their coins on the table as well as the moneychanger. [Hence, realizing that the finder will not know to whom it belongs, the one who lost the money will despair of it.] In this way, the case of the moneychanger differs from that of the storekeeper, according to *Tur* (*Choshen Mishpat* 260), who rules that in the preceding case, if the article is found on the counter, it belongs to the storekeeper, since no one puts anything on the counter except the storekeeper (*Tos. Yom Tov*).

בֵּין הַכִּסֵּא וְלַשֻּׁלְחָנִי, — *between the stool and the moneychanger,*

[45]   THE MISHNAH/BAVA METZIA – Chapter Two: *Eilu Metzios*

לַשֻּׁלְחָנִי. הַלּוֹקֵחַ פֵּרוֹת מֵחֲבֵרוֹ, אוֹ שֶׁשָּׁלַח לוֹ חֲבֵרוֹ פֵּרוֹת, וּמָצָא בָהֶן מָעוֹת, הֲרֵי אֵלּוּ שֶׁלּוֹ. אִם הָיוּ צְרוּרִין, נוֹטֵל וּמַכְרִיז.

[ה] **אַף הַשִּׂמְלָה** הָיְתָה בִּכְלַל כָּל־אֵלֶּה. לָמָּה יָצָאת? לְהַקִּישׁ אֵלֶיהָ, לוֹמַר לָךְ מַה־שִּׂמְלָה מְיֻחֶדֶת שֶׁיֶּשׁ־בָּהּ סִימָנִים וְיֶשׁ־לָהּ תּוֹבְעִים, אַף כָּל־דָּבָר שֶׁיֶּשׁ־בּוֹ סִימָנִים וְיֶשׁ־לוֹ תּוֹבְעִים חַיָּב לְהַכְרִיז.

יד אברהם

[That is, the money was found between the moneychanger and the stool upon which he places the table top to do his transactions.]

הֲרֵי אֵלּוּ לַשֻּׁלְחָנִי — *they belong to the moneychanger.*

[They were obviously lost by the moneychanger.]

הַלּוֹקֵחַ פֵּרוֹת מֵחֲבֵרוֹ, אוֹ שֶׁשָּׁלַח לוֹ חֲבֵרוֹ פֵּרוֹת, וּמָצָא בָהֶן מָעוֹת, הֲרֵי אֵלּוּ שֶׁלּוֹ. — *[If] one purchases produce from another, or if another sends him produce, and he finds money inside it, it belongs to him.*

[The finder may keep the money.]

This applies only if the person that sold or gave the produce was a merchant who purchases from many farmers or dealers and does not know whose money this is; since it has no distinguishing feature, the original owner has certainly despaired of it. However, if the produce was gathered by the seller or giver from his own land, the money is surely his and must be returned to him (*Rav* from *Gem.* 27a).

Similarly, if the produce had been threshed while in the merchant's possession, the money is returned to him only if the threshing was done by him or by his gentile slaves, since — even if the money had been lost by the latter — all the possessions of a gentile slave belong to his master. Should the produce be threshed by hired workers, however, the money may have been lost by them. Consequently, whoever did, in fact, lose the money despairs of recovering it, since he realizes that the finder will not know whose it is. Therefore, the finder may keep it (*Tos. Yom Tov*).

Should the merchant himself discover the money, if — since he bought the produce — not enough time has elapsed for him to mix it with the produce of other farmers, the farmer who lost the money has not despaired of recovering it. If sufficient time to mix them had already passed, however — even if the merchant has not actually done so — the farmer assumes that it was already mixed, and despairs of recovering his money, since he thinks that the merchant will not know to whom to return it (ibid. from *Tos.*).

אִם הָיוּ צְרוּרִין, — *If it is tied,*

[The money was tied in a bundle.]

נוֹטֵל וּמַכְרִיז. — *[he must] take [it] and announce [it].*

The distinguishing feature with which to identify it would be either the type of knot or the number of coins (*Rav*; *Rashi*).

belong to the moneychanger.

[If] one purchases produce from another, or if another sends him produce, and he finds money inside it, it belongs to him. If it is tied, [he must] take [it] and announce [it].

5. The garment, too, was included in all of these. Why was it singled out? To compare to it, to tell you [that] just as a garment is distinguished in that it has distinguishing features and it has claimants, so, too, anything which has distinguishing features and which has claimants must be announced.

YAD AVRAHAM

5.

After stating the precept of returning lost articles, Scripture (*Deut.* 22:1-3; see preface to this chapter) adds: וְכֵן תַּעֲשֶׂה לַחֲמֹרוֹ וְכֵן תַּעֲשֶׂה לְשִׂמְלָתוֹ וְכֵן תַּעֲשֶׂה לְכָל־אֲבֵדַת אָחִיךָ, *And so shall you do with his donkey, and so shall you do with his garment, and so shall you do with any lost article belonging to your brother.*

This mishnah discusses why *garment* is singled out by the verse, when it is, in fact, included in the generality of *any lost article belonging to your brother.*

אַף הַשִּׂמְלָה הָיְתָה בִּכְלָל כָּל־אֵלֶּה. — *The garment, too, was included in all of these.*

Although a garment is not a living creature like the others mentioned previously in the passage (*Meiri*), it is nevertheless included in the phrase: לְכָל־אֲבֵדַת אָחִיךָ, *with any lost article belonging to your brother* (ibid.; *Rav* from *Gem.* 27a). [Indeed, the *Gemara* seeks to explain why the Torah finds it necessary to specify each of the living creatures mentioned.]

לָמָה יָצָאת? — *Why was it singled out?*

Why did the Torah state specifically: וְכֵן תַּעֲשֶׂה לְשִׂמְלָתוֹ, *and so shall you do with his garment?* (*Rav; Rashi*).

לְהַקִּישׁ אֵלֶיהָ, — *To compare to it,*

That is, to compare all types of lost articles to the garment (*Meiri*).

לוֹמַר לָךְ מַה־שִּׂמְלָה מְיֻחֶדֶת שֶׁיֶּשׁ־בָּהּ סִמָנִים וְיֶשׁ־לָהּ תּוֹבְעִים, — *to tell you [that] just as a garment is distinguished in that it has*

distinguishing features and it has claimants,

A garment usually has distinguishing features, and always has owners claiming it as their own, since it does not originate from the wilds (*Rav; Rashi*).

Tosafos and *Rambam* (*Commentary*) explain that since the garment has distinguishing features, it has claimants, because — knowing that he can identify it — the owner does not despair of recovering it, and he comes and claims it.

אַף כָּל־דָּבָר שֶׁיֶּשׁ־בּוֹ סִמָנִים וְיֶשׁ־לוֹ תּוֹבְעִים חַיָּב לְהַכְרִיז. — *so, too, anything which has distinguishing features and which has claimants must be announced.*

This excludes anything of which the owner has surely despaired (*Rav; Rashi*). We know that a person has despaired when we hear him bemoaning his misfortune of having lost the item (*Rav* from *Gem.* 23a).

Tosafos explain that we learn from

[ו] **וְעַד מָתַי** חַיָּב לְהַכְרִיז? עַד כְּדֵי שֶׁיֵּדְעוּ בּוֹ
שְׁכֵנָיו; דִּבְרֵי רַבִּי מֵאִיר. רַבִּי
יְהוּדָה אוֹמֵר: שְׁלֹשָׁה רְגָלִים, וְאַחַר הָרֶגֶל
הָאַחֲרוֹן שִׁבְעָה יָמִים, כְּדֵי שֶׁיֵּלֵךְ לְבֵיתוֹ שְׁלֹשָׁה,
וְיַחֲזֹר שְׁלֹשָׁה, וְיַכְרִיז יוֹם אֶחָד.

[ז] **אָמַר** אֶת־הָאֲבֵדָה, וְלֹא אָמַר סִימָנֶיהָ, לֹא

יד אברהם

the mention of the garment that anything having a distinguishing feature
must be returned, because it has
claimants. This excludes any article not
having a distinguishing feature, since
the owner surely despairs of it. [It
follows logically that if the owner
despairs of recovering an article having
a distinguishing feature, the article
belongs to its finder.]

Although this mishnah seems to imply
that the institution of identifying lost articles
by stating their distinguishing features is of
Biblical origin (see preface to this chapter), it
is possible that the *Tanna* did not mean this
literally. His intention may have been that
only the law that anything which has
claimants must be announced is Scripturally
derived, and that the distinguished-feature
institution is a Rabbinical innovation which
he mentions only incidentally *(Gem. 27b)*.

6.

וְעַד מָתַי חַיָּב לְהַכְרִיז? — *Until when is he
required to announce?*

If, after finding an article with a
distinguishing feature, the finder announced it, but the owner did not come
forward, how long must he continue to
announce it *(Meiri)?*

עַד כְּדֵי שֶׁיֵּדְעוּ בּוֹ שְׁכֵנָיו; דִּבְרֵי רַבִּי מֵאִיר. —
*Until there is time for its neighbors to
know of it; [these are] the words of R'
Meir.*

R' Meir maintains that it is sufficient
to announce the article for the time it
takes for those who live near the place
where the object has been found to
become aware that the finder has it,
since it may belong to one of them *(Rav
from Gem. 28a).*

רַבִּי יְהוּדָה אוֹמֵר: שְׁלֹשָׁה רְגָלִים, — *R'
Yehudah says: Three festivals,*

R' Yehudah rules that the finder of
the article must announce it in
Jerusalem during the three pilgrimage
festivals — Pesach, Shavuos, Succos —
when the entire nation is present. It is

not enough to make the announcement
during one or two such festivals, since
some individuals may have found it
impossible to make the pilgrimage then
(Meiri). [After three consecutive
festivals, however, it is assumed that
everyone has been in Jerusalem at least
once and heard the announcement.
Therefore, if no one claimed it by then,
the finder need not announce it any
longer.]

The *Gemara* (28b) relates that there was a
stone in Jerusalem known as אֶבֶן הַטּוֹעֵן, *the
Stone of the Claimants*, where finders and
losers of items would gather. The finder
would announce the items and give them to
those who properly identified them. In
Taanis (3:8) the stone is called אֶבֶן הַטּוֹעִים
(הַתּוֹעִים), *the Stone of the Strayers*, referring
to those who have strayed from their
belongings.

וְאַחַר הָרֶגֶל הָאַחֲרוֹן שִׁבְעָה יָמִים, — *and
seven days after the last festival,*

After the last of the three festivals
during which he announces the article
(Tif. Yis.), he must remain in Jerusalem
seven more days and continually

2
6-7

6. Until when is he required to announce? Until there is time for its neighbors to know of it; [these are] the words of R' Meir. R' Yehudah says: Three festivals, and seven days after the last festival, so that he [have] three [days to] go home, three [days to] return, and one day [to] announce.

7. [If] he mentioned the lost article, but did not

announce it *(Meiri).*

כְּדֵי שֶׁיֵּלֵךְ לְבֵיתוֹ שְׁלֹשָׁה, — *so that he [have] three [days to] go home,*

That is, so that everyone who heard the announcement should have time to go home and determine if he had lost such an item *(Rav).* Although there were places in *Eretz Yisrael* that were further away than a three-day journey from Jerusalem, as mentioned in *Taanis* 1:3, the Rabbis did not wish to impose an unreasonable burden on the finder by having him announce the article for a longer period of time *(Tos. Yom Tov* from *Gem.* 28a).

וְיַחֲזֹר שְׁלֹשָׁה, — *three [days to] return,*

[The one who lost the article is given three days to return to Jerusalem.]

וְיַכְרִיז יוֹם אֶחָד. — *and one day [to] announce.*

He announces his claim to the item and states its distinguishing features *(Rav; Rashi; Meiri).*

Alternatively, this refers to the finder's announcing the article. When the one who lost the article returns, the finder will be announcing it for one more day, so that the loser will be able to claim and identify it *(Tif. Yis.; Tos.*

22b; *Rabbeinu Chananel; Rambam Commentary).*

Others render: *and one day to search —* i.e., those who heard the announcement are given one day to search through their belongings to ascertain whether they lost such an article *(Rabbeinu Tam* and *Rabbeinu Yehonasan* quoted by *Shitah Mekubetzes, Chiddushei HaRitva Hachadashim).*

The *Gemara* states that after the destruction of the Temple, the Rabbis enacted that one who finds a lost item should announce it in the synagogues and in study halls. When many oppressors came along, insisting that lost articles belong to the king, the Rabbis enacted that the finder of an article should merely notify his neighbors and acquaintances, and that would suffice *(Rav; Choshen Mishpat* 267:3; see *Sma* ad loc.).

If the finder has announced the item for the required period, and no one has claimed it and properly identified it, he should put it away until Elijah comes [see commentary to 1:8] *(Shulchan Aruch* §15). He may not take the item for his own use, since there is always the chance that the owner may come and claim it *(Shach* ad loc.).

7.

אָמַר אֶת־הָאֲבֵדָה, וְלֹא אָמַר סִימָנֶיהָ, — *[If] he mentioned the lost article, but did not mention its distinguishing features,*

[After someone had found an article, another person claimed that he had lost that type of item, but did not give any

valid means of identification.]

Although the one who claims the object states its color and whether it is long or short, these do not suffice to properly identify it [see preface to this chapter, s.v. *Types of Distinguishing*

בבא מציעא
ב/ז
יִתֶּן־לוֹ. וְהָרַמַּאי — אַף־עַל־פִּי שֶׁאָמַר סִימָנֶיהָ, לֹא יִתֶּן־לוֹ, שֶׁנֶּאֱמַר: "עַד דְּרֹשׁ אָחִיךָ אֹתוֹ," עַד שֶׁתִּדְרֹשׁ אֶת־אָחִיךָ, אִם רַמַּאי הוּא אִם אֵינוֹ רַמַּאי.

כָּל־דָּבָר שֶׁעוֹשֶׂה וְאוֹכֵל יַעֲשֶׂה וְיֹאכַל; וְדָבָר

יד אברהם

Features] (Ravad, Maggid Mishneh to Hil. Gezeilah 13:13).

Alternatively, this means that if there is a superior distinguishing feature and the claimant does not mention it, this proves that the item is not his, although those that he states are ordinarily adequate (Ravad, quoted in Shitah Mekubetzes). [This view is not quoted by Shulchan Aruch, and is rejected by the Halachah.]

לֹא יִתֶּן־לוֹ. — he should not give it to him.

In the Gemara (28b), there is a controversy regarding the announcement of a lost article. R' Yehudah rules that the finder should announce merely that he found a lost article, but not specify what it is. This is to prevent the possibility that someone will have heard the one who lost the item bemoaning his loss, and if he happens to know the distinguishing features of that item, he may claim it as his own (Rashi). R' Nachman contends that the finder must specify the item that he found; he maintains that we do not fear deceivers. According to R' Yehudah, the mishnah is interpreted very simply as telling us that if someone announces that he found an article, and another claims, for example, that he lost a shirt, even though he correctly stated that the lost article is a shirt, he is not given the item on the basis of such a meager description. According to R' Nachman, however, the mishnah seems to be incomprehensible, since it apparently states the obvious fact that if, for example, someone announces that he found a shirt and another claims that he lost a shirt, it is not given to him. The Gemara therefore explains that, according to R' Nachman, the mishnah

means that the claimant does indeed present distinguishing features, but not those that are conclusive evidence that the article is his.

The halachah is in accordance with the view of R' Nachman (Choshen Mishpat 267:4,5). [It is surprising that Rav and Rambam (Commentary) are silent here, and that Tiferes Yisrael explains the mishnah according to R' Yehudah's opinion. Cf. Tos. R' Akiva.]

וְהָרַמַּאי — As for a deceiver —

That is, one known to be a deceiver (Tos. 27b; Shitah Mekubetzes quoting Rabbeinu Yehonasan, Ritva, Ramach).

אַף־עַל־פִּי שֶׁאָמַר סִימָנֶיהָ, לֹא יִתֶּן־לוֹ, — although he mentions its distinguishing features, he should not give it to him,

The item is not given to him unless he produces witnesses to attest that he is its owner (Tif. Yis.; Rambam, Hil. Gezeilah 13:3).

If the deceiver identifies the article with a totally unmistakable distinguishing feature (see preface to this chapter), Tur, quoting Rosh, and Ravad (loc. cit., as explained by Bach) rule that he is believed that it is his. Maggid Mishneh, however, interprets Ravad as meaning that even in such an instance, a deceiver is not believed. See Shach (267:2).

When the number of deceivers increased, the Rabbis decreed that anyone claiming a lost article must produce character witnesses attesting to his honesty (Gem. 28b). Should he be unable to produce such witnesses, he is treated as a deceiver and is not given the article unless he brings witnesses that it belongs to him, or — according to many authorities — identifies it with totally

2
7

mention its distinguishing features, he should not give it to him. As for a deceiver — although he mentions its distinguishing features, he should not give it to him, as it is said *(Deuteronomy* 22:2): *'Until your brother seeks it'* [which is interpreted as meaning:] until you test your brother [to determine] whether he is a deceiver or whether he is not a deceiver.

Anything that works and eats shall work and eat;

YAD AVRAHAM

unmistakable distinguishing features *(Choshen Mishpat* 267:6, *Rama, Shach* ad loc. §2).

שֶׁנֶּאֱמַר: ,,עַד דְּרשׁ אָחִיךָ אתו,`` עַד שֶׁתִּדְרֹשׁ אֶת־אָחִיךָ, אִם רַמַּאי הוּא אִם אֵינוֹ רַמַּאי. — *as it is said (Deuteronomy* 22:2): *'Until your brother seeks it'* [which is interpreted as meaning:] *until you test your brother [to determine] whether he is a deceiver or whether he is not a deceiver.*

The *Gemara* (28a) rejects the simple meaning of the verse, *You shall take it*

[the lost item] *until your brother seeks it,* since it is obvious that the finder cannot return the item until the one who lost it comes and identifies it. [This verse deals with a case in which the finder does not know the owner of the item. If he does, he must return it although the owner is not even aware that he has lost it.] These words are therefore interpreted to mean that you must determine if the one who claims the item is a deceiver and if it is indeed his.

◆§ Caring for a Lost Item

If one finds an item which he is required to return, as discussed in the previous mishnayos of this chapter, it is his obligation to care for it to the best of his ability and to see to it that it should not decrease in value. If he must spend some money to properly maintain the item, he should do so, and the owner — upon claiming it — will reimburse him for the expenses. However, he should see to it that these expenses do not exceed the income generated by the item during this time — such as that of a work animal — which belongs to the owner. If it seems that this will happen, he should sell the item and hold the money for the owner, as outlined below.

The following segment of the mishnah discusses how one should care for an animal that he found and must return, if he does not know who its owner is.

כָּל־דָּבָר שֶׁעוֹשֶׂה וְאוֹכֵל — *Anything that works and eats*

That is, if one finds an animal that can work and thereby earn enough money to cover the cost of feeding it — e.g., a donkey *(Rav; Rashi).*

יַעֲשֶׂה וְיֹאכַל; — *shall work and eat;*

Rather than sell it immediately [and hold the money for the owner], the finder must let the animal work and feed it from the proceeds of its labors,

holding the surplus money — if any — for the owner when he claims the animal *(Rashbam loc. cit.* §15). This is because the owner prefers to retain this animal, rather than buy another one of equal value, since the animal recognizes its master, who has trained it according to his desire. However, the finder need not care for this type of animal for more than twelve months. The same applies to hens, which earn their keep by laying eggs *(Rav* from *Gem.* 28b).

שֶׁאֵינוֹ עוֹשֶׂה וְאוֹכֵל יִמָּכֵר, שֶׁנֶּאֱמַר: ,,וַהֲשֵׁבֹתוֹ **בבא** לוֹ,'' רְאֵה הֵיאַךְ תְּשִׁיבֶנּוּ לוֹ. **מציעא** מַה־יְּהֵא בַּדָּמִים? רַבִּי טַרְפוֹן אוֹמֵר: יִשְׁתַּמֵּשׁ **ב/ח** בָּהֶן; לְפִיכָךְ, אִם אָבְדוּ, חַיָּב בְּאַחֲרָיוּתָן. רַבִּי עֲקִיבָא אוֹמֵר: לֹא יִשְׁתַּמֵּשׁ בָּהֶן; לְפִיכָךְ, אִם אָבְדוּ, אֵינוֹ חַיָּב בְּאַחֲרָיוּתָן.

[ח] מָצָא סְפָרִים, קוֹרֵא בָהֶן אַחַת לִשְׁלֹשִׁים

יד אברהם

וְדָבָר שֶׁאֵינוֹ עוֹשֶׁ.ה וְאוֹכֵל — *anything that does not work, but eats,*

For example, ganders, roosters, calves, young donkeys, kids, and lambs (ibid.).

יִמָּכֵר, — *shall be sold,*

This does not mean that they are sold immediately; rather, each type of animal is given a different limit, according to the expense involved in feeding it. Calves and young donkeys — depending on the circumstances — must be kept for either three months or thirty days.[1] Kids and lambs, too, must be kept for three months. Young ganders and roosters are kept thirty days; old ones, however — that eat large quantities of food — need be kept only three days (*Rav; Rashi*).

Others rule contrarily that young ganders and roosters, which require much care, are kept for three days, whereas the older ones, which require little care, must be kept for thirty days (*Rambam* loc. cit. §16; *Nimmukei Yosef* quoting *Rabbeinu Chananel*).

After any of the time periods mentioned above elapses, the finder may sell the animal. According to *Rashi*, this must be done through a court. *Ramah* (quoted in *Tur* 267) and *Rav* hold that he may purchase them for himself, since the court appraises their value (*Tos. Yom Tov*). Others rule that he may purchase them for himself, even

without the court's appraisal (*Tif. Yis.* from *Tur* ad loc.).

שֶׁנֶּאֱמַר: ,,וַהֲשֵׁבֹתוֹ לוֹ,'' רְאֵה הֵיאַךְ תְּשִׁיבֶנּוּ לוֹ. — *as it is said* (ibid.): *'And you shall return it to him,'* [*which is interpreted as meaning:*] *see how you shall return it to him.*

[See to it that you do not spend more on it than it earns, since the owner will then owe you money, and that is not considered returning the item in its entirety (see *Rashi, Gem.* 28b).]

Shoshannim LeDavid explains that the *Tanna* bases this ruling on Scripture's use of the word לוֹ, *to him,* instead of the usual אֵלָיו. The intention is: Return it in a manner that is in his best interests.

מַה־יְּהֵא בַּדָּמִים? — *What shall be with the money?*

[What shall be with the money received from the sale of the lost animals?]

רַבִּי טַרְפוֹן אוֹמֵר: יִשְׁתַּמֵּשׁ בָּהֶן; — *R' Tarfon says: He may use it;*

Since he went to the trouble of caring for the lost animal and selling it, the Rabbis permitted him to use the money (*Gem.* 29b) [as long as he returns the full amount to the owner when he claims it].

לְפִיכָךְ, אִם אָבְדוּ, חַיָּב בְּאַחֲרָיוּתָן. — *therefore, if it is lost, he is responsible for it.*

Since he is permitted to use the

1. This distinction is made by the *Gemara. Rashi* construes it as meaning that if the calves and young donkeys are able to graze, so that the cost of sustaining them will be minimal, they must be kept for three months. If feed — which is expensive — however, must be brought to them,

anything that does not work, but eats, shall be sold, as it is said (ibid.): *'And you shall return it to him,'* [which is interpreted as meaning:] see how you shall return it to him.

What shall be with the money? R' Tarfon says: He may use it; therefore, if it is lost, he is responsible for it. R' Akiva says: He may not use it; therefore, if it is lost, he is not responsible for it.

8. [If] he found scrolls, he may read them once in

YAD AVRAHAM

money, even if he does not avail himself of that privilege, he is given the status of a borrower [see preface to chapter 3], who is liable for any accidents occurring to the borrowed item (*Rav* from *Gem.* 29a).

Accordingly, the term אָבְדוּ, *lost*, is not to be construed here as it usually is. Rather, it means that even if the money is lost due to an accident, such as a ship sinking at sea, the finder is nevertheless responsible to reimburse the owner (*Tos. Yom Tov* from *Gem.* 29b).

רַבִּי עֲקִיבָא אוֹמֵר: לֹא יִשְׁתַּמֵשׁ בָּהֶן; — *R'*
Akiva says: He may not use it;
[The finder may not use the money; he must put it away and hold it for the owner.]

לְפִיכָךְ, אִם אָבְדוּ, אֵינוּ חַיָּב בְּאַחֲרָיוּתָן. — *therefore, if it is lost, he is not responsible for it.*
[He does not have the status of a bor-

rower, who is responsible for accidents. Rather, he has the same responsibility to watch the money as he does for the lost article itself. According to Rabbah, he is deemed a שׁוֹמֵר חִנָּם, *unpaid guardian,* who is not liable for loss or damage to the item, except if it occurs due to his neglect. According to Rav Yosef, he is considered a שׁוֹמֵר שָׂכָר, *paid guardian,* who is liable for theft and loss. See *Gem.* 29a, *Bava Kamma* 56b.]

The halachah is in accordance with the view of R' Tarfon, that one may use the money he receives for selling a lost animal. However, should one find money which he is obligated to return, such as money in a purse, or three coins piled one on top of the other, even R' Tarfon agrees that he may not use it (*Rav* from *Gem.* 29b). Since he did not go to any trouble with that money, the Rabbis did not grant him the privilege of using it (*Tos. Yom Tov* from *Gem.*).

As a continuation of the preceding mishnah, which discusses the care required for lost animals, the *Tanna* now proceeds to delineate the care required for other types of lost articles and in what manner the finder should use them in order to care for them properly (*Meiri*).

מָצָא סְפָרִים, קוֹרֵא בָהֶן אַחַת לִשְׁלֹשִׁים יוֹם; — [*If*] *he found scrolls, he may read them once in thirty days;*
If scrolls are left unopened for any length of time, they become moldy.

Therefore, he must open them and roll them every thirty days. Since the Rabbis required the finder to open the scrolls, they permitted him to read them, although reading may cause them to

the thirty-day limit applies. *Shoshannim LeDavid* interprets *Rav* as offering a different explanation of the *Gemara*, maintaining that *Rav's* view coincides with that of *Rambam* (loc. cit. §16). *Sma*, however, contends that *Rambam's* explanation is the same as *Rashi's*.

בָּבָא מציעא: יוֹם; וְאִם אֵינוֹ יוֹדֵעַ לִקְרוֹת, גּוֹלְלָן. אֲבָל לֹא יִלְמֹד
בָּהֶן בַּתְּחִלָּה, וְלֹא יִקְרָא אַחֵר עִמּוֹ.
מָצָא כְסוּת, מְנַעֲרָה אַחַת לִשְׁלֹשִׁים יוֹם,
וְשׁוֹטְחָהּ לְצָרְכָּהּ, אֲבָל לֹא לִכְבוֹדוֹ.
כְּלֵי כֶסֶף וּכְלֵי נְחֹשֶׁת — מִשְׁתַּמֵּשׁ בָּהֶן לְצָרְכָּן,
אֲבָל לֹא לְשָׁחֳקָן.
כְּלֵי זָהָב וּכְלֵי זְכוּכִית — לֹא יִגַּע בָּהֶן עַד שֶׁיָּבֹא
אֵלִיָּהוּ.

יד אברהם

deteriorate if he touches the parchment too much or pulls it from both sides (Meiri).

All their written works were made into a scroll (Rav).

וְאִם אֵינוֹ יוֹדֵעַ לִקְרוֹת, גּוֹלְלָן — if he does not know how to read, he should roll them.

He should roll them from beginning to end in order to air them out (ibid.; Rashi).

The same applies to printed books — he should open them and allow the wind to blow between the pages (Aruch Hashulchan, Choshen Mishpat 267:13).

אֲבָל לֹא יִלְמֹד בָּהֶן בַּתְּחִלָּה — However, he should not study in them for the first time,

He may not use one of these scrolls to study something he has not yet learned, since this will take time, and he will have to keep it open longer than is necessary to air it out (Rav; Rashi).

This ruling applies only to scrolls of Scripture, which — if one has already learned and is familiar with the text — can be read without touching or pulling the parchment. If one finds a Gemara, however, since it requires intensive study to master, even after one has learned it one hundred times — on the contrary, the better one knows it, the more one is equipped to delve into it — he should not use it (Tos. Yom Tov from Nimmukei Yosef, quoting Ramban).

Actually, the ruling of Ramban, cited by Tos. Yom Tov, is stated regarding one who borrows a Gemara. Although the halachah is

that if one borrows a Torah scroll, he may not read it if he has not yet learned it, Ramban reasons that if he borrows a Gemara — since it receives the same wear when being studied the hundredth time as the first time, and since it was lent to him in order to study it — he may use it even if he has never before learned that tractate. Tos. Yom Tov appears to deduce from this reasoning that, in the case of one who finds a Gemara, the reverse is true: he may not use the Gemara even if he is familiar with it, as explained above. See Sma 267:28. Aruch Hashulchan interprets Ramban as meaning that printed books do not require touching and pulling as do parchment scrolls; therefore, the finder may study them, even for the first time. [This, however, does not appear to be Ramban's intention.]

R' Moshe Feinstein maintains that if one finds printed books that are relatively new, he should not open them, since they retain their good condition even if they are not opened for many years (Hashovas Aveidah by R' Moshe Goldberger).

וְלֹא יִקְרָא אַחֵר עִמּוֹ — nor should another read with him.

If two people read, one will pull the parchment to one side, and the other to the other side, eventually tearing it (Rav; Rashi).

According to Rashi, the Gemara (29b) qualifies this ruling as referring to an instance in which both persons would study the same column. Since they must sit close to each other, they will pull the parchment. Should they study two different columns, however, since they

2
8

thirty days; if he does not know how to read, he should roll them. However, he should not study in them for the first time, nor should another read with him.

[If] he found a garment, he should shake it out once in thirty days, and spread it out for its benefit, but not for his honor.

[As for] silverware and copperware — he should use them for their benefit, but not to wear them out.

[As for] gold utensils and glassware — he may not touch them until Elijah comes.

YAD AVRAHAM

would sit apart, they would not pull the parchment, and there is no danger of the scroll tearing. *Rif* and *Rambam (Hil. Gezeilah* 13:13), however, interpret the *Gemara* contrarily: if they are both studying the same column, they may use the scroll, but if they are studying different columns, they may not use it, since it is likely that each one will pull the parchment to his side.

מָצָא כְסוּת, מְנַעֲרָהּ — [If] *he found a garment, he should shake it out*

According to *Rambam (Commentary,* ed. Kafich), the *Gemara* (29b) qualifies this as referring to woolen clothing; it must be shaken out to prevent its becoming moldy or moth-eaten. If he found linen clothing, however, he should not shake it out at all.

Rashi, however, construes the *Gemara* as meaning the opposite: woolen clothes should not be shaken out, since they become stretched and will tear; only linen clothing should be shaken out.

אַחַת לִשְׁלשִׁים יוֹם, — *once in thirty days,*

Shaking the garment this often is beneficial to it; doing it less or more frequently is detrimental to it *(Tos. Yom Tov* from *Tur* 267).

וְשׁוֹטְחָהּ לְצָרְכָּהּ, — *and spread it out for its benefit,*

He should spread it out so that the air

should get to it, and it should not disintegrate or become moth-eaten *(Rav; Rashi).*

אֲבָל לֹא לִכְבוֹדוֹ. — *but not for his honor.*

He should not spread it out for his own purposes, even if the garment benefits thereby. For example, he should not spread it out on his bed to air it, and, simultaneously, warm himself with it or gain esteem from his friends *(Meiri* from *Gem.).*

כְּלִי כֶסֶף וּכְלֵי נְחֹשֶׁת — מִשְׁתַּמֵּשׁ בָּהֶן לְצָרְכָּן, — [As for] *silverware and copperware — he should use them for their benefit,*

Since — in order to guard them properly — they must be kept in the ground, where they tarnish, he should take them out periodically and use them *(Rav; Rashi).*

אֲבָל לֹא לְשָׁחֳקָן. — *but not to wear them out.*

He should not use them to the point of wearing them out *(Rav; Rashi).*

Meiri and *Tiferes Yisrael* explain that this is an allusion to the *Gemara's* ruling that silverware may be used with cold water, but not with hot water, since that blackens it. Copperware, on the other hand, may be used with hot water, but not on the fire, since that wears it out.

כְּלֵי זָהָב וּכְלֵי זְכוּכִית — לֹא יִגַּע בָּהֶן עַד שֶׁיָּבֹא אֵלִיָּהוּ. — [As for] *gold utensils and glassware — he may not touch them*

מָצָא שַׂק אוֹ קֻפָּה, וְכָל־דָּבָר שֶׁאֵין דַּרְכּוֹ לִטּוֹל,
הֲרֵי זֶה לֹא יִטֹּל.

[ט] אֵיזוֹ הִיא אֲבֵדָה? מָצָא חֲמוֹר אוֹ פָרָה
רוֹעִין בַּדֶּרֶךְ — אֵין זוֹ אֲבֵדָה; חֲמוֹר
וְכֵלָיו הֲפוּכִין, פָּרָה רָצָה בֵּין הַכְּרָמִים — הֲרֵי זוֹ
אֲבֵדָה.
הֶחֱזִירָהּ וּבָרְחָה, הֶחֱזִירָהּ וּבָרְחָה — אֲפִלּוּ
אַרְבָּעָה וַחֲמִשָּׁה פְעָמִים — חַיָּב לְהַחֲזִירָהּ,
שֶׁנֶּאֱמַר: ,,הָשֵׁב תְּשִׁיבֵם."

until Elijah comes.

These should be put into the ground and left there, even if it takes very long to determine who the owner is, since neither of them tarnish, and the glassware can easily break (Rav; Rashi).

מָצָא שַׂק אוֹ קֻפָּה, — [If] he found a sack or a basket,

Mussaf heAruch defines קֻפָּה as any large receptacle.

וְכָל־דָּבָר שֶׁאֵין דַּרְכּוֹ לִטּוֹל, — or anything he is not accustomed to taking,

That is, anything degrading for him to carry in the street. For example, he is an important person [a sage or a respected older person (Rambam, Hil. Gezeilah 11:13)] and not accustomed to

carry his own sack or basket from the street to a safe place (Rav, Tos. Yom Tov from Rashi).

הֲרֵי זֶה לֹא יִטֹּל. — he need not take [it].

The Gemara (30a) derives this from Scripture's use of an affirmative expression (Deut. 22:1): וְהִתְעַלַּמְתָּ, and hide yourself, which implies that sometimes it is permitted for one to pretend that he does not see a lost article [as in the example mentioned above].

Despite the fact that the Torah does not require one to return a lost article if it is beneath his dignity, it is proper for one to go beyond the requirements of the law, and return it (Gem.; Rambam loc. cit. §17).

9.

אֵיזוֹ הִיא אֲבֵדָה? — What is [considered] a lost article?

In what situation is an animal assumed to be lost, meaning that the owner is unaware of its whereabouts (Rav; Rashi; Meiri)?

מָצָא חֲמוֹר אוֹ פָרָה רוֹעִין בַּדֶּרֶךְ — אֵין זוֹ אֲבֵדָה; — [If] he finds a donkey or a cow grazing by the road — this is not [considered] a lost article;

Although there is no proper pasture there, since an animal sometimes goes

by itself to graze in such places, it is not considered lost, and we assume that the owner knows of its whereabouts (Meiri). Therefore, one who sees it is not obligated to return it to its owner (Rav; Rashi).

Should the animal be running, however, it depends upon which way it is running. If it is running toward the city, it is not considered lost; if toward the fields, it is considered lost, and the finder is obligated to return it to its owner (Tos. Yom Tov from Gem. 31a).

2
9

[If] he found a sack or a basket, or anything he is not accustomed to taking, he need not take [it].

9. What is [considered] a lost article? [If] he finds a donkey or a cow grazing by the road — this is not [considered] a lost article; a donkey with its gear overturned, [or] a cow running among the vineyards — this is [considered] a lost article.

[If] he returned it and it ran away, returned it [again] and it ran away — even four or five times — he is obligated to return it, as it is said (*Deuteronomy* 22:1): 'You shall surely return them.'

חֲמוֹר וְכֵלָיו הֲפוּכִין, — *a donkey with its gear overturned,*

Its saddle is on its belly or on its side (*Meiri*).

פָּרָה רָצָה בֵּין הַכְּרָמִים — [*or*] *a cow running among the vineyards —*

It thereby injures its feet (*Rav* from *Gem.* 31a).

הֲרֵי זוּ אֲבֵדָה. — *this is* [*considered*] *a lost article.*

[And he is obligated to return it to its owner.]

Should the cow be seen *grazing* among the vineyards, however, it is not considered lost. Nevertheless, if the vineyards belong to Jews, the finder is required to return the cow, so that it should not damage the vineyards (*Tos. Yom Tov* from *Gem.*).

If a gentile owns the vineyard, and the finder fears that he will kill the cow for damaging his property, it must be returned (*Gem.* ad loc.).

The same applies in places where the government imposes a fine on the owners of animals that damage others' property (*Rama, Choshen Mishpat* 261:2).

הֶחֱזִירָהּ וּבָרְחָה, הֶחֱזִירָהּ וּבָרְחָה — אֲפִלּוּ אַרְבָּעָה וַחֲמִשָׁה פְעָמִים — [*If*] *he returned it and it ran away, returned it* [*again*] *and it ran away — even four or five times —*

These numbers are not definitive. The *Gemara* adds: *even one hundred times* (*Tos. Yom Tov*).

חַיָּב לְהַחֲזִירָהּ, — *he is obligated to return it,*

We do not assume that since it ran away several times, the owner is negligent by not having guarded it better (*Tif. Yis.*).

שֶׁנֶּאֱמַר: ,,הָשֵׁב תְּשִׁיבֵם.'' — *as it is said* (*Deuteronomy 22:1*): *'You shall surely return them.'*

Rambam (*Commentary*) explains that הָשֵׁב is an infinitive, which can refer to doing the action once or many times.

The double expression הָשֵׁב תְּשִׁיבֵם is used to denote that one may return the lost article even to the owner's garden or to his ruins, although the latter is unaware that the article is being returned (*Tos. Yom Tov* from *Gem.* 31a).

◆§ Taking Off from Work to Return a Lost Item

The Torah does not require one to lose money in the process of returning a lost article. This is why, as discussed above, if the finder spends money in caring for the item, the owner must repay him for this. Similarly, one is not required to take time

הָיָה בָּטֵל מִסֶּלַע, לֹא יֹאמַר לוֹ: ,,תֵּן לִי סֶלַע";
אֶלָּא, נוֹתֵן לוֹ שְׂכָרוֹ כְּפוֹעֵל בָּטֵל. אִם יֵשׁ שָׁם בֵּית-
דִּין, מַתְנֶה בִּפְנֵי בֵית-דִּין; אִם אֵין שָׁם בֵּית-דִּין,
בִּפְנֵי מִי יַתְנֶה? שֶׁלּוֹ קוֹדֵם.

[י] מְצָאָהּ בְּרֶפֶת, אֵינוֹ חַיָּב בָּהּ; בִּרְשׁוּת
הָרַבִּים, חַיָּב בָּהּ. וְאִם הָיְתָה בֵית

off from work to return a lost item if this will cause him a loss.

The mishnah now tells us what one's options are before returning a lost article, and what the halachah is once he returns it without making any prior stipulations.

הָיָה בָּטֵל מִסֶּלַע, — [If] he refrained from [earning] a sela,

A person saw a lost article, which was worth many selaim, and he took time off from his work — during which he would have earned a sela — to return it (Meiri).

לֹא יֹאמַר לוֹ: ,,תֵּן לִי סֶלַע"; — he shall not say to him: 'Give me a sela';

[The one who returned the lost article cannot demand that its owner reimburse him for the sela he lost by returning the lost article.]

אֶלָּא, נוֹתֵן לוֹ שְׂכָרוֹ כְּפוֹעֵל בָּטֵל. — rather, he pays him his wage like an idle worker.

That is, the salary a person would be willing to take for doing light work, like returning the article, instead of earning more to do his usual, harder work (Rav; Rashi).

[Apparently, the Rabbis maintained that, unless one specifically stipulates otherwise — as discussed below — he is satisfied to do lighter work at a lesser wage — at least, occasionally — than harder work at a higher wage. Therefore, the owner need pay him only the lesser wage.] For example, a person was working at a job for which he would receive four dinars. To comply with a request that he leave it completely and sit idle, he would ask for

one dinar. To leave his work and return the lost article, he would ask for two dinars. Thus, in our case, he is entitled to two dinars. Although he is receiving one of these dinars for returning the lost article, since he was not obligated to forsake his work in order to return it, he may accept wages for the act (Tos. Yom Tov quoting Tur, Choshen Mishpat 265).

Others explain that he may indeed demand the wages he receives for his usual work, but only what he would have earned during the slow season, not during the busy season, when workers are at a premium (Rabbeinu Chananel; Meiri).

אִם יֵשׁ שָׁם בֵּית-דִּין, מַתְנֶה בִּפְנֵי בֵית-דִּין; — If there is a court, he may stipulate before the court;

That is, if he does not wish to forgo his usual earnings in order to return the lost item, as long as three men are present [even laymen suffice to form this 'court'] he may stipulate that he will return the article only if he is paid his usual wages (Rav; Rashi). [If this is done, when the owner claims his object, he must comply with the stipulation.]

אִם אֵין שָׁם בֵּית-דִּין, בִּפְנֵי מִי יַתְנֶה? שֶׁלּוֹ קוֹדֵם. — if there is no court, before whom shall he stipulate? His own takes precedence.

[If three men are not present, he

2
10

[If] he refrained from [earning] a sela, he shall not say to him: 'Give me a *sela*'; rather, he pays him his wage like an idle worker. If there is a court, he may stipulate before the court; if there is no court, before whom shall he stipulate? His own takes precedence.

10. [I]f] he finds it in a stable, he is not responsible for it; in a public domain, he is responsible

cannot make this stipulation.] Therefore, he is permitted to do his own work and is not obligated to return the item *(Rav)*.

10.

מְצָאָהּ בְּרֶפֶת, — *[If] he finds it in a stable,*

The mishnah cannot be referring to a normal stable in which the animal is locked securely, since, in such a case, it is obvious that the finder need not return it to its owner. It also cannot be dealing with a stable that encourages the animal to run away — such as one which is open on all sides — for, in such an instance, the finder would certainly be obligated to return it. The *Gemara* therefore concludes that the mishnah refers to a stable which is not locked, yet is not open on all sides; hence, it does not encourage the animal to run away *(Rav, Tos. Yom Tov* from *Tur, Choshen Mishpat* 261). *Meiri* explains that the animal does not find a wide opening, enabling it to escape easily, but there is no locked door preventing its escape.

אֵינוּ חַיָּב בָּהּ; — *he is not responsible for it;*

[Since it is not considered lost, he is not obligated to return it.]

Some rule that if the animal is found in a stable more than two thousand cubits from the city's border, it is considered lost and must be returned [*Rosh, Tur;* cf. *Rama loc. cit. §3] (Tif. Yis.).*

בִּרְשׁוּת הָרַבִּים, חַיָּב בָּהּ. — *in a public domain, he is responsible for it.*

This applies only if the animal was found in a public domain, apparently astray. Otherwise, it would not be considered lost, similar to the case discussed in the commentary to mishnah 9, in which a cow running on the road is deemed lost only if it is running toward the fields.

Ravad interprets the mishnah as meaning that the animal was found on a large highway, frequented by crowds. Since it fears the crowds, it is likely to run away. Moreover, it may fall into the hands of dishonest people, who will not return it. The preceding mishnah, however, does not deal with this type of highway, but with a public path, which is not frequented by crowds *(Tos. Yom Tov* from *Rosh).*

◄§ עֲשֵׂה דּוֹחֶה לֹא תַעֲשֶׂה §►
Supersedure of a Negative Commandment by a Positive Commandment

There is a general principle in Biblical law that if, in any situation, a positive precept stated in the Torah dictates that one should do a certain act, while that act is prohibited by a negative precept, he may — or in some cases, must — do the act, since the negative precept is superseded by the positive one. There are, however, exceptions to this rule *(Yevamos* 3b; see *Ramban* to *Exodus* 20:8).

הַקְּבָרוֹת, לֹא יִטַּמֵּא לָהּ.

אִם אָמַר לוֹ אָבִיו: ,,הִטַּמֵּא,'' אוֹ שֶׁאָמַר לוֹ:

,,אַל־תַּחֲזִיר,'' לֹא יִשְׁמַע לוֹ.

פָּרַק וְטָעַן, פָּרַק וְטָעַן — אֲפִלּוּ אַרְבָּעָה וַחֲמִשָּׁה

פְּעָמִים — חַיָּב, שֶׁנֶּאֱמַר: ,,עָזֹב תַּעֲזֹב.'' הָלַךְ וְיָשַׁב

יד אברהם

וְאִם הָיְתָה בֵית הַקְּבָרוֹת,[1] — *If it is [in] a
graveyard,*

The intention is that the finder is a
Kohen, who is Biblically forbidden to
contaminate himself by coming into
contact with a corpse. This is prohibited
by both a positive commandment (Lev.
21:6): קְדֹשִׁים יִהְיוּ, *they shall be holy,* and
a negative commandment (ibid., v. 1):
לְנֶפֶשׁ לֹא־יִטַּמָּא בְעַמָּיו, *no one shall
contaminate himself with a dead body
among his people.* On the other hand,
there is a positive commandment
obligating him to return the lost article
(Deut. 22:1): הָשֵׁב תְּשִׁיבֵם לְאָחִיךָ, *you
shall surely return them to your brother*
(Rav, Tos. Yom Tov from Gem. 30a).

Rambam (Commentary) adds that the
mishnah may be referring also to a
Nazirite, who — like a Kohen — is
prohibited to contaminate himself by
virtue of a positive commandment
(Num. 6:8), קָדֹשׁ הוּא, *he is holy,* and a
negative commandment (ibid., v. 6):
עַל־נֶפֶשׁ מֵת לֹא יָבֹא, *upon the body of a
dead person he shall not come* (Tos.
Yom Tov).

לֹא יִטַּמֵּא לָהּ. — *he may not contaminate
himself for it.*

This is based on the rule that אֵין
עֲשֵׂה דּוֹחֶה עֲשֵׂה וְלֹא תַעֲשֶׂה, *a positive
commandment does not supersede the
combination of a positive commandment and a negative commandment.*
Therefore, the positive precept of
returning the lost article does not
supersede the positive and negative
precepts restricting the Kohen or the
Nazirite (Rav from Gem.).

Although there is also a negative
commandment involved in returning a
lost article (Deut. 22:3): לֹא תוּכַל
לְהִתְעַלֵּם, *you shall not hide yourself,* a
negative commandment cannot even
contribute to the supersedure of other
commandments [so that even a combination of a positive precept and a
negative precept does not supersede
another such combination, nor does it
supersede even a positive precept alone]
(Tos. Yom Tov from Rashi 30a).

אִם אָמַר לוֹ אָבִיו: ,,הִטַּמֵּא,'' — *If his father
says to him: 'Contaminate yourself,'*

The father of the Kohen or Nazirite
tells him to contaminate himself in order
to return the lost article that is in the
graveyard. Thus, by doing so, he would
be fulfilling an additional positive commandment, that of אִישׁ אִמּוֹ וְאָבִיו
תִּירָאוּ, *each man shall fear his mother
and his father* [Lev. 19:3] (Tif. Yis.).

אוֹ שֶׁאָמַר לוֹ: ,,אַל־תַּחֲזִיר,'' — *or he says to
him: 'Do not return [it],'*

This refers to a new case: a person
sees an object that he is obligated to
return in a place where he is permitted
to go, but his father forbids him to
return it (Rav; Rashi).

לֹא יִשְׁמַע לוֹ. — *he should not obey him.*

This is based on the verse (Lev. 19:3):
אִישׁ אִמּוֹ וְאָבִיו תִּירָאוּ וְאֶת־שַׁבְּתֹתַי תִּשְׁמֹרוּ
אֲנִי ה' אֱלֹהֵיכֶם, *Each man shall fear his
mother and his father, and you shall
keep My Sabbaths; I am HASHEM your
God.* The intention is that if a person is
ordered by his parent to desecrate the

1. Some editions (Rav; Rambam, Hil. Rotzeach 13:7) read: בְּבֵית הַקְּבָרוֹת, while others
(Choshen Mishpat 272:1) read: בֵּין הַקְּבָרוֹת, *among the graves* (Tos. Yom Tov). [All these
versions have the same meaning, although the latter two are more explicit.]

2
10

for it. If it is [in] a graveyard, he may not contaminate himself for it.

If his father says to him: 'Contaminate yourself,' or he says to him: 'Do not return [it],' he should not obey him.

[If] he unloaded and loaded, unloaded and loaded — even four or five times — he is obligated, as it is said (*Exodus* 23:5): 'You shall surely help.' [If] he

YAD AVRAHAM

Sabbath, he should not obey, because *I am HASHEM, your God* — that is to say — 'both you and your father are obligated to honor Me.' This applies not only to the Sabbath, but to all the other commandments as well (*Gem.*, as explained by *Nimmukei Yosef*).

[It appears that according to *Rav*, this derivation is made from the beginning of the verse, since he does not cite the words *I am HASHEM, your God.*] *R' Nissan Alpert*, in his glosses to *Meiri*, states that this seems to be the opinion of *Meiri* and *Rambam* (*Mamrim* 6:12).

Although the obligation to return a lost article stems from both a positive commandment and a negative commandment and, as discussed above, would not be superseded by the positive obligation of obeying one's parents, we might have thought that this case is an exception to the rule, because the honor of one's parents is compared by Scripture to the honor of God. Therefore, it is necessary for the verse to tell us that even in this case, the supersedure does not apply (*Tos. Yom Tov* from *Gem.* 32a).

⋅§ Loading and Unloading Another's Animal

The final segment of this mishnah deals with the precepts of helping the animal of another Jew with its load when it is in need, which is based on two verses: (1) *Exodus* 23:5 — כִּי־תִרְאֶה חֲמוֹר שׂנַאֲךָ רֹבֵץ תַּחַת מַשָּׂאוֹ וְחָדַלְתָּ מֵעֲזֹב לוֹ עָזֹב תַּעֲזֹב עִמּוֹ, *Should you see your enemy's donkey lying under its burden and refrain from helping him? You shall surely help him.* (2) *Deuteronomy* 22:4 — לֹא־תִרְאֶה אֶת־חֲמוֹר אָחִיךָ אוֹ שׁוֹרוֹ נֹפְלִים בַּדֶּרֶךְ וְהִתְעַלַּמְתָּ מֵהֶם הָקֵם תָּקִים עִמּוֹ, *You shall not see your brother's donkey or his ox falling by the road and hide yourself from them; you shall surely pick them up with him.*

The first verse refers to an animal which falls under its burden and must be unloaded; the second, to an animal whose burden fell off and must be reloaded. In either case, the one who sees this situation is obligated to help unload and/or reload the animal. Of course, the intention of the words, *your enemy*, in the first verse is *even your enemy*.

Although the verses specify a donkey or an ox, the same applies to all animals. Scripture chose these as examples because they are usually used as beasts of burden (*Bava Kamma* 5:7; see ArtScroll comm. ad loc.).

פָּרַק וְטָעַן — *[If] he unloaded and loaded,*

[A person saw another's animal lying under its burden, and he unloaded it and then reloaded it.]

פָּרַק וְטָעַן — אֲפִלּוּ אַרְבָּעָה וַחֲמִשָּׁה פְעָמִים — *— unloaded and loaded — even four or five times —*

As in mishnah 9, these numbers are

not definitive; the ruling applies regardless of how many times he repeated the process (*Meiri* from *Gem.* 31a).

חַיָּב, — *he is obligated,*

[He must nevertheless continue to unload the animal and reload it each time it falls under its burden.]

שֶׁנֶּאֱמַר: ,,עָזֹב תַּעֲזֹב.'' — *as it is said (Exodus*

בבא
מציעא
ב/יא

לוֹ, וְאָמַר: ,,הוֹאִיל וְעָלֶיךָ מִצְוָה, אִם רְצוֹנְךָ לִפְרֹק,
פְּרֹק,'' פָּטוּר, שֶׁנֶּאֱמַר: ,,עִמּוֹ.'' אִם הָיָה זָקֵן אוֹ
חוֹלֶה, חַיָּב.

מִצְוָה מִן־הַתּוֹרָה לִפְרֹק, אֲבָל לֹא לִטְעֹן. רַבִּי
שִׁמְעוֹן אוֹמֵר: אַף לִטְעֹן. רַבִּי יוֹסֵי הַגְּלִילִי אוֹמֵר:
אִם הָיָה עָלָיו יָתֵר עַל מַשָּׂאוֹ, אֵינוֹ זָקוּק לוֹ,
שֶׁנֶּאֱמַר: ,,תַּחַת מַשָּׂאוֹ'' — מַשָּׂאוּי שֶׁיָּכוֹל לַעֲמֹד
בּוֹ.

[יא] אֲבֵדָתוֹ וַאֲבֵדַת אָבִיו — אֲבֵדָתוֹ קוֹדֶמֶת;

יד אברהם

23:5): 'You shall surely help.'
As explained in the commentary to mishnah 9, an infinitive — in this case, עֲזֹב — can refer to doing the action once or many times. The double expression עָזֹב תַּעֲזֹב is used to denote that even if the owner of the animal is not present, the passerby is nevertheless required to unload and reload his animal. The same is true of the double expression, cited above, used with regard to loading: הָקֵם תָּקִים (*Gem.* 31a).

הָלַךְ וְיָשַׁב לוֹ, — *[If] he walked away and sat down,*
The owner of the animal impudently walked away and sat down (*Rav; Rashi; Meiri*).

וְאָמַר: — *and said:*
He said to the passerby (*Meiri*).

,,הוֹאִיל וְעָלֶיךָ מִצְוָה, אִם רְצוֹנְךָ לִפְרֹק, פְּרֹק,'' — *'Since the commandment is [incumbent] upon you, if you want to unload, unload,'*
['Since the Torah requires you to unload my animal, if you want to do it, go ahead, but I will not help you.']

פָּטוּר, — *he is exempt,*
[The passerby is exempt from unloading the animal.]

שֶׁנֶּאֱמַר: ,,עִמּוֹ.'' — *as it is said (ibid.): 'With him.'*

[This implies that the passerby is obligated to help unload the animal only if its owner is prepared to join him.]

אִם הָיָה זָקֵן אוֹ חוֹלֶה, — *If he is old or sick,*
The owner of the animal has no strength to help, and he refrains from helping not out of impudence, but because of illness or old age (*Meiri*).

חַיָּב. — *he is obligated.*
The passerby is obligated to unload and reload the animal without the owner's assistance (ibid.; see *Rambam Commentary*).

מִצְוָה מִן־הַתּוֹרָה לִפְרֹק, — *It is a commandment in the Torah to unload,*
That is, one is obligated by the Torah to help unload another animal without receiving pay (*Rav* from *Gem.* 32a) unless he is engaged in his own work and would lose money by doing so. In that case, he may follow the procedure discussed in mishnah 9 with regard to returning a lost article (*Tos. Yom Tov* from *Rosh*).

אֲבָל לֹא לִטְעֹן. — *but not to load.*
He is not obligated to load the animal unless he is paid to do so (*Rav* from *Gem.*).
The *Gemara* deduces this from the fact that the Torah states commandments both to unload and load. Had only the precept to load been stated, we

walked away and sat down, and said: 'Since the commandment is [incumbent] upon you, if you want to unload, unload,' he is exempt, as it is said (ibid.): 'With him.' If he is old or sick, he is obligated.

It is a commandment in the Torah to unload, but not to load. R' Shimon says: Even to load. R' Yose the Galilean says: If it bore more than its [proper] burden, he is not bound to him, for it is said (ibid.): 'under its burden' — a burden which it can bear.

11. [B]etween] his own lost article and his father's lost article — his own lost article takes

would know that one is obligated to unload as well, for if it is required that one load another's animal although the animal suffers no pain and the owner suffers no loss, it is surely required to unload another's animal, since the animal suffers pain and the owner sustain a loss. [The animal may die or be injured if the load is not removed from it.] The only reason the Torah states the commandment to unload, as well, is to tell us that he must do so without being compensated for it (Tos. Yom Tov from Gem.).

רַבִּי שִׁמְעוֹן אוֹמֵר: אַף לִטְעֹן. — R' Shimon says: Even to load.

One must even load without compensation (Rav from Gem.).

R' Shimon asserts that the two verses are obscure in their meaning. We cannot know definitely which one deals with loading and which one with unloading. Thus, if only the verse in Deuteronomy were written, we might have thought that it means that the animal is falling with the burden upon it, and the passerby is obligated to unload it. The verse in Exodus, therefore, is needed to reveal to us that the other verse refers to loading. Hence, there is no superfluous verse to

teach us that there is a distinction between the obligations of loading and unloading (Tos. Yom Tov from Gem.).

The halachah is not in accordance with the view of R' Shimon (Rav; Rambam Commentary and Hil. Rotzeach 13:7).

רַבִּי יוֹסִי הַגְּלִילִי אוֹמֵר: אִם הָיָה עָלָיו יֶתֶר עַל מַשָּׂאוֹ, אֵינוֹ זָקוּק לוֹ, — R' Yose the Galilean says: If it bore more than its [proper] burden, he is not bound to him,

If the owner overloaded the animal, the passerby is not obligated to help him unload it, since it is the owner's negligence that caused this situation (Meiri).

שֶׁנֶּאֱמַר: ,,תַּחַת מַשָּׂאוֹ'' — מַשּׂאוּי שֶׁיָּכוֹל לַעֲמֹד בּוֹ. — for it is said (ibid.): 'under its burden' — a burden which it can bear.

Its burden implies a burden fit for it, not an oversized one that it cannot bear. R' Yose rules that the prohibition of cruelty to animals is a Rabbinical prohibition. Therefore, although the animal suffers pain, the passerby is not obligated by Biblical law to unload it (Gem. 32b).

The halachah is not in accordance with R' Yose (Rav; Rambam Commentary).

11.

אֲבֵדָתוֹ וַאֲבֵדַת אָבִיו — — [Between] his own lost article and his father's lost article —

That is, if one found two lost articles,

אֲבֵדָתוֹ וַאֲבֵדַת רַבּוֹ — שֶׁלּוֹ קוֹדֶמֶת. אֲבֵדַת אָבִיו
וַאֲבֵדַת רַבּוֹ — שֶׁל־רַבּוֹ קוֹדֶמֶת, שֶׁאָבִיו הֱבִיאוֹ
לָעוֹלָם הַזֶּה, וְרַבּוֹ — שֶׁלִּמְּדוֹ חָכְמָה — מְבִיאוֹ
לְחַיֵּי הָעוֹלָם הַבָּא. וְאִם אָבִיו חָכָם, שֶׁל־אָבִיו
קוֹדֶמֶת.

הָיָה אָבִיו וְרַבּוֹ נוֹשְׂאִין מַשָּׂאוּי, מַנִּיחַ אֶת־שֶׁל־
רַבּוֹ, וְאַחַר־כָּךְ מַנִּיחַ אֶת־שֶׁל־אָבִיו.

הָיוּ אָבִיו וְרַבּוֹ בְּבֵית הַשֶּׁבִי, פּוֹדֶה אֶת־רַבּוֹ,
וְאַחַר־כָּךְ פּוֹדֶה אֶת־אָבִיו. וְאִם הָיָה אָבִיו חָכָם,

יד אברהם

one belonging to him and one belonging
to his father, and he cannot retrieve
them both at once (Rambam, Hil.
Gezeilah 12:1).

אֲבֵדָתוֹ קוֹדֶמֶת; — his own lost article takes
precedence;

It surely takes precedence over lost
articles belonging to strangers. To be
sure, if it is possible to recover the item
belonging to his father or the stranger,
as well as his own, he is not freed from
the obligation to do so. If he recovered
the stranger's article and neglected his
own — even if his was very expensive —
he is entitled only to wages for the work
he did, similar to the case in *Bava
Kamma* 10:4 (*Meiri*; *Rambam* loc. cit.;
Choshen Mishpat 264:1).

The *Gemara* (33a) bases this ruling on
the verse (*Deut.* 15:4): אֶפֶס כִּי לֹא יִהְיֶה־בְּךָ
אֶבְיוֹן, *Only there shall not be among you
a needy one*, which it construes as
meaning that one should try not to
become impoverished. Hence, his own
interests take precedence (*Rav*).
Nevertheless, a person should conduct himself beyond the letter of the law
in this regard, and not insist on giving
precedence to his own interests, unless
this would cause him a definite loss.
[Otherwise, each time an opportunity
arises to save something belonging to
another, he would avoid doing so with
the pretext that this will prevent him
from doing something profitable for

himself (*Sma* 264:2).] One who
constantly insists on putting his own
needs before those of others thereby
rejects the responsibility of performing
kind deeds, and — as a punishment —
will himself eventually require the help
of others (*Choshen Mishpat* ibid. §1
from *Gem.*).

אֲבֵדָתוֹ וַאֲבֵדַת רַבּוֹ — שֶׁלּוֹ קוֹדֶמֶת. —
[between] his own lost article and his
teacher's lost article — his own takes
precedence.

This, too, applies only if he cannot
retrieve them both (*Meiri*).

אֲבֵדַת אָבִיו וַאֲבֵדַת רַבּוֹ — שֶׁל־רַבּוֹ קוֹדֶמֶת, —
[Between] his father's lost article and his
teacher's lost article — his teacher's
takes precedence,

This applies only to the teacher from
whom he has learned most of his
knowledge, whether it be Scripture,
Mishnah or *Gemara* (*Rav*, *Tos. Yom
Tov* from *Gem.* 33a; *Rashi*; *Rambam*
loc. cit. §2).

However, if the father or someone
else paid the teacher for his services, the
student must give precedence to that
person's articles over those of the
teacher (*Tif. Yis.* from *Yoreh Deah*
242:34; *Rama* ad loc. from *Sefer
Chasidim*; *Sma* 264:5).

שֶׁאָבִיו הֱבִיאוֹ לָעוֹלָם הַזֶּה, וְרַבּוֹ — שֶׁלִּמְּדוֹ
חָכְמָה — מְבִיאוֹ לְחַיֵּי הָעוֹלָם הַבָּא. — *for his
father brought him into this world,*

precedence; [between] his own lost article and his teacher's lost article — his own takes precedence. [Between] his father's lost article and his teacher's lost article — his teacher's takes precedence, for his father brought him into this world, whereas his teacher — who taught him wisdom — brings him into the life of the World to Come. If his father is a scholar, however, his father's takes precedence.

[If] his father and his teacher were carrying a load, he should put down his teacher's, and afterwards put down his father's.

[If] his father and his teacher were in captivity, he should ransom his teacher, and afterwards ransom his father. If his father was a scholar, however, he

YAD AVRAHAM

whereas his teacher — who taught him wisdom — brings him into the life of the World to Come.

[Therefore, he deserves precedence.]

וְאִם אָבִיו חָכָם, — *If his father is a scholar, however,*

His father is as great in Torah scholarship as his teacher *(Tos. Yom Tov).*

Tos. Yom Tov's comment is based on the reading of *Rambam (Hil. Gezeilah* 12:2): אם הָיָה אָבִיו שָׁקוּל כְּרַבּוֹ, *if his father was equal to his teacher.* See also *Choshen Mishpat* 264:2. Cf. *Rav (Kereisos* 6:9), cited below.

שֶׁל־אָבִיו קוֹדֶמֶת. — *his father's takes precedence.*

Although he learned much more from his teacher than from his father, since the father is as great a scholar as the teacher, he must give precedence to the father's article *(Pnei Yehoshua).*

הָיָה אָבִיו וְרַבּוֹ נוֹשְׂאִין מַשָּׂאוּי, מַנִּיחַ אֶת־שֶׁל־רַבּוֹ, — [If] his father and his teacher were carrying a load, he should put down his teacher's,

[He must first help his teacher with his load.]

This, too, refers only to a teacher from whom he learned most of his

knowledge *(Rav).*

וְאַחַר־כָּךְ מַנִּיחַ אֶת־שֶׁל־אָבִיו. — *and afterwards put down his father's.*

[This ruling, too, is based on the reasoning stated above.]

The mishnah does not state that in such a case, if the father is equal in scholarship to the teacher, he is given precedence. *Beis Yosef (Yoreh Deah* 242) is undecided whether this case is different from the previous one.

Rav (Kereisos 6:9) and *Tur* (ibid.), quoting *Rosh,* state that if the father is a Torah scholar, he takes precedence, even if he is not as erudite as the teacher *(Tos. Yom Tov). Tur* states that this applies only with regard to putting down their loads and ransoming them, as discussed below, but not to the return of lost articles, in which case the father's takes precedence only if he is equal in scholarship to the teacher, as mentioned above. *Rav (Kereisus* 6:9), however, maintains that the halachah is the same with regard to all these cases.

הָיוּ אָבִיו וְרַבּוֹ בְּבֵית הַשֶּׁבִי, — [If] his father and his teacher were in captivity,

[And he cannot redeem both of them together.]

פּוֹדֶה אֶת־רַבּוֹ, וְאַחַר־כָּךְ פּוֹדֶה אֶת־אָבִיו. — he should ransom his teacher, and af-

יד אברהם

terwards ransom his father.

As in the cases above, this refers only to a teacher from whom he learned most of his knowledge (Rav).

וְאִם הָיָה אָבִיו חָכָם, פּוֹדֶה אֶת־אָבִיו, וְאַחַר־כָּךְ פּוֹדֶה אֶת־רַבּוֹ. — If his father was a scholar, however, he should ransom his father, and afterwards ransom his teacher.

In this case, when their lives are in danger, the father must be redeemed first even if he is not as great a scholar as the teacher. This is different from the case of returning the lost article, in which case, even if he displeases his father slightly in favor of his teacher, there is no harm done (Tos. Yom Tov from Beis Yosef).

We have explained the mishnah according to R' Yehudah, since the halachah follows his view. There are, however, other opinions mentioned in the Gemara: R' Meir rules that the teacher who deserves precedence over one's father is not the one who taught him Scripture or Mishnah, but only one who taught him reasons for the halachos in the Mishnah, and the reconciliation of seemingly contradictory mishnayos. R' Yose contends that even if someone enlightened a person with the explanation of one mishnah, he is deemed his teacher.

Although the halachah is not in accordance with R' Yose's view, that is only with regard to giving him precedence over his father. However, his ruling is accepted with regard to such a person being considered his teacher, and he is obligated to honor him (Rambam Commentary; see Avos 6:3).

Chapter 3

◆§ אַרְבָּעָה שׁוֹמְרִים / The Four Shomerim (Guardians)

If someone has in his possession an item belonging to another person with the latter's permission, he falls under one of the following four categories:

◆§ שׁוֹמֵר חִנָּם / The Unpaid Shomer

כִּי־יִתֵּן אִישׁ אֶל־רֵעֵהוּ כֶּסֶף אוֹ־כֵלִים לִשְׁמֹר וְגֻנַּב מִבֵּית הָאִישׁ אִם־יִמָּצֵא הַגַּנָּב יְשַׁלֵּם שְׁנָיִם. אִם־לֹא יִמָּצֵא הַגַּנָּב וְנִקְרַב בַּעַל־הַבַּיִת אֶל־הָאֱלֹהִים אִם־לֹא שָׁלַח יָדוֹ בִּמְלֶאכֶת רֵעֵהוּ. עַל־כָּל־דְּבַר־פֶּשַׁע עַל־שׁוֹר עַל־חֲמוֹר עַל־שֶׂה עַל־שַׂלְמָה עַל־כָּל־אֲבֵדָה אֲשֶׁר יֹאמַר כִּי־הוּא זֶה עַד הָאֱלֹהִים יָבֹא דְּבַר־שְׁנֵיהֶם אֲשֶׁר יַרְשִׁיעֻן אֱלֹהִים יְשַׁלֵּם שְׁנַיִם לְרֵעֵהוּ.

If a man gives another person money or utensils to watch, and it is stolen from the house of the man, if the thief is found, he shall pay twofold. If the thief is not found, then the householder shall approach the judges if he has not put forth his hand upon the other's goods. For every matter of trespass, for an ox, for a donkey, for a lamb, for a garment, for any loss, concerning which he will say, 'This is it,' the matter of the two of them shall come before the judges; whomever the judges convict shall pay twofold to the other (Exodus 22:6-8).

The Rabbis interpret this passage as referring to a man who agreed to watch another person's article gratis. Such a shomer is not liable if the item is stolen or lost, unless it occurred due to his negligence. If he claims that the theft or loss took place although he had watched the item properly, but he has no witnesses to corroborate this, the Torah requires him to swear that the item had indeed been stolen or lost.

According to some authorities, this is the only Biblical oath he must take;[1] the

---

1. Accordingly, the meaning of verse 7 in the passage quoted above is: If he has not put forth his hand upon the other's goods, then the householder should approach the judges — i.e.,

should ransom his father, and afterwards ransom his
teacher.

YAD AVRAHAM

others mentioned below were instituted by the Rabbis in accordance with the principle of גִּלְגּוּל שְׁבוּעָה, *attaching oaths* — i.e., a person who must swear an oath may be required to take additional oaths which he would otherwise not have had to [see commentary to 1:1, s.v. זֶה יִשָּׁבַע] (*Tif. Yis.* from *Choshen Mishpat* 294:2). Others (*Tos.* 6a; *Rosh*, quoting *Yerushalmi*) maintain that the Torah also requires him to swear that he had not been negligent in watching the item, but rather, had watched it in the usual manner of *shomerim.* A practical difference between these two opinions would occur in a case in which witnesses testify that the item had been stolen, thereby freeing the *shomer* from swearing to that effect. Since he need not take this primary oath, he is exempt also from all other 'attached oaths.' If, however, the oath regarding negligence is Biblical, he must take it notwithstanding the witnesses' testimony regarding the theft (*Tos.* 6a).

If the *shomer* is required to take a Biblical oath, he must swear also the 'attached oath' that he did not use the item for his own purposes. Had he done so, he would be considered a גַּזְלָן, *robber,* who is liable for anything that occurs to the item (*Gem.* 41a, *Rashi* 41b). Some authorities contend that another 'attached oath' which the *shomer* must take is that the item is not presently in his possession. This is to avoid the possibility that the item had indeed been stolen, but had since been returned (*Meiri*). If the article in question is a speciality item or one that is not generally available, even if the *shomer* wishes to pay rather than swear that the article was stolen or lost, he is nevertheless required to take the oath that it is not presently in his possession, because we fear that he may have it, and would rather keep it and pay for it than return it. The same applies to the other three *shomerim* as well (*Choshen Mishpat* 295:1).

‪שׁוֹמֵר שָׂכָר‬ / The Paid Shomer

כִּי־יִתֵּן אִישׁ אֶל־רֵעֵהוּ חֲמוֹר אוֹ־שׁוֹר אוֹ־שֶׂה וְכָל־בְּהֵמָה לִשְׁמֹר וּמֵת אוֹ־נִשְׁבַּר אוֹ־נִשְׁבָּה אֵין רֹאֶה. שְׁבֻעַת ה' תִּהְיֶה בֵּין שְׁנֵיהֶם אִם־לֹא שָׁלַח יָדוֹ בִּמְלֶאכֶת רֵעֵהוּ וְלָקַח בְּעָלָיו וְלֹא יְשַׁלֵּם. וְאִם־גָּנֹב יִגָּנֵב מֵעִמּוֹ יְשַׁלֵּם לִבְעָלָיו. אִם־טָרֹף יִטָּרֵף יְבִאֵהוּ עֵד הַטְּרֵפָה לֹא יְשַׁלֵּם.

If a man gives another a donkey or an ox or a lamb or any animal to watch, and it dies, or fractures a limb or is captured, without anyone seeing it, Hashem's oath shall be between them if he did not put forth his hand upon the other's goods, and its owner shall accept it, and he shall not pay. But if it is stolen from him, he shall pay its owner. If it is torn, he shall bring witness; the torn one he shall not pay (*Exodus* 22:9-12).

This passage is construed by the Rabbis (*Gem.* 94b) as dealing with one who is paid to watch another's item. Such a *shomer* is liable for theft, loss, or damage to the item unless it occurs accidentally — for example, it is seized by armed bandits, or — if it is an animal — it dies a natural death or breaks a leg. If the *shomer* claims that such an accident took place but has no witnesses to verify this, he must swear to that effect (mishnah 7:8). This is the oath referred to in the verse. Should the *shomer* have used the item for his own purpose, he is deemed a robber and is liable even in the case of an accident.

‪שׁוֹאֵל‬ / The Borrower

וְכִי־יִשְׁאַל אִישׁ מֵעִם רֵעֵהוּ וְנִשְׁבַּר אוֹ־מֵת בְּעָלָיו אֵין־עִמּוֹ שַׁלֵּם יְשַׁלֵּם.

---

swear that it was indeed stolen. The intention is not that he must swear that he had not used the article for his own purposes. The same would apply to the verse regarding the paid *shomer* that is discussed below (*Tif. Yis.; Ramban, Exodus* 22:8).

[א] **הַמַּפְקִיד** אֵצֶל חֲבֵרוֹ בְּהֵמָה אוֹ כֵלִים,
וְנִגְנְבוּ אוֹ שֶׁאָבְדוּ, שָׁלֵם, וְלֹא
רָצָה לִשָּׁבַע — שֶׁהֲרֵי אָמְרוּ: שׁוֹמֵר חִנָּם נִשְׁבָּע
וְיוֹצֵא — נִמְצָא הַגַּנָּב, מְשַׁלֵּם תַּשְׁלוּמֵי כֶפֶל; טָבַח
וּמָכַר, מְשַׁלֵּם תַּשְׁלוּמֵי אַרְבָּעָה וַחֲמִשָּׁה. לְמִי
מְשַׁלֵּם? לְמִי שֶׁהַפִּקָּדוֹן אֶצְלוֹ.

יד אברהם

If a man borrows from another, and it fractures a limb or dies, if its owner is not with him, he shall surely pay (Exodus 22:13).

If a person borrows an item or animal from another, he is liable for anything that occurs to it, even unavoidable accidents, except if it breaks or dies as a result of his using it for the purpose for which he borrowed it. Since the owner was well aware that it would be used in this manner, he himself is considered to have been negligent in lending it out for that purpose. If there are no witnesses to verify the borrower's claim, he must swear that what he said is true (*Choshen Mishpat 340:4*).

⊷§ שׂוֹכֵר / The Renter

אִם־שָׂכִיר הוּא בָּא בִּשְׂכָרוֹ.

If it is rented, it came through its rent (ibid. v. 14).

Scripture is telling us that since a renter pays for the use of the item, unlike a borrower who uses it gratuitously, his liabilities differ from the latter's in that he is not responsible for accidents occurring to the article (*Rashi* ad loc.). According to R' Meir, the renter has the same liabilities as the unpaid *shomer*; according to R' Yehudah, the paid *shomer* (*Gem.* 80b). The halachah follows the view of R' Yehudah (*Choshen Mishpat 307:1*).

1.

הַמַּפְקִיד אֵצֶל חֲבֵרוֹ בְּהֵמָה אוֹ כֵלִים, — [*If*] *one deposits an animal or utensils with another,*

[He asks another person to watch them for him.] This mishnah deals with an unpaid *shomer* (*Tif. Yis.*).

וְנִגְנְבוּ אוֹ שֶׁאָבְדוּ, — *and they are stolen or lost,*

Some versions omit the phrase *or lost,* because the mishnah continues below: *if the thief is found ...* which obviously does not apply had the article been lost. Those readings which do contain this phrase can be explained as meaning that although the *shomer* claimed that the article had been lost, it was later discovered to have been stolen. Alternatively, the mishnah's statement is

construed as follows: *And they are stolen* — that is, it is known that the object had been stolen from the *shomer's* house, but it is not known if this was due to his neglect; *or lost* — that is, it is known that the object is missing from the *shomer's* house, but it is not known if this was due to theft or some other cause (*Tos.*). [Other explanations of the mishnah are given below.]

שָׁלֵם, וְלֹא רָצָה לִשָּׁבַע — *and, not wishing to swear,* [*the shomer*] *pays* —

[He pays the value of the item to the owner.] This is because he did not wish to take *the oath of the shomerim* — viz., that he had not been neglectful in watching the item, nor had he used it for his own purposes. Had he sworn thus,

3
1

1. [If] one deposits an animal or utensils with another, and they are stolen or lost, and, not wishing to swear, [the *shomer*] pays — for they said: An unpaid *shomer* [may] swear and be quit — [if] the thief is found, he pays the twofold payment; [if] he has slaughtered or sold [the animal], he pays the fourfold or fivefold payment. Whom does he pay? The one to whom the deposit was entrusted.

he would not have had to pay (*Rav; Rashi*).

The mishnah's ruling, stated below, applies not only if the *shomer* actually pays, but even if he merely states in court that he intends to pay (*Rav from Gem. 34a*).

Even if the *shomer* elects to pay, he is nevertheless required to swear that the article is not in his possession. This is done to avoid the possibility that he desired to have it for himself and therefore claimed that it had been stolen, so that he can pay and keep it against the will of the owner (*Gem. 34b*).

שֶׁהֲרֵי אָמְרוּ: שׁוֹמֵר חִנָּם נִשְׁבָּע וְיוֹצֵא — — *for they said: An unpaid shomer [may] swear and be quit —*

[*They* refers to the Rabbis, who derive from the Torah that if such a *shomer* swears, he need not pay.]

Literally, the mishnah's statement means: *An unpaid shomer swears and leaves* — that is, he leaves the court where the oath was administered [and need not pay] (*Shoshannim LeDavid*).

נִמְצָא הַגַּנָּב, מְשַׁלֵּם תַּשְׁלוּמֵי כֶפֶל; — [if] the thief is found, he pays the twofold payment;

[If the one who stole the item from the *shomer* is found, he must pay double the value of the item, as stated in *Exodus 22:9*. The laws of the twofold, fourfold and fivefold payments are discussed in *Bava Kamma, ch. 7.*]

טָבַח וּמָכַר, מְשַׁלֵּם תַּשְׁלוּמֵי אַרְבָּעָה וַחֲמִשָּׁה. — [if] he has slaughtered or sold [the

animal], he pays the fourfold or fivefold payment.

[As specified in *Exodus 21:37*, this applies only if the stolen item is an ox or a lamb.]

לְמִי מְשַׁלֵּם? — Whom does he pay?

[To whom does the thief make these payments?]

לְמִי שֶׁהַפִּקָּדוֹן אֶצְלוֹ. — The one to whom the deposit was entrusted.

That is, the *shomer*. By paying — or, as mentioned above, by merely stating in court that he intends to pay — he acquires the rights to all payments relating to the item, whether it be the twofold payment or the four/fivefold payment (*Rav*).

The Rabbis instituted that an unpaid *shomer* may pay for the item and thereby acquire the rights to payments relating to it, because they assumed that the owner of the item would rather accept payment for it and give over the rights to the two/four/fivefold payments to the *shomer* than risk losing the principal amount itself [for if he would refuse payment from the *shomer*, and the thief would not be found, he would be left with nothing] (*Tos. Yom Tov*).

The *Gemara (34a)* explains that when the owner gives the item over to the *shomer*, it is as if he stipulates that in the event the item is stolen and the *shomer* pays for it, it shall be retroactively considered as having belonged to the latter from the time it was deposited with him. Others maintain that it is deemed the *shomer's*

נִשְׁבַּע וְלֹא רָצָה לְשַׁלֵּם — נִמְצָא הַגַּנָּב, מְשַׁלֵּם
תַּשְׁלוּמֵי כֶפֶל; טָבַח וּמָכַר, מְשַׁלֵּם תַּשְׁלוּמֵי
אַרְבָּעָה וַחֲמִשָּׁה. לְמִי מְשַׁלֵּם? לְבַעַל הַפִּקָּדוֹן.

[ב] הַשּׂוֹכֵר פָּרָה מֵחֲבֵרוֹ וְהִשְׁאִילָהּ לְאַחֵר,
וּמֵתָה כְּדַרְכָּהּ, יִשָּׁבַע הַשּׂוֹכֵר
שֶׁמֵּתָה כְּדַרְכָּהּ, וְהַשּׂוֹאֵל יְשַׁלֵּם לַשּׂוֹכֵר. אָמַר רַבִּי

יד אברהם

immediately prior to the theft. According to both views, the item
belonged to the *shomer* at the time of
the theft; hence, the payments are due
him. The difference between the two
opinions is whether the *shomer* acquires
the fleece and offspring of the animal
between the time of the deposit and
shortly before the theft (*Tos. R' Akiva*).

It is necessary for the *Tanna* to
specify that this ruling applies to both
animals and utensils. In the former case,
he is teaching us that the owner is willing to give over even the rights to the
four/fivefold payment in order to be
sure of receiving the principal.
Regarding utensils, he is telling us that
although there is little trouble involved
in watching them, the owner is
nevertheless willing to give over the
right to the twofold payment if the
shomer pays him the principal amount
(*Tos. Yom Tov* from *Gem.* 33b).

Not only the two/four/fivefold
payments are awarded to the *shomer*,
but also any increase in the value of the
item. This explains why the mishnah
mentions the case of the item being lost
[see commentary above, s.v. וְנִגְנְבוּ]
although the payments described do not
apply to it. The *Tanna* is implying that
in such a case any increase in the
article's value belongs to the *shomer*
(*Tos. Yom Tov* from *Nimmukei Yosef*).

As mentioned above, the mishnah is
dealing with the case of an unpaid
shomer. The same applies also to a paid
shomer who claims that an accident had
occurred, but pays rather than swears.

If it is subsequently discovered that the
item had been stolen, the twofold
payment belongs to the *shomer*. The
reason the ruling is stated with regard to
the unpaid *shomer* is to tell us that
although the item was held by him
solely for the owner's benefit — when it
is given over to him, it is as if he
acquires the article in the event that it is
stolen and he chooses to pay for it.
Surely, this is so in the case of the paid
shomer, who watches the item because
he is paid to do so.

Another reason is to teach us that
even if the unpaid *shomer* admits that
the article was stolen or lost as a result
of his negligence, and he pays, he
nevertheless acquires thereby the rights
to the two/four/fivefold payments,
since he could have sworn falsely and
been exempt from paying. Surely, this is
so in the case of the paid *shomer*, who
claims that he is exempt, yet pays
nevertheless (*Tif. Yis.*).

נִשְׁבַּע וְלֹא רָצָה לְשַׁלֵּם — [If] he swore
and did not wish to pay —

[The unpaid *shomer* chose to swear
that the article was stolen or lost, rather
than pay.]

נִמְצָא הַגַּנָּב, מְשַׁלֵּם תַּשְׁלוּמֵי כֶפֶל; טָבַח וּמָכַר,
מְשַׁלֵּם תַּשְׁלוּמֵי אַרְבָּעָה וַחֲמִשָּׁה. לְמִי מְשַׁלֵּם?
לְבַעַל הַפִּקָּדוֹן. — [if] *the thief is found, he*
pays the twofold payment; [if] *he has*
slaughtered or sold [*the animal*], *he pays*
the fourfold or fivefold payment.
Whom does he pay? The owner of the
deposit.

[If] he swore and did not wish to pay — [if] the thief is found, he pays the twofold payment; [if] he has slaughtered or sold [the animal], he pays the fourfold or fivefold payment. Whom does he pay? The owner of the deposit.

2. [If] one rents a cow from another and lends it to someone else, and it dies naturally, the renter must swear that it died naturally, and the borrower must pay the renter. Said R' Yose: How does that

YAD AVRAHAM

Although it is obvious that if the *shomer* does not pay, he does not receive the multiple payments, the mishnah states this to point out that it applies only if the *shomer* does not subsequently pay. If he does, however, although he had originally troubled the owner to take him to court to swear, the latter willingly gives over the rights to the multiple payments in exchange for the principal amount. This is Rava's view in *Bava Kamma* 108a, which the halachah follows *(Tos. Yom Tov from Nimmukei Yosef).*

2.

הַשּׂוֹכֵר פָּרָה מֵחֲבֵרוֹ וְהִשְׁאִילָהּ לְאַחֵר, — [If] one rents a cow from another and lends it to someone else,

The renter lends it out to another person with the owner's permission [for the duration of the rental *(Tos. Yom Tov from Rashi)*]. Had the owner not given permission, the renter would be liable for anything that occurs to the animal, because the halachah is that a *shomer* who gives over the deposit to another *shomer* is liable *(Rav from Gem.* 36a).

וּמֵתָה כְּדַרְכָּהּ, — and it dies naturally,

[The cow dies while in the borrower's possession. This is an accident for which a borrower is liable, but a renter is exempt.]

יִשָּׁבַע הַשּׂוֹכֵר שֶׁמֵּתָה כְּדַרְכָּהּ, — the renter must swear that it died naturally,

He must swear to the owner that the animal did not die as a result of negligence, and he is exempt, for a renter is not liable for accidents *(Rav; Rashi).*

וְהַשּׂוֹאֵל יְשַׁלֵּם לַשּׂוֹכֵר. — and the borrower must pay the renter.

Since the borrower is liable for accidents, he must pay the renter *(Rav).*

When the animal dies, the renter becomes exempt from paying and acquires the animal, since he is not liable for accidents; he takes the oath merely to placate the owner. Therefore, the borrower — who *is* responsible for accidents — must pay the renter *(Tos. Yom Tov from Gem.* 35b).

As mentioned above, this applies only if the owner permitted the renter to lend out the cow. Otherwise, the renter is liable for anything that occurs to the animal just as is any *shomer* who gives over his deposit to another *shomer (Rav from Gem.* 36b).

The *Gemara's* qualification of the mishnah as referring to an instance in which the renter had permission to lend the deposit is in accordance with the view of Abaye, who explains that had he not been permitted to do so, he would be liable, because the owner can claim

יוֹסֵי: כֵּיצַד הַלָּה עוֹשֶׂה סְחוֹרָה בְּפָרָתוֹ שֶׁל־חֲבֵרוֹ?
אֶלָּא, תַּחֲזֹר פָּרָה לַבְּעָלִים.

[ג] **אָמַר** לִשְׁנַיִם: „גָּזַלְתִּי לְאֶחָד מִכֶּם מָנֶה,
וְאֵינִי יוֹדֵעַ אֵיזֶה מִכֶּם,״ אוֹ „אָבִיו
שֶׁל־אֶחָד מִכֶּם הִפְקִיד לִי מָנֶה, וְאֵינִי יוֹדֵעַ אֵיזֶה
הוּא״ — נוֹתֵן לָזֶה מָנֶה וְלָזֶה מָנֶה, שֶׁהוֹדָה מִפִּי
עַצְמוֹ.

יד אברהם

that he did not wish the deposit to be in another's possession. The intention is, according to *Tosafos*, that giving a deposit to another *shomer* without permission is deemed negligence, and for any accident that can be attributed to it having been given to the second *shomer*, the first *shomer* is liable. For example, if the animal dies, since it is possible that the air in the borrower's house was not as healthful as that in the renter's house, the renter is liable.

Rava, however, explains that if one *shomer* gives over the deposit to another, the first one is liable, because the owner may claim that — never having dealt with the second *shomer* — he does not believe the latter's oath. In our case, however, since the first *shomer* — i.e., the renter — takes the oath, claiming to know that the animal died a natural death, this reason does not apply. Therefore, even if he had lent out the cow without the owner's permission, he is still exempt. Since the halachah follows Rava's opinion, it is unnecessary to qualify the mishnah as

referring to an instance in which the animal was lent out without permission.

[Perhaps *Rav* — who does make this qualification — rules in accordance with Abaye's view, as does *Rabbeinu Chananel*, quoted by *Tosafos* (s.v. את). Although *Rambam* (Commentary) makes the same qualification of the mishnah as *Rav* — which seems to indicate that he follows the view of Abaye — in *Hil. Sechirus* (1:4) he rules in accordance with Rava's opinion. See *Shoshannim LeDavid*.]

אָמַר רַבִּי יוֹסֵי: כֵּיצַד הַלָּה עוֹשֶׂה סְחוֹרָה בְּפָרָתוֹ שֶׁל־חֲבֵרוֹ? — *Said R' Yose: How does that person do business with another's cow?*

R' Yose regards the renter who lends out the deposit as the agent of the owner. Therefore, the latter litigates directly with the borrower (ibid. from *Rosh*).

אֶלָּא, תַּחֲזֹר פָּרָה לַבְּעָלִים. — *Rather, the cow should be returned to the owner.*

[That is, the payment for the cow should be given to the owner, not to the renter.]

The halachah is in accordance with R' Yose (*Rav; Rambam Commentary*).

3.

אָמַר לִשְׁנַיִם: — [If] one says to two:

[One person approaches two others and tells them:]

„גָּזַלְתִּי לְאֶחָד מִכֶּם מָנֶה, — 'I robbed one of you of a maneh,

[A maneh equals one hundred zuz.]

וְאֵינִי יוֹדֵעַ אֵיזֶה מִכֶּם,״ — but I do not know which one of you,'

[He does not remember which one of them he robbed.] They, too, do not know (*Tif. Yis.* from *Gem. 37a*).

Although neither of them had demanded the money from him, he

person do business with another's cow? Rather, the
cow should be returned to the owner.

3. [If] one says to two: 'I robbed one of you of a
maneh, but I do not know which one of you,'
or 'The father of one of you deposited a maneh with
me, but I do not know which one he is' — he gives
this one a maneh and that one a maneh, because he
admitted by himself.

YAD AVRAHAM

admits to the crime in order to fulfill his
duty toward Heaven *(Rav* from *Gem.*
37a; see *Rashi* ad loc.).

אוֹ — *or*
[This is another case. A person
approached two people and said the
following:]

,אָבִיו שֶׁל־אֶחָד מִכֶּם הִפְקִיד לִי מָנֶה, וְאֵינִי יוֹדֵעַ
אֵיזֶה הוּא" — *'The father of one of you
deposited a maneh with me, but I do not
know which one he is'* —
[He does not remember whose father
it was.] They, too, do not know, as in
the preceding case *(Tif. Yis.).*

,נוֹתֵן לָזֶה מָנֶה וְלָזֶה מָנֶה — *he gives this one
a maneh and that one a maneh,*
[He must give each one a hundred
zuz.]

שֶׁהוֹדָה מִפִּי עַצְמוֹ. — *because he admitted
by himself.*
That is, since the motive of the robber
or *shomer* is to discharge his obligation
toward Heaven — as evidenced by his
admitting that he owes the money — he
can do so only by giving a *maneh* to
each of the persons in question, thereby
assuring that it has been returned to its
rightful owner. By law, however, he is
required only to give one *maneh,* and
the two persons divide it between them
(Rambam, Hil. Gezeilah 4:10; see
Lechem Mishneh ad loc.).
However, should two people accuse a
certain person — each one claiming that
the latter stole a *maneh* from him — and
the person admits to having stolen that

amount from only one of them, but he
does not know which one, the halachah
is that each of the two accusers must
swear that the robber had stolen a
maneh from him, and the robber must
then pay each one. This is a
Rabbinically ordained fine for
transgressing the negative commandment *(Lev.* 19:13), לֹא תִגְזֹל, *You shall
not rob (Rav; Rambam Commentary).*
The accusers must swear, because —
as a general rule — one who seeks to
exact money from another merely on the
basis of his word must swear that he is
saying the truth. Alternatively, since the
robber or *shomer* would not have to pay
both accusers were it not for the
Rabbinical fine, it would not be proper
to fine him if the accusers do not take an
oath *(Kesef Mishneh* loc. cit. §9). In the
previous case, on the other hand, the
Rabbis did not impose any fine, since he
had admitted the crime without anyone
demanding the money from him
(Rambam ibid. §10).
Likewise, if each of two persons claim
that his father had deposited a *maneh*
with a certain individual, and the latter
admits that one of their fathers had
indeed done so, but he has forgotten
which one, each of the claimants must
swear that his father had deposited the
maneh with that *shomer,* and the latter
must then pay each one. This is because
the *shomer* is at fault for not
remembering which one gave him the
money *(Rav).*
The same applies if each one claims

[ד] **שְׁנַיִם** שֶׁהִפְקִידוּ אֵצֶל אֶחָד — זֶה מָנֶה,
וְזֶה מָאתַיִם — זֶה אוֹמֵר: ,,שֶׁלִּי
מָאתַיִם,'' וְזֶה אוֹמֵר: ,,שֶׁלִּי מָאתַיִם,'' נוֹתֵן לָזֶה
מָנֶה וְלָזֶה מָנֶה, וְהַשְּׁאָר יְהֵא מֻנָּח עַד שֶׁיָּבֹא
אֵלִיָּהוּ.
אָמַר רַבִּי יוֹסֵי: אִם־כֵּן, מַה הִפְסִיד הָרַמַּאי?
אֶלָּא, הַכֹּל יְהֵא מֻנָּח עַד שֶׁיָּבֹא אֵלִיָּהוּ.

that he himself had entrusted the *shomer* with a *maneh*. Rav chooses an instance involving fathers to parallelize the case in the mishnah (*Tos. Yom Tov*). The mishnah itself deliberately states a case in which it was one of the fathers who had deposited the money with the *shomer*, because had the case been that the *shomer* admitted of his own accord that he had accepted a *maneh* from one of the persons themselves, he would not be obligated to pay more than a *maneh*, even in order to fulfill his duty to Heaven. This is because the depositor should have noted to whom he gave the money, and he obviously did not, since he did not claim it (ibid. from *Rosh*). Because the depositor did not come to claim the money, the *shomer* became negligent and forgot who the depositor was. Hence, the *shomer's* negligence was caused by the depositor (*Sma* 76:5). *Nesivos Hamishpat* (ibid. §11) com-

ments: Since the depositor, too, was negligent, the *shomer* is not obligated to pay both claimants and take a loss so that the depositor is assured of receiving the money. See *Shach*, *Ketzos Hachoshen* ad loc.

Should each of two persons claim that a certain individual had purchased an item from him, but did not pay for it, and the latter admits that he had indeed bought such an item from one of them, but does not remember which one, the buyer need pay only the purchase price, and the two who claim to be the seller must decide what to do with it. The buyer is not penalized for not remembering the seller, since purchases are usually paid for immediately. In the case of a deposit, however, since it is generally kept for a length of time, the *shomer* is penalized for not remembering who gave it to him (*Tos. Yom Tov* from *Nimmukei Yosef*).

4.

שְׁנַיִם שֶׁהִפְקִידוּ אֵצֶל אֶחָד — — *[If] two deposited with one —*
[Two people deposited money with one person.]

זֶה מָנֶה, וְזֶה מָאתַיִם — *one a maneh, and one two hundred [zuz] —*
One of the people gave the *shomer* one hundred *zuz*, and the other gave him two hundred *zuz*. According to *Rif* and *Rambam* (Commentary and Hil. She'elah 5:4), the mishnah is dealing with a case in which both people give

their money to the *shomer* in one package. According to *Rav* and *Rashi*, the same applies even if they give it in two packages — as long as they do so in each other's presence (*Tif. Yis.*).

זֶה אוֹמֵר: ,,שֶׁלִּי מָאתַיִם,'' וְזֶה אוֹמֵר: ,,שֶׁלִּי מָאתַיִם,'' — *[and] this one says: 'The two hundred are mine,' and that one says: 'The two hundred are mine,'*
[Subsequently, each one claims to have been the one who gave the *shomer* two hundred *zuz*.]

4. [If] two deposited with one — one a *maneh*, and one two hundred [*zuz*] — [and] this one says: 'The two hundred are mine,' and that one says: 'The two hundred are mine,' he gives this one a *maneh* and that one a *maneh*, and the remainder should be put away until Elijah comes.

Said R' Yose: If so, what does the deceiver lose? Rather, everything should be put away until Elijah comes.

YAD AVRAHAM

נוֹתֵן לָזֶה מָנֶה וְלָזֶה מָנֶה, — *he gives this one a maneh and that one a maneh,*

[Since there is no question that each of them had given at least a *maneh*, he must return a *maneh* to each one.]

וְהַשְּׁאָר יְהֵא מֻנָּח — *and the remainder should be put away*

Rambam (Hil. She'elah 5:4) rules that it is held by the *shomer*. Mordechai maintains that it is held by the court (Tif. Yis. from Choshen Mishpat 300:1).

עַד שֶׁיָּבֹא אֵלִיָּהוּ. — *until Elijah comes.*

That is, until Elijah the prophet comes and resolves the matter. Of course, it can be settled earlier if the two litigants arrive at a compromise, or one of them admits that the other is right (Meiri).

In this case, the *shomer* is not obligated to pay two hundred *zuz* to each of them, because the two persons brought their deposits together [according to *Rav* and *Rashi* simultaneously; according to *Rif* and *Rambam*, in one bundle]. Since it is obvious that such a situation often leads to subsequent disputes as to who gave the larger amount, and the two of them did not find it necessary to take precautions to avoid this, the *shomer* assumed that they trust each other, and was therefore not careful to note who gave him the larger amount (Gem. 37a).

In such a case, he is not required to pay each one even if he wishes to fulfill his obligation to Heaven, according to Tosafos (37a), Maggid Mishneh (Hil.

She'elah 4:4), and Meiri. Rosh and Tur (300), however, contend that this applies only if the depositors did not claim the two hundred; it was the *shomer* who mentioned it to them. Should they claim it, the *shomer* must pay each of them that amount if he wishes to discharge his duty toward Heaven. If the money was given to the *shomer* in two separate bundles [or, according to *Rav* and *Rashi*, at separate times], and each of the depositors claims that the two hundred are his, they must both swear to that effect, and the *shomer* must pay each one two hundred, because of his negligence in not writing the name of the owners on their property, as in the preceding mishnah (Rambam Commentary).

אָמַר רַבִּי יוֹסֵי: אִם־כֵּן, — *Said R' Yose: If so,*

That is, if both of those who claim that the two hundred *zuz* is theirs — one of which is obviously lying — receive a *maneh* each (Meleches Shlomo).

מָה הִפְסִיד הָרַמַּאי? — *what does the deceiver lose?*

The liar will never admit his deceit, since he loses nothing by lying (Rav; Rashi).

אֶלָּא, הַכֹּל יְהֵא מֻנָּח עַד שֶׁיָּבֹא אֵלִיָּהוּ. — *Rather, everything should be put away until Elijah comes.*

That is, the entire three hundred *zuz*. Thus, knowing that he will lose his hundred *zuz*, the deceiver will be motivated to confess (Meleches Shlomo).

[ה] **וְכֵן שְׁנֵי** כֵּלִים — אֶחָד יָפֶה מָנֶה וְאֶחָד
יָפֶה אֶלֶף זוּז. זֶה אוֹמֵר: ,,יָפֶה
שֶׁלִּי,'' וְזֶה אוֹמֵר: ,,יָפֶה שֶׁלִּי,'' נוֹתֵן אֶת־הַקָּטָן
לְאֶחָד מֵהֶן, וּמִתּוֹךְ הַגָּדוֹל נוֹתֵן דְּמֵי קָטָן לַשֵּׁנִי,
וְהַשְּׁאָר יְהֵא מֻנָּח עַד שֶׁיָּבֹא אֵלִיָּהוּ.
אָמַר רַבִּי יוֹסֵי: אִם כֵּן, מָה הִפְסִיד הָרַמַּאי?
אֶלָּא, הַכֹּל יְהֵא מֻנָּח עַד שֶׁיָּבֹא אֵלִיָּהוּ.

[ו] **הַמַּפְקִיד** פֵּרוֹת אֵצֶל חֲבֵרוֹ, אֲפִלּוּ הֵן
אֲבוּדִין, לֹא יִגַּע בָּהֶן. רַבָּן

יד אברהם

5.

וְכֵן שְׁנֵי כֵּלִים — *And so it is [with] two
utensils* —

[The law stated in the previous
mishnah applies also to a case in which
each of two people deposited a utensil
with a third party.]

אֶחָד יָפֶה מָנֶה וְאֶחָד יָפֶה אֶלֶף זוּז. — *one
worth a maneh and one worth a
thousand zuz.*

[One deposited a utensil worth a
hundred zuz, and the other deposited a
utensil worth a thousand zuz.]

זֶה אוֹמֵר: ,,יָפֶה שֶׁלִּי,'' וְזֶה אוֹמֵר: ,,יָפֶה שֶׁלִּי,''
*[If] this one says: 'The more expensive
one is mine,' and that one says: 'The
more expensive one is mine,'*

[Each of them claims that the utensil
worth one thousand zuz is his, and the
shomer does not remember who gave it
to him.]

נוֹתֵן אֶת־הַקָּטָן לְאֶחָד מֵהֶן, — *he gives the
smaller one to one of them,*

[The shomer must give the utensil
worth one hundred zuz to one of the
claimants.]

וּמִתּוֹךְ הַגָּדוֹל נוֹתֵן דְּמֵי קָטָן לַשֵּׁנִי, — *and from
the larger one he gives the value of the
smaller one to the other,*

Rav and Rashi explain that the more
expensive utensil is to be broken, and a
portion of it equaling the value of the
cheaper utensil is given to the other
claimant. This is done despite the fact
that the breakage will surely cause a loss
in its value. *Rashba* and *Meiri* add that,
according to this opinion, the mishnah
must be qualified as dealing only with
utensils that will not suffer a great loss
by breaking them. Otherwise, the item
would be sold, rather than broken, as in
the case of the cloak in 1:1. *Rashba*,
himself, disagrees with this qualification, maintaining that the mishnah is
dealing with all types of utensils.
Rather, he and *Rambam* (Hil. She'elah
5:4) explain that in all such cases, the
more expensive utensil is sold, and the
second claimant is given a part of the
price received, equal to the value of the
cheaper utensil.

וְהַשְּׁאָר יְהֵא מֻנָּח עַד שֶׁיָּבֹא אֵלִיָּהוּ. — *and the
remainder should be put away until
Elijah comes.*

[See commentary to 1:8. Of course, if
they wish, they can settle the matter
between themselves.]

אָמַר רַבִּי יוֹסֵי: אִם כֵּן, מָה הִפְסִיד הָרַמַּאי? אֶלָּא,

5. **A**nd so it is [with] two utensils — one worth a *maneh* and one worth a thousand *zuz*. [If] this one says: 'The more expensive one is mine,' and that one says: 'The more expensive one is mine,' he gives the smaller one to one of them, and from the larger one he gives the value of the smaller one to the other, and the remainder should be put away until Elijah comes.

Said R' Yose: If so, what does the deceiver lose? Rather, everything should be put away until Elijah comes.

6. [**I**f] one deposits produce with another, even if it is becoming ruined, he may not touch it.

YAD AVRAHAM

הַכֹּל יְהֵא מֻנָּח עַד שֶׁיָּבֹא אֵלִיָּהוּ. — *Said R' Yose: If so, what does the deceiver lose? Rather, everything should be put away until Elijah comes.*

[As in the previous mishnah, R' Yose contends that the deceiver's true share of the contested item must be withheld from him in order to encourage him to admit that he had lied.]

Although this mishnah seems to superfluously state the same ruling as the preceding one, it teaches us that according to the first, anonymous *Tanna*, even in the case of the two utensils, which involves a loss [see below], the more expensive utensil must be divided so that a segment equal to the value of the cheaper utensil can be given to one claimant. Were it not for this

mishnah stating otherwise, we would think that, in such a case, all agree that both utensils are put away (*Gem.* 37b).

[The loss referred to by the *Gemara* is explained by the commentators in accordance with their aformentioned interpretations of the mishnah.] *Rav, Rashba and Rashi,* explain that in order to divide the more expensive utensil it is broken, thereby causing a loss. *Rambam* (*Hil. She'elah* 5:4, according to *Lechem Mishneh* loc. cit.) and *Rashba,* however, explain that the loss is that the more expensive utensil is sold and perhaps its owner may never be able to find another one like it.

The halachah is in accordance with the first *Tanna* (*Rav; Rambam* ibid. and *Commentary* 5:4).

6.

The following mishnah deals with a deposit of produce which is being ruined because of mice or decay, and its owner cannot be contacted (*Maggid Mishneh, Hil. She'elah* 7:1).

הַמַּפְקִיד פֵּרוֹת אֵצֶל חֲבֵרוֹ, אֲפִלּוּ הֵן אֲבוּדִין, — *[If] one deposits produce with another, even if it is becoming ruined,*

[Some editions read: אוֹבְדִין. The meaning is the same.]

For example, it is being ruined because of mice or decay (*Rav; Rashi*).

לֹא יִגַּע בָּהֶן. — *he may not touch it.*

[If the owner of the deposit cannot be

שִׁמְעוֹן בֶּן־גַּמְלִיאֵל אוֹמֵר: מוֹכְרָן בִּפְנֵי בֵית דִּין,
מִפְּנֵי שֶׁהוּא כְּמֵשִׁיב אֲבֵדָה לַבְּעָלִים.

[ז] הַמַּפְקִיד פֵּרוֹת אֵצֶל חֲבֵרוֹ, הֲרֵי זֶה יוֹצִיא
לוֹ חֲסֵרוֹנוֹת: לְחִטִּין וּלְאֹרֶז,
תִּשְׁעַת חֲצָאֵי קַבִּין לְכוֹר; לִשְׂעוֹרִין וּלְדֹחַן, תִּשְׁעָה
קַבִּין לְכוֹר; לְכֻסְמִין וּלְזֶרַע פִּשְׁתָּן, שָׁלֹשׁ סְאִין

יד אברהם

contacted, the *shomer* should not touch
it.]

The *Gemara* accounts for this ruling
by citing a popular maxim: A person
prefers one *kav* (a certain measure) of
his own to nine of another. The
intention is that if a person had a choice
of having something produced by his
own toil or nine times the amount of
that item produced by someone else, he
would opt for the former. In our case,
therefore, if, for example, the amount of
the deposit is ten *kavs*, even if nine of
them will be ruined if the *shomer* holds
on to them, he should do so nevertheless
and retain the remaining one, rather
than sell them and purchase nine *kavs*
produced by someone else.

This is not to be taken literally, but as
an exaggeration. [The expression
probably originates from *Sotah* 3:4.]
Actually, this first, anonymous *Tanna*
holds that as long as the produce will
not be ruined more than the usual
amount — as listed in the following
mishnah — the *shomer* may not sell it.
However, if it will be ruined more than
that amount, even this *Tanna* concurs
with Rabban Shimon ben Gamliel [cited
below] that the shomer should sell it
before a court (*Rav, Tos. Yom Tov* from
Gem. 38a).

Tosafos explain that the controversy
between the first *Tanna* and Rabban
Shimon ben Gamliel applies only if the
produce is ruined in one or two months
to the extent that it would normally be
ruined in a year. The first *Tanna* rules
that since it might not continue being

ruined during the remainder of the year,
the *shomer* may not sell it. Rabban
Shimon ben Gamliel, however, contends
that since it has been ruined to such an
extent in a short time, it will probably
continue at that rate; therefore, the
shomer should sell it (*Bach, Choshen
Mishpat* 292). Should it be ruined more
than this amount in one or two months,
all agree that the *shomer* should sell it.

This is the interpretation given by R'
Kahana in the *Gemara*. Another explanation is that of R' Nachman bar Yitzchak. He maintains that the first *Tanna*
prohibits the sale of the produce because of the possibility that the owner
had designated it as *terumah* (the
Kohen's portion) for other produce.
Accordingly, it may never be sold. *Rosh*
and *Ravad* rule in accordance with R'
Nachman's view. *Ravad*, therefore,
adds that outside of the Holy Land —
where no *terumah* or tithes are given —
the produce may be sold. *Rosh*, however, contends that R' Nachman is not
disagreeing with R' Kahana, but is
merely adding another reason to prohibit the sale of the produce, which may
be valid even if the produce is being
ruined to a greater extent than usual.

רַבָּן שִׁמְעוֹן בֶּן־גַּמְלִיאֵל אוֹמֵר: מוֹכְרָן בִּפְנֵי
בֵּית דִּין, מִפְּנֵי שֶׁהוּא כְּמֵשִׁיב אֲבֵדָה לַבְּעָלִים. —
*Rabban Shimon ben Gamliel says: He
should sell it in the presence of a court,
because he is as one who returns a lost
item to the owner.*

[By selling the remaining produce, the
shomer salvages its value for the

Rabban Shimon ben Gamliel says: He should sell it in the presence of a court, because he is as one who returns a lost item to the owner.

7. [If] one deposits produce with another, he may deduct for decreases: for wheat and rice, nine half *kavs* per *kor;* for barley and for millet, nine *kavs* per *kor;* for spelt and for linseed, three *se'in* per *kor;*

YAD AVRAHAM

owner.]
    According to *Rif* and *Rambam* (*Commentary* and *Hil. She'elah* 7:1), the halachah is in accordance with the

first *Tanna's* opinion. *Rosh,* however, follows the view of Rabban Shimon ben Gamliel. See *Gateway to the Talmud,* p. 95 §11.

7.

If one deposits produce with another person, the latter may not mingle it with his own produce (*Rambam, Hil. She'elah* 5:5). Should he do so unlawfully, and use an unknown amount of the produce, when he pays for what he used, he may deduct the amount that the produce is usually ruined (*Rav* from *Gem.* 40a).
    The following table, excerpted from *Gateway to the Talmud,* p. 118, will be helpful in understanding this and the following mishnah. The modern equivalencies given are based on the calculations of *Chazon Ish.*

MEASURES OF VOLUME		
MEASURE	EQUIVALENT	U.S. EQUIVALENT
לֹג, *log;* pl. לֻגִּין	6 eggs	21.2 fl. oz.
קַב, *kav;* pl. קַבִּין, *kavs*	4 *lugin*	2.65 quarts
סְאָה, *seah;* pl. סְאִין, *se'in*	6 *kavs*	4 gallons
כּוֹר, *kor;* pl. כּוֹרִין, *korin*	30 *se'in*	120 gallons

הַמַּפְקִיד פֵּרוֹת אֵצֶל חֲבֵרוֹ, — *[If] one deposits produce with another,*
    And, as explained above, the *shomer* mingled the produce with his own, and then used it without knowing how much he had used (ibid.).

הֲרֵי זֶה יוֹצִיא לוֹ חֶסְרוֹנוֹת: — *he may deduct for decreases:*
    When repaying the owner, the *shomer* may deduct the amount the produce usually decreases in value by becoming ruined (*Rav; Rashi*).

לְחִטִּין וּלְאֹרֶז, — *for wheat and rice,*
    That is, peeled rice (*Gem.* 40a) The translation of אֹרֶז as *rice* follows *Tosafos* to *Berachos* 37a. According to

Rashi, it is a type of millet. See *Mishnah Berurah* 208:25, that *rice* is the generally accepted definition.

תִּשְׁעַת חֲצָאֵי קַבִּין לְכוֹר; — *nine half kavs per kor;*
    [A *kor* equals thirty *se'in,* and a *seah* equals six *kavs;* hence, a *kor* equals 180 *kavs.* From each *kor,* the *shomer* may deduct 4½ *kavs,* which is one-fortieth of the *kor.*]

לִשְׂעוֹרִין וּלְדֹחַן, תִּשְׁעָה קַבִּין לְכוֹר; — *for barley and for millet, nine kavs per kor;*
    [Nine *kavs* is one-twentieth of a *kor.* All agree that דֹחַן is a type of millet.]

לְכֻסְמִין וּלְזֶרַע פִּשְׁתָּן, שְׁלֹשׁ סְאִין לְכוֹר; — *for spelt and for linseed, three se'in per kor;*

לְכוֹר; הַכֹּל לְפִי הַמִּדָּה, הַכֹּל לְפִי הַזְּמָן. אָמַר רַבִּי
יוֹחָנָן בֶּן־נוּרִי: וְכִי מָה אִכְפַּת לָהֶן לָעַכְבָּרִין; וַהֲלֹא
אוֹכְלוֹת בֵּין מֵהַרְבֵּה וּבֵין מִקִּמְעָא? אֶלָּא, אֵינוֹ
מוֹצִיא לוֹ חֶסְרוֹנוֹת אֶלָּא לְכוֹר אֶחָד בִּלְבָד. רַבִּי
יְהוּדָה אוֹמֵר: אִם הָיְתָה מִדָּה מְרֻבָּה, אֵינוֹ מוֹצִיא
לוֹ חֶסְרוֹנוֹת, מִפְּנֵי שֶׁמּוֹתִירוֹת.

יד אברהם

[Three *se'in* constitutes one-tenth of a kor.]

The linseed mentioned here is qualifed by the *Gemara* as those which are in capsules. Since the capsules dry up and fall off, the value of the linseed decreases greatly (*Rashi*).

The value of pure linseed, without capsules, does not decrease to this extent. *Meiri* conjectures that it decreases to the same extent as that of barley — namely, nine *kavs* per kor.

The amounts listed above were applicable in *Eretz Yisrael* during the time of the *Tannaim*. In other countries and at other times, however, the *shomer* deducts the amount each species is known to decrease in value (*Rav; Rambam Commentary*).

הַכֹּל לְפִי הַמִּדָּה, — *everything according to the measure,*

The amounts stated above are deducted for each kor of produce in the deposit (*Rav from Gem.*).

הַכֹּל לְפִי הַזְּמָן. — *everything according to the time.*

That amount is then multiplied by the number of years the produce was lying in the possession of the *shomer* (ibid. from *Gem., Rashi*).

אָמַר רַבִּי יוֹחָנָן בֶּן־נוּרִי: וְכִי מָה אִכְפַּת לָהֶן לָעַכְבָּרִין; — *Said R' Yochanan ben Nuri: What difference does it make to the mice;*

[Since the deduction is being made based on the amount the mice usually

eat, why is *everything according to the measure?* What difference does it make to the mice how much produce is in the bin?] R' Yochanan ben Nuri differs with the first, anonymous *Tanna's* opinion that the total amount of the deposit is a factor in determining what the *shomer* may deduct (*Rashi*).

וַהֲלֹא אוֹכְלוֹת בֵּין מֵהַרְבֵּה וּבֵין מִקִּמְעָא? אֶלָּא, אֵינוֹ מוֹצִיא לוֹ חֶסְרוֹנוֹת אֶלָּא לְכוֹר אֶחָד בִּלְבָד. — *do they not eat whether from much or from little? Rather, he deducts for decreases for one kor only.*

They eat the same amount regardless of the total volume. Therefore, the *shomer* may deduct only the amount prescribed by the mishnah (*Rav; see Ravad quoted in Shitah Mekubetzes*).

If the deposit consisted of less than a kor, *Tosafos* maintain that he does not deduct the full prescribed amount. This is because the mice have less space to hide; hence, fewer of them will gather, and less of the produce will be eaten. *Meiri*, however, does not differentiate between a case involving a kor and one involving less than a kor.

The *Gemara* (40a) relates that the Sages — i.e., the first *Tanna* — replied to R' Yochanan ben Nuri that the larger the deposit, the more produce that is ruined or lost. *Yerushalmi* (3:5), however, states that the Sages' reasoning is that the mice do indeed eat more from a larger quantity, because when they see much produce they call others to join them. *Tosafos* explain that the

3
7
everything according to the measure, everything according to the time. Said R' Yochanan ben Nuri: What difference does it make to the mice; do they not eat whether from much or from little? Rather, he deducts for decreases for one *kor* only. R' Yehudah says: If it had been a large measure, he does not deduct for decreases, because it increases.

YAD AVRAHAM

retort given by our *Gemara* was meant to demonstrate that even according to R' Yochanan's own view that the total volume does not affect the amount eaten by the mice, it certainly affects the amount that is ruined or lost. The Sages themselves, however, contend that the mice eat more from a larger quantity (*Tos. Yom Tov*).

Meiri, on the other hand, reconciles *Yerushalmi* with our *Gemara*. He explains that when there is much produce, many factors cause it to decrease in value. Much of it is ruined, much of it is lost, and more mice gather when they see plentiful produce. That is the intention of both our *Gemara* and the *Yerushalmi*.

The halachah is in accordance with the first *Tanna* (*Rav; Rambam Commentary*).

רַבִּי יְהוּדָה אוֹמֵר: אִם הָיְתָה מִדָּה מְרֻבָּה, — *R' Yehudah says: If it had been a large measure,*

The owner had entrusted the *shomer* with a large measure of produce — namely, from ten *korin* and over (*Rav, Tos. Yom Tov* from *Gem.*).

אֵינוּ מוֹצִיא לוֹ חֶסְרוֹנוֹת, — *he does not deduct for decreases,*

[Upon returning the deposit, the *shomer* does not deduct for the usual decreases in the amount of produce.]

מִפְּנֵי שֶׁמּוֹתִירוֹת. — *because it increases.*

If produce is deposited with a *shomer*, it is usually stored in the summer, when the grain is dry, and returned in the winter, the rainy season,

when — due to the cold and rainy weather — the grain is moist. It therefore expands to the extent that it compensates for the amount eaten by the mice. Although R' Yehudah does not subscribe completely to R' Yochanan ben Nuri's view, he agrees that in any volume of produce ten *korin* and above, the mice do not eat the usual amount per *kor*. Therefore, the expansion of the grain offsets the loss caused by the mice (*Rav; Rashi,* as explained by *Maharsha;* see *Tos. HaRosh*). *Rabbeinu Peretz* and *Tiferes Yisrael* construe *Rashi* as meaning that R' Yehudah concurs totally with R' Yochanan ben Nuri's opinion.

Tosafos maintain that R' Yehudah concurs with the first *Tanna's* opinion, that the *shomer* may deduct for decreases from each *kor*. They explain that the expansion of the ten *korin* offsets the decreases that usually occur in one *kor*. Therefore, if the deposit consisted of ten *korin*, the *shomer* may deduct for the decreases usually occurring in nine of them. [See *Maharam.*]

Meiri explains that when one deposits a large amount like ten *korin*, he does not give exactly that much; he always gives more. Therefore, when the *shomer* returns it, he may not deduct for decreases, since the amount of the decrease offsets the surplus given him by the owner.

The halachah is not in accordance with R' Yehudah (*Rav; Rambam Commentary*).

[ח] **יוֹצִיא** לוֹ שְׁתוּת לַיַּיִן. רַבִּי יְהוּדָה אוֹמֵר:
חֹמֶשׁ.

יוֹצִיא לוֹ שְׁלֹשֶׁת לְגִין שֶׁמֶן לְמֵאָה: לֹג וּמֶחֱצָה
שְׁמָרִים, לֹג וּמֶחֱצָה בֶּלַע. אִם הָיָה שֶׁמֶן מְזֻקָּק,
אֵינוֹ מוֹצִיא לוֹ שְׁמָרִים. אִם הָיוּ קַנְקַנִּים יְשָׁנִים,
אֵינוֹ מוֹצִיא לוֹ בֶּלַע.

רַבִּי יְהוּדָה אוֹמֵר: אַף הַמּוֹכֵר שֶׁמֶן מְזֻקָּק
לַחֲבֵרוֹ כָּל־יְמוֹת הַשָּׁנָה, הֲרֵי זֶה מְקַבֵּל עָלָיו לֹג
וּמֶחֱצָה שְׁמָרִים לְמֵאָה.

יד אברהם

8.

The following mishnah is a continuation of the previous one, discussing a case in which someone deposited wine with another person, and the latter mixed it with his own wine, not knowing how much of the other's he had used (*Rav; Rashi*).

יוֹצִיא לוֹ שְׁתוּת לַיַּיִן — *He may deduct a sixth for wine.*

When the *shomer* wishes to return the original amount of the deposit, he may deduct a sixth of the amount to compensate for the wine that is usually absorbed by the vessel (*ibid.*).

Others explain that this deduction is based also on the amount of lees (*Tos. Rabbeinu Peretz; Tos. HaRosh; see Lechem Shamayim*).

רַבִּי יְהוּדָה אוֹמֵר: חֹמֶשׁ. — *R' Yehudah says: A fifth.*

The earth from which vessels were made in R' Yehudah's region was more absorbent than that of the first *Tanna's* region (*Rav from Gem.* 40a). [In other words, R' Yehudah is not disagreeing with the first *Tanna.* He is merely stating what the halachah would be in his area.]

Another interpretation found in the *Gemara* is that in the first *Tanna's* locale, they would line the barrels with wax, which is not very absorbent, whereas in R' Yehudah's area, they would do so with pitch, which is more absorbent.

Rambam (Commentary) explains that

the wine manufactured in the first *Tanna's* region was not absorbed as readily as that of R' Yehudah's. Therefore, the first *Tanna* allows for the deduction of one sixth of the original amount, while R' Yehudah permits the deduction of one fifth. This seems not to follow either of the *Gemara's* interpretations (*Shoshannim LeDavid*).

Surprisingly, the authorities do not differentiate between various regions and the earth found in each. They state unqualifiedly that the *shomer* may deduct one sixth. Since we are not familiar with the various types of earth, we cannot judge which regions have the type that absorbs a fifth of the original volume of wine. Therefore, the *shomer* — who brought about the doubt by mingling the other person's wine with his own — may deduct only one sixth, as in the first *Tanna's* region (*Bach Choshen Mishpat* 292).

יוֹצִיא לוֹ שְׁלֹשֶׁת לְגִין שֶׁמֶן לְמֵאָה — *He may deduct three lugin of oil per hundred:*

[If a person entrusts another with a hundred *lugin* of oil, and he mingles it with his own oil and uses it without knowing how much he used, when he

8. He may deduct a sixth for wine. R' Yehudah says: A fifth.

He may deduct three *lugin* of oil per hundred: a *log* and a half for sediment, and a *log* and a half for absorption. If it was refined oil, he may not deduct for sediment. If the vessels were old, he may not deduct for absorption.

R' Yehudah says: Also [if] one sells refined oil to another [for] all the days of the year, the latter must accept upon himself a *log* and a half sediment per hundred.

YAD AVRAHAM

wishes to return the original amount, he may deduct three *lugin* per hundred.]

Since oil is thick, it is not absorbed as much as wine, and three *lugin* is the entire decrease in its volume *(Meiri; Tif. Yis.)*.

לֹג וּמֶחֱצָה שְׁמָרִים, — *a log and a half for sediment,*

[A *log* and a half is deducted to offset the sediment that usually settles on bottom of the barrel.]

לֹג וּמֶחֱצָה בֶּלַע. — *and a log and a half for absorption.*

[Another *log* and a half is deducted to offset the oil that is usually absorbed in the walls of the barrel.]

אִם הָיָה שֶׁמֶן מְזֻקָּק, — *If it was refined oil,*

[That is, oil from which the sediment has been removed.]

אֵינוֹ מוֹצִיא לוֹ שְׁמָרִים. — *he may not deduct for sediment.*

[The *shomer* may deduct only a *log* and a half to offset the absorption.]

אִם הָיוּ קַנְקַנִּים יְשָׁנִים, — *If the vessels were old,*

[He had poured the oil into old vessels that were already saturated with oil; hence, they will no longer absorb any more of it.]

אֵינוֹ מוֹצִיא לוֹ בֶלַע. — *he may not deduct for absorption.*

[He may deduct only a *log* and a half to offset the sediment.]

In the case of wine, however, even old vessels absorb the wine in them *(Tos.* 40b).

רַבִּי יְהוּדָה אוֹמֵר: אַף הַמּוֹכֵר שֶׁמֶן מְזֻקָּק לַחֲבֵרוֹ כָּל-יְמוֹת הַשָּׁנָה, — *R' Yehudah says: Also [if] one sells refined oil to another [for] all the days of the year,*

Just as the depositor of oil in our case must accept a deduction of a *log* and a half per hundred to offset the sediment, so in the case of a purchaser: Someone sold another person enough oil for the entire year. Although they did not stipulate the type of oil to be given, the seller gives him refined oil. It remains in the seller's barrels, and the buyer comes and takes little by little as he needs it *(Rav; Rashi; Meiri)*.

הֲרֵי זֶה מְקַבֵּל עָלָיו לֹג וּמֶחֱצָה שְׁמָרִים לְמֵאָה. — *the latter* (lit., *this one*) *must accept upon himself a log and a half sediment per hundred.*

The buyer must allow the seller to deduct a *log* and a half per hundred *lugin* to account for the sediment that settled on the bottom of the barrel. The halachah is not in accordance with R' Yehudah. Should the purchaser specify that he wishes to buy refined oil, the seller may not deduct a *log* and a half to offset the sediment. This is *Ravad's*

[ט] **הַמַּפְקִיד** חָבִית אֵצֶל חֲבֵרוֹ, וְלֹא יִחֲדוּ
לָהּ הַבְּעָלִים מָקוֹם, וְטִלְטְלָהּ,
וְנִשְׁבְּרָה — אִם מִתּוֹךְ יָדוֹ נִשְׁבְּרָה לְצָרְכּוֹ, חַיָּב;
לְצָרְכָּהּ, פָּטוּר. אִם מִשֶּׁהִנִּיחָהּ נִשְׁבְּרָה — בֵּין
לְצָרְכּוֹ בֵּין לְצָרְכָּהּ — פָּטוּר.
יִחֲדוּ לָהּ הַבְּעָלִים מָקוֹם, וְטִלְטְלָהּ, וְנִשְׁבְּרָה
— בֵּין מִתּוֹךְ יָדוֹ וּבֵין מִשֶּׁהִנִּיחָהּ — לְצָרְכּוֹ,

יד אברהם

view, quoted by *Rashba*, based on *Yerushalmi*.

Meiri cites others who explain that even if the purchaser specifies that he wishes refined oil, he must accept the deduction of a *log* and a half for sediment. Should he purchase oil without specifying, even the first *Tanna* concurs with R' Yehudah that he must accept the deduction of a *log* and a half

per hundred. This is *Rambam's* ruling (*Hil. Mechirah* 18:9, according to *Maggid Mishneh*).

Meiri himself concurs with this opinion only if the seller supplies the purchaser with the oil in one installment. Should he dole it out to him over a period of time, however, the purchaser need not agree to the deduction. [See glosses of *R' Nissan Alpert* ad loc.]

9.

This following mishnah, according to R' Sheshes in the *Gemara* (41a), is based on the principle that הַשּׁוֹאֵל שֶׁלֹּא מִדַּעַת גַּזְלָן הֲוֵי, *one who borrows without permission is deemed a robber*, and is liable for any accident that occurs to the article. Although the item may be in his possession in the capacity of an unpaid *shomer*, who is exempt for all losses unless it happened as a result of his negligence, since he is now classified as a robber, he no longer has these exemptions, and is liable for any occurrence.

Consequently, in order to revert to his previous status of an unpaid *shomer*, he must make a valid return of the stolen article, or — as in our case — the borrowed article. Whether the thief must notify the owner when he returns the stolen article is the subject of a controversy between R' Yishmael and R' Akiva. R' Yishmael rules that he need not inform the owner when he returns it. Therefore, when he does so, he is no longer liable for accidents. R' Akiva rules that he must inform the owner when he returns the article. Should he do so without his knowledge, he retains his status as a thief and is still liable for all types of accidents.

הַמַּפְקִיד חָבִית אֵצֶל חֲבֵרוֹ, וְלֹא יִחֲדוּ לָהּ
הַבְּעָלִים מָקוֹם, — [*If*] *one deposits a cask with another, and its owner had not designated a place for it,*

The owner of the cask did not ask the *shomer* to lend him a specific place where the cask would be kept (*Rav; Rashi*).

וְטִלְטְלָהּ, — *and he moved it,*
[The *shomer* moved the cask from

one place to another.]

וְנִשְׁבְּרָה — *and it broke* —
It broke by accident (*Tif. Yis.*).

אִם מִתּוֹךְ יָדוֹ נִשְׁבְּרָה — *if it broke from his hand*
[The cask fell and broke while the *shomer* was moving it.]

לְצָרְכּוֹ, — [*and he had moved it*] *for his benefit,*

9. [If] one deposits a cask with another, and its owner had not designated a place for it, and he moved it, and it broke — if it broke from his hand [and he had moved it] for his benefit, he is liable; for its benefit, he is exempt. If it broke after he put it down — whether [he had moved it] for his benefit or for its benefit — he is exempt.

[If] the owner had designated a place for it, and he moved it, and it broke — whether from his hand or whether after he put it down — [if he had moved it]

YAD AVRAHAM

He had moved it for his own use — e.g., to stand on it to take down birds from a high nest — and indeed used it for that purpose (*Rav, Tos. Yom Tov* from *Gem.* 41a).

חַיָּב; — *he is liable;*
Since the *shomer* borrowed the cask without permission, he is deemed a thief, and as long as he did not return it to its place, he was responsible for it and liable for any accidents occurring to it (*Rashi to Gem.* 41a; *Meiri*).

לְצָרְכָּה, — *for its benefit,*
The cask broke while he was moving it, but his purpose in moving it had been that it was standing in an unsafe place, where it would likely break (*Rav; Rashi*).

פָּטוּר. — *he is exempt.*
[Since the *shomer* had not borrowed the item, he is exempt from any accidents happening to it, just as is every paid or unpaid *shomer*.]

אִם מִשֶּׁהִגִּיחָה נִשְׁבְּרָה — *If it broke after he put it down —*
After the *shomer* finished using the cask, he put it in a safe place (ibid.).

בֵּין לְצָרְכּוֹ בֵּין לְצָרְכָּה — *whether [he had moved it] for his benefit or for its benefit —*
Regardless of whether the *shomer* had moved the cask for his own benefit or for the benefit of the cask (ibid.).

פָּטוּר. — *he is exempt.*

Since the *shomer* put the cask in a safe place, it is once again considered to be in the possession of the owner, and the *shomer* reverts to his previous status as an unpaid *shomer*, who is not liable for accidents. Although he did not inform the owner that he had put the cask back, it is nevertheless regarded as a valid return of the item. This follows the view of R' Yishmael, who rules that if one steals a lamb from a flock or a coin from a purse, and returns it, he is no longer responsible for it, although he did not inform the owner.

The mishnah qualifies this case as one in which the owner did not designate a place for the cask to teach us that not only if the owner had designated a place for it and the *shomer* put it back there is the latter exempt from accidents, but even if the owner did not designate a place, and the *shomer* put it back in any safe place, the latter is nevertheless exempt, since it is not necessary to inform the owner that he returned it (*Rav from Gem.* 41a).

יִחֲדוּ לָהּ הַבְּעָלִים מָקוֹם, — [If] *the owner had designated a place for it,*
[The owner of the item had asked the *shomer* to lend him a certain place in his house to put the cask.]

וְטִלְטְלָהּ, וְנִשְׁבְּרָה — *and he moved it, and it broke —*
[The *shomer* moved the cask from its place, and it broke by accident.]

בֵּין מִתּוֹךְ יָדוֹ — *whether from his hand*

[י] **הַמַּפְקִיד** מָעוֹת אֵצֶל חֲבֵרוֹ, צְרָרָן
וְהִפְשִׁילָן לַאֲחוֹרָיו, אוֹ שֶׁמְּסָרָן
לִבְנוֹ וּלְבִתּוֹ הַקְּטַנִּים, וְנָעַל בִּפְנֵיהֶם שֶׁלֹּא כָרָאוּי,

יד אברהם

[That is, while he was moving it.]

וּבֵין מִשֶּׁהִנִּיחָהּ — *or whether after he put it down* —

That is, after he returned it to its designated place *(Gem. 41a).*

לְצָרְכּוֹ, — *[if he had moved it] for his benefit,*

[The *shomer* had moved the cask to use for his own purposes, such as to take down birds from a high nest, as above.]

חַיָּב; — *he is liable;*

Since he did not inform the owner that he was returning the item, he is still deemed a thief, and is responsible for accidents. This segment of the mishnah follows R' Akiva's view, that even if a thief returns the stolen article, he is still responsible for it until he informs the owner that he returned it. Therefore, in our case, the *shomer* who took the cask for his own use without the owner's permission acquires the status of a thief until he notifies the owner that he is returning it. This is because if the owner had realized that the *shomer* used the item for his own purposes, he would not have wanted him to continue serving as a *shomer* for it *(Tos. Yom Tov from Gem., Rashi).* [However, once the *shomer* notifies the owner that the item has been put back in a safe place, and the latter does not insist that it be returned to him immediately, he is obviously agreeable that the *shomer* should continue watching the item.]

According to R' Akiva, this ruling applies also if the owner did not designate a place for the cask. The reason the mishnah chooses the instance that the owner did designate a place is to teach us that not only if he did not designate a place is the *shomer* liable, since there is no place for him to return the item, but even if the owner did designate a place, and the *shomer* returned the cask to that place, the latter is liable nevertheless until he informs the owner that he returned it *(Rav from Gem.).*

לְצָרְכָּהּ, — *for its benefit,*

[That is, if the *shomer* had moved the cask because it had been in an unsafe place.]

פָּטוּר. — *he is exempt.*

[He is not liable for accidents, just as every paid or unpaid *shomer.*]

We have explained the mishnah according to R' Yochanan, who interprets it to mean that the *shomer* returned the cask to its designated place. He must therefore attribute the latter half of the mishnah to R' Akiva, who requires that the thief notify the owner upon returning the stolen article. Others attribute the entire mishnah to R' Yishmael, who does not require such notification. They explain that in the mishnah's last case, the *shomer* returned the cask to another place, not the one that had been designated. It is therefore not deemed a return even according to R' Yishmael *(Gem. 41a).*

10.

The Mishnah now defines the concept of פְּשִׁיעָה, *negligence,* for which even an unpaid *shomer* is liable.

for his benefit, he is liable; for its benefit, he is exempt.

10. [I]f] one deposits money with another [and] he tied it up and slung it behind him, or gave it over to his minor son or daughter, and locked [the door] before them inadequately, he is liable, since he

---

YAD AVRAHAM

הַמַּפְקִיד מָעוֹת אֵצֶל חֲבֵרוֹ, צְרָרָן — [If] one deposits money with another [and] he tied it up

The latter is traveling, and he ties the money in his kerchief to carry it home (Rav, Rashi, Meiri).

This refers to a headdress, tied around the head, with two ends hanging loose which can hang to the front or to the back (Shitah Mekubetzes from Rabbeinu Yehonasan).

וְהִפְשִׁילָן לַאֲחוֹרָיו, — and slung it behind him,

He slung the money tied up in the ends of his kerchief over his shoulder, rather than in front of him (Rabbeinu Yehonasan). Although this is generally considered watching the money properly, he is nevertheless liable for any accidents, because one who takes money that has been entrusted to him from one place to another must carry it in his hand, just as was done with money used to redeem the second tithe and brought to Jerusalem [see preface to 4:8]. This is derived from Deuteronomy 14:25: וְצַרְתָּ הַכֶּסֶף בְּיָדְךָ, and you shall tie the money in your hand — that is, although the money is tied, it must be in your hand (Rav from Gem. 42a).

אוֹ שֶׁמְּסָרָן לִבְנוֹ וּלְבִתּוֹ הַקְּטַנִּים, — or gave it over to his minor son or daughter,

The shomer gave over the money to his minor son or daughter for safekeeping, although minors are not considered responsible (Gem. 36a). Should the shomer give over the money to his son or daughter who is of age, however, the son or daughter must swear that they watched it in the usual

manner of shomrim, and the father is exempt. The rule that a shomer who gives over the deposit to another shomer is liable for it does not apply here, since one who gives a deposit to a shomer does so with the knowledge that the latter will give it over to his wife and children for safekeeping (Rav from Gem.).

וְנָעַל בִּפְנֵיהֶם שֶׁלֹּא כָּרָאוּי, — and locked [the door] before them inadequately,

Should the shomer give over the money to his child and lock the door properly, however, he is exempt. Although the Gemara rules that money is considered safe only if it is hidden under the ground, since the children have the money, the thieves fear that they will scream if they attempt to seize it (Tos. HaRosh).

Others read: אוֹ נָעַל בִּפְנֵיהֶם שֶׁלֹּא כָּרָאוּי, or locked [the door] before it inadequately (Rif). The versions of Meiri and Tiferes Yisrael are the same as ours, but they construe the mishnah as if it stated the conjunction אוֹ, or. According to these authorities, this case — separate from that of the minor child above — is that the shomer placed the money in a room and locked the door with an inadequate lock, or placed it in a box with an inadequate lock. Should he lock it properly, however, he is exempt in the event of theft. Although the Gemara states that money is considered safe only if it is hidden under the ground, that refers only to the time of the Amoraim (sages mentioned in the Gemara), when thievery was rampant, and burying the money was the only way to be certain that it would be safe

חַיָּב, שֶׁלֹּא שָׁמַר כְּדֶרֶךְ הַשּׁוֹמְרִים. וְאִם שָׁמַר
כְּדֶרֶךְ הַשּׁוֹמְרִים, פָּטוּר.

[יא] הַמַּפְקִיד מָעוֹת אֵצֶל שֻׁלְחָנִי, אִם
צְרוּרִין, לֹא יִשְׁתַּמֵּשׁ בָּהֶן;
לְפִיכָךְ, אִם אָבְדוּ, אֵינוֹ חַיָּב בְּאַחֲרָיוּתָן. מֻתָּרִין,
יִשְׁתַּמֵּשׁ בָּהֶן; לְפִיכָךְ, אִם אָבְדוּ, חַיָּב בְּאַחֲרָיוּתָן.
אֵצֶל בַּעַל הַבַּיִת, בֵּין צְרוּרִין וּבֵין מֻתָּרִים, לֹא
יִשְׁתַּמֵּשׁ בָּהֶן; לְפִיכָךְ, אִם אָבְדוּ, אֵינוֹ חַיָּב
בְּאַחֲרָיוּתָן.

יד אברהם

(Rashba; Ritva; Nimmukei Yosef).

It is also possible that the mishnah is dealing with one who gives his money to a *shomer* on Friday afternoon, when the latter has no time to bury it (*Tos. HaRosh*).

חַיָּב, — *he is liable*,
[The *shomer* is liable to pay the owner, even if he is an unpaid *shomer*.]

שֶׁלֹּא שָׁמַר כְּדֶרֶךְ הַשּׁוֹמְרִים. — *since he did not watch as shomrim do*.
As explained above, one who is transporting money that has been deposited with him must do so in his

hand, where it is visible to him. If he hides it in his house, it must be buried in the ground, or placed in the wall within a handbreadth from the ground or the ceiling, where thieves seldom search (*Rav* from *Gem.*).

וְאִם שָׁמַר כְּדֶרֶךְ הַשּׁוֹמְרִים, — *But if he watched as shomrim do*,
[And the money was stolen or lost.]

פָּטוּר. — *he is exempt*.
[As long as an unpaid *shomer* is not guilty of negligence, he is exempt for theft or loss.]

11.

This mishnah deals with an unpaid *shomer* who receives a deposit of money, and tells us under which circumstances he is adjudged as a paid *shomer* to be liable for theft and loss.

הַמַּפְקִיד מָעוֹת אֵצֶל שֻׁלְחָנִי, — *[If] one deposited money with a moneychanger*,
He entrusted his money with a moneychanger, who constantly needs coins for his business (*Rashi; Tif. Yis.*).

אִם צְרוּרִין, — *[and] it is tied up*,
The money is tied with an unusual knot or is tied and sealed (*Rav* from *Gem.* 43a).

לֹא יִשְׁתַּמֵּשׁ בָּהֶן; — *he may not use it;*
By tying it with an unusual knot or sealing the bundle, the owner indicated

that he does not want the *shomer* to use the money (*Tos. Yom Tov* from *Rashi*).

לְפִיכָךְ, אִם אָבְדוּ, אֵינוֹ חַיָּב בְּאַחֲרָיוּתָן. — *therefore, if it is lost, he is not responsible for it.*
If the money is lost while in the possession of the moneychanger, the latter is exempt, since he is only an unpaid *shomer* (*Tif. Yis.*).

מֻתָּרִין, — *[If it is] untied*,
The money is not tied, or even if it is tied, but not with an unusual knot, and

did not watch as *shomerim* do. But if he watched as *shomerim* do, he is exempt.

11. [If] one deposited money with a money-changer, [and] it is tied up, he may not use it; therefore, if it is lost, he is not responsible for it. [If it is] untied, he may use it; therefore, if it is lost, he is responsible for it. With a householder [however], whether it is tied or untied, he may not use it; therefore, if it is lost, he is not responsible for it.

YAD AVRAHAM

it is not sealed (*Rav*).

יִשְׁתַּמֵּשׁ בָּהֶן; — *he may use it;*
The fact that the money is tied is no indication that the owner does not want the *shomer* to use it, because it is customary for a person to tie up his money. Since the owner is aware of the moneychanger's immediate need for coins, unless he indicates that he objects to the objects for the latter's use of it, we assume that he does not (*Tos. Yom Tov* from *Rashi*).

Similarly, if a Torah scholar is entrusted with a book, a copy of which he does not own, he may study with it. An ignoramus, however, may not even copy a letter from a book deposited in his care (*Tif. Yis.* quoting *Choshen Mishpat* 292:20 from *Mordechai*).

לְפִיכָךְ, אִם אָבְדוּ, — *therefore, if it is lost,*
Even if he has not yet used it (*Rav; Rashi* to *Gem.* 43a).

חַיָּב בְּאַחֲרָיוּתָן. — *he is responsible for it.*
The privilege of being allowed to use the coins makes the moneychanger a paid *shomer*, and he is therefore responsible for theft or loss. Should he use the money, he becomes a borrower and is responsible for accidents as well (*Rav* from *Gem., Rashi*).

In 2:7 it is stated that the proceeds realized from selling a lost article may be used by the finder, and that this privilege makes him a borrower even before he avails himself of it. This is because the finder expects that it will be a long time before the owner comes to

claim the item. In our case, however, since the *shomer* fears that the owner will come at any time and demand his deposit, he will not buy merchandise with the money. Consequently, the privilege of being able to use the money is of little value (*Tos. Yom Tov* from *Rosh*, quoting *Ravad*).

אֵצֶל בַּעַל הַבַּיִת, — *With a householder [however],*
[That is, if one deposits money with a person who is not a moneychanger.]

בֵּין צְרוּרִין וּבֵין מֻתָּרִים, לֹא יִשְׁתַּמֵּשׁ בָּהֶן; — *whether it is tied or untied, he may not use it;*
[Since he is not constantly in need of coins, even if the money is not tied, there is no indication that the owner is willing to allow him to use his money.]

Mordechai asserts that this ruling applied only in the time of the *Tannaim*, when the vast majority of Jews earned their livelihood from agriculture. Only the moneychangers — or, according to R' Yehudah — the storekeepers as well — were constantly in need of coins for their business. In our times, however, when most people earn their living from commerce, any person may use the money with which he is entrusted [unless the owner indicated that he is not to do so] (*Tif. Yis.* from *Choshen Mishpat* 292:7 *Sma* § 18, *Shach* § 12).

לְפִיכָךְ, אִם אָבְדוּ, אֵינוּ חַיָּב בְּאַחֲרָיוּתָן. — *therefore, if it is lost, he is not*

חֶנְוָנִי כְּבַעַל הַבַּיִת; דִּבְרֵי רַבִּי מֵאִיר. רַבִּי יְהוּדָה אוֹמֵר: חֶנְוָנִי כַּשֻּׁלְחָנִי.

[יב] הַשּׁוֹלֵחַ יָד בְּפִקְדוֹן — בֵּית שַׁמַּאי אוֹמְרִים: יִלְקֶה בְחָסֵר וּבְיָתֵר. וּבֵית הִלֵּל אוֹמְרִים: כִּשְׁעַת הוֹצָאָה. רַבִּי עֲקִיבָא אוֹמֵר: כִּשְׁעַת הַתְּבִיעָה.

יד אברהם

responsible for it.

That is, provided he hides it in the ground, as explained above (*Tos. Yom Tov* from *Rambam, Hil. She'elah* 7:8).

חֶנְוָנִי כְּבַעַל הַבַּיִת; דִּבְרֵי רַבִּי מֵאִיר — *A storekeeper is like a householder; [these are] the words of R' Meir.*

[R' Meir maintains that just as a householder may not use the money entrusted with him, neither may a storekeeper.]

Although he requires much money to purchase various types of fruit, oil, and wine with which to stock up his store, so that nothing should be missing, he is nevertheless adjudged as a householder insofar as even if the owner gives him the money untied, he may not use it (*Shitah Mekubetzes* from *Rabbeinu Yehonasan*).

[Rabbeinu Yehonasan's intention

appears to be that the storekeeper, unlike the moneychanger, does not always require coins. Although, in order to keep his shelves well stocked with all sorts of merchandise, he does need ready cash, R' Meir does not deem this adequate grounds for permitting him to use the money.]

רַבִּי יְהוּדָה אוֹמֵר: חֶנְוָנִי כַּשֻּׁלְחָנִי — *R' Yehudah says: A storekeeper is like a moneychanger.*

R' Yehudah disagrees, maintaining that the storekeeper is regarded in this respect like a moneychanger, since the cash he has on hand never suffices, and he must borrow (*Shitah Mekubetzes* from *Rabbeinu Yehonasan*). [Hence, unless the owner of the money indicated to the storekeeper that he does not want him to use the deposit for his own purposes, the storekeeper may do so.]

12.

שְׁלִיחוּת יָד / Unlawful Use of a Deposit

A *shomer* who uses a deposit entrusted with him for his own purposes — whether he actually takes part of it, or merely intends to do so — is known as a שׁוֹלֵחַ יָד, *one who puts forth his hand.* This act confers upon him the status of a robber, thereby making him liable for any accident occuring to the deposit (*Rambam, Hil. Gezeilah* 3:11). This is based on *Exodus* 22:9,10: וּמֵת אוֹ־נִשְׁבַּר ... *and it dies, or fractures a limb, or is captured, without anyone seeing it.* HASHEM's oath shall be between them if he did not put forth his hand upon the other's goods ... From here it is deduced that if the *shomer* did put forth his hand upon the other's goods, he is liable even if the animal dies, fractures a limb, or is captured, although all of these are unavoidable accidents (*Tos. Yom Tov* from *Rashi* 41b).

הַשּׁוֹלֵחַ יָד בְּפִקְדוֹן — *[If] one uses a deposit for his own purposes (lit., puts*

forth his hand upon a deposit) —

Should the intended use of the

A storekeeper is like a householder; [these are] the words of R' Meir. R' Yehudah says: A storekeeper is like a moneychanger.

12. [If] one uses a deposit for his own purposes — Beis Shammai say: He must suffer whether it loses [value] or it gains. Beis Hillel say: As of the time of its being taken out. R' Akiva says: As of the time of the claim.

YAD AVRAHAM

deposit involve the loss of part of the item, then as soon as he lifts it up, he immediately becomes responsible for accidents. If it does not involve a loss to the item, he is liable only from the time he commences to use it unlawfully.

In the latter case, the *shomer* is liable because he is borrowing the article without permission — hence acquiring the status of a robber — not because of the special halachah of שְׁלִיחוּת יָד, *unlawful use of a deposit*, which applies only to *shomrim* (*Tif. Yis.* from *Choshen Mishpat* 292:1).

בֵּית שַׁמַּאי אוֹמְרִים: יִלְקֶה בְּחָסֵר — *Beis Shammai say: He must suffer whether it loses [value]*

For example, if the deposit was an ewe laden with wool that was shorn after the *shomer* used it, or a pregnant ewe which gave birth after the *shomer* used it [and subsequently, both the ewe and its fleece or its young become lost or die *(Tif. Yis.)*], the *shomer* must pay for the ewe according to its value at the time he used it — i.e., for both the animal and its fleece or young. Thus, he suffers a loss in an instance of the animal losing value [by giving birth or being shorn] (*Rav* from *Gem.* 43b).

וּבְיָחֵר. — *or it gains.*

Should the *shomer* take an ewe that becomes laden with wool or impregnated after he uses it [and both the animal and its fleece or young are lost or die], he must pay for its complete value, including the wool or fetus, although it

was worth less when he used it. Hence, he suffers also in an instance of the animal gaining in value (*ibid.*).

וּבֵית הִלֵּל אוֹמְרִים: כִּשְׁעַת הוֹצָאָה. — *Beis Hillel say: As of the time of its being taken out.*

The *shomer* must pay for the deposit according to its value at the time he appropriated it. If the deposit was an animal, and it was laden with wool at that time, he pays for an animal laden with wool; if shorn of its wool, he pays for it accordingly (*Rav, Tos. Yom Tov* from *Gem.*, as explained by *Rashi*).

רַבִּי עֲקִיבָא אוֹמֵר: בִּשְׁעַת הַתְּבִיעָה. — *R' Akiva says: As of the time of the claim.*

That is, according to the value of the deposit at the time the *shomer* is brought to court. This ruling is based on the verse (*Lev.* 5:24): ... לַאֲשֶׁר הוּא לוֹ יִתְּנֶנּוּ בְּיוֹם אַשְׁמָתוֹ ... *to him to whom it belongs shall he give it on the day of his guilt*, which means that he must pay according to its value on the day he is declared guilty (*Rav* from *Gem.*).

Tosafos explain that R' Akiva does not refer to a case in which a change takes place in the item — as in the instances involving an animal, described above — but to one in which it gains or loses in its market value. According to both Beis Shammai and Beis Hillel, if the article appreciates between the time the *shomer* uses it and the time he is brought to court, and it was lost or destroyed in the interim, he must pay according to its value as of the time of its loss or

הַחוֹשֵׁב לִשְׁלוֹחַ יָד בְּפִקָּדוֹן — בֵּית שַׁמַּאי
אוֹמְרִים: חַיָּב. וּבֵית הִלֵּל אוֹמְרִים: אֵינוֹ חַיָּב עַד
שֶׁיִּשְׁלַח בּוֹ יָד, שֶׁנֶּאֱמַר: ",...,, אִם־לֹא שָׁלַח יָדוֹ
בִּמְלֶאכֶת רֵעֵהוּ." כֵּיצַד? הִטָּה אֶת־הֶחָבִית וְנָטַל
הֵימֶנָּה רְבִיעִית, וְנִשְׁבְּרָה, אֵינוֹ מְשַׁלֵּם אֶלָּא
רְבִיעִית, הִגְבִּיהָהּ וְנָטַל הֵימֶנָּה רְבִיעִית, וְנִשְׁבְּרָה,
מְשַׁלֵּם דְּמֵי כֻלָּהּ.

יד אברהם

destruction. Should it depreciate, he must pay according to its value at the time of the appropriation. R' Akiva differs with both Beis Hillel and Beis Shammai, maintaining that whether the article gains or loses in value, the *shomer* must pay what it was worth at the time of the claim (*Tos. Yom Tov*).

The halachah follows the view of Beis Hillel (*Rav*).

הַחוֹשֵׁב לִשְׁלוֹחַ יָד בְּפִקָּדוֹן — — [*If*] *one intends to take a deposit for his own use* —

The *shomer* tells witnesses that he will use this person's deposit for his own purposes (*Rav ibid.; Rashi*).

Meiri explains that he states that he needs the type of item which is in his trust and is going to use it. Either witnesses heard him say this, or he admitted having said it.

בֵּית שַׁמַּאי אוֹמְרִים: חַיָּב. — *Beis Shammai say: He is liable.*

He is liable for any accidents that occurred after he made that statement (*Rashi*).

Beis Shammai base this ruling on a phrase in *Exodus* 22:8: עַל־כָּל־דְּבַר־פֶּשַׁע, *for every matter of trespass* [which can also be translated: *for every word of trespass* — i.e., once the *shomer* states that he intends to use the deposit for his own purposes, he becomes liable for any accidents occurring to it subsequently]. Beis Hillel, however, interpret this phrase as meaning that the *shomer* instructs another person to appropriate the deposit (*Rav from Gem. 44a*).

Although the general rule is that אֵין

שָׁלִיחַ לִדְבַר עֲבֵרָה, *there is no agent in matters of sin* — i.e., if one tells another to sin, the latter is liable if he complies (*Bava Kamma* 6:4; see ArtScroll commentary ad loc.). Beis Hillel derive from the above phrase that the case of taking a deposit for one's own use is an exception to the rule (*Gem. 44a*).

וּבֵית הִלֵּל אוֹמְרִים: אֵינוֹ חַיָּב עַד שֶׁיִּשְׁלַח בּוֹ יָד, — *Beis Hillel say: He is not liable until he uses it for his own purposes,*

According to Beis Hillel, a *shomer's* stating that he intends to appropriate the deposit does not incur liability; only the act of appropriation itself does so.

שֶׁנֶּאֱמַר: ",...,, אִם־לֹא שָׁלַח יָדוֹ בִּמְלֶאכֶת רֵעֵהוּ." — *as it is said (Exodus 22:7): '... if he has not put forth his hand on the other's goods.'*

[This indicates that he becomes liable for accidents only after he actually uses the deposit for his own purposes.]

כֵּיצַד? — *How?*

The mishnah now explains the view of Beis Hillel, that the *shomer* becomes liable only after the actual appropriation. In some editions, this word is omitted, indicating that this is a separate case, and is not intended as an illustration of Beis Hillel's opinion (*Rav*).

הִטָּה אֶת־הֶחָבִית — [*If*] *he tilted the cask*

A *shomer*, who had been entrusted with a cask, tilted it without lifting it. The mishnah teaches us that tilting is not deemed lifting (*Tif. Yis.*).

**3
12**
[If] one intends to take a deposit for his own use —
Beis Shammai say: He is liable. Beis Hillel say: He is
not liable until he uses it for his own purposes, as it is
said (*Exodus* 22:7): ... *if he has not put forth his
hand on the other's goods.* How? [If] he tilted the
cask and took a quarter [of a *log*] from it, and it
broke, he pays only for the quarter [of a *log*]. [If] he
lifted it and took a quarter [of a *log*] from it, and it
broke, he must pay its entire value.

YAD AVRAHAM

וְנָטַל הֵימֶנָּה רְבִיעִית, — *and took a quarter
[of a log] from it,*
[In Talmudic nomenclature the term a
רְבִיעִית, a *quarter*, refers to a quarter of a
log [see preface to mishnah 7] unless
otherwise specified. In our case, the
shomer appropriated such an amount
from the deposit.]

וְנִשְׁבְּרָה, — *and it broke,*
Subsequently, the cask broke by
accident (*Tif. Yis.*) [and its entire
contents spilled out].

אֵינוֹ מְשַׁלֵּם אֶלָּא רְבִיעִית. — *he pays only
for the quarter [of a log].*
[He must pay only for the quarter of a
log which he actually took. This is
because a *shomer* is liable for using a
deposit for his own purposes only if he
lifts it or pulls it, thereby performing an
act of acquisition. Since, in this case, he
merely tilted the cask, but did not lift it,
he is not liable for accidents occurring to
it.]
However, if the cask contained wine,
and after he took a quarter of a *log* the
remainder of it became sour, he is liable
for the remainder as well, since he was
instrumental in its souring (*Rav* from
Gem.). *Rashi* explains that a full cask of
wine does not sour as readily as one that
is not completely full (*Tos. Yom Tov*).

הִגְבִּיהָהּ וְנָטַל הֵימֶנָּה רְבִיעִית, — [*If*] *he lifted
it and took a quarter* [*of a log*] *from it,*
Actually, even if he did not take out
the quarter of a *log*, but merely lifted the
cask with the intention of taking it, he is

liable for subsequent accidents (*Rav*
from *Gem*. 44a). Should he lift it
without the intention of taking
anything out, however, he is not liable.
Although the halachah is that a *shomer*
becomes liable for accidents occurring to
a deposit if he appropriates it even
without causing a loss to it, this is only
so if he had at least intended to cause a
loss to it.
In the case of mishnah 9 the *shomer* is
responsible if he stands on the cask to
bring birds from a high nest, although
he causes no loss to the cask [nor does
he intend to], because that is an instance
of borrowing the deposit without
permission, not one of appropriation,
each of which has its own halachah.
This is the reason for the ruling of
Tur (292) that in such a case the *shomer*
becomes liable only when he actually
uses the item and not before that; since
he has no intention of causing any loss
to the cask or its contents, he does not
become liable from the time he lifted the
cask, as he would if he had intended to
cause a loss to it (*Tos. Yom Tov*).

וְנִשְׁבְּרָה, — *and it broke,*
The *shomer* lifted the cask with the
intention of taking it, and it subsequently broke by accident (*Tif. Yis*).

מְשַׁלֵּם דְּמֵי כֻלָּהּ. — *he must pay its entire
value.*
[Since he is guilty of using the deposit
for his own purposes, he is liable for the
entire article — not only for the amount
he actually took — as though he had

[א] הַזָּהָב קוֹנֶה אֶת־הַכֶּסֶף, וְהַכֶּסֶף אֵינוֹ קוֹנֶה אֶת־הַזָּהָב. הַנְּחֹשֶׁת קוֹנָה אֶת־הַכֶּסֶף, וְהַכֶּסֶף אֵינוֹ קוֹנֶה אֶת־הַנְּחֹשֶׁת. מָעוֹת הָרָעוֹת קוֹנוֹת אֶת־הַיָּפוֹת, וְהַיָּפוֹת אֵינָן קוֹנוֹת אֶת־הָרָעוֹת. אֲסִימוֹן קוֹנֶה אֶת־הַמַּטְבֵּעַ, וְהַמַּטְבֵּעַ

יד אברהם

stolen it.]

Ravad (Hil. Gezeilah 3:12) adds that he is liable for the entire value only if he originally intended to take the entire contents of the cask, but later decided to take only a quarter of a *log.* Otherwise, he is liable only for the amount he actually took.

Chapter 4

◄§ Money as a Method of Acquisition

According to Jewish law, whenever a transaction — such as a sale — is performed, it can be consummated only through a קִנְיָן, *act of acquisition;* otherwise either of the parties involved may retract. One method of acquisition, for example, is מְשִׁיכָה, *meshichah* (pulling): the buyer takes hold of the article and draws it to him. He thereby becomes indebted to the seller and must give him the purchase price agreed upon. The transfer of money, however, is not a valid act of acquisition, as stated in mishnah 2. In effect, therefore, the commodity acquires the money, rather than the money acquiring the commodity.

Should an exchange of two types of money be transacted, the one that is less acceptable as a medium of exchange and less frequently minted is deemed the commodity, and the other one is deemed the money.

R' Yochanan maintains that according to Biblical law, the transfer of money is indeed a valid act of acquisition; it is only due to a Rabbinical enactment that another such act is required in order to acquire chattels. Resh Lakish, however, rules that the Torah requires *meshichah* to consummate a transaction; hence, the transfer of money is totally inefficacious in the acquisition of movables *(Gem.* 47a). [All agree that it is generally effective in acquiring real property *(Kiddushin* 1:5; see ArtScroll commentary ad loc.).]

1.

הַזָּהָב — *Gold*
That is, a gold coin *(Tif. Yis.).*

קוֹנֶה אֶת־הַכֶּסֶף, — *acquires silver,*
If an exchange is made of gold coins for silver coins, as soon as the gold coins are transferred, the other party acquires the silver coins. The one who receives the gold coins becomes obligated to give the silver coins that had been agreed upon — whether they are new coins or old ones. Should they have stipulated that he would give him new coins, he

must do so — although the old ones may be better — since the recipient can claim that he wishes to keep them for a long time, and old silver coins tarnish excessively *(Rav, Tos. Yom Tov* from *Gem.* 45b).

As explained above, the medium of exchange used more commonly is considered the coin, and the other one is considered the commodity for the purpose of the transaction. In our case, silver coins are used more commonly than gold coins; therefore, the silver is

1. **G**old acquires silver, but silver does not acquire gold. Copper acquires silver, but silver does not acquire copper. Disqualified coins acquire current ones, but current ones do not acquire disqualified ones. Unstamped metal acquires coins,

considered the 'money,' and the gold, the commodity (Rav from Gem. 44b).

וְהַכֶּסֶף אֵינוֹ קוֹנֶה אֶת־הַזָּהָב. — but silver does not acquire gold.

Since silver is the more common medium of exchange, it is considered the 'money,' and, as explained above, the transfer of money in a transaction does not prevent either party involved from retracting (ibid.).

הַנְּחֹשֶׁת קוֹנָה אֶת־הַכֶּסֶף, — Copper acquires silver,

In this case, too, the copper coins are considered the commodity, and the silver coins, the money. Therefore, when the copper coins are transferred, the recipient is obligated to pay with the silver coins, as stipulated (ibid.).

וְהַכֶּסֶף אֵינוֹ קוֹנֶה אֶת־הַנְּחֹשֶׁת. — but silver does not acquire copper.

Since silver is the 'money' and copper is the commodity, even after the silver is transferred, either of the parties may retract, as explained above (ibid.).

Although copper coins, in certain areas where they circulate, are a more common medium of exchange than silver coins, since they are not accepted in all areas, they are deemed a commodity vis-à-vis the latter (Tos. Yom Tov from Gem. 44b).

In a transaction involving gold coins and copper coins, there are varying opinions as to which is considered the commodity. The silver coins made of an alloy, which are used today, are regarded as 'money' in relation to pure silver coins (Tif. Yis. from Choshen Mishpat 203:5,6).

מָעוֹת הָרָעוֹת — Disqualified (lit., bad) coins

[That is, coins disqualified by either the entire kingdom or the province.]

קוֹנוֹת אֶת־הַיָּפוֹת, — acquire current [lit., nice] ones,

[The disqualified coins are considered the commodity; the current coins, the 'money.']

וְהַיָּפוֹת אֵינָן קוֹנוֹת אֶת־הָרָעוֹת. — but current ones do not acquire disqualified ones.

[Since the current coins constitute the 'money' in the exchange, it is not their transfer that consummates the sale, but an act of acquisition on the commodity being sold.]

The translation of מָעוֹת הָרָעוֹת as disqualified coins is given by Rav, Rashi, and Rambam (Hil. Mechirah 7:6).

Tosafos, however, question this definition on the grounds that if it were correct, the mishnah's statement would be self-evident: if copper coins — which do circulate — are regarded as commodities in relation to silver coins, disqualified coins are surely regarded as commodities in relation to current coins. They therefore explain instead that מָעוֹת הָרָעוֹת are coins which are used as a medium of exchange, but are not as readily accepted as others (Tos. Yom Tov). Ravad, too, construes this term as referring to coins which are abraded and red, and are not as acceptable as other coins (Chiddushei HaRashba; Maggid Mishneh loc. cit.).

אֲסִימוֹן — Unstamped metal

That is, metal which has been made according to the dimensions of a current coin, but has not yet been stamped (Rav; Rashi).

This term is derived from the Greek, but given a Hebrew form (Tif. Yis.).

קוֹנָה אֶת־הַמַּטְבֵּעַ, וְהַמַּטְבֵּעַ אֵינוֹ קוֹנֶה אֶת־

אֵינוֹ קוֹנֶה אֶת־אֲסִימוֹן. הַמִּטַּלְטְלִין קוֹנִים אֶת־
הַמַּטְבֵּעַ, וְהַמַּטְבֵּעַ אֵינוֹ קוֹנֶה אֶת־הַמִּטַּלְטְלִין.
זֶה הַכְּלָל: כָּל הַמִּטַּלְטְלִין קוֹנִין זֶה אֶת־זֶה.

[ב] **כֵּיצַד?** מָשַׁךְ הֵימֶנּוּ פֵרוֹת וְלֹא נָתַן לוֹ
מָעוֹת, אֵינוֹ יָכוֹל לַחֲזֹר בּוֹ. נָתַן לוֹ
מָעוֹת, וְלֹא מָשַׁךְ הֵימֶנּוּ פֵרוֹת, יָכוֹל לַחֲזֹר
בּוֹ.

יד אברהם

אֲסִימוֹן. — *acquires coins, but coins do not acquire unstamped metal.*

Although unstamped coins can easily be converted into coins acceptable for circulation, in their present state they are not regarded as money, but as commodities (*Tos. Yom Tov* from *Tos. 44a*).

הַמִּטַּלְטְלִין קוֹנִים אֶת־הַמַּטְבֵּעַ, וְהַמַּטְבֵּעַ אֵינוֹ קוֹנֶה אֶת־הַמִּטַּלְטְלִין. — *Movables acquire coins, but coins do not acquire movables.*

[Obviously, the chattels are the commodity in such a transaction.] The mishnah teaches us that they acquire even disqualified and unstamped coins, which are adjudged commodities vis-à-vis regular coins. In relation to movables, however, they are regarded as 'money' (*Tos. Yom Tov* from *Tos. 44a*).

זֶה הַכְּלָל: כָּל הַמִּטַּלְטְלִין קוֹנִין זֶה אֶת־זֶה. — *This is the rule: All movables acquire each other.*

This segment of the mishnah deals

with חֲלִיפִין, *chalifin*, a method of acquisition by which one chattel is exchanged for another. In such an instance, too, as soon as one of the parties pulls the other's object to himself, the latter acquires the former's object. The *Gemara* (46b) construes the expression *all movables* as teaching us that two purses containing coins may be exchanged for each other. Although a coin cannot be used for *chalifin*, nor acquired thereby, a disqualified coin may be used for either purpose since it is not regarded as normal currency (*Rav, Tos. R' Akiva*).

The words זֶה הַכְּלָל, *this is the rule*, are not found in *Rif* or *Rosh*. Indeed, it seems that they should be omitted, because this expression usually prefaces a principle that includes the previously stated rulings, but adds other cases to them as well. In our mishnah, however, the principle that follows these words deals with the exchange of movables for movables, whereas the aforementioned rulings deal with cases including both movables and coins (*Tos. Yom Tov*).

2.

The following mishnah is a continuation of the preceding one, stating that even if one pays for an item, it is not yet his until he performs an act of acquisition. Only once that is done can neither of the parties involved retract. Nevertheless, to retract from such a transaction after the money has been given is unbecoming conduct for a Jew, and a Rabbinical curse is pronounced upon one who does so.

כֵּיצַד? — *How?*

What is the case referred to by the previous mishnah in which gold and copper — regarded as commodities — acquire silver — deemed the 'money,' but not vice versa (*Tif. Yis.*)?

מָשַׁךְ הֵימֶנּוּ פֵרוֹת, — *[If] he took [lit., pulled] produce from him,*

[The mishnah uses the example of produce, but actually refers to any commodity, even those coins that are adjudged as the commodity of the trans-

4
2

but coins do not acquire unstamped metal. Movables acquire coins, but coins do not acquire movables. This is the rule: All movables acquire each other.

2. **H**ow? [If] he took produce from him, but did not give him money, he cannot retract. [If] he gave him money, but did not take the produce from him, he can retract. They said, however: He Who

YAD AVRAHAM

action.]

The commodity was transferred to the buyer's possession (Meiri).

וְלֹא נָתַן לוֹ מָעוֹת, — but did not give him money,

The buyer did not yet give the seller the money — whatever metal coinage is adjudged as the 'money' — in this transaction (ibid.).

אֵינוֹ יָכוֹל לַחֲזֹר בּוֹ. — he cannot retract.

Neither of the parties involved can retract (ibid.; Tif. Yis.), because once an act of acquisition — in this case, meshichah (pulling) — is performed, the transaction is consummated (Tos. Yom Tov from Nimmukei Yosef).

נָתַן לוֹ מָעוֹת, — [If] he gave him money,

The buyer gave the seller money or any coin adjudged as the 'money' (Meiri).

וְלֹא מָשַׁךְ הֵימֶנּוּ פֵּרוֹת, — but did not take the produce from him,

He did not take possession of the merchandise or any coin that is adjudged as the commodity in the transaction (ibid.).

יָכוֹל לַחֲזֹר בּוֹ. — he can retract.

[As long as the commodity had not been properly acquired, the transaction is not complete] and either the buyer or the seller can retract (Rav from Gem. 47b).

As mentioned in the preface to this chapter, R' Yochanan maintains that the transfer of money does indeed consummate a sale according to Biblical law. Rashi explains that he derives this from

the redemption of consecrated articles, which is effected by the transfer of money.

Nimmukei Yosef, however, contends that R' Yochanan does not base his opinion on any verse, but rather on the universal custom of consummating sales with money.

Tosafos (Bechoros 13b) assert that R' Yochanan's source is a phrase in Leviticus 25:14: אוֹ קָנֹה, or buy. Since the usual method of buying mentioned in Scripture is with money (e.g., Lev. 25:41, Jeremiah 32:44), we assume that this is the Torah's intention with regard to the purchase of movables.

In order to purchase an article according to Rabbinical law, however, an act of acquisition is required, and until such an act is performed, either of the parties involved may retract. This was enacted so that in the event the purchaser leaves his merchandise with the seller for a long time after having paid him for it, the latter will protect it if, for example, a fire breaks out. Had the transaction been considered complete — as it would be under Biblical law — the seller would have no interest in saving the merchandise from being destroyed, since it already belongs to the purchaser. Due to the Rabbinical enactment, however, the seller may retract from the sale at any time, as long as the buyer has not performed an act of acquisition. Since the seller will consider retracting if the price on the item rises, so that he can resell it for a higher price, he will always have an interest in protecting the item (Rav from Gem.

[97]   THE MISHNAH/BAVA METZIA – Chapter Four: HaZahav

אֲבָל אָמְרוּ: מִי שֶׁפָּרַע מֵאַנְשֵׁי דוֹר הַמַּבּוּל וּמִדּוֹר
הַפְלָגָה הוּא עָתִיד לְהִפָּרַע מִמִּי שֶׁאֵינוֹ עוֹמֵד
בְּדִבּוּרוֹ. רַבִּי שִׁמְעוֹן אוֹמֵר: כָּל שֶׁהַכֶּסֶף בְּיָדוֹ יָדוֹ
עַל הָעֶלְיוֹנָה.

46b).

Rashi gives the above reason only before the Gemara concludes that both the purchaser and the seller may retract. Once that is established, the efficacy of the enactment is obvious: the seller will surely see to it that the item does not become damaged, because if it does, the buyer will certainly retract. Perhaps Rav, who cites Rashi's reason after stating the Gemara's conclusion, maintains — as does Ramban in Milchamos Hashem — that the original enactment had dictated only that the seller may retract; it was only later that the enactment was broadened to include the purchaser as well (Tos. Yom Tov).

Similarly, the Rabbis ruled that once the buyer performs an act of acquisition, he acquires the item although he did not yet give the money. Were it not so, he would have no interest in protecting the item from being destroyed, since he could always retract from the sale (ibid., quoting Tos. 47b).

We do not fear that since the transfer of money does not consummate the sale, the seller will not protect the money properly, because the seller is at the very least considered an unpaid guardian to watch the money and would be liable for negligence if it is destroyed, since he did not hide the money in the ground, as discussed in 3:10 (Tos. to Kiddushin 28b). Alternatively, there is less trouble involved in saving money than there is in saving merchandise. Therefore, it is not feared that the seller will not expend the effort necessary to protect the money [Sma 198:7] (Tos. Yom Tov).

Tosafos (47b) wonder why the Rabbis would make such an enactment for the sake of those who would retract were the item to appreciate, when such

persons thereby bring upon themselves the Rabbinical curse stated below. They reply that indeed this law was enacted precisely because of such people; others would not sit by and watch another person's property go up in flames, but will strive to salvage it. Therefore, as an incentive for the former type, they enacted the rule that the transfer of money does not consummate the sale, in order that the seller should have an interest in saving the wheat, viz. that he should be able to sell it at a higher price (Tos. Yom Tov).

אֲבָל אָמְרוּ — They said, however:

The Rabbis said that although a seller can legally retract if the buyer has paid him but has not performed an act of acquisition, if the seller does so, the court pronounces the following curse on him, and then he returns the money to the purchaser (Rav from Gem. 48b).

מִי שֶׁפָּרַע מֵאַנְשֵׁי דוֹר הַמַּבּוּל וּמִדּוֹר הַפְלָגָה — He Who exacted retribution from the people of the generation of the Flood and from the generation of the Dispersion

[The latter term refers to the generation that built the Tower of Babel and was dispersed all over the face of the earth.]

A baraisa, quoted in the Gemara (48a), adds to the wording of the curse: ... and from the people of Sodom and Amorah [see Gen. 19:24] and from the Egyptians who were drowned in the sea [see Exodus 14:28] (Rav).

Tif. Yis. (in Boaz) expounds on the mention of these four groups. They represent the four reasons people sin: (1) sensual lust; (2) desire for honor; (3) desire for earthly riches; (4) denial of God's providence. The generation of the Flood was guilty mainly of

**4
2**   exacted retribution from the people of the generation of the Flood and from the generation of the Dispersion will exact retribution from one who does not abide by his spoken word.

R' Shimon says: Whoever has the money in his possession has the upper hand.

YAD AVRAHAM

immorality, due to their lust. The generation of the Dispersion was motivated by self-aggrandizement. The people of Sodom and Amorah neglected the poor lest they consume their money. The Egyptians denied God's providence.

הוּא עָתִיד לְהִפָּרֵעַ מִמִּי שֶׁאֵינוֹ עוֹמֵד בְּדִבּוּרוֹ. — *will exact retribution from one who does not abide by his spoken word.*

Whether he does so because of any of the reasons that motivated the groups mentioned above, or any other reason, he will be punished (ibid.).

רַבִּי שִׁמְעוֹן אוֹמֵר: כָּל שֶׁהַכֶּסֶף בְּיָדוֹ יָדוֹ עַל הָעֶלְיוֹנָה. — *R' Shimon says: Whoever has the money in his possession has the upper hand.*

R' Shimon rules that only the seller — who has received the money — can retract, not the purchaser, who has already paid. He differs with the first *Tanna*, who rules that both the seller and the purchaser can retract as long as the latter has not performed an act of acquisition (*Tos. Yom Tov; Tif. Yis.*).

Rav explains that R' Shimon disagrees with the first *Tanna* in one instance. Since the first *Tanna* rules that both the seller and the purchaser can revoke the sale if the latter had not yet performed an act of acquisition, R' Shimon states that in one case, the seller can revoke the sale, but not the purchaser. This is so if the item being

sold is in a place that is owned by the purchaser and rented to the seller, in which case if the purchaser wishes to revoke the sale, the seller can prevent him from doing so, even if he had not yet performed an act of acquisition. R' Shimon argues that the Rabbis' reason for enacting that the transfer of money does not consummate the sale — so that the seller will protect the item properly — does not apply here. Since the item is in premises owned by the buyer, he will be sure to protect the item himself.

The halachah is in accordance with the first *Tanna* — that in all cases, even the one described above, as long as the buyer did not perform an act of acquisition, both he and the seller may revoke the sale.

Tos. Yom Tov maintains that according to R' Shimon, in the case that the loft owned by the purchaser is rented to the seller, since the reason for the enactment does not apply, the transfer of money should consummate the sale, and neither one should be able to revoke it.

Tos. Yom Tov, however, construes R' Shimon as meaning that in *every* case in which the buyer has paid but not performed an act of acquisition, only the seller may retract, since the entire objective of the Rabbis' enactment was only to give the seller an incentive to protect the item properly.

3.

From here to the end of the chapter, the *Tanna* deals with the laws of אוֹנָאָה, *fraud*, that is perpetrated in transactions of buying and selling. The Torah (*Lev.* 25:14) states: וְכִי־תִמְכְּרוּ מִמְכָּר לַעֲמִיתֶךָ אוֹ קָנֹה מִיַּד עֲמִיתֶךָ אַל־תּוֹנוּ אִישׁ אֶת־אָחִיו, *If you sell anything to another, or buy from the hand of another, you shall not wrong each*

[ג] **הָאוֹנָאָה** אַרְבָּעָה כֶּסֶף מֵעֶשְׂרִים וְאַרְבַּע
כֶּסֶף לַסֶּלַע — שְׁתוּת לַמִּקָּח.
עַד מָתַי מֻתָּר לְהַחֲזִיר? עַד כְּדֵי שֶׁיַּרְאֶה לְתַגָּר
אוֹ לִקְרוֹבוֹ.

יד אברהם

other. From here we learn that the seller and buyer may not defraud or wrong each other by overcharging or underpaying for the article being sold. The Rabbis divided the laws dealing with fraud into three levels, depending on the amount that was overcharged or underpaid. Regarding the lowest level, since the amount is small and most people would not make a claim to recover it, the wronged party is assumed to have relinquished his claim to it. In a case involving the medium level, the overcharge or undercharge must be returned, but the sale remains in force. If the fraud was in an amount of the highest level, and either of the parties prefers that the sale be invalidated rather than the money be returned, his wishes are complied with.

This mishnah deals with the medium level. Once we know that amount, we understand that anything less is relinquished, and anything more invalidates the sale (*Meiri*).

The following table, based on *Gateway to the Talmud*, p. 119, will be helpful in understanding this mishnah, as well as mishnah 5.

CURRENCIES	
NAME	**EQUIVALENT IN PURE SILVER**
פְּרוּטָה, *perutah*	½ barleycorn
אִסָּר, *issar*	8 *perutos*
פֻּנְדְּיוֹן, *pundeyon*	2 *issarin*
מָעָה, *ma'ah*	2 *pundeyonos*
זוּז, zuz, or דִּינָר, *dinar*[1]	6 *ma'os*
סֶלַע, *sela*	4 dinars
מָנֶה, *maneh*	100 *dinars* or 25 *selaim*

הָאוֹנָאָה — *The [amount that constitutes] fraud*

[That is, if one overcharges or underpays by this amount, he must return it to the other party.]

אַרְבָּעָה כֶּסֶף — *is four silver [ma'os]*

[The over/under payment was four silver *ma'os*.]

מֵעֶשְׂרִים וְאַרְבָּעָה כֶּסֶף לַסֶּלַע — *out of twenty-four silver [ma'os which are equivalent] to a sela —*

The value of the purchased article was a *sela*, which equals twenty-four silver *ma'os* (*Rav*).

A *sela* equals four *dinars*, each equaling six *ma'os* (*Rashi; Tif. Yis.*).

שְׁתוּת לַמִּקָּח. — *a sixth of the purchase.*

The amount of over/underpayment equals one-sixth of the true value of the purchased article. For example, if the article is worth twenty-four *ma'os*, and it is sold for twenty-eight, the purchaser has been overcharged one-sixth of the true value. Should the article be sold for twenty *ma'os*, the seller has been underpaid by one-sixth of the true value. According to Rav (the *Amora*), these are the only cases in which the sale remains in force, while the amount of

1. The unqualified term דִּינָר refers to a silver *dinar*, not to be confused with a gold *dinar* which is worth twenty-five times as much.

3. The [amount that constitutes] fraud is four silver [*ma'os*] out of twenty-four silver [*ma'os* which are equivalent] to a *sela* — a sixth of the purchase.

Until when can one revoke [the sale]? Until he is able to show [the item] to a merchant or to his relative.

YAD AVRAHAM

over/underpayment must be returned. According to Shmuel, however, even if the fraud amounts to one-sixth of the price actually *paid*, that, too, is considered fraud, and the amount overcharged or underpaid must be returned. For example, if the item was worth twenty-eight *ma'os* and was sold for twenty-four, or worth twenty and sold for twenty-four — in which case the fraud equals one-sixth of the actual purchase price — the sale remains in force, but the over/underpayment must be returned. The halachah follows the view of Shmuel (*Tos. Yom Tov* from *Gem.* 49b).

Whether one may deliberately overcharge or underpay *less* than one-sixth is questionable. A God-fearing person should not do so (*Tur* 227:5 quoting *Rosh*).

In any of these cases, which are of the medium level [see preface], the victim of the fraud can insist only that he be reimbursed for the amount he was defrauded, but not that the sale be invalidated. The perpetrator, too, cannot demand that the victim either return the article or accept it for the price charged (*Rashi* 50b).

עַד מָתַי מֻתָּר לְהַחֲזִיר? — *Until when can one revoke [the sale]?*

Until when can the one who was defrauded return to the perpetrator and demand that the sale be invalidated — in a case that the fraud exceeds a sixth — or that the amount of which he was defrauded be refunded to him? The term מֻתָּר, *can* [lit., *permitted*] — rather than the usual יָכוֹל — is used to intimate that the defrauded party can revoke the sale without having the curse of *He Who*

exacted restitution ... imposed upon him (*Rav; Rashi*).

עַד כְּדֵי שֶׁיַּרְאֶה — *Until he is able to show [the item]*

The buyer is given the time it usually takes to show it to one of the persons mentioned below and ask him about the item and its price. Whether the particular person he wishes to show it to is far or near does not affect the allotted time (*Tos. Yom Tov* from *Tos.* 49b).

לַתַּגָּר — *to a merchant*

[That is, one who is familiar with the merchandise and the price that should be charged for it.]

אוֹ לִקְרוֹבוֹ. — *or to his relative.*

[That is, a relative who is familiar with this type of merchandise. See *Shoshannim LeDavid*.]

If the buyer waits longer than this period of time, it is as if he has relinquished his claim. However, if he was legitimately unable to find a merchant or kinsman knowledgeable about this merchandise during this period, he is given an extension of time (*Tif. Yis.* from *Choshen Mishpat* 227:7).

Should the seller have been the one who was defrauded, however, he has unlimited time to make his claim. Since he does not have the merchandise, he must wait until he acquires a similar item. Nevertheless, if he does learn what the proper price is, and yet neglects to make his claim, he is considered to have relinquished it (*Rav* from *Gem.* 50b, 51a).

Rambam (*Hil. Mechirah* 12:6) asserts that in the case of commodities that are uniform and all are sold for the same price, the seller need only find out the

הוֹרָה רַבִּי טַרְפוֹן בְּלֹד: הָאוֹנָאָה שְׁמֹנָה כֶּסֶף
לַסֶּלַע — שְׁלִישׁ לַמִּקָּח — וְשָׂמְחוּ תַגְּרֵי לֹד. אָמַר
לָהֶם: כָּל הַיּוֹם מֻתָּר לְהַחֲזִיר. אָמְרוּ לוֹ: יַנִּיחַ לָנוּ
רַבִּי טַרְפוֹן בִּמְקוֹמֵנוּ. וְחָזְרוּ לְדִבְרֵי חֲכָמִים.

[ד] **אֶחָד** הַלּוֹקֵחַ וְאֶחָד הַמּוֹכֵר יֵשׁ לָהֶן אוֹנָאָה.
כְּשֵׁם שֶׁאוֹנָאָה לַהֶדְיוֹט, כָּךְ אוֹנָאָה
לַתַּגָּר. רַבִּי יְהוּדָה אוֹמֵר: אֵין אוֹנָאָה לַתַּגָּר.

יד אברהם

present market price. Should he have
time for that and neglect to make his
claim, he has relinquished it. *Rashba*,
however, disagrees, maintaining that
the Sages established only one rule, and
it is applicable equally to all sellers
(*Maggid Mishneh* ad loc.).

הוֹרָה רַבִּי טַרְפוֹן בְּלֹד: הָאוֹנָאָה — *R' Tarfon
ruled in Lod: The [amount that
constitutes] fraud*

[That is, the amount of overcharge or
underpayment necessary in a sale which
would require that the extra money be
returned, although the sale would
remain in force.]

שְׁמֹנָה כֶּסֶף לַסֶּלַע — *is eight silver
[ma'os] out of a sela —*

[The discrepant amount is eight
ma'os on an item worth a *sela*.]

שְׁלִישׁ לַמִּקָּח — *a third of the
purchase —*

[Since a *sela* equals twenty-four
ma'os, eight ma'os equals a third of a
sela.]

וְשָׂמְחוּ תַגְּרֵי לֹד. — *and the merchants of
Lod rejoiced.*

They were knowledgeable about the
merchandise and sold their wares for
high prices (*Rav; Rashi*). [Therefore,
they welcomed R' Tarfon's ruling that if
they overcharged any amount less than
a third of the price, it need not be
returned.]

אָמַר לָהֶם: — *He said to them:*

[R' Tarfon said to the merchants of
Lod.]

כָּל הַיּוֹם מֻתָּר לְהַחֲזִיר. — *For a whole day,
one may revoke [the sale].*

[R' Tarfon ruled that in a sale
involving fraud, both parties have a full
day to revoke the sale or claim the
amount of over/underpayment.]

אָמְרוּ לוֹ: — *They said to him:*

[The merchants replied to R' Tarfon.
Some editions read merely: אָמְרוּ, *they
said*. According to that version, the use
of the third person in this statement is
indeed more appropriate.]

יַנִּיחַ לָנוּ רַבִּי טַרְפוֹן בִּמְקוֹמֵנוּ. — *Let R'
Tarfon leave us alone in our place.*

Although R' Tarfon rules that the law
of fraud applies only if the over/under-
payment is one-third of the price, since
he extended the time of revoking the
sale, the merchants of Lod preferred to
follow the first opinion of the mishnah
— that of the Sages — which limited the
period of revocability to the time the
buyer is able to show the article to a
merchant or relative (*Gem. 50b*).

וְחָזְרוּ לְדִבְרֵי חֲכָמִים. — *And they went
back to the words of the Sages.*

[They adhered to the view of the
Sages that even if the discrepant amount
is one-sixth of the price, it must be
returned.]

The halachah follows the Sages'
opinion (*Rav; Rambam Commentary*).

R' Tarfon ruled in Lod: The [amount that constitutes] fraud is eight silver [*ma'os*] out of a *sela* — a third of the purchase — and the merchants of Lod rejoiced. He said to them: For a whole day, one may revoke [the sale]. They said to him: Let R' Tarfon leave us alone in our place. And they went back to the words of the Sages.

4. Both the buyer and the seller are governed by the [law of] fraud. Just as [the law of] fraud [applies] to a layman, so does [the law of] fraud [apply] to a merchant. R' Yehudah says: [The law of] fraud does not [apply] to a merchant.

YAD AVRAHAM
4.

אֶחָד הַלּוֹקֵחַ וְאֶחָד הַמּוֹכֵר יֵשׁ לָהֶן אוֹנָאָה. — *Both the buyer and the seller are governed by [the law of] fraud.*

[Whether one defrauds a person who sells to or buys from him, he infracts the negative commandment prohibiting fraud, as explained in the preface to mishnah 3.]

Should the Torah have stated this prohibition with regard to a seller only, we would think that only a seller is forbidden to perpetrate a fraudulent sale; since — having bought it — he is familiar with the price of the item, and if he is overcharging for it, he is obviously doing so intentionally. The buyer, however, is not familiar with the price; therefore we would think that even if he underpays, he is not doing so deliberately, and it is not considered fraud. On the other hand, should the Torah state the prohibition only with regard to a buyer, we would think that it does not apply to a seller, because the buyer is the one considered to have truly gained by the transaction — that is, he remains with something permanent, while the seller is left with money, which is easily, and therefore most likely, spent. As the proverb goes:

Buyers gain, sellers lose. This might lead us to believe that the seller is permitted to overcharge. Therefore, the Torah tells us that both the buyer and the seller are included in the laws of fraud (*Tos. Yom Tov* from *Gem.* 51a).

כְּשֵׁם שֶׁאוֹנָאָה לַהֶדְיוֹט, כָּךְ אוֹנָאָה לַתַּגָּר. — *Just as [the law of] fraud [applies] to a layman, so does [the law of] fraud [apply] to a merchant.*

[That is, just as one infracts a negative commandment for defrauding a layman, so is he prohibited to defraud a merchant, although the latter is familiar with his wares and knows their prices.]

רַבִּי יְהוּדָה אוֹמֵר: אֵין אוֹנָאָה לַתַּגָּר. — *R' Yehudah says: [The law of] fraud does not [apply] to a merchant.*

R' Yehudah refers to a middleman, who buys from one person and immediately sells to a second one. Since he has just purchased the merchandise, he certainly did not forget the price. If he sells it for a low price, it is probably because he wishes to purchase another article, and he sells this one with the full knowledge of its true price, intentionally forgoing it. Now, he has decided to

מִי שֶׁהֻטַּל עָלָיו יָדוֹ עַל הָעֶלְיוֹנָה. רָצָה, אוֹמֵר
לוֹ: ,,תֶּן־לִי מָעוֹתַי אוֹ תֶּן־לִי מַה־שֶּׁאוֹנִיתָנִי.''

[ה] כַּמָּה תְּהֵא הַסֶּלַע חֲסֵרָה, וְלֹא יְהֵא בָהּ
אוֹנָאָה? רַבִּי מֵאִיר אוֹמֵר: אַרְבַּע
אִסָּרִין — אִסָּר לַדִּינָר. רַבִּי יְהוּדָה אוֹמֵר: אַרְבַּע
פֻּנְדְּיוֹנוֹת — פֻּנְדְּיוֹן לַדִּינָר. רַבִּי שִׁמְעוֹן אוֹמֵר:
שְׁמֹנֶה פֻּנְדְּיוֹנוֹת — שְׁנֵי פֻּנְדְּיוֹנוֹת לַדִּינָר.

יד אברהם

retract, and wishes to recover the difference between his price and the true price (Rav, Tos. Yom Tov from Gem. 51a). [But, according to R' Yehudah, we do not allow him to do so.]

The halachah is in accordance with the view of the first, anonymous Tanna (Rav; Rosh; Tif. Yis. from Choshen Mishpat 227:14).

מִי שֶׁהֻטַּל עָלָיו יָדוֹ עַל הָעֶלְיוֹנָה. — The one who has been imposed upon has the upper hand.

That is, the one who was defrauded (Rav; Rashi). [He has the advantage of being able to plead what he wishes.]

רָצָה, אוֹמֵר לוֹ: — If he wishes, he may say

to him:

If the buyer was defrauded, he may say the following to the seller (Rav; Rashi).

,,תֶּן־לִי מָעוֹתַי אוֹ תֶּן־לִי מַה־שֶּׁאוֹנִיתָנִי.'' — 'Give me my money or give me what you defrauded me.'

'Return my money and let the sale be revoked, or let the sale remain and give me the amount you overcharged me' (Meiri).

If the seller was the one who was defrauded, he may tell the buyer: 'Return the item to me or give me the amount you underpaid me' (Tos. Yom Tov, Tif. Yis. from Gem. 51a).

5.

Just as there is fraud in the price of merchandise, so is there fraud in the use of coins. A coin that is constantly used becomes worn and loses some of its weight. This mishnah tells us the maximum amount that may be missing from a coin for it to continue being circulated at its face value.

כַּמָּה תְּהֵא הַסֶּלַע חֲסֵרָה, וְלֹא יְהֵא בָהּ אוֹנָאָה? — How much may a sela be defective, and yet there should still be no [infraction of the law of] fraud?

That is, how much may wear off the sela through its use, and yet it may still be circulated for its original value without infracting the law of fraud (Rav; Rashi)?

The intention of Rav and Rashi based on the Gemara (52a) is that the mishnah's question is: Until what point may the sela be worn down? Each

answer given below, therefore, states the amount that would be considered fraud (Tos. Yom Tov). Indeed, some versions of the mishnah (Meiri; see Shenuyei Nuschaos) read: עַד כַּמָּה .... Until which amount ... From the Gemara it would seem that this is the correct reading (R' Nissan Alpert in glosses to Meiri).

רַבִּי מֵאִיר אוֹמֵר: אַרְבַּע אִסָּרִין — R' Meir says: Four issarin —

That is, four issarin out of the sela

4
5　The one who has been imposed upon has the upper hand. If he wishes, he may say to him: 'Give me my money or give me what you defrauded me.'

5. How much may a *sela* be defective, and yet there should still be no [infraction of the law of] fraud? R' Meir says: Four *issarin* — an *issar* to a *dinar*. R' Yehudah says: Four *pundeyonos* — a *pundeyon* to a *dinar*. R' Shimon says: Eight *pundeyonos* — two *pundeyonos* to a *dinar*.

(Rav; Rashi).

אִסָּר לַדִּינָר — *an issar to a dinar.*

In other words, 1/24 of the original *sela* has been rubbed off. A *dinar* equals 6 *ma'os*; a *ma'ah* equals two *pundeyonos*, and a *pundeyon* equals two *issarin* (ibid.).

רַבִּי יְהוּדָה אוֹמֵר: אַרְבַּע פֻּנְדְיוֹנוֹת — *R' Yehudah says: Four pundeyonos —*

[That is, four *pundeyonos* out of a *sela*.]

פֻּנְדְיוֹן לַדִּינָר — *a pundeyon to a dinar.*

In other words, one-twelfth of the original *sela* became rubbed off *(Rav; Rashi).*

[According to R' Yehudah, if that amount of a *sela* has been rubbed off, circulating the *sela* for its original value constitutes fraud.]

רַבִּי שִׁמְעוֹן אוֹמֵר: שְׁמֹנָה פֻּנְדְיוֹנוֹת — *R' Shimon says: Eight pundeyonos —*

[Eight *pundeyonos* out of a *sela*.]

שְׁנֵי פֻּנְדְיוֹנוֹת לַדִּינָר — *two pundeyonos to a dinar.*

This is equivalent to one-sixth of the original amount, the same ratio that is deemed fraud with regard to selling merchandise [as explained above] *(Rav; Rashi).*

Although R' Shimon could have stated his view in terms of *ma'os*, by saying a *ma'ah* to a *dinar*, he converted it to *pundeyonos* to conform with R'

Yehudah, who stated his view in terms of *pundeyonos (Tos. Yom Tov* from *Tos.).* Why R' Yehudah did not state his view in terms of *issarin* as R' Meir did is indeed puzzling *(Tos. R' Akiva).*

In order to reconcile this mishnah, which presents three views on the ratio constituting fraud, with mishnah 3, which states that the ratio is 1:6, the *Gemara* (52a) presents two solutions, those of Rava and Abaye. Rava holds that there is no difference between the laws governing fraud as regards the selling of merchandise and as regards the circulation of a defective coin. Therefore, he concludes that mishnah 3 follows the view of R' Shimon, that a 1:6 ratio constitutes fraud. Abaye contends that there is a distinction between the two types of fraud. In certain cases of buying merchandise — specifically a garment — the purchasers are willing to overpay if necessary, but they are not willing to accept a defective coin which they will have difficulty in passing on (see *Tos.* ad loc. s.v. עשיק).

Accordingly, *Rif, Rambam (Commentary* and *Hil. Mechirah* 12:10), and *Rav* rule in accordance with the view of R' Shimon, since it coincides with the decision in mishnah 3, according to Rava, whose opinion the halachah usually follows. *Rosh* and *Rambam,* however, attribute this view to Rabbah rather than Rava. Consequently, they rule in accordance with the opinion of Abaye, who flourished after Rabbah,

[ו] עַד מָתַי מֻתָּר לְהַחֲזִיר? בַּכְּרַכִּים, עַד כְּדֵי
שֶׁיַּרְאֶה לְשֻׁלְחָנִי; וּבַכְּפָרִים, עַד
עַרְבֵי שַׁבָּתוֹת. אִם הָיָה מַכִּירָהּ, אֲפִלּוּ לְאַחַר
שְׁנֵים עָשָׂר חֹדֶשׁ מְקַבְּלָהּ הֵימֶנּוּ. וְאֵין לוֹ עָלָיו
אֶלָּא תַּרְעֹמֶת. וְנוֹתְנָהּ לְמַעֲשֵׂר שֵׁנִי, וְאֵינוּ חוֹשֵׁשׁ,
שֶׁאֵינוֹ אֶלָּא נֶפֶשׁ רָעָה.

יד אברהם

and whose rulings are therefore considered more authoritative. With regard to our mishnah they follow the view of R' Yehudah, who maintains that the ratio of 1:12 is adjudged fraud in the case of the defective coins, and this is not inconsistent with mishnah 3. See *Choshen Mishpat* 227:16.

With regard to a coin sold by weight, however, any small amount missing is deemed fraud (*Tif. Yis.* from *Shulchan Aruch* ad loc.).

6.

עַד מָתַי מֻתָּר לְהַחֲזִיר? — *Until when may one return* [*it*]?

[Until when may one return a defective coin?]

בַּכְּרַכִּים, — *In big cities,*

Where moneychangers are found (*Rav; Rashi*).

עַד כְּדֵי שֶׁיַּרְאֶה לְשֻׁלְחָנִי; — *until he can show* [*it*] *to a moneychanger;*

Since no one but a moneychanger is familiar with the value of coins (*Tos. Yom Tov* from *Gem.* 52b), unlike merchandise, regarding which even one's relatives may be able to advise him, as mentioned in mishnah 3 (*Meiri*).

וּבַכְּפָרִים, — *in villages,*

Where moneychangers are not found (*Rav; Rashi*).

עַד עַרְבֵי שַׁבָּתוֹת. — *until the eve of the Sabbath.*

When he attempts to spend the *sela* to purchase food for the Sabbath repasts, he will discover whether or not it is acceptable (*Rav; Rashi*). At that time, moneychangers or their apprentices would come to the villages and provide change for the residents, so that they could buy their Sabbath needs. Alternatively, the villagers would go to the big cities for that purpose (*Meiri*).

In mishnah 3, with regard to overcharge, the *Tanna* does not differentiate between big cities and villages, whereas in this case of the defective coins, he does differentiate. Indeed, Abaye qualifies mishnah 3 as referring only to big cities, where there are many people who are familiar with the prices of garments and other commodities. Rava, however, contends that even in the villages, everyone is familiar with the prices of garments, while only moneychangers are familiar with coins. Therefore, unlike the mishnah above, this mishnah differentiates between big cities and villages (*Gem.* 52b).

אִם הָיָה מַכִּירָהּ, — *If he recognizes it* [*however*],

The one who originally gave the coin recognizes that this is the coin he had given (*Rav; Rashi*).

אֲפִלּוּ לְאַחַר שְׁנֵים עָשָׂר חֹדֶשׁ מְקַבְּלָהּ הֵימֶנּוּ. — *he should accept it from him even after twelve months.*

That is, if he is especially pious and wishes to do beyond the letter of the law, even if the one to whom he gave the coin returns it to him after a long time, he should accept it from him (*Rav* from *Gem.* 52b).

6. Until when may one return [it]? In big cities, until he can show [it] to a moneychanger; in villages, until the eve of the Sabbath. If he recognizes it [however], he should accept it from him even after twelve months. But he has only resentment against him. He may give it for the second tithe, and he need not fear, for it is only [out of] evil disposition [that one refuses this coin].

YAD AVRAHAM

וְאֵין לוֹ עָלָיו אֶלָּא תַרְעֹמֶת. — *But he has only resentment against him.*

If, however, one is not especially pious, and does not wish to accept the coin after the time limit set by the mishnah, the person who received the coin can have no claim against him, only resentment. The latter himself is at fault, since he did not return the coin during the allotted time (ibid.).

וְנוֹתְנָהּ לְמַעֲשֵׂר שֵׁנִי, — *He may give it for the second tithe,*

[As prescribed by the Torah (Deut. 14:22-27), מַעֲשֵׂר שֵׁנִי, the second tithe, is to be transported to Jerusalem and eaten within the walls of the Holy City. Should one live far from Jerusalem, making it difficult to transport the produce, he may redeem it instead, and take the money to Jerusalem, where he purchases food to be eaten with the sanctity of the second tithe. See preface to mishnah 8.]

Rav interprets the Gemara (52b) as construing our mishnah to mean that even if a certain coin may not be circulated at its face value, and were one to do so, he would be guilty of fraud, it may nevertheless be used to redeem tithe for that value. *Rambam (Hil. Maaser Sheni* 411a) and *Rivan* (quoted in *Tosafos* loc. cit.) concur with this view.

Other authorities (*Rashi, Tos., Meiri*) contend that since people do not accept such a coin for its value, but for somewhat less, the second tithe cannot be redeemed with such a coin at its full value, but for the amount given by everyone.

Rivam (cited in *Tosafos*) understands the mishnah as referring to a coin that is lacking less than the amount which would render its circulation at face value as fraudulent. He explains that a *sela*, worn off in this manner, may be used to redeem one's second tithe for slightly less than a *sela*. Since a complete, unworn *sela* is not computed at its full value, but for slightly less, so is this worn *sela*.

וְאֵינוֹ חוֹשֵׁשׁ, — *and he need not fear,*

He need not fear that the coin has been reduced to the status of unstamped metal, which is unacceptable for the redemption of the second tithe, since the Torah requires money which is stamped (*Rav; Rashi; Tos.*).

שֶׁאֵינוֹ אֶלָּא נֶפֶשׁ רָעָה. — *for it is only [out of] evil disposition [that one refuses this coin].*

If one refuses to accept this coin at its true value as currency, but only as silver bullion, it is out of evil disposition that he does so (*Rav*). In other words, he is a stingy person.

7.

Most of this mishnah and the entire one following it are not directly related to the topic of our chapter. They are introduced here incidentally after the mention of the four silver *ma'os* as the amount that is deemed fraud (*Meiri*).

[ז] הָאוֹנָאָה אַרְבָּעָה כֶּסֶף. וְהַטַּעֲנָה שְׁתֵּי כֶּסֶף. וְהַהוֹדָאָה שָׁוֶה פְרוּטָה. חָמֵשׁ פְּרוּטוֹת הֵן: הַהוֹדָאָה שָׁוֶה פְרוּטָה; וְהָאִשָּׁה מִתְקַדֶּשֶׁת בְּשָׁוֶה פְרוּטָה; וְהַנֶּהֱנֶה בְשָׁוֶה פְרוּטָה מִן הַהֶקְדֵּשׁ, מָעַל; וְהַמּוֹצֵא שָׁוֶה פְרוּטָה, חַיָּב לְהַכְרִיז; וְהַגּוֹזֵל אֶת חֲבֵרוֹ שָׁוֶה פְרוּטָה וְנִשְׁבַּע לוֹ, יוֹלִיכֶנּוּ אַחֲרָיו אֲפִלּוּ לְמָדָי.

יד אברהם

הָאוֹנָאָה אַרְבָּעָה כֶּסֶף. — *Four silver [ma'os] constitutes fraud.*

As explained above this refers to an overcharge of four *ma'os* on an item worth a *sela* — which equals twenty-four *ma'os* — so that the overpayment constitutes one-sixth of the true price. Although this has already been clearly stated above, and the mishnah's next statement is repeated in *Shevuos* 6:1, both statements are intended merely to lead up to the five laws involving a *perutah* listed below (*Tos. Yom Tov* from *Gem.* 55a). [This is obviously *Rav's* intention as well.]

וְהַטַּעֲנָה שְׁתֵּי כֶּסֶף, — *Two silver [ma'os] constitutes a claim,*

If one claims that another person owes him two *ma'os* or more, and the person confesses owing part of it, the latter must take a Biblical oath that he does not owe him more. Should the claim be for less than this amount, however, no oath is required (*Rav* from *Shevuos* 39b).

וְהַהוֹדָאָה שָׁוֶה פְרוּטָה. — *and the worth of a perutah constitutes a confession.*

The oath mentioned above is imposed only if the person confesses that he owes a *perutah* or more. Should he confess to the entire claim with the exception of one *perutah*, he is likewise liable (*Rav*).

This interpretation is in accordance with Shmuel (loc. cit.). Rav [the *Amora*], however, while agreeing with Shmuel's interpretation of this latter

half of the mishnah's statement, construes the first half as meaning that the *denial* of the claim must be for at least two *ma'os*. Accordingly, the claim must equal at least two *ma'os* and a *perutah*. In this regard, the halachah is in accordance with Rav (*Tif. Yis.* from *Choshen Mishpat* 88:1).

As shown on the table above, a *perutah* contains half a barleycorn of pure silver. Hence, two *ma'os* equal thirty-two barleycorns of pure silver, a *ma'ah* equaling thirty-two *perutos* or sixteen barleycorns (ibid.).

חָמֵשׁ פְּרוּטוֹת הֵן: — *There are five [laws involving a] perutah:*

[Regarding the following laws, the Rabbis set the minimum at a *perutah*.]

הַהוֹדָאָה שָׁוֶה פְרוּטָה; — *The worth of a perutah constitutes confession;*

[This has been explained above.]

וְהָאִשָּׁה מִתְקַדֶּשֶׁת בְּשָׁוֶה פְרוּטָה; — *a woman may be married with the worth of a perutah;*

[As stated in *Kiddushin* 1:1, a man can marry a woman by giving her a minimum of a *perutah* or something worth a *perutah*.]

וְהַנֶּהֱנֶה בְשָׁוֶה פְרוּטָה מִן הַהֶקְדֵּשׁ, מָעַל; — *[if] one derives benefit worth a perutah from consecrated things, he has committed me'ilah;*

[If one benefits from items consecrated to be offered upon the Altar, or those belonging to the Temple, and that benefit is worth at least a *perutah*, he is

7. **F**our silver [*ma'os*] constitutes fraud. Two silver [*ma'os*] constitutes a claim, and the worth of a *perutah* constitutes a confession.

There are five [laws involving a] *perutah:* The worth of a *perutah* constitutes confession; a woman may be married with the worth of a *perutah;* [if] one derives benefit worth a *perutah* from consecrated things, he has committed *me'ilah;* [if] one finds the worth of a *perutah*, he is required to announce [it]; and [if] one robs another of the worth of a *perutah* and swears to him, he must follow him with it even to Media.

YAD AVRAHAM

required to bring a guilt-offering and repay the amount that he benefited, as well as an additional fifth, as stated in the following mishnah.]

וְהַמּוֹצֵא שָׁוֶה פְרוּטָה, חַיָּב לְהַכְרִיז; — *[if] one finds the worth of a perutah, he is required to announce [it];*

Chapter 2 discusses at length the halachah that in certain instances one who finds a lost object must announce it. Here the mishnah adds that only an object worth a *perutah* or more need be announced. This is based on *Deuteronomy* 22:3, אֲשֶׁר־תֹּאבַד מִמֶּנּוּ, *which he loses*, which implies that only something important enough to be considered a loss must be announced. An item worth less than a *perutah* is not deemed a loss (*Rav from Gem.* 27a).

This ruling is found nowhere else in the Mishnah. As the *Tanna* teaches it to us, he mentions incidentally the other four laws involving the *perutah*, and the two laws involving *ma'os* (*Tos. Yom Tov*).

וְהַגּוֹזֵל אֶת חֲבֵרוֹ שָׁוֶה פְרוּטָה וְנִשְׁבַּע לוֹ. — *and [if] one robs another of the worth of a perutah and swears to him,*

[The robber swears falsely to his victim, denying the theft.]

יוֹלִיכֶנּוּ אַחֲרָיו אֲפִלוּ לְמָדִי. — *he must follow him with it even to Media.*

If the robber subsequently confesses that he swore falsely, he cannot expiate his sin unless he returns the stolen article into the hand of the one who was robbed; it is not sufficient for him to give it to the latter's agent. We derive this from *Numbers* 5:7, וְנָתַן לַאֲשֶׁר אָשַׁם לוֹ, *and he shall give [it] to him against whom he is guilty* (*Rav from Bava Kamma* 103b).

[The mishnah informs us that this applies only if the stolen article is worth at least a *perutah*. This halachah is stated also in *Bava Kamma* 9:5. See ArtScroll commentary there.]

Media is chosen as an example of a distant land (*Tif. Yis.* ibid.).

8.

⋘§The Portions Separated from Produce

The following mishnah touches upon virtually all of the portions that must be separated from crops:

תְּרוּמָה / Terumah

The first portion separated is the *terumah* (lit., *separation*) — usually between

חֲמִשָּׁה [ח] חֲמִשִּׁין הֵן: הָאוֹכֵל תְּרוּמָה,
וּתְרוּמַת מַעֲשֵׂר, וּתְרוּמַת מַעֲשֵׂר
שֶׁל־דְּמַאי, וְהַחַלָּה, וְהַבִּכּוּרִים, מוֹסִיף חֹמֶשׁ;

יד אברהם

one-fortieth and one-sixtieth of the total crop — which is given to a *Kohen* (priest) and is forbidden to a non-*Kohen*. This portion is sometimes called תְּרוּמָה גְדוֹלָה, *the great terumah*, to differentiate it from תְּרוּמַת מַעֲשֵׂר, *terumah of the [first] tithe*, which is given by Levites and is also a form of *terumah*, as discussed below.

מַעֲשֵׂר רִאשׁוֹן — The First Tithe

After the *terumah* has been separated, מַעֲשֵׂר רִאשׁוֹן, *the first tithe*, is taken from the remainder of the crop and presented to a Levite.

מַעֲשֵׂר מִן הַמַּעֲשֵׂר / Tithe from the Tithe

From the first tithe that he receives, the Levite separates an additional *terumah* that he gives to a *Kohen*. The amount of this *terumah* is exactly one-tenth of his first tithe. It is referred to also as תְּרוּמַת מַעֲשֵׂר, *terumah of the tithe*, and all the laws peculiar to *terumah* apply to it as well. Before this *terumah* is separated, the first tithe — like all produce before the separation of *terumah* — may not be eaten. Thus, before the first tithe may be eaten, two *terumos* must be taken from it: the regular *terumah*, which was separated from the entire crop before the Levite's share was taken from it, and the special tithe separated by the Levite.

מַעֲשֵׂר שֵׁנִי / The Second Tithe

In the first, second, fourth and fifth years of the seven-year *Shemittah* (Sabbatical) cycle, a second tithe is separated from what remains of the produce after the *Kohen's* and Levite's shares have been removed. This tithe must be brought to Jerusalem by the owner and eaten there. If this is not convenient, the owner may redeem the produce for money, which he takes to Jerusalem and uses there for the purchase of food, which then assumes the sanctity previously resident in the produce and redemption money. He then eats the food in Jerusalem.

[The only portion that must be separated, but is not mentioned in our mishnah, is מַעֲשֵׂר עָנִי, *the tithe of the poor*, which — in the third and sixth years of the Sabbatical cycle — is separated instead of the second tithe, and is distributed to the poor.]

חַלָּה / Challah

Dough requires yet an additional *terumah*. This is called חַלָּה, *challah* (lit., *loaf*), and all the laws of *terumah* apply to it.

דְּמַאי / Demai

With the passage of time, it became apparent to the Rabbis that many עַמֵּי הָאָרֶץ, *ignorant* [and, in this case, greedy] *people*, were becoming less scrupulous in the separation of the various tithes. Although they continued to separate *terumah* carefully and treat it with the proper seriousness, and most of them were just as careful with the other tithes, significant numbers of them no longer separated any tithes except for *terumah*. As a result, anyone who purchased produce from an ignorant person — unless the latter was known to be fully observant — could not assume that it had been tithed, and the seller could not be trusted to give an honest answer even if he were asked directly. Such a product was called דְּמַאי *(demai)*, a contraction of דָּא מַאי, *what is this?* In view of the possibility that the *demai* might not have been tithed, the Rabbis forbade purchasers to eat it unless they tithed it themselves. However, since the tithe is separated merely because of a doubt, it need not be given to a Levite, and may be eaten by anyone (see ArtScroll *Sotah* p. 174).

8. **F**ive [laws require the addition of] a fifth: [If] one eats *terumah, terumah* of the tithe, *terumah* of the tithe of *demai, challah,* or *bikkurim,*

בְּכּוּרִים / The First-fruit Offering

The first ripe fruits of wheat, barley, grapes, figs, pomegranates, olives, and dates are brought to the Temple, and after the ceremony prescribed by the Torah (*Deut.* 26:1-11), it is given to a *Kohen.* In many respects, the laws of *terumah* apply to it.

חֲמִשָּׁה חֹמְשִׁין הֵן: — *Five [laws require the addition of] a fifth:*

[In the following five instances, in addition to paying the principal, one must also pay an additional fifth. The 'fifth' mentioned refers to a fourth of the principal amount. It is called a 'fifth,' because when the fourth is added to the principal, the additional amount constitutes a fifth of the new sum. See *Bava Kamma* 65b.]

Each of these halachos is repeated elsewhere in the Mishnah. They are grouped together here to tell us that the Torah requires the addition of a fifth only in these instances, and in no others. Alternatively, since the *Tanna* listed the five laws involving a *perutah* in the previous mishnah, he deemed it appropriate to continue by listing this other group of five laws (*Tos. Yom Tov*).

הָאוֹכֵל תְּרוּמָה, — *[If] one eats terumah,*

A non-*Kohen* eats *terumah gedolah* [or one of the other portions listed below] inadvertently (*Rav; Rashi*).

וּתְרוּמַת מַעֲשֵׂר, — *terumah of the tithe,*

The tithe from the tithe, given by the Levite to the *Kohen* (ibid.).

וּתְרוּמַת מַעֲשֵׂר שֶׁל-דְּמַאי, — *terumah of the tithe of demai,*

As explained in the preface, if one purchases produce from an עַם הָאָרֶץ, *ignoramus,* he is obligated to separate the first tithe, from which he must separate *terumah* of the tithe. This is because many of the ignoramuses do not separate the first tithe. It is not necessary to separate *terumah gedolah,* since all are scrupulous in doing so

(ibid.).

וְהַחַלָּה, — *challah,*

[*Challah,* too, is referred to in the Torah (*Num.* 15:17-21) as *terumah.*]

וְהַבִּכּוּרִים, — *or bikkurim,*

The first-fruit offering, too, is called *terumah* in the Torah, as the *Gemara* (*Makkos* 17a) construes the phrase (*Deut.* 12:17) וּתְרוּמַת יָדֶךָ, *and the separation of your hand,* as referring to *bikkurim* (*Rashi; Meiri*).

מוֹסִיף חֹמֶשׁ: — *he must add a fifth;*

[Since all of the portions enumerated above are called *terumah,* a non-*Kohen* who eats any of them inadvertently must pay the principal amount, as well as an additional fifth to a *Kohen,* as prescribed in *Leviticus* 22:14]

Because they share the same appellation, and the obligations of paying an additional fifth in all the cases are derived from one source, the *Tanna* teaches them all as only one instance in his list of cases requiring an additional fifth (*Rav; Rashi; Meiri*).

Some deem the additional fifth as an atonement for the sin (*Tos. to Pesachim* 29a).

If a non-*Kohen* eats one of these portions deliberately, he pays the principal amount, but not the additional fifth. He is liable for מִיתָה בִּידֵי שָׁמַיִם, [premature] *death at the hands of Heaven;* if he had been forewarned by two witnesses he is liable to מַלְקוֹת, *lashes.*

Although, as explained in the preface, the laws of *demai* are of Rabbinic origin, the Rabbis nevertheless imposed the Biblically derived additional fifth on one

וְהַפּוֹדֶה נֶטַע רְבָעִי וּמַעֲשֵׂר שֵׁנִי שֶׁלּוֹ, מוֹסִיף
חֹמֶשׁ; הַפּוֹדֶה אֶת־הֶקְדֵּשׁוֹ, מוֹסִיף חֹמֶשׁ; הַנֶּהֱנֶה
בְשָׁוֶה פְרוּטָה מִן־הַהֶקְדֵּשׁ, מוֹסִיף חֹמֶשׁ; וְהַגּוֹזֵל
אֶת־חֲבֵרוֹ שָׁוֶה פְרוּטָה וְנִשְׁבַּע לוֹ, מוֹסִיף חֹמֶשׁ.

יד אברהם

who eats *terumah of the tithe of demai* to strengthen their enactment, making it as stringent as Torah law.

In the *Gemara* (55b), R' Nachman, quoting Shmuel, attributes this mishnah to R' Meir, who maintains that a *get* (bill of divorce) not delivered according to Rabbinic laws is completely invalid, to the extent that the offspring of any marriage following a divorce based on such a document has the status of a *mamzer* (loosely, *bastard*). R' Meir's reason is that the Rabbis strengthened their laws by making them as stringent as those of the Torah. Accordingly, our mishnah — which agrees with this principle — is attributed to R' Meir. The Sages, who dispute R' Meir's opinion with regard to a *get*, would not require the addition of a fifth when repaying *terumah of the tithe of demai*.

Yerushalmi (*Demai* 1:2), however, contends that our mishnah is not necessarily in contradiction with the view of the Sages regarding a *get*. The Rabbis may have been stringent only in our case of *terumah of the tithe of demai* in order that people should treat it with the proper sanctity. *Rambam* (*Hil. Terumah* 10:4) cites our mishnah as halachah, adding: *so that they should not treat it lightly*, apparently alluding to the reason given by *Yerushalmi*. According to our *Gemara*, however, the halachah does not follow the view of this mishnah, since we do not rule in accordance with R' Meir's opinion regarding a *get* (*Tos. Yom Tov*).

וְהַפּוֹדֶה נֶטַע רְבָעִי — [if] one redeems his *revai* plantings

[In *Leviticus* 19:23-24, the Torah states that it is forbidden to eat or derive any benefit from the fruit produced by a newly planted tree during its first three years. Rather, the fruit must be burned. (See *Temurah* 33b.) This fruit is called עָרְלָה, *orlah* (lit., *closed off* from benefit). Fruit that grows during the fourth year — called רְבָעִי, *revai* (four-year-old) — must be brought to Jerusalem and eaten there. Should it be inconvenient to take the fruit to Jerusalem, the owner may redeem it, take the money to Jerusalem, and purchase food with it there, as explained in the preface with regard to the second tithe. This is derived from the phrase (ibid.) קֹדֶשׁ הִלּוּלִים, *holy for praises*, which is similar to חִלּוּלִים, *for redemptions*, implying that it must be redeemed. Now, just as when one redeems his second tithe, he must add a fifth, as discussed below, so must he do so when he redeems his *revai* plantings. See *Berachos* 35a.] This is derived from a גְזֵרָה שָׁוָה, *an analogous wording* (see *Gateway to the Talmud*, p. 129). Just as the second tithe is called קֹדֶשׁ, *holy* (*Lev.* 27:30), so are *revai* plantings (ibid. 19:24). We therefore deduce that just as the redemption of the second tithe requires the addition of a fifth, so does the redemption of *revai* plantings (*Rav, Rashi* from *Kiddushin* 44b).

וּמַעֲשֵׂר שֵׁנִי שֶׁלּוֹ, — or *his second tithe*,

[As explained above, if one finds it inconvenient to bring his second tithe to Jerusalem, he may redeem it and bring the money — which has assumed the sanctity of the tithe — to Jerusalem, and with it, purchase food to eat.]

The *Tanna* specifies *his revai plantings* or *his second tithe*, since one who redeems another's *revai* plantings or second tithe need not add a fifth. This is derived from *Leviticus* 27:31: וְאִם־גָּאֹל יִגְאַל אִישׁ מִמַּעֲשְׂרוֹ חֲמִשִׁיתוֹ יֹסֵף עָלָיו,

he must add a fifth; [if] one redeems his *revai* plantings or his second tithe, he must add a fifth; [if] one redeems his consecrated objects, he must add a fifth; [if] one derives benefit the worth of a *perutah* from consecrated articles, he must add a fifth; and [if] one robs another of the worth of a *perutah* and swears to him, he must add a fifth.

YAD AVRAHAM

Should a man redeem any of his tithe, he shall add its fifth to it, indicating that this applies only to his tithe, and his *revai* plantings, which — as mentioned above — have the same status as the second tithe (*Rav; Rashi*).

מוֹסִיף חֹמֶשׁ; — *he must add a fifth;*

The *Tanna* reckons these two cases — the second tithe and the *revai* plantings — as only one instance in which a fifth must be added, since the fact that a fifth must be paid is derived for both cases from one source — the verse regarding the second tithe, from which we deduce that it applies also to *revai* plantings, as explained above (*Rav*).

הַפּוֹדֶה אֶת־הֶקְדֵּשׁוֹ, — [if] *one redeems his consecrated articles,*

That is, the same person who consecrated the article redeems it, not someone else (*Rav; Rashi*).

מוֹסִיף חֹמֶשׁ; — *he must add a fifth;*

This is based on *Leviticus* 27:15: וְאִם־ הַמַּקְדִּישׁ יִגְאַל אֶת־בֵּיתוֹ וְיָסַף חֲמִישִׁית כֶּסֶף־ עֶרְכְּךָ עָלָיו וְהָיָה לוֹ, *And if the one who consecrated it redeems his house, he shall add a fifth of the money of its value to it, and it shall become his.* Should the item be redeemed by a person other than one who consecrated it, however, he need not add a fifth (*Rav; Rashi*).

Rambam (*Hil. Temurah* 4:13) offers a reason for this ruling. The Torah realized that by nature a person seeks to increase his possessions, while spending

as little money as possible. In our case, although the person has consecrated an item, it is possible that he regrets doing so and will therefore redeem it for less than its value. Consequently, the Torah states that if he redeems it for himself, he shall add a fifth. Laws such as these are intended to subdue one's temptation and improve his character traits. Indeed, most of the Torah's laws are pieces of advice from the Great Counselor to improve character traits and to refine deeds, as stated in *Proverbs* 22:20,21.

הַנֶּהֱנֶה בְּשָׁוֶה פְרוּטָה מִן־הַהֶקְדֵּשׁ, מוֹסִיף חֹמֶשׁ; — [if] *one derives benefit the worth of a perutah from consecrated objects, he must add a fifth;*

As explained above, if one inadvertently derives benefit worth a *perutah* from consecrated objects, he must repay it to the Temple, add a fifth, and bring a guilt-offering [as derived from *Leviticus* 5:14-16] (*Rav*).

וְהַגּוֹזֵל אֶת־חֲבֵרוֹ שָׁוֶה פְרוּטָה וְנִשְׁבַּע לוֹ, מוֹסִיף חֹמֶשׁ. — *and [if] one robs another of the worth of a perutah and swears to him, he must add a fifth.*

[He swears that he did not rob him and later confesses that he did.] Although this applies also to one who denies a deposit, a loan, or any of the other instances mentioned in *Leviticus* 5:20-26, the *Tanna* follows the language of the mishnah in *Bava Kamma* 9:7, where robbery is the principal topic. Moreover, robbery is the first instance mentioned in the verse (*Tos. Yom Tov*).

9.

This mishnah delineates the articles to which the rules of fraud do not apply.

[ט] אֵלוּ דְבָרִים שֶׁאֵין לָהֶם אוֹנָאָה:

הָעֲבָדִים, וְהַשְּׁטָרוֹת,
וְהַקַּרְקָעוֹת, וְהַהֶקְדֵּשׁוֹת. אֵין לָהֶן תַּשְׁלוּמֵי כֶפֶל,
וְלֹא תַשְׁלוּמֵי אַרְבָּעָה וַחֲמִשָּׁה. שׁוֹמֵר חִנָּם אֵינוֹ

יד אברהם

אֵלוּ דְבָרִים שֶׁאֵין לָהֶם אוֹנָאָה: — *The
following things are not governed by*
[*the law of*] *fraud:*

[In other words, even if the buyer or
seller of one of these items is defrauded
by more than a sixth of the price, the
sale is final, and he cannot recover the
amount of the over/underpayment.]

הָעֲבָדִים, — *Slaves,*

[That is, gentile slaves, as explained
below.]

וְהַשְּׁטָרוֹת — *deeds,*

One sells a deed of indebtedness —
i.e., the right to collect the debt — to
another (*Tos. Yom Tov* from *Rashi*).

וְהַקַּרְקָעוֹת, — *land,*

[This includes also anything attached
to the ground, such as houses.]

וְהַהֶקְדֵּשׁוֹת. — *and consecrated articles.*

Such an instance can occur when the
Temple treasurer sells a consecrated
article or when one sells his עוֹלָה,
elevation offering, that had developed a
blemish (*Rashi*).

Things dedicated to the synagogue,
the poor, or any other charity, are not
regarded as consecrated in this sense,
and are therefore not excluded from the
law of fraud (*Tif. Yis.* from *Sma*
227:49).

The exclusion of these things from
the law of fraud is derived from
Leviticus 25:14: וְכִי־תִמְכְּרוּ מִמְכָּר לַעֲמִיתֶךָ *If
you sell anything to another, or buy
from the hand of another, you shall not
wrong each other.* The expression *from
the hand of another* indicates that the
verse is dealing only with articles
handed over from the seller to the
buyer. This excludes real estate, which
cannot be moved, and also gentile

slaves, which are compared to real estate
in *Leviticus* 25:46. Since the Torah
speaks of articles that have intrinsic
value, deeds — which do not — are
excluded. From the phrase אַל־תּוֹנוּ אִישׁ
אֶת־אָחִיו — lit., *one man shall not wrong
his brother,* we deduce that only items
belonging to another person come under
the law of fraud, and not consecrated
items, which belong to the Almighty
(*Rav* from *Gem.* 56b).

However, even in the above cases, if
the over/underpayment constituted
more than half of the price paid — for
example, any article worth one *sela* was
sold for more than two — some rule that
the sale is revoked. Others maintain that
even if the over/underpayment was
exactly half of the price paid — e.g., an
article worth one *sela* was sold for two —
the sale is revoked (*Choshen Mishpat*
227:29; see *Sma, Shach* ad loc.).

אֵין לָהֶן תַּשְׁלוּמֵי כֶפֶל, — [*The rule of*]
twofold payment does not [*apply*] *to
them,*

If someone steals any of the items
listed above, he need not pay the
twofold payment [usually required of a
thief; see ArtScroll *Bava Kamma* 7:1, p.
140] (*Tif. Yis.*).

This is derived from the verse dealing
with an unpaid *shomer* who claims that
the deposit entrusted to him had been
stolen (*Ex.* 22:8): עַל־כָּל־דְּבַר־פֶּשַׁע
עַל־שׁוֹר עַל־חֲמוֹר עַל־שֶׂה עַל־שַׂלְמָה עַל־כָּל־
אֲבֵדָה ... יְשַׁלֵּם שְׁנַיִם לְרֵעֵהוּ, *For any article
of trespass, for an ox, for a donkey, for
a lamb, for a garment, for any lost
article ... he shall pay twofold to the
other person.* The opening phrase, *for
any article of trespass,* is all inclusive, as
is the phrase *for any lost article.* The
articles listed between them are

4
9

9. The following things are not governed by [the law of] fraud: Slaves, deeds, land, and consecrated articles. [The rule of] twofold payment does not [apply] to them, nor [that of] the fourfold and fivefold payment. An unpaid *shomer* need not

specifications of these generalizations, thereby forming a כְּלָל וּפְרָט וּכְלָל, *a generalization followed by a specification, followed in turn by another generalization*, which is one of the thirteen rules of Biblical exegesis. This rule dictates that in such an instance, the specification qualifies the two generalities to include only such things that are similar to the specified items [see ArtScroll Siddur *(Ashkenaz, p.49)* and *Gateway to the Talmud*, p. 140]. In our case, just as the items specified in the verse are movable and have intrinsic value, so do the generalizations include only chattels with intrinsic value. This excludes real estate, which is not movable; slaves, which are compared to real estate; and deeds, which have no intrinsic value. Since the verse concludes: *he shall pay twofold to the other person*, consecrated objects — which belong to the Almighty, and not to any person — are excluded as well *(Rav* from *Gem.* 47b).

It is necessary for the Torah to tell us that real estate is not included in the rule of twofold payment, although it seems impossible to steal real properties, because such theft is indeed possible in the following cases: (1) when one moves the boundary marker of another's field, making it smaller; (2) things attached to the ground, such as grapes on vines *(Tos. Yom. Tov* from *Tos.).*

וְלֹא תַשְׁלוּמֵי אַרְבָּעָה וַחֲמִשָּׁה. — *nor [that of] the fourfold and fivefold payment.*

As stated in *Exodus* 21:37 [and explained in ArtScroll *Bava Kamma*, p. 141], someone who steals a lamb and slaughters or sells it, must pay four times its value to the owner; one who steals an ox and slaughters or sells it

must pay five times its value. As the verse specifies, these laws apply exclusively to a lamb and an ox. Hence, it is not applicable to real estate, slaves, and deeds *(Tos. Yom Tov* from *Nimmukei Yosef).* Even if one steals a lamb or an ox belonging to the Temple, he need not pay the four/fivefold payment. This is because the latter is applicable only if it includes the general twofold payment applying to thieves and — as explained above — one who steals consecrated items is exempt from paying the twofold payment *(Rav* from *Gem.* 57b).

שׁוֹמֵר חִנָּם אֵינוֹ נִשְׁבָּע, — *An unpaid shomer need not take an oath,*

[Although, as stated in 3:1, an unpaid *shomer* must take an oath if he claims that the deposit entrusted to him had been stolen or lost, this does not apply if the deposit consisted of slaves, deeds, real estate, or consecrated objects.]

The *Gemara* (57b) derives this from another כְּלָל וּפְרָט וּכְלָל, *generalization, specification, generalization sequence,* in a verse regarding the unpaid *shomer:* כִּי-יִתֵּן אִישׁ אֶל-רֵעֵהוּ כֶּסֶף אוֹ-כֵלִים לִשְׁמֹר, *If a man gives another person silver or utensils to be watched … (Ex.* 22:6). The phrase *if a man gives another person* [implying that whatever he gives is included] is a generalization; *silver or utensils* is a specification; *to be watched* [implying that whatever can be watched is included] is a second generalization. Hence, the hermeneutical rule teaches us that only things that are similar to silver and utensils are included in the generalizations — i.e., they must be chattels having intrinsic value. Slaves, deeds and real estate are therefore excluded.

נִשְׁבָּע, וְנוֹשֵׂא שָׂכָר אֵינוֹ מְשַׁלֵּם.
רַבִּי שִׁמְעוֹן אוֹמֵר: קָדָשִׁים שֶׁהוּא חַיָּב
בְּאַחֲרָיוּתָן יֵשׁ לָהֶן אוֹנָאָה; וְשֶׁאֵינוֹ חַיָּב בְּאַחֲרָיוּתָן
אֵין לָהֶן אוֹנָאָה. רַבִּי יְהוּדָה אוֹמֵר: אַף הַמּוֹכֵר
סֵפֶר תּוֹרָה, בְּהֵמָה, וּמַרְגָּלִית אֵין לָהֶם אוֹנָאָה.

יד אברהם

Actually, according to most authorities (Tos.; Ravad, Hil. Sechirus 2:3; Ramban; Rif; Ri Migash; Rama, Choshc̣n Mishpat 301:1) the intent of the mishnah is that even if due to the shomer's neglect in watching the item properly, it is lost, stolen, or damaged — in which case he would usually be liable for it — he is exempt if the deposit consisted of slaves, deeds, real estate, or consecrated items. The reason the mishnah states merely that the shomer is exempt from the oath is that it is based on the above verse, which discussed only the oath that the shomer must take (Tos. Yom Tov). Meiri and Ritva suggest that according to this view, the Tanna does not discuss what the halachah would be in the event that it is known that the loss occurred due to the shomer's neglect, because this is a rare case. However, Meiri himself and Rambam (loc. cit.) maintain that if an unpaid shomer is negligent in watching even the types of deposits listed above, he is liable, since negligence is equivalent to directly destroying the article. They derive this from the Tanna's statement that the shomer is exempt from taking an oath, which they construe as implying that if it is known that he had been neglectful in watching the item, he is liable to pay for it (Maggid Mishneh ad loc.). [The authorities do not equate neglectful watching with direct damage. They therefore contend that the shomer is exempt from such payment as he is from taking the oath.]

וְנוֹשֵׂא שָׂכָר אֵינוֹ מְשַׁלֵּם. — nor need a paid shomer pay.

If slaves, deeds, real estate, or consecrated items that have been entrusted to a paid shomer are stolen or lost, the shomer is exempt from paying for them (Meiri).

[The term נוֹשֵׂא שָׂכָר is synonymous with שׁוֹמֵר שָׂכָר, paid shomer. Literally, it means: one who receives payment.]

This ruling, too, is derived from a כְּלָל וּפְרָט וּכְלָל / generalization, specification, generalization sequence in a verse dealing with the paid shomer. The Torah states (Exodus 22:9): כִּי־יִתֵּן אִישׁ אֶל־רֵעֵהוּ חֲמוֹר אוֹ־שׁוֹר אוֹ־שֶׂה וְכָל־בְּהֵמָה לִשְׁמֹר ..., If a man gives another a donkey or a bull or a lamb or any animal to watch. The opening clause, If a man gives another, implying that whatever is given is included, is a generalization. Likewise, the final phrase, to watch, includes all types of deposits. The items listed between them are specifications, indicating that the two generalizations include only such articles similar to these examples — i.e., chattels having intrinsic vlaue. Therefore — as explained above — slaves, land, and real estate are excluded. Since the Torah, in the next verse, specifies ... he did not stretch forth his hand to the property of the other person, consecrated objects — which are the property of the Almighty — are excluded (Rav from Gem. 57b).

The mishnah does not mention the renter and the borrower — the remaining two of the four shomerim (see preface to chapter 3) — since consecrated objects can neither be borrowed nor rented (Meiri).

רַבִּי שִׁמְעוֹן אוֹמֵר: קָדָשִׁים שֶׁהוּא חַיָּב בְּאַחֲרָיוּתָן — R' Shimon says: Consecrated articles

take an oath, nor need a paid *shomer* pay.

R' Shimon says: Consecrated articles for which one is responsible are governed by [the law of] fraud; but those for which he is not responsible are not governed by [the law of] fraud. R' Yehudah says: Also one who sells a Torah scroll, an animal, or a pearl is not governed by [the law of] fraud. They said

YAD AVRAHAM

for which one is responsible

This refers to a case in which, for example, one said, „הֲרֵי עָלַי עוֹלָה‟ — *'I take upon myself to bring an elevation-offering'* (Rav; Rashi).

[As explained in *Megillah* 1:6, one who uses the expression „... הֲרֵי עָלַי‟ — *'I take upon myself ...'* when pledging to bring an offering obligates himself to bring the sacrifice even if the animal he designated dies, is stolen, or becomes blemished — thus invalidating it — in which case he must bring another animal to replace it.]

יֵשׁ לָהֶן אוֹנָאָה; — *are governed by [the law of] fraud;*

If the animal he designated became blemished, and he is selling it — since he is responsible to replace it, it is considered his property, and the exhortation of אַל-תּוֹנוּ אִישׁ אֶת-אָחִיו, *you shall not wrong each other (Lev. 25:14)* — i.e., the law of fraud — applies to it (Rav; Rashi).

The same applies to the fourfold and fivefold payments as stated in *Bava Kamma 7:4*, where R' Shimon rules that if one steals an offering from the one who pledged to bring it, and it is of the type which the owner is responsible to replace, the thief is liable for the four/fivefold payment where applicable. It follows, obviously, that if the thief merely steals the animal, but does not slaughter or sell it, he pays the twofold payment, since — as explained above — if there is no twofold payment for the theft, there can be no four/fivefold payment for slaughtering or selling (Tos. Yom Tov).

וְשֶׁאֵינוּ חַיָּב בְּאַחֲרָיוּתָן — *but those for which he is not responsible*

This refers to a case in which one said, „הֲרֵי זוּ קָרְבָּן‟, — *'This animal shall be an offering'* (Rav; Rashi). [As explained in *Megillah* 1:6, this expression does not impose a personal obligation upon the one who pledged to bring the offering, but merely consecrates the animal as a sacrifice. Should that animal die, become blemished, or be stolen, the one who consecrated it is not obligated to replace it.]

אֵין לָהֶן אוֹנָאָה. — *are not governed by [the law of] fraud.*

[Since the one who consecrated the animal is not responsible to replace it, it is considered as the property of the Temple, and is not included in the exhortation *you shall not wrong each other*, and hence, is not subject to the law of fraud. For the same reason, the two/four/fivefold payments do not apply to it, as explained above.]

The halachah is not in accordance with R' Shimon (Rav; Rambam Commentary).

רַבִּי יְהוּדָה אוֹמֵר: אַף הַמּוֹכֵר סֵפֶר תּוֹרָה, בְּהֵמָה, וּמַרְגָּלִית אֵין לָהֶם אוֹנָאָה. — *R' Yehudah says: Also one who sells a Torah scroll, an animal, or a pearl is not governed by [the law of] fraud.*

R' Yehudah reasons that a Torah scroll has limitless value. [Therefore, no matter how much one overcharges for it, it is not deemed fraud (Tif. Yis).] The same applies if one has a pearl and he seeks another one like it so that he can set both of them together (Rav from

אָמְרוּ לוֹ: לֹא אָמְרוּ אֶלָּא אֶת־אֵלּוּ.

[י] **כְּשֵׁם** שֶׁאוֹנָאָה בְּמִקָּח וּמִמְכָּר, כָּךְ אוֹנָאָה
בִּדְבָרִים. לֹא יֹאמַר לוֹ: ,,בְּכַמָּה חֵפֶץ
זֶה?" וְהוּא אֵינוֹ רוֹצֶה לִקַּח. אִם הָיָה בַּעַל תְּשׁוּבָה,
לֹא יֹאמַר לוֹ: ,,זְכֹר מַעֲשֶׂיךָ הָרִאשׁוֹנִים!" אִם הוּא
בֶּן־גֵּרִים, לֹא יֹאמַר לוֹ: ,,זְכֹר מַעֲשֵׂה אֲבוֹתֶיךָ!"
שֶׁנֶּאֱמַר: ,,וְגֵר לֹא־תוֹנֶה וְלֹא תִלְחָצֶנּוּ."

יד אברהם

Gem., Rashi 58b).

The halachah is not in accordance
with R' Yehudah (Rav; Rambam Commentary).

אָמְרוּ לוֹ: לֹא אָמְרוּ אֶלָּא אֶת־אֵלּוּ. — They

said to him: They stated only these.

The Sages said to R' Yehudah that
only those items listed above — slaves,
deeds, real estate, and consecrated
articles — are excluded from the law of
fraud (Meiri).

10.

כְּשֵׁם שֶׁאוֹנָאָה בְּמִקָּח וּמִמְכָּר, כָּךְ אוֹנָאָה
בִּדְבָרִים. — Just as there is wronging in
buying and selling, so is there wronging
with words.

[Just as the Torah prohibits a person
to wrong another by overcharging or
underpaying in business, so does it
prohibit him to wrong another with
words, as explained below.] This is
derived from Leviticus 25:17: וְלֹא תוֹנוּ
אִישׁ אֶת־עֲמִיתוֹ וְיָרֵאתָ מֵאֱלֹהֶיךָ כִּי אֲנִי ה'
אֱלֹהֵיכֶם, You shall not wrong each
other, and you shall fear your God, for I
am HASHEM, your God. This refers to
wronging with words, a sin apparent
only to God Himself, Who knows
whether a person's intention in saying
something is for good or bad (Rav from
Gem. 58b).

לֹא יֹאמַר לוֹ: ,,בְּכַמָּה חֵפֶץ זֶה?" וְהוּא אֵינוֹ
רוֹצֶה לִקַּח. — One shall not say to
another: 'How much does this article
cost?' if he does not wish to purchase
[it].

[One should not ask a merchant the
price of one of his wares, making the

impression that he wishes to purchase
it, if he actually has no intention of
buying it.]

Since a person who did this can
always claim that he had indeed
considered buying the item, he cannot
be judged by a human court. For this
reason, the Torah states: and you shall
fear your God, because He knows your
thoughts and recognizes whether you
asked about the price with good intent
or merely to bother the merchant (Tos.
Yom Tov).

Meiri explains that since the one who
asked the price is embarrassed to admit
to the merchant that he never intended
to buy the article, the latter assumes that
he is not buying it because the price
quoted was too high. The merchant will
therefore lower the price, and — since
this will be heard by potential customers
— he will be forced to sell the item for
less. Thus, the first 'customer' has
caused the merchant a loss with his
words. Even if no one overhears the
merchant lowering his price, the would-
be customer causes him unnecessary

to him: They stated only these.

10. Just as there is wronging in buying and selling, so is there wronging with words. One shall not say to another: 'How much does this article cost?' if he does not wish to purchase [it]. If he was a penitent, he shall not say to him: 'Remember your former deeds!' If he was the son of proselytes, he shall not say to him: 'Remember your ancestors' deeds!' for it is said (*Exodus* 22:20): *You shall neither wrong a proselyte nor oppress him.*

YAD AVRAHAM

trouble and anguish.

The *Gemara* (loc. cit.) gives other instances of אוֹנָאַת דְּבָרִים, *wronging with words:*

(1) If a person comes to someone to purchase grain, he should not send him to one who never sold grain in his life, thus embarrassing either the customer or the person he sent him to (*Kesef Mishneh, Hil. Mechirah* 14:14).

(2) If a person is afflicted with pains or diseases, one should not tell him what Job was told by his friends (*Job* 4:7): *Recall, now, who that was innocent ever perished?*

Rambam (ibid. and *Commentary*) mentions also the example of one who asks another person a difficult question, knowing full well that the latter is not a scholar.

For several reasons, wronging another with words is a graver sin than wronging in business. This is evidenced by the fact that the Torah adds the admonition *you shall fear your God* with regard to the former and not the latter. Moreover, wronging with words is a sin committed with one's body, which is worse than a sin committed with one's belongings. Also the latter can be rectified by returning the overcharge, but there is obviously nothing he can return in the former case (*Gem.* 58b).

אִם הָיָה בַּעַל תְּשׁוּבָה, לֹא יֹאמַר לוֹ: ,,זְכֹר מַעֲשֶׂיךָ הָרִאשׁוֹנִים!" — *If he was a penitent, he shall not say to him: 'Remember your former deeds!'*

This instance is in no way related to business transactions. The sin is that he embarrasses the person (*Meiri; Beis David*).

Although he may seek to exonerate himself by saying that he did this for the penitent's good, so that the latter be embarrassed by his sins and thereby attain forgiveness, God knows that his true intention was to gain honor from the person's disgrace and to cause him to revert to his former ways by showing him that his repentance has not been accepted and that people still mention his former sins (*Maskil LeDavid to Lev.* 25:17).

אִם הוּא הָיָה בֶּן־גֵּרִים, לֹא יֹאמַר לוֹ: ,,זְכֹר מַעֲשֵׂה אֲבוֹתֶיךָ!" שֶׁנֶּאֱמַר: ,,וְגֵר לֹא־תוֹנֶה וְלֹא תִלְחָצֶנּוּ." — *If he was the son of proselytes, he shall not say to him: 'Remember your ancestors' deeds!' for it is said (Exodus 22:20): 'You shall neither wrong a proselyte nor oppress him.'*

We may not even mention his ancestors' deeds, let alone his own deeds (*Tos. Yom Tov* from *Tos.*).

If he wishes to study Torah, do not tell him 'Shall a mouth that ate non-kosher food study Torah that was said by the Almighty?' (*Gem.* loc. cit.).

[יא] אֵין מְעָרְבִין פֵּרוֹת בְּפֵרוֹת — אֲפִלּוּ
חֲדָשִׁים בַּחֲדָשִׁים; וְאֵין
צָרִיךְ לוֹמַר חֲדָשִׁים בִּישָׁנִים. בֶּאֱמֶת, בַּיַּיִן, הִתִּירוּ
לְעָרֵב קָשֶׁה בְּרַךְ, מִפְּנֵי שֶׁהוּא מַשְׁבִּיחוֹ.
אֵין מְעָרְבִין שִׁמְרֵי יַיִן בְּיַיִן, אֲבָל נוֹתֵן לוֹ אֶת־
שְׁמָרָיו. מִי שֶׁנִּתְעָרֵב מַיִם בְּיֵינוֹ לֹא יִמְכְּרֶנּוּ בְּחָנוּת,
אֶלָּא אִם־כֵּן הוֹדִיעוֹ; וְלֹא לְתַגָּר — אַף־עַל־פִּי
שֶׁהוֹדִיעוֹ — שֶׁאֵינוֹ אֶלָּא לְרַמּוֹת בּוֹ.
מְקוֹם שֶׁנָּהֲגוּ לְהָטִיל מַיִם בַּיַּיִן, יַטִּילוּ.

יד אברהם

11.

This mishnah discusses various types of deception practiced in business to mislead the buyers. The *Tanna* gives the guidelines as to what is deemed deception and what is considered legitimate business practice.

אֵין מְעָרְבִין פֵּרוֹת בְּפֵרוֹת — *Produce may not be mixed with [other] produce —*

If one stipulates to sell a person the produce of a certain field, he may not mix the produce of another field with it (*Rav; Rashi*).

Others explain that one who sells produce may not mingle a small amount of inferior produce with a large amount of superior produce in order to make it appear that all the produce is of superior quality (*Tif. Yis.; Rosh*).

אֲפִלּוּ חֲדָשִׁים בַּחֲדָשִׁים; — *even new [produce] with [other] new [produce];*

According to *Rav* and *Rashi*, this means: even if the produce of both fields is new. According to *Rosh*, it means even if the good and the bad are both new.]

וְאֵין צָרִיךְ לוֹמַר חֲדָשִׁים בִּישָׁנִים. — *and, certainly, new with old.*

Needless to say, the seller may not mix new produce with old produce, since old produce is dry and makes more flour than the new (*Rav; Rashi*).

Others explain that old produce is better for eating than the new (*Rosh; Tos. 60a*)

Rosh rules that one may also not mix old produce with new produce, since the buyer may wish to store it for a long time, and the old produce may rot. *Rashi*, however, maintains that old produce may be mixed with fresh produce.

בֶּאֱמֶת, — *Truly,*

Wherever the *Tanna* uses the expression *truly*, he is stating a definite halachah which cannot be questioned (*Tos. Yom Tov from Gem. 60a*).

בַּיַּיִן, הִתִּירוּ לְעָרֵב קָשֶׁה בְּרַךְ, — *in [the case of] wine, they permitted to mix strong [wine] with mild [wine],*

If one stipulated to sell mild wine, he may blend strong wine with it (*Rashi*).

מִפְּנֵי שֶׁהוּא מַשְׁבִּיחוֹ. — *because it improves it.*

The strong wine improves the mild wine in that it preserves it for a longer time (*Tos. Yom Tov from Rosh*). Therefore, it is permitted to be mixed in. Should one stipulate to sell strong wine, *Rav* and *Rashi* rule that he may not blend mild wine into it. *Rosh*, however, contends that — on the contrary — he may surely mix mild wine with strong

11. **P**roduce may not be mixed with [other] produce — even new [produce] with [other] new [produce]; and, certainly, new with old. Truly, in [the case of] wine, they permitted to mix strong [wine] with mild [wine], because it improves it.

The lees of [one] wine may not be mixed with [another] wine, but he may give him its own lees. One whose wine was mixed with water may not sell it in a store, unless he notifies him; and not to a merchant — even if he notifies him — for this is only to deceive with it.

Wherever they are accustomed to put water into wine, they may put.

YAD AVRAHAM

wine. The halachah (*Choshen Mishpat* 228:11; *Tif. Yis.*) follows the latter view.

The *Gemara* (60a) qualifies this ruling as referring only to the season when wines are in the presses, because when the two wines that are being mixed ferment together, they form one taste. Afterwards, however, when each one already has its own distinct aroma and flavor, they may not be mingled, since one spoils the other, rather than enhances its flavor. Nevertheless, in places where the wine is tasted before being purchased, the seller may mix the wines even after they are no longer in the presses (*Tos. Yom Tov; Tif. Yis.*).

Meiri explains that while the wine is in the presses, it is sweet, and the strong wine permanently improves the flavor of the mild wine. When the wine is no longer in the presses, however, adding strong wine to it would effect only a temporary improvement, and if it would be sold when the flavor is at its best, the buyer would be cheated, since it will deteriorate after the purchase. Indeed, once the deterioration of the flavor is perceptible to the taste, the wine may be sold.

אֵין מְעָרְבִין שִׁמְרֵי יַיִן בְּיַיִן, — *The lees of [one] wine may not be mixed with*

[another] wine,

That is, one who sells wine may not mix lees from another cask into it (*Rav*), since the lees will spoil the wine (*Tos. Yom Tov* from *Tur* 228).

אֲבָל נוֹתֵן לוֹ אֶת־שְׁמָרָיו. — *but he may give him its own lees.*

If he sells a certain amount of wine, he may include the sediment of that wine as part of the amount (*Tif. Yis.*).

מִי שֶׁנִּתְעָרֵב מַיִם בְּיֵינוֹ לֹא יִמְכְּרֶנּוּ בַחֲנוּת, אֶלָּא אִם־כֵּן הוֹדִיעוֹ; — *One whose wine was mixed with water may not sell it in a store, unless he notifies him;*

He may not sell it retail, unless he notifies each customer that the wine has been diluted with water (*Rav; Rashi*).

וְלֹא לְתַגָּר — אַף־עַל־פִּי שֶׁהוֹדִיעוֹ— *and not to a merchant — even if he notifies him —*

He may not sell all of it together to a merchant, even if he notifies him that the wine is diluted (ibid.).

שֶׁאֵינוֹ אֶלָּא לְרַמּוֹת בּוֹ. — *for this is only to deceive with it.*

The merchant is buying it from him in order to resell it on a retail level and deceive the customers [by not informing them that it is diluted] (ibid.).

מָקוֹם שֶׁנָּהֲגוּ לְהָטִיל מַיִם בַּיַּיִן, — *Wherever they are accustomed to put water into*

[יב] **הַתַּגָּר** נוֹטֵל מֵחָמֵשׁ גְּרָנוֹת וְנוֹתֵן לְתוֹךְ מְגוּרָה אַחַת; מֵחָמֵשׁ גִּתּוֹת, וְנוֹתֵן לְתוֹךְ פִּיטָס אֶחָד, וּבִלְבַד שֶׁלֹּא יְהֵא מִתְכַּוֵּן לְעָרֵב. רַבִּי יְהוּדָה אוֹמֵר: לֹא יְחַלֵּק הַחֶנְוָנִי קְלָיוֹת וֶאֱגוֹזִין לַתִּינוֹקוֹת, מִפְּנֵי שֶׁהוּא מַרְגִּילָן לָבֹא אֶצְלוֹ. וַחֲכָמִים מַתִּירִין.

וְלֹא יִפְחֹת אֶת־הַשַּׁעַר. וַחֲכָמִים אוֹמְרִים: זָכוּר לַטּוֹב.

לֹא יָבֹר אֶת־הַגְּרִיסִין; דִּבְרֵי אַבָּא שָׁאוּל. וַחֲכָמִים מַתִּירִין. וּמוֹדִים שֶׁלֹּא יָבֹר מֵעַל־פִּי

יד אברהם

wine,

That is, each locale according to its custom — the water constituting either a half, third, or a fourth of the mixture (Gem.).

יַטִּילוּ. — *they may put.*

[The seller need not inform the buyer that he has diluted the wine.]

This, too, applies only during the season when the wine is in the presses.

Since this is the custom, all wines are expected to be diluted in this manner, and there is no deception involved (*Rav*).

Maggid Mishneh (Hil. *Mechirah* 18:6) explains that when the wine is in the presses and water is mixed in, the water assumes the flavor of the wine. After the wine comes out of the presses, however, the water merely dilutes it (*Tos. Yom Tov*).

12.

הַתַּגָּר — *A merchant*

This refers to one who purchases grain from many farmers and sells it (*Rav; Rashi*).

נוֹטֵל מֵחָמֵשׁ גְּרָנוֹת וְנוֹתֵן לְתוֹךְ מְגוּרָה אַחַת; — *may take from five threshing-floors and put [it] into one bin;*

Since everyone knows that the grain did not grow in the seller's own fields, and that he purchases it from many different farmers, and the purchasers buy it from him with this knowledge, he may mix it all in one bin (ibid.; *Meiri*).

מֵחָמֵשׁ גִּתּוֹת, — *from five winepresses,*

[One may take wine from five different winepresses.]

וְנוֹתֵן לְתוֹךְ פִּיטָס אֶחָד, — *and put [it] into*

one cask,

[He may blend the various wines in one cask or vat and sell it from there.]

Some editions read פִּיטָם, but it appears that ours is the correct spelling. See *Shinnuyei Nuschaos, Aruch, Meleches Shlomo.* The latter two cite other editions which read: פִּתָּס.

וּבִלְבַד שֶׁלֹּא יְהֵא מִתְכַּוֵּן לְעָרֵב. — *as long as he does not intend to mix.*

He may not intentionally mix in inferior produce. The mishnah means that the merchant may not purchase most of his produce from a source known for its high quality — intending to spread a rumor that all his produce originates from there — while actually mixing in produce from an inferior

12. A merchant may take from five threshing-floors and put [it] into one bin; from five winepresses, and put [it] into one cask, as long as he does not intend to mix.

R' Yehudah says: A storekeeper may not distribute parched corn or nuts to the children, because he accustoms them [to come] to him. The Sages, however, permit [it].

He may not lower the price. The Sages, however, say: He is remembered for good.

He may not sift crushed beans; [these are] the words of Abba Shaul. The Sages, however, permit [it]. They agree, however, that he may not sift from

YAD AVRAHAM

source (Rav; Rashi; Meiri).

רַבִּי יְהוּדָה אוֹמֵר: לֹא יְחַלֵּק הַחֶנְוָנִי קְלָיוֹת וֶאֱגוֹזִין לַתִּינוֹקוֹת, מִפְּנֵי שֶׁהוּא מַרְגִּילָן לָבֹא אֶצְלוֹ. — R' Yehudah says: A storekeeper may not distribute parched corn or nuts to the children, because he accustoms them [to come] to him.

He thereby deprives his competitors of their livelihood (Meiri).

וַחֲכָמִים מַתִּירִין. — The Sages, however, permit [it].

The Sages reason that this storekeeper can tell his competitors that they have the option of distributing plums (Tos. Yom Tov from Gem. 60a).

Meiri explains that plums were more expensive than nuts. He can therefore tell them that while he distributes cheap fruit to attract customers, they can distribute more expensive fruit and take the customers away from him.

וְלֹא יִפְחֹת אֶת־הַשַּׁעַר. — He may not lower the price.

A merchant may not sell his wares below the current market price in order to attract customers, since he is depriving his competitors of their livelihood (Rav; Rashi).

This is the opinion of R' Yehudah (Meleches Shlomo).

וַחֲכָמִים אוֹמְרִים: זָכוּר לַטוֹב. — The Sages, however, say: He is remembered for good.

The Sages contend that the merchant who lowers his prices is deserving of praise, because — as a result of this — those who store produce will follow suit and sell their produce cheaply (Rav from Rashi 60b).

The halachah follows the view of the Sages (Rav; Tif. Yis. from Choshen Mishpat 288:18).

לֹא יָבֹר אֶת־הַגְּרִיסִין; דִּבְרֵי אַבָּא שָׁאוּל. — He may not sift crushed beans; [these are] the words of Abba Shaul.

He may not pick out the inferior beans from among the good ones. Since this enhances their appearance, he will raise the price more than is commensurate to the ones that have been removed (Rav; Rashi).

וַחֲכָמִים מַתִּירִין. — The Sages, however, permit [it].

They reason that there is no deception involved, since the customers can compute the amount of undesirable matter that had been removed and how much that amount of beans should cost. In fact, the storekeeper is entitled to raise the price because of the labor involved in sifting the beans (Rav from

בבא
מציעא
ה/א
הַמְגוּרָה, שֶׁאֵינוֹ אֶלָּא כְּגוֹנֵב אֶת־הָעַיִן. אֵין
מְפַרְכְּסִין לֹא אֶת־הָאָדָם, וְלֹא אֶת־הַבְּהֵמָה, וְלֹא
אֶת־הַכֵּלִים.

[א] **אֵיזֶהוּ** נֶשֶׁךְ וְאֵיזֶהוּ תַרְבִּית? אֵיזֶהוּ נֶשֶׁךְ?
הַמַּלְוֶה סֶלַע בַּחֲמִשָּׁה דִינָרִין,

יד אברהם

Rashi 60b).

The halachah is in accordance with the view of the Sages (*Rav; Tif. Yis.* from *Choshen Mishpat* 228:17).

ומודים שֶׁלֹא יָבֹר מֵעַל־פִּי הַמְּגוּרָה, — *They agree, however, that he may not sift from the opening of the bin,*

The Sages concur with Abba Shaul that the merchant may not sift the beans at the top of the bin and leave over the refuse on the bottom (*Rav; Rashi*).

שֶׁאֵינוֹ אֶלָּא כְּגוֹנֵב אֶת־הָעַיִן. — *for he is only like one who deceives the eye.*

Even if he informs the customer that he has sifted only the beans lying on the top of the bin, he is still compared to one who deceives the eye, since the customer — looking at the good beans — does not always think of the refuse lying beneath them (*Tos. Yom Tov*), or he may think that there is not much refuse below (*Tif. Yis.*).

אֵין מְפַרְכְּסִין — *We may not beautify*

[We may not enhance the appearance of anything being sold in order to make it look better than it really is.]

לֹא אֶת־הָאָדָם, — *either man,*

For example, one may not enhance the appearance of a gentile slave offered for sale by dyeing his white hair black (*Rav* from *Gem.* 60b).

וְלֹא אֶת־הַבְּהֵמָה, — *beast,*

One may not feed an animal bran broth, which would inflate the intestines — giving it a bloated appearance — and stiffen the hair, in order to make it look better before selling it.

Similarly, it is prohibited to inflate the entrails of a slaughtered animal or soak the meat to give it a white appearance, making it seem that it is fat (*Gem.*).

וְלֹא אֶת־הַכֵּלִים. — *or utensils.*

One may not paint old utensils to make them appear new before selling them (*Tif. Yis.* from *Gem.* 60b).

New ones, however, may be painted, since the painting is done merely to beauty them, and the buyer is willing to pay extra for the beauty (*Gem., Rashi*).

[From *Rambam* (*Hil. Mechirah* 18:2) it appears that the same laws apply to shining and polishing utensils.]

Chapter 5

◄§ רְבִּית / Interest on Loans

The following chapter deals with the prohibition of taking interest for a loan. It is prohibited not only to lend money with interest, but to borrow with interest and to take any part in such a transaction as well (see mishnah 11). The interdict is found in *Leviticus* 25:35-37:

וְכִי־יָמוּךְ אָחִיךָ וּמָטָה יָדוֹ עִמָּךְ ... אַל־תִּקַּח מֵאִתּוֹ נֶשֶׁךְ וְתַרְבִּית ... אֶת־כַּסְפְּךָ לֹא־תִתֵּן
לוֹ בְּנֶשֶׁךְ וּבְמַרְבִּית לֹא־תִתֵּן אָכְלֶךָ.
Should your brother become impoverished and his hand waver beside you ... you shall take from him neither interest nor increase ... Your money you shall not give him with interest, nor shall you give your

the opening of the bin, for he is only like one who deceives the eye.
We may not beautify either man, beast, or utensils.

1. **W**hat is interest and what is increase? What is interest? [If] one lends a *sela* for five dinars,

YAD AVRAHAM

food with increase.

Thus, the Torah refers to interest — both for loans of money and loans of food — by using two terms: (1) נֶשֶׁךְ (lit., *biting*), since the interest accumulates and consumes the property of the debtor very much like the venom of a serpent, which slowly spreads through the entire body of the victim of its bite; and (2) מַרְבִּית, *increase*, since the property of the creditor increases through this loan. The *Gemara* (60b) states that these two terms are synonymous, since — regarding this type of interest — it is impossible for the creditor to 'bite' the debtor without increasing his own property.

Although Scripture uses the latter term only with regard to interest involving food, the *Gemara* deduces that both terms apply to interest on loans involving any type of item. The Torah uses both expressions to indicate that one who transgresses this prohibition thereby violates two negative commandments *(Tos. Yom Tov)*. The mishnah, however, uses the term תַּרְבִּית to refer to the Rabbinically prohibited form of interest that applies to transactions of buying and selling, in which the seller does not 'bite' the purchaser, but his property increases nevertheless.

The Biblical prohibition applies only if it is stipulated beforehand exactly how much interest will be paid (רִבִּית קְצוּצָה) *(Rambam, Hil. Malveh 4:3)*.

The practical difference between interest prohibited Biblically and that prohibited Rabbinically is that only the former can be recovered in court. Rabbinically prohibited interest, however, need not be returned by a lender unless he wishes to fulfill his duty to Heaven. Yet, if the borrower seized even this back from the lender, he need not return it *(Tif. Yis. from Yoreh Deah 161:15).*

[Note: We have deliberately avoided using the familiar term *usury*, because in modern usage it refers to an exorbitant rate or amount of interest or one in excess of that permitted by law. In contrast, the Torah prohibition of interest applies to any rate or amount.]

1.

אֵיזֶהוּ נֶשֶׁךְ — *What is interest*
What interest is Biblically prohibited? *(Tif. Yis. from Gem. 60b).*

וְאֵיזֶהוּ תַּרְבִּית? — *and what is increase?*
What is the Rabbinically prohibited interest, known as תַּרְבִּית, *increase?* It is called by this name since the increase comes of itself, without the creditor taking away from the debtor *(Tif. Yis.).*

אֵיזֶהוּ נֶשֶׁךְ? הַמַּלְוֶה סֶלַע בַּחֲמִשָּׁה דִינָרִין, — *What is interest?* [If] one lends a sela for five dinars,

[One person lends another a *sela*, which equals four *dinars*. See table of currencies in preface to 4:3.]

Actually, the *Tanna* could have given the simpler example of lending two *dinars* in return for three, similar to the next case of two *se'in* for three. He deliberately chose the example of a *sela* for five *dinars* so that we not think that since this case involves two different types of coins, and due to fluctuations in value, a *sela* is sometimes indeed worth five *dinars*, it is not considered a

סָאתַיִם חִטִּין בְּשָׁלֹש, מִפְּנֵי שֶׁהוּא ,,נוֹשֵׁךְ.'' וְאֵיזֶהוּ
תַרְבִּית? הַמַּרְבֶּה בְּפֵרוֹת. כֵּיצַד? לָקַח הֵימֶנּוּ חִטִּין
בְּדִינַר זָהָב הַכּוֹר, וְכֵן הַשַּׁעַר. עָמְדוּ חִטִּין
בִּשְׁלֹשִׁים דִּינָרִין, אָמַר לוֹ: ,,תֶּן־לִי חִטַּי, שֶׁאֲנִי
רוֹצֶה לְמָכְרָן וְלִקַּח בָּהֶן יָיִן.'' אָמַר לוֹ: ,,הֲרֵי חִטֶּיךָ
עֲשׂוּיוֹת עָלַי בִּשְׁלֹשִׁים דִּינָרִין, וַהֲרֵי לְךָ אֶצְלִי בָּהֶן
יָיִן;'' וְיַיִן אֵין לוֹ.

יד אברהם

loan, but a transaction of buying and
selling, which is prohibited only by
Rabbinic law. Rather, the *Tanna* teaches
us that since the two items involved in
this transaction are both coins, it is
considered a loan and is Biblically
prohibited.

To be sure, if one gave another gold
coins on the condition that silver coins
amounting to a larger value be returned
to him, since — as explained in 4:1 — the
silver coins are considered the medium
of exchange, whereas the gold coins are
considered the item purchased, it would
not be Biblically prohibited (*Tos. R'
Akiva* quoting *Pnei Yehoshua*).

סָאתַיִם חִטִּין בְּשָׁלֹש, — [*or*] *two se'in of
wheat for three*,

[One lends two *se'in* of wheat with
the stipulation that three *se'in* be repaid
to him.]

מִפְּנֵי שֶׁהוּא ,,נוֹשֵׁךְ.'' — *because he 'bites.'*

That is, this type of interest is called
נֶשֶׁךְ, *biting*, since the lender takes from
the borrower more than what he gave
him (*Rav; Rashi*).

וְאֵיזֶהוּ תַרְבִּית? הַמַּרְבֶּה בְּפֵרוֹת. — *And what
is increase? One who increases through
produce.*

The Rabbinically prohibited interest
applies when one increases his property
through certain transactions involving
produce. Although, as explained above,
both loans involving money and those
involving produce are equally prohibited by the laws of interest, the mishnah's intention is to use the word תַרְבִּית

to refer to Rabbinically prohibited
interest, which is applicable only in a
transaction of buying or selling (*Rav*).

כֵּיצַד? לָקַח הֵימֶנּוּ חִטִּין בְּדִינַר זָהָב — *How?*
[*If*] *he purchased wheat from him at
[the rate of] a golden dinar*

[For example, Reuven purchased
wheat from Shimon at this price.]

A golden *dinar* is equivalent to
twenty-five silver *dinars* (*Rav; Rashi*).

הַכּוֹר, — *per kor,*

A *kor* is a dry measure equivalent to
thirty *se'in* (*Tif. Yis.*). [See table in
preface to 3:7.]

וְכֵן הַשַּׁעַר. — *and that was the market
price.*

Since wheat was available in the city
at that price, it was permissible for
Reuven to give Shimon money, stipulating that the latter supply him with
wheat at this price throughout the year.
Although the price may rise, he may
nevertheless supply him with the wheat
at the original price, and it is not considered interest. [This is because when
Reuven gives the money, the wheat
becomes his to the extent that the
prohibition against interest is not
transgressed. Although, as explained in
4:1, giving money is not a sufficient
means of acquiring an object, the Rabbis
chose to consider it sufficient with
regard to the prohibition of interest that
they themselves enacted (*Tos. Yom
Tov*).] Even if Shimon, the seller, has no
wheat at this time, as long as others do
and the market price has been

5
1

[or] two *se'in* of wheat for three, because he 'bites.'
And what is increase? One who increases through
produce. How? [If] he purchased wheat from him at
[the rate of] a golden *dinar* per *kor*, and that was the
market price. [Then] wheat rose to thirty *dinars*,
[and] he said to him: 'Give me my wheat, for I wish
to sell it and purchase wine for it.' He replied: 'Your
wheat shall be considered [a debt of] thirty *dinars*
upon me, and you have [a claim of] wine upon me for
them'; but he has no wine.

YAD AVRAHAM

publicized, since he can purchase it at
the price they agreed upon, it is
regarded as though he already has the
wheat, as stated in mishnah 7 (Rav;
Rashi).

עָמְדוּ חִטִּין בִּשְׁלֹשִׁים דִּינָרִין, — [Then] wheat
rose to thirty dinars,
[The price of wheat rose from
twenty-five dinars per kor to thirty
dinars per kor.]

אָמַר לוֹ: — [and] he said to him:
[Reuven said to Shimon.]

"תֶּן־לִי חִטַּי, שֶׁאֲנִי רוֹצֶה לְמָכְרָן וְלִקַּח בָּהֶן יָיִן".
— 'Give me my wheat, for I wish to sell
it and purchase wine for it.'
Should he give him wheat, it would
be permissible, as explained above (Rav;
Rashi). Tosafos (62b), however, construe the mishnah's entire case differently. According to them, Shimon had
owed Reuven a golden dinar from a
previous debt. With that money,
Reuven wishes to purchase wheat from
Shimon, although the latter does not
have any in his possession at the time.
This is prohibited, since Shimon neither
has wheat nor is receiving money, and if
the price subsequently would rise, it
would constitute Rabbinically forbidden interest (Tos. Yom Tov).

אָמַר לוֹ: — He replied:
[Shimon replied to Reuven.]

"הֲרֵי חִטֶּיךָ עֲשׂוּיוֹת עָלַי בִּשְׁלֹשִׁים דִּינָרִין, —
'Your wheat shall be considered [a debt

of] thirty dinars upon me,
'Instead of the wheat that I owe you, I
accept upon myself a debt the rate of
thirty dinars per kor of wheat, as
though you were lending me this
amount of money now' (Meiri).

וַהֲרֵי לְךָ אֶצְלִי בָהֶן יָיִן". — and you have [a
claim of] wine upon me for them';
'I obligate myself to give you wine
corresponding to the value of the wheat
that I owe you, ten se'in at the time of
vintage, a seah costing three dinars'
(ibid.).

וְיַיִן אֵין לוֹ. — but he has no wine.
[Shimon, who owes Reuven the
wheat or its equivalent, has no wine in
his possession at the time.] Accordingly,
this agreement is prohibited although he
pledges to supply Reuven with wine at
the current market price, which is already known. Since he does not give
him money with which he can purchase
wine at the present, but rather he wishes
to make the money he received for the
wheat a debt and to obligate himself to
supply Reuven with wine for the money
he owes him, it is prohibited if he has no
wine. This is because if the price of wine
rises, it is considered that the purchaser
is receiving more value than he had paid
for, which constitutes Rabbinical interest.
Should Shimon have wine, however,
it is as though the wine already belongs
to Reuven, as explained above, and if
the price rises, it is the latter's wine that

[ב] **הַמַּלְוֶה** אֶת־חֲבֵרוֹ, לֹא יָדוּר בַּחֲצֵרוֹ חִנָּם,
וְלֹא יִשְׂכֹּר מִמֶּנּוּ בְּפָחוֹת, מִפְּנֵי
שֶׁהוּא רִבִּית.
מַרְבִּין עַל־הַשָּׂכָר, וְאֵין מַרְבִּין עַל־הַמֶּכֶר. כֵּיצַד?
הִשְׂכִּיר לוֹ אֶת־חֲצֵרוֹ, וְאָמַר לוֹ: ,,אִם מֵעַכְשָׁיו
אַתָּה נוֹתֵן לִי, הֲרֵי הוּא לְךָ בְּעֶשֶׂר סְלָעִים לַשָּׁנָה,
וְאִם שֶׁל־חֹדֶשׁ בְּחֹדֶשׁ, בְּסֶלַע לַחֹדֶשׁ,'' מֻתָּר. מָכַר

יד אברהם

has gained in value (Rav).

Although, in fact, a purchaser does
not gain possession of the item until he
performs an act of acquisition — e.g.,
מְשִׁיכָה, pulling (see General Introduction) — once he gives the money for it, if
he subsequently retracts from the sale,
he incurs upon himself the Rabbinical
curse of ... מִי שֶׁפָּרַע, He Who exacted
retribution from the generation of the
Flood and from the generation of the
Dispersion will exact retribution from
one who does not abide by his spoken
word (4:2). Most authorities, including

Rav, Rashi, and Rambam, maintain that
this applies even in a transaction in
which money was not paid directly for
the merchandise, but is based on a
previous debt. See Rambam, Hil.
Mechirah 7:4. Ravad (ad loc.), however,
rules that although Reuven has not
acquired the wine according to the rules
of acquisition, since the entire question
here involves only Rabbinical interest,
the Rabbis deemed it as though he has
already acquired the wine, and has
therefore not transgressed at all (see
Tos. R' Akiva).

2.

The following mishnah delineates various types of Rabbinical interest, known as
אֲבַק רִבִּית, a minor form (lit., dust) of interest.

הַמַּלְוֶה אֶת־חֲבֵרוֹ, לֹא יָדוּר בַּחֲצֵרוֹ חִנָּם, — [If]
one lends to another, he may not dwell
in his courtyard gratis,

The lender may not dwell in the
borrower's courtyard gratis, even if the
courtyard is not customarily rented out
and the lender is not looking for a dwelling to rent, in which case he derives no
benefit from the courtyard and the
borrower suffers no loss (Tif. Yis. from
Yoreh Deah 166:1).

Rosh (§16-17) quotes authorities who
rule that if the borrower and the lender
were known to be close friends, who
would do favors for one another even
before the loan, the latter may dwell in
the former's courtyard gratis. Accordingly, the mishnah deals only with

ordinary people, who are not such close
friends. This is the view of most
authorities. Maharshal (Bava Kamma
9:9) contends that even in the case of
close friends, only such favors that are
not known publicly, such as lending
animals or utensils, are permitted.
Giving him a place to live gratis —
which will be known by the public —
however, is prohibited (Shach, Yoreh
Deah 166:1).

Similarly, the borrower may not
honor the lender by calling him to the
Torah or purchasing gelilah [the honor
of rolling the Torah together] for him,
since these honors are bestowed upon
their recipients in public (Shach ad loc.
from Maharshal loc. cit. §11).

5
2

2. [If] one lends to another, he may not dwell in his courtyard gratis, nor may he rent it from him for less, because it is increase.

The rent may be increased, but the sale price may not be increased. How? [If] he rented him his courtyard, and said to him: 'If you pay me now, you may have it for ten *selaim* per year, but if [you pay] for each month in its month, [you must pay] a *sela* per month,' it is permissible. [If] he sold him his field,

וְלֹא יִשְׂכֹּר מִמֶּנּוּ בְּפָחוֹת, — *nor may he rent it from him for less,*

Not only may he not dwell in his courtyard gratis, but he may not even rent it from him for less than the usual rent (*Meiri*).

מִפְּנֵי שֶׁהוּא רִבִּית. — *because it is increase.*

Both of these cases are Rabbinically prohibited, since it appears that the borrower is doing these favors because of the lender's loan. This is known as אֲבַק רִבִּית, *a minor form of interest.* Should it be stipulated at the time of the loan that the borrower do this favor, it constitutes רִבִּית קְצוּצָה, *stipulated interest,* and is prohibited by the Torah (ibid.).

[The mishnah now proceeds to discuss whether certain other instances are considered minor forms of interest. These cases do not involve loans.]

מַרְבִּין עַל-הַשָּׂכָר, — *The rent may be increased,*

A landlord may increase the rent to compensate for his waiting to receive payment (*Rav; Rashi*).

וְאֵין מַרְבִּין עַל-הַמֶּכֶר. — *but the sale price may not be increased.*

A seller may not demand a higher price from the purchaser for waiting to receive payment (ibid.).

כֵּיצַד? הִשְׂכִּיר לוֹ אֶת-חֲצֵרוֹ, וְאָמַר לוֹ: — *How?* [If] *he rented him his courtyard, and said to him:*

The same applies if he hired himself out as a laborer or rented out his animal

or utensils (*Tif. Yis.*).

אִם מֵעַכְשָׁיו אַתָּה נוֹתֵן לִי, הֲרֵי הוּא לְךָ בְּעֶשֶׂר סְלָעִים לַשָּׁנָה, — *'If you pay me now, you may have it for ten selaim per year,*

['If you pay the rent in advance, I will rent it to you for ten *selaim* per year.']

וְאִם שֶׁל-חֹדֶשׁ בְּחֹדֶשׁ, בְּסֶלַע לַחֹדֶשׁ," — *but if* [you pay] *for each month in its month,* [you must pay] *a sela per month,'*

['If you pay me the rent on a monthly basis, you will have to pay me a *sela* per month, thus totaling twelve *selaim* per year.']

מֻתָּר. — *it is permissible.*

This leniency is based on the rule that שְׂכִירוּת אֵינָהּ מִשְׁתַּלֶּמֶת אֶלָּא לְבַסּוֹף, *rent is payable only at the end of the term.* Therefore, if one rents a courtyard at a *sela* per month, the rent is due at the end of each month. Accordingly, if the tenant pays a *sela* at the end of each month, he is paying the true rental of the courtyard, without any charge for delaying the payment. If he pays in advance, however, the owner — in appreciation for his early payment — lowers the rate and relinquishes two months' rent (*Rav from Gem.* 64b).

Although the halachah is that יֶשְׁנָהּ לְשְׂכִירוּת מִתְּחִלָּה וְעַד סוֹף, *there is a progressive liability for renting from beginning to end,* as in Kiddushin 3:6, the intention is merely that the owner has earned the money for the rental from the beginning of the period until the end. It is, however, not payable until the end (*Tos. Yom Tov* from *Nimmukei Yosef*).

לוֹ אֶת־שָׂדֵהוּ, וְאָמַר לוֹ: ,,אִם מֵעַכְשָׁיו אַתָּה נוֹתֵן
לִי, הֲרֵי הִיא שֶׁלְּךָ בְּאֶלֶף זוּז, אִם לַגֹּרֶן, בִּשְׁנֵים
עָשָׂר מָנֶה,'' אָסוּר.

[ג] **מָכַר לוֹ** אֶת־הַשָּׂדֶה, וְנָתַן לוֹ מִקְצָת
דָּמִים, וְאָמַר לוֹ: ,,אֵימָתַי
שֶׁתִּרְצֶה, הָבֵא מָעוֹת וְטֹל אֶת־שֶׁלְּךָ,'' אָסוּר.
הִלְוָהוּ עַל־שָׂדֵהוּ, וְאָמַר לוֹ: ,,אִם אִי אַתָּה נוֹתֵן
לִי מִכָּאן וְעַד שָׁלֹשׁ שָׁנִים, הֲרֵי הִיא שֶׁלִּי,'' הֲרֵי

יד אברהם

מָכַר לוֹ אֶת־שָׂדֵהוּ, וְאָמַר לוֹ: ,,אִם מֵעַכְשָׁיו אַתָּה
נוֹתֵן לִי, הֲרֵי הִיא שֶׁלְּךָ בְּאֶלֶף זוּז, — [If] he
sold him his field, and said to him: 'If
you pay me now, it is yours for a
thousand zuz,

[In contrast, if one person sold
another his field, telling him, 'If you pay
me for the field immediately, I will
charge you only one thousand zuz.']

אִם לַגֹּרֶן, בִּשְׁנֵים עָשָׂר מָנֶה,'' — [but] if at the
time of threshing, [I give it to you] for
twelve maneh,'

'If you wait to pay me at the time of
threshing, when you will sell your grain
(Tif. Yis.) [since I have to wait for my
money, I will charge you twelve hundred zuz].'

אָסוּר. — it is prohibited.

Since the money is due at the time of
the sale, the price he charges him when
he pays immediately is the true price;
the extra two hundred zuz is a charge
for giving him credit. This is Rabbinically prohibited interest, and may not be
taken. Should the seller have already
taken it, however, the buyer cannot
recover it from him in court (Rav).

The same ruling applies to sales of
movables. The reason the Tanna states

it in a case involving land is that since
the law of אוֹנָאָה, fraud, does not apply
to real property, as stated in 4:9, we
might think that the seller is not
charging him for credit, but is merely
raising the price (Tif. Yis.).

Should he raise the price at the time
of the sale without stipulating that it is
because of the buyer's failure to pay immediately, it is permissible. In the case
of movables, however, if the price is
known, since the law of fraud applies,
he may not sell them for a higher price
(Tif. Yis. from Yoreh Deah 173:1).
According to Tur, even if it is not
stipulated that the increase in price is
due to the credit, it is permitted only if it
is a small increase. Should there be a
large increase in the price, it is obvious
that it is a credit charge, and it is
prohibited.

The mishnah commences with the case of
renting a courtyard and concludes with the
case of selling a field. It was more customary
to rent out courtyards than to rent out fields,
since the owner of a field usually tills his own
field to earn a livelihood rather than rent it to
others. When one was forced to sell his property, however, he was more likely to sell his
field than his courtyard, as in Leviticus
25:25,29 (Tos. Yom Tov, Tif. Yis.).

3.

מָכַר לוֹ אֶת־הַשָּׂדֶה, וְנָתַן לוֹ מִקְצָת דָּמִים,
[If] he sold him a field, and he gave him

part of the money,

[This is a new case. In the sale of a

5
3

and said to him: 'If you pay me now, it is yours for a thousand *zuz*, [but] if at the time of threshing, [I give it to you] for twelve *maneh*,' it is prohibited.

3. **[I**f] he sold him a field, and he gave him part of the money, and he said to him: 'Whenever you wish, bring the money and take yours,' it is prohibited.

[If] he lent him on [the security of] his field, and said to him: 'If you do not pay me within three years,

YAD AVRAHAM

field, the purchaser gave the seller a down payment.]

וְאָמַר לוֹ: — *and he said to him:*
[The seller said to the purchaser.]

"אֵימָתַי שֶׁתִּרְצֶה, הָבֵא מָעוֹת וְטֹל אֶת־שֶׁלָּךְ," — *'Whenever you wish, bring the money and take yours,'*
Whenever you wish, you may pay the balance, and you will acquire the field retroactively (Rav, Rashi from Gem. 65b).

אָסוּר. — *it is prohibited.*
Since it is not known whether the buyer will subsequently pay the balance and thereby acquire the field retroactively, the ownership of the field at this time is in question, and therefore, neither the seller nor the buyer may benefit from its produce. The seller may not benefit from it, because in the event the buyer acquires the field retroactively, the seller will have, in effect, taken the produce as payment for waiting for his money. The buyer may not benefit from the produce, because if he does not make the final payment and does not acquire the field, he will have taken the produce only because his money was in the seller's possession until he decided whether or not to make the final payment. In both cases, there is an infraction of the prohibition of taking interest (Rav from Gem. 65b).

Therefore, in order that such trans-

actions be permitted, the produce must be held in escrow until it is clarified to whom it belongs. Should they stipulate that the purchaser takes title to the field when he makes the final payment, there is no problem, since the seller may enjoy the benefits of the field until that payment is made. If they stipulate that the purchaser acquires a part of the field in proportion to the amount of the price he has paid, he may benefit from the field to that extent. Similarly, should they agree that the sale is final at the time of the down payment, and that the balance of payment is regarded as a loan, the purchaser may enjoy the benefits of the field immediately, since it is already his (Gem. 65b).

הִלְוָהוּ עַל־שָׂדֵהוּ, — *[If] he lent him on [the security of] his field,*
[This is a new case.]
For example, a person lent another one thousand *zuz* on the security of his field, which was worth two thousand *zuz* (Meiri).

וְאָמַר לוֹ: — *and said to him:*
[The lender said to the borrower.]

"אִם אִי אַתָּה נוֹתֵן לִי מִכָּאן וְעַד שָׁלֹשׁ שָׁנִים, הֲרֵי הִיא שֶׁלִּי," — *'If you do not pay me within three years, it is mine,'*
That is, 'I will take title to the field retroactively from the time of the loan' (Rav from Gem. 66a).

[131] THE MISHNAH/BAVA METZIA – Chapter Five: *Eizehu Neshech*

הִיא שֶׁלּוֹ. וְכָךְ הָיָה בַּיְתּוֹס בֶּן־זוּנִין עוֹשֶׂה, עַל־פִּי
חֲכָמִים.

[ד] **אֵין** מוֹשִׁיבִין חֶנְוָנִי לְמַחֲצִית שָׂכָר, וְלֹא יִתֵּן
מָעוֹת לִקַּח בָּהֶן פֵּרוֹת לְמַחֲצִית שָׂכָר,

יד אברהם

הֲרֵי הִיא שֶׁלּוֹ. — *it is his.*

[The transaction is valid, and if the borrower does not pay the debt within three years, the lender acquires the field retroactively.]

As in the preceding case, since the ownership of the field is in question, the produce must be held in escrow until the borrower either repays the loan or allows the three years to elapse. Were the lender allowed to enjoy the produce before the time, if the borrower subsequently repays the loan — in which case, the field will have always remained his — the produce will have been interest on the loan (*Rav;* see *Meiri, Sma* 207:18).

⋙ אַסְמַכְתָּא / An Insincere Transaction

If a person makes a conditional commitment to another, and it is obvious that he has done so only because he assumes that the condition will not be fulfilled, the halachah is that the commitment is not binding, even if the condition is subsequently fulfilled (see *Yad Avraham* commentary to ArtScroll *Bava Basra* 10:5).

For example, if a transaction is made with the stipulation that it will take effect only if and when a certain condition is fulfilled, it is void, because we assume that the stipulator never wanted it to be valid (*Rashi* 63a). Had he been

sincere about the transaction, he would have agreed that it should be valid immediately. Even if he wished it to be subject to a condition that must be fulfilled subsequently, once that condition is met, the transaction should become retroactively valid from the time it was made. Since he stipulated instead that the transaction is valid only if and *when* the condition is fulfilled, his intention is obviously that the condition will not be met, thus invalidating the transaction. This is called an אַסְמַכְתָּא, *asmachta* (lit., *reliance*) — i.e., he relies on the assumption that the condition will not be met. Because he was never truly sincere from the outset, the transaction is void even if the condition is fulfilled.[1]

The case in our mishnah is a valid transaction, and is not considered an *asmachta*. Since the borrower agrees that if he fails to pay the lender, the latter should acquire the field retroactively, it is considered as if the field is being sold by the borrower to the lender for the money that was lent — although it is much below the market price — on condition that if the borrower wishes to give back the money within three years, the lender will accept it and the field will return to the borrower's possession.

Indeed, should the stipulation be that

---

1. Some maintain that this applies only if the transaction involves selling something for well below its price, indicating that the seller is not serious (*Rashi* 66a; *Choshen Mishpat* 207:9). *Rav,* who — in the comment cited below — construes the mishnah as referring to a case in which the loan was for considerably less than the price of the field, seems to concur with this view. Others contend that even if the sale is for the market price, as long as the seller stipulates that it will be effective only if and when the condition is fulfilled, it is void (*Rama* ad loc.). This is because no one wishes to part with his property, even for a fair price, unless he is forced to. Therefore, in our case, we assume that he made the stipulation only because he is not serious about the transaction (*Sma* ibid. §16).

it is mine,' it is his. And so was Baisos the son of Zonin wont to do, with the consent of the Sages.

4. A storekeeper may not be set up for half the profit, nor may money be given with which to buy produce at half profit, unless he gives him his

if the borrower does not pay within three years, the field becomes the lender's *at that time*, the transaction is void, since it is an *asmachta* — the borrower never intends to give up the field; rather, he is certain that he will repay the loan during the three years (*Rav* from *Gem.*).

Although the gist of both cases in this mishnah is that such instances are permissible only if the produce is held in escrow, in the first case the *Tanna* stresses that benefiting from the produce is prohibited, while in our case he stresses that the transaction itself is valid. This is because he wishes to point out that although the first case deals with a sale — and not a loan — benefiting from the produce would be

prohibited because of interest; and although the second case deals with a loan, it is permissible if the produce is held in escrow. Alternatively, the second case is maintained to introduce the mishnah's next statement regarding Boesus — who dealt with loans — indicating that this practice is sanctioned by the Sages (*Tos. Yom Tov*).

וְכָךְ הָיָה בַּיְתוֹס בֶּן־זוֹנִין עוֹשֶׂה, עַל־פִּי חֲכָמִים. — *And so was Baisos the son of Zonin wont to do, with the consent of the Sages.*

[He would lend money on the security of a field worth more than the loan, and would take title to it if the debtor was delinquent in his payment, although it appeared to be interest.]

4.

אֵין מוֹשִׁיבִין חֶנְוָנִי לְמַחֲצִית שָׂכָר, — *A storekeeper may not be set up for half the profit,*

One may not commission a storekeeper to sell produce for him, offering him half the profit. For example, he may not buy produce wholesale and give it to the storekeeper to sell retail, and divide the profits earned thereby. The reason for this prohibition is based on the principle that this type of investment, known in the Gemara (104b) as עִיסְקָא, *iska*, is considered a half loan and a half פִּקָּדוֹן, *deposit*. Since half of it is a loan to the storekeeper, he receives the profits or suffers the losses of that portion. Since half of it is a deposit belonging to the investor, the profits or losses of that half are his. This is prohibited because the storekeeper manages the investor's

portion to compensate him for his loan of the other half, which is regarded as interest (*Rav; Rashi*).

וְלֹא יִתֵּן מָעוֹת לִקַּח בָּהֶן פֵּרוֹת לְמַחֲצִית שָׂכָר, — *nor may money be given with which to buy produce at half profit,*

[One should also not give money to a storekeeper to purchase produce in the market and to sell it retail, with the understanding that the storekeeper will receive the profit of half the investment and give the profit of the other half to the investor. As explained above, this is prohibited because it constitutes interest.]

אֶלָּא אִם־בֵּן נוֹתֵן לוֹ שְׂכָרוֹ — *unless he gives him his wages*

[The only permissible manner of making either of the above arrange-

אֶלָּא אִם־כֵּן נוֹתֵן לוֹ שְׂכָרוֹ כְּפוֹעֵל.
אֵין מוֹשִׁיבִין תַּרְנְגוֹלִין לְמֶחֱצָה, וְאֵין שָׁמִין
עֲגָלִין וּסְיָחִין לְמֶחֱצָה, אֶלָּא אִם־כֵּן נוֹתֵן לוֹ שָׂכָר
עֲמָלוֹ וּמְזוֹנוֹ. אֲבָל מְקַבְּלִין עֲגָלִין וּסְיָחִין לְמֶחֱצָה,

יד אברהם

ments is by giving the storekeeper wages for managing the half of the investment that is a deposit. Since he is compensated for managing it, he is not doing so as compensation for the loan he is getting; hence, there is no problem of interest.]

כְּפוֹעֵל. — *as a laborer.*

The *Gemara* (68 a-b) explains this to mean that, for example, if he customarily works at a trade which involves difficult work and pays accordingly, he must be paid how much he would be willing to accept for leaving his difficult work and engaging in the easier, but less lucrative work of managing the investment *(Rav; Rashi)*. [For further elaboration, see commentary to 2:9, s.v. אֶלָּא.]

Tosafos (ad loc.) disagree with *Rashi* and construe the *Gemara* differently. According to *Beis Yosef* (*Yoreh Deah* 177), they explain that he is paid as a laborer who has work to do, but instead agrees to leave his work and sit idle. *Tos. Yom Tov* supports *Beis Yosef's* interpretation of *Tosafos* by citing *Tosafos* to *Berachos* 29b. According to *Chochmas Shlomo*, based on *Tur* (*Yoreh Deah* 177), however, *Tosafos* means that he is paid what an unemployed laborer would accept for doing this work.

Since the storekeeper is being paid merely to avoid the transgression of Rabbinically prohibited interest, this nominal wage is sufficient *(Tos. Yom Tov* from *Rosh)*.

Although these two cases — giving the storekeeper the produce and giving him money to purchase produce — seem to be identical, the *Tanna* found reason to state both of them. Should he have

stated only the case of giving produce, we would think that only in that case is it sufficient to pay the storekeeper as an idle worker, since there is little toil involved. But if he gives him money to purchase produce, a more arduous task, we would be inclined to believe that he must pay him his full wage. On the other hand, if the *Tanna* had stated only the case of giving money, we would think that only in this instance — which involves much toil — must the storekeeper be paid as an idle laborer. But if he gives him produce, since less work is required, even that much is unnecessary, and as long as he gives him any meager compensation — even that of allowing him to dip bread in his vinegar, or sharing a dried fig with him — it would be sufficient. Therefore, both cases must be stated (ibid. from *Gem.* 68b).

אֵין מוֹשִׁיבִין תַּרְנְגוֹלִין לְמֶחֱצָה, — *Hens may not be set to brood at half [profit],*

One may not assess eggs and then give them to someone to have his hen sit on them until they hatch, with the understanding that they will share the added value of the fledglings over the value of the eggs. Since the owner of the hen is responsible for half the loss — e.g., if the eggs spoil or the fledglings die — it is considered that half the eggs are a loan and half are a deposit, as in the above cases. Accordingly, he is managing the investor's share in appreciation for the loan of the other half, which is Rabbinically prohibited interest *(Rav; Rashi)*.

וְאֵין שָׁמִין עֲגָלִין וּסְיָחִין לְמֶחֱצָה, — *nor may calves or foals be assessed at half [profit],*

5
4

wages as a laborer.

Hens may not be set to brood at half [profit], nor may calves or foals be assessed at half [profit], unless he gives him the wage of his toil and his feed. But calves or foals may be accepted for half profit and

YAD AVRAHAM

One may not assess these animals to determine their value and then assign them to someone to raise them for two years with the understanding that they will divide the profits, or — should they die — the loss (ibid.).

אֶלָּא אִם־כֵּן נוֹתֵן לוֹ — *unless he gives him*
[The above two cases are permissible only if the investor gives the one who takes care of the animals the following.]

שְׂכַר עֲמָלוֹ — *the wage of his toil*
As in the cases above, he is paid as a 'laborer' [see the various interpretations of the phrase above, s.v. וּכְפוֹעֵל] *(Rambam, Commentary* and *Hil. Sheluchim* 8:1). *Tosafos,* however, reason that in our case, since all he must do is feed the animals, and the feeding takes but a short time every day, it would be inappropriate to pay him as a 'laborer.' Such an amount is appropriate only in the case of the storekeeper who must sit all day in his store to sell his merchandise *(Tos. Yom Tov).*

וּמְזוֹנוּ. — *and his feed.*
The one who takes care of the fledglings must be paid what he spends for feeding them *(Rav; Rashi).* Needless to say, in the case of the calves of foals as well, the owner must pay for their feed. It was necessary for the mishnah to state this only to tell us that even in the case of the fledglings, although only a minimal amount is required to feed them, it is assumed that the one who raises them relinquishes this amount; rather the owner must pay him for it in order to avoid the transgression of taking interest *(Tos. Yom Tov).*

אֲבָל מְקַבְּלִין עֲגָלִין וּסְיָחִין לִמְחֱצָה, — *But calves or foals may be accepted for half*

profit
One may undertake to care for them if no assessment of them is made, so that he is not responsible for them if they die; but if they live, he shares the profits *(Rav; Rashi).*

[Hence, there is no loan involved here, and he therefore need not be paid for his work or the cost of feeding the animals.]

From this segment of the mishnah we learn that unless stipulated otherwise, one who agrees to raise animals does not take any responsibility for loss. This arrangement is not regarded as a half loan, half deposit, since the animals were not assessed from the outset but only when the time comes to divide the profits. By using the expression *may be accepted,* rather than *may be assessed,* as in the preceding segment of the mishnah, the *Tanna* indicates that no assessment was made at the time the animals were accepted. If, however, the animals *are* assessed at the outset, it is assumed that the one who will care for them accepts half the responsibility for losses *(Tos. Yom Tov from Tos.).*

The same applies in the case of hens (ibid. from *Nimmukei Yosef).*

Rambam (Commentary) explains that the expression *may be accepted* denotes that the one who raises the animal receives a share of the animal itself. In such a case, he is working to take care of his own share, not repaying the investor for a loan. Therefore, he may receive half the profit.

Foals mentioned in the mishnah are *young donkeys.* This is *Tos. Yom Tov's* definition, and so it appears from *Rambam (Hil. Sheluchim* 8:1). *Rashi,* however, explains it as *colts.*

וּמְגַדְּלִין אוֹתָן עַד שֶׁיִּהְיוּ מְשֻׁלָּשִׁין; וַחֲמוֹר, עַד שֶׁתְּהֵא טוֹעֶנֶת.

[ה] שָׁמִין פָּרָה וַחֲמוֹר וְכָל־דָּבָר שֶׁהוּא עוֹשֶׂה
וְאוֹכֵל לְמֶחֱצָה. מְקוֹם שֶׁנָּהֲגוּ
לַחֲלוֹק אֶת־הַוְּלָדוֹת מִיָּד, חוֹלְקִין; מְקוֹם שֶׁנָּהֲגוּ
לְגַדֵּל, יְגַדְּלוּ. רַבָּן שִׁמְעוֹן בֶּן־גַּמְלִיאֵל אוֹמֵר: שָׁמִין

יד אברהם

וּמְגַדְּלִין אוֹתָן עַד שֶׁיִּהְיוּ מְשֻׁלָּשִׁין; — and
raised until they reach a third of their
growth;

This refers to the calves (Beis David).
[According to Rashi, it applies to the
colts, as well.]

At that stage of their growth, the
meat is very tasty [and it was therefore
customary to terminate the partnership
and sell the calves] (Tos. Yom Tov).

Rambam (loc. cit. and Commentary) explains that they would raise the
calves until they were three years old.
Prior to this time, neither one may sell
his share.

וַחֲמוֹר, עַד שֶׁתְּהֵא טוֹעֶנֶת. — and a donkey,
until it can bear [a burden].

[One may accept a donkey to raise it
until this time at half profit. Rambam
(Hil. Sheluchim 8:1) construes this as
referring to the young donkeys mentioned above (Beis David). [According
to Rashi, this is another case, not the
one mentioned previously in the
mishnah.]

It was customary to raise the donkeys
to this age before dividing the profits
(Rav; Rashi).

Before this age, neither one may sell
the donkey without the other's consent
(Rambam, loc. cit.).

Tos. Yom Tov notes that the verb
form טוֹעֶנֶת, bear, is feminine, whereas
the noun חֲמוֹר, donkey, is masculine. He
concludes that the noun — although
grammatically masculine — may refer to
a female donkey, as we find in many
places, both in the Bible and the

Mishnah. Beis David explains that the
female donkeys are later in their development, and reach the stage of bearing
burdens later than males. Therefore, if
one is given male and female donkeys to
raise, he may not terminate the
partnership when the male donkeys are
able to bear burdens, but must wait until
the females are able to do so. He
suggests also that the Tanna alludes to
the practice of raising female donkeys,
since that is more profitable than raising
male donkeys, the former being kept for
reproduction.

Although the mishnah states that in
the case of the half loan, half deposit,
the one who receives the item must be
paid for his toil if he is to receive half
the profit, the Gemara (68b) states that
if they had not made such an agreement
at the outset, and at the end of the
partnership, the investor does not want
to pay the one who raised the animals
for his work, an alternative is that the
worker should receive two-thirds of the
profit if there was one, but if there was a
loss, he is responsible for only half of it.
This extra one-sixth of the profit which
he receives in addition to the half which
is actually due him serves as a remuneration for his caring for the investor's
share of the animals, and thus, there is
no problem with interest. This is the
ruling of most authorities. Rambam
(Hil. Sheluchim 6:3) and Shulchan
Aruch (Yoreh Deah 177:4), however,
interpret the Gemara to mean that in the
case of loss, the investor would be
responsible for two-thirds of the loss,

raised until they reach a third of their growth; and a
donkey, until it can bear [a burden].

5. A cow or a donkey or anything that works and
eats may be assessed at half profit. [In] a place
where they are accustomed to divide the offspring
immediately, they divide [them]; [in] a place where
they are accustomed to raise [them], they must raise
[them]. Rabban Shimon ben Gamliel says: A calf

YAD AVRAHAM

since the recipient must receive his wage
in any case — even if there is a loss —
and, in such an event, his wage would
be that the investor would suffer one-
sixth of the loss above the half that is his
(*Shach* ad loc. §14).

5.

שָׁמִין פָּרָה וַחֲמוֹר וְכָל־דָּבָר שֶׁהוּא עוֹשֶׂה וְאוֹכֵל
לְמֶחֱצָה. — *A cow or a donkey or*
anything that works and eats may be
assessed at half profit.

This refers to a full-grown cow or
full-grown donkey, which is capable of
working (*Rav; Rashi*) [or anything
which does sufficient work to pay for its
keep]. The work belongs to the one who
raises it, and the investor and the
worker share the increase, should the
animal become fatter; or the young,
should it give birth (ibid.).

In contrast to the previous mishnah,
which states that calves or foals may not
be assessed at half profit, unless the
worker is paid for his toil and the feed,
this case deals with older animals, which
do sufficient work to pay for their up-
keep. The work done by the animal is
given to the worker in lieu of the payment for his toil and the feed (*Meiri*).

מְקוֹם שֶׁנָּהֲגוּ לַחֲלוֹק אֶת־הַוְּלָדוֹת מִיָּד, חוֹלְקִין;
— [*In*] *a place where they are*
accustomed to divide the offspring
immediately, they divide [*them*];
[That is, if two persons agreed to the
transaction described above, and the
animal bore offspring, and the custom is
that] after a minimum time period —
viz., for small animals [e.g., sheep and
goats] thirty days, and for large animals

[e.g., cows] fifty days (*Rav, Rashi* from
Gem. 69a) [the offspring are divided
between them, then that is what is done,
and the worker is not obligated to
continue raising the young].

Should the recipient agree to raise the
young of the animals, however, they are
assessed, and he receives three-fourths
of the increase of his partner's share,
since his share is now a half loan, half
deposit. Since he owns part of the
animal, the investor need not pay him
for his toil or for the feed (*Gem.* 69b,
Rashi ad loc.).

מְקוֹם שֶׁנָּהֲגוּ לְגַדֵּל, יְגַדְּלוּ. — [*in*] *a place*
where they are accustomed to raise
[*them*], *they must raise* [*them*].
[If the custom is that the worker
raises the offspring longer than the
minimum period mentioned above, he
must do so.]

Others explain that in those places
where they are accustomed to divide the
offspring immediately, that is done. In
places where the worker raises them, he
must raise them for thirty days, as
above. A custom to raise the young for a
longer period than this, however, need
not be followed (*Rosh; Tur, Yoreh*
Deah 177).

רַבָּן שִׁמְעוֹן בֶּן־גַּמְלִיאֵל אוֹמֵר: שָׁמִין עֵגֶל עִם־

עֵגֶל עִם־אִמּוֹ, וְסֽיָח עִם־אִמּוֹ. וּמַפְרִיז עַל־שָׂדֵהוּ,
וְאֵינוֹ חוֹשֵׁשׁ מִשּׁוּם רִבִּית.

[ו] אֵין מְקַבְּלִין צֹאן בַּרְזֶל מִיִּשְׂרָאֵל, מִפְּנֵי
שֶׁהוּא רִבִּית. אֲבָל מְקַבְּלִין צֹאן בַּרְזֶל
מִן־הַנָּכְרִים, וְלֹוִין מֵהֶן וּמַלְוִין אוֹתָן בְּרִבִּית. וְכֵן

יד אברהם

אָמוֹ, וְסֽיָח עִם־אִמּוֹ.— *Rabban Shimon ben Gamliel says: A calf may be assessed with its mother, and a foal with its mother.*

[Although the previous mishnah states that *calves or foals may not be assessed at half profit,* such an agreement can be made if it is done together with the mother animal.]

The investor need pay only for the toil and feed involved in caring for the mother, not for the offspring (*Rav; Rashi*), since the calf or the foal constantly follows its mother, and the worker has very little to do in caring for it. The little work he does is compensated for by the droppings of the animal, which are used for manure (*Tos. Yom Tov, Tif. Yis.* from *Gem.* 68b, *Rashi*).

Tosafos (ad loc.) explain that although Rabban Shimon ben Gamliel does not mention it, the investor must surely pay for the mother animal's feed, since the droppings cannot compensate for that.

The Sages differ with Rabban Shimon ben Gamliel and maintain that the droppings are of no value, since the owner abandons them (*Tos. Yom Tov* from *Gem.*).

The halachah is not in accordance with Rabban Shimon ben Gamliel (*Rav; Rambam, Commentary* and *Hil. Sheluchim* 8:3).

וּמַפְרִיז עַל־שָׂדֵהוּ, — *One may increase the rent of his field,*

If a landlord is accustomed to rent out his field for ten *korin* per annum, and the tenant offers him twelve *korin* on condition that he lends him two hundred *zuz* with which to purchase fertilizer for the field, he may accept it. Others read: וּמַפְרִין עַל־שָׂדֵהוּ, *One may make his field fruitful* — that is, he may lend the tenant the money to fertilize the field and make it produce more crops (*Rav; Rashi*).

וְאֵינוֹ חוֹשֵׁשׁ מִשּׁוּם רִבִּית. — *and he need not fear that it is interest.*

The tenant may pay the additional two *korin*, since the landlord is renting him a more fertile field, one which can produce more crops (ibid.).

6.

אֵין מְקַבְּלִין צֹאן בַּרְזֶל מִיִּשְׂרָאֵל, — *Fixed-value property* (lit., *iron sheep*) *may not be accepted from a Jew,*

The term צֹאן בַּרְזֶל, *fixed-value property,* refers to property given to a worker for which the latter accepts full responsibility. [As long as the worker does not return the property or the value for which it had been assessed at the time he accepted it, all profits are divided between him and the owner

(*Rav; Rashi*).] Such property is compared to iron, because like iron, its owner — who does not risk suffering a loss — need not worry that it will die, or become ill or the like. It is compared to sheep, since it may bring profit to its owner, like sheep, which give wool, milk, and offspring (*Tif. Yis.; Lechem Shamayim*).

מִפְּנֵי שֶׁהוּא רִבִּית. — *because it is interest.*

5
6
may be assessed with its mother, and a foal with its mother. One may increase the rent of his field, and he need not fear that it is interest.

6. Fixed-value property may not be accepted from a Jew, because it is interest. But fixed-value property may be accepted from gentiles, and we may borrow from them and lend them with interest. And

[Such an agreement is forbidden because of the prohibition of interest.] Since the worker is completely responsible for the investment, it is deemed a loan, and the share of the profits he must give the investor is considered interest (*Rav; Rashi*). *Rambam* (*Hil. Malveh* 8:12) maintains that it is not Biblically prohibited, since the amount of interest had not been stipulated. The Rabbis, however, forbade such an arrangement, since profit is likely and loss is unlikely. *Tosafos* (70b), too, explain that according to *Rashi*, it is prohibited only by Rabbinic law.

Although it is stated in mishnah 4 that it is prohibited to make such an agreement even if the worker accepts only half the responsibility, and it is therefore obvious that this instance — in which he accepts full responsibility — would be prohibited, the *Tanna* states our case as well to teach us that even such an agreement may be made with a gentile investor, as mentioned below (*Rav; Rashi*).

Nimmukei Yosef adds that in this case, even if the investor pays for the toil and the feed, it is prohibited (*Tos. Yom Tov*).

Rabbeinu Tam construes the case as being one in which the sheep are assessed at the time of the agreement, and a certain amount of profit is anticipated. Nevertheless, the worker agrees to pay a fixed amount whether or not there is any profit. Accordingly, this would involve Biblically prohibited interest (*Tos.*).

אֲבָל מְקַבְּלִין צֹאן בַּרְזֶל מִן־הַנָּכְרִים, — *But fixed-value property may be accepted from gentiles,*

[Since one may borrow from gentiles for interest, as stated below, he may also accept fixed-value property from them.] The *Tanna* deemed it necessary to specifically state that this case is permitted, so that we should not think that accepting an investment in which the recipient must bear the full loss while receiving only a share of the profit is tantamount to giving the gentile a free gift, which is prohibited because of לֹא תְחָנֵּם, *You shall not favor them* (*Deut.* 7:2).

וְלֹוִין מֵהֶן וּמַלְוִין אוֹתָן בְּרִבִּית. — *and we may borrow from them and lend them with interest.*

This is derived from the verse (*Deut.* 23:21), לַנָּכְרִי תַשִּׁיךְ, *from the gentile you may take interest.* The *Gemara* (70b) explains that this applies both to a lender and a borrower. The Rabbis, however, prohibited lending money to gentiles for interest, lest one become intimate with them and be attracted to their ways. They permitted it only to those who need it for their livelihood, and scholars, who are not likely to learn from the gentiles' ways. *Tosafos*, noting that we are not scrupulous in our observance of this prohibition, explain that perhaps the halachah is in accordance with other *Amoraim* in the *Gemara* who rule that there was never any prohibition enacted in this matter. Alternatively, since we live among the

תּוֹשָׁב.
מַלְוֶה יִשְׂרָאֵל מָעוֹתָיו שֶׁל־נָכְרִי מִדַּעַת הַנָּכְרִי,
אֲבָל לֹא מִדַּעַת יִשְׂרָאֵל.

[ז] **אֵין** פּוֹסְקִין עַל־הַפֵּרוֹת עַד שֶׁיֵּצֵא הַשַּׁעַר.
יָצָא הַשַּׁעַר, פּוֹסְקִין, וְאַף־עַל־פִּי שֶׁאֵין
לָזֶה, יֵשׁ לָזֶה.

יד אברהם

gentiles and have no other means of earning money other than by doing business with them, there is no reason to prohibit lending them for interest in order not to learn from their ways any more than to prohibit doing any other type of business with them.

וְכֵן בְּגֵר תּוֹשָׁב. — And so it is with a resident alien.

[This term refers to a gentile who lives in the Holy Land and observes the Seven Noachide Commandments which are binding upon all of mankind. They include the prohibitions of idolatry, illicit sexual relations, murder, eating the limbs of a live animal, cursing God's Name, and robbery, as well as the responsibility of establishing a judicial system.

The mishnah tells us that a resident alien is judged as a gentile with regard to the prohibition of interest.]

It is necessary for the Tanna to teach us this, since the precept of sustaining a person in need applies to a resident alien as it does to any Jew, and we would think the same is true of the prohibition of interest stated in the very next verse (Beis David; Shoshannim LeDavid).

מַלְוֶה יִשְׂרָאֵל מָעוֹתָיו שֶׁל־נָכְרִי מִדַּעַת הַנָּכְרִי, — A Jew may lend out a gentile's money with the knowledge of the gentile,

For example, Reuven borrowed money with interest from a gentile and wished to pay him. Shimon then met Reuven and requested that he give him the money, offering to pay Reuven the interest for the amount of time he holds the money, so that Reuven will give this

to the lender when he repays the loan. As long as Reuven introduces Shimon to the gentile and the latter consents to the request, this is permitted, although Reuven is the one who is actually handing over the money to Shimon (Rav).

The Gemara, however, rejects this interpretation, since a Jew cannot serve as a שָׁלִיחַ, agent, for a gentile, and hence it is as if Reuven were lending to Shimon with interest. Instead, the mishnah's case is construed as being one in which the gentile took the money from Reuven and gave it to Shimon. The Tanna teaches us that this is permitted although the gentile is doing so at the behest of Reuven (Tos. Yom Tov; see Tos. R' Akiva).

אֲבָל לֹא מִדַּעַת יִשְׂרָאֵל. — but not with the knowledge of a Jew.

This refers to a case in which, for example, a gentile borrowed money with interest from Reuven and wished to pay him. Shimon then met the gentile, and requested that he give him the money, offering to pay the gentile the interest for the amount of time that he holds the money, so that the gentile will give this to Reuven when he repays the loan. As long as the gentile does not introduce Shimon to Reuven and ask his consent to lend the money to Shimon, it is permitted, although he has lent him money that he owes Reuven. The mishnah is telling us here that if the gentile brings Shimon to Reuven before granting him the loan, he may not pay him the interest. According to Rashi and

so it is with a resident alien.

A Jew may lend out a gentile's money with the knowledge of the gentile, but not with the knowledge of a Jew.

7. A price for produce may not be fixed until the market price is known. When the market price is known, a price may be fixed, and although this one does not have, someone else does have.

YAD AVRAHAM

Rabbeinu Chananel, this is because the gentile is lending the money as Reuven's agent, making Reuven the lender and Shimon the borrower. Although there is a principle in Biblical law that a gentile cannot serve as an agent, the Rabbis instituted that in cases in which granting the power of agency to the gentile would prove to be a stringency [for the Jews involved] — as in our case, since it would thereby be prohibited for him to give the money to Shimon — he is granted that power.

Rabbeinu Tam, however, qualifies this case in a manner similar to the previous case — i.e., it is prohibited only

if Reuven took the money from the gentile and gave it to Shimon. Otherwise, the gentile may lend it to Shimon with interest, since he has no power of agency whatever *(Tos. Yom Tov).*

Rav and *Meiri* explain this phrase in the mishnah as referring to the previous case, in which a Jew borrowed from the gentile. The *Tanna* is telling us that if Reuven does not return the money to the gentile before the latter lends it to Shimon, Reuven would be considered the lender, and Shimon, the borrower. Such an arrangement would therefore be prohibited.

7.

אֵין פּוֹסְקִין עַל־הַפֵּרוֹת — *A price for produce may not be fixed*

One may not stipulate with a merchant to supply him with produce at a certain time for a certain rate and pay him for it in advance *(Tos. Yom Tov from Nimmukei Yosef).*

עַד שֶׁיֵּצֵא הַשַּׁעַר. — *until the market price is known.*

Since the market price is not yet known, it is possible that it will be higher than the stipulated price. If it is, the purchaser will have received the produce at the lower price because he paid in advance, and in effect, received interest for lending money to the vendor (ibid.; *Tif. Yis.*).

יָצָא הַשַּׁעַר, — *When the market price is known,*

That is, when there is already a set price *(Tif. Yis.).*

פּוֹסְקִין, — *a price may be fixed,*

[The vendor may stipulate to supply the merchant produce at the present market price.]

Some editions delete this sentence, since it can be deduced from the preceding one *(Tos. 62b).*

וְאַף־עַל־פִּי שֶׁאֵין לָזֶה, — *and although this one does not have,*

Although this vendor does not have the produce at the time of the stipulation, they may nevertheless agree to such a transaction at the market price, and there is no problem of interest *(Tif. Yis.).*

יֵשׁ לָזֶה. — *someone else does have.*

הָיָה הוּא תְּחִלָּה לַקּוֹצְרִים, פּוֹסֵק עִמּוֹ עַל־
הַגָּדִישׁ, וְעַל־הֶעָבִיט שֶׁל־עֲנָבִים, וְעַל הַמַּעֲטָן שֶׁל־
זֵיתִים, וְעַל־הַבֵּיצִים שֶׁל־יוֹצֵר, וְעַל־הַסִּיד
מִשֶּׁשִּׁקְעוֹ בַּכִּבְשָׁן. וּפוֹסֵק עִמּוֹ עַל־הַזֶּבֶל כָּל־יְמוֹת
הַשָּׁנָה. רַבִּי יוֹסֵי אוֹמֵר: אֵין פּוֹסְקִין עַל־הַזֶּבֶל,
אֶלָּא אִם־כֵּן הָיָה לוֹ זֶבֶל בָּאַשְׁפָּה; וַחֲכָמִים
מַתִּירִין.

יד אברהם

Even if the price rises subsequently, the purchaser can claim that the vendor did him no favor by giving him the produce at the earlier market price, since had he not paid him, he would have been able to purchase it elsewhere at that price (*Tos. Yom Tov* from *Gem.* 63b).

Although the purchaser did not yet take possession of the produce, it is not considered interest if the price rises. Since the seller cannot retract without being subject to the Rabbinical curse of מִי שֶׁפָּרַע ..., *May He Who exacted retribution* ... (4:2), it is considered as though he had taken possession of the produce, and it gained value in his possession (*Tos.* 62b).

Apparently, *Tosafos* hold that without some act of acquisition, the prohibition of interest still applies. This view coincides with those of *Rashi* and *Maggid Mishneh* (*Hil. Mechirah* 22:3), as was discussed at the beginning of this chapter. *Ravad* (ibid. 7:4), however, rules that the transaction is permitted even without any act of acquisition. Since the prohibition of interest in this case would be Rabbinical, the Rabbis have the power to deal leniently with a prohibition that they themselves instituted. Therefore, in our case, they regard it as though the purchaser has the produce in his possession at the time of the transaction, since it is available elsewhere (*Tos. Yom Tov*). When the price rises, if both parties agree, they may assess the produce in question at a higher price, and the vendor can give the purchaser other produce for that amount. Whether he may give him money instead of produce is questionable (*Tif. Yis.* from *Yoreh Deah* 175:6).

הָיָה הוּא תְּחִלָּה לַקּוֹצְרִים, — [If] *he was the first of the reapers,*

The seller was the first of the reapers, and he already has a stack of grain although the market price is not yet known (*Rav; Rashi*).

פּוֹסֵק עִמּוֹ — *he may fix a price with him*

The seller may make an agreement with the purchaser at any price he desires (*Rav; Rashi*).

עַל־הַגָּדִישׁ, — *on the stack of grain,*

Since the seller has the grain in his possession, even if the price they fixed is higher than the market price, it is not considered interest. Although the purchaser did not yet perform an act of acquisition — since it involves only Rabbinical interest, the Rabbis dealt leniently in the case that the seller has the grain in his possession (*Rav; Rashi*). [The same applies to all the other items listed below.]

As explained above, this is only because the seller is subject to the Rabbinical curse if he retracts on the transaction. In this context, that is regarded as an act of acquisition (*Tos. Yom Tov*).

וְעַל־הֶעָבִיט שֶׁל־עֲנָבִים, וְעַל־הַמַּעֲטָן שֶׁל־זֵיתִים, — *or on the vat of grapes, or on the vat of olives,*

[A seller may fix a price for these

5
7

[If] he was the first of the reapers, he may fix a price with him on the stack of grain, or on the vat of grapes, or on the vat of olives, or on the clay balls of a potter, or on lime after it has been sunk into the kiln. He may fix a price on manure all the days of the year. R' Yose says: A price may not be fixed on manure, unless he had manure in the dung heap; the Sages, however, permit [it].

YAD AVRAHAM

even if the market price is not yet known.]

According to *Rav* and *Rashi*, these are large vats in which grapes or olives are gathered prior to their being pressed for wine or oil. In them, the fruits become warm, and the extraction of the juice is facilitated *(Rav; Rashi)*.

Rambam (Commentary to Tahoros 10:4) defines these as pits dug in the ground where the fruits are placed before being pressed.

וְעַל־הַבֵּיצִים שֶׁל־יוֹצֵר, — *or on the clay balls of a potter,*

If a potter has taken earth and formed clay balls from which to make pots, he may agree to supply a purchaser with pots at a certain price, although the market price is still unknown *(Rav; Rashi)*.

וְעַל־הַסִּיד מִשֶּׁשְּׁקָעוֹ בַכִּבְשָׁן. — *or on lime after it has been sunk into the kiln.*

The same applies to lime after the wood and limestones have already been lowered into the furnace to be burnt and made into quicklime (ibid.).

Although all the aforementioned items are not yet completed, the manufacturer may nevertheless agree to supply his customer with them at a certain price. This is permitted only if no more than two steps in the production are missing. Should three steps be missing, such an agreement may not be made. The *Gemara* (74a) explains that the grain in the mishnah's case has already been spread out and dried; it requires merely threshing and winnowing. The grapes need only be

placed in the press and trodden. Although there is a third step — drawing the wine into the pit — the case is one in which it is customary for the buyer to do this step. [The maximum two steps refer to those done by the seller.] The olives are already a heated mass. They require to be placed between the boards and pressed; drawing the oil into the pit is done by the purchaser. The clay balls have already been molded and dried. They need only be placed in the oven and baked; the purchaser takes them out of the oven. In the case of lime, it requires only to be burnt and removed from the kiln; the purchaser crushes it.

וּפוֹסֵק עִמּוֹ עַל־הַזֶּבֶל — *He may fix a price on manure*

[One may agree to supply his customer with manure for fertilizer at a certain price.]

כָּל־יְמוֹת הַשָּׁנָה. — *all the days of the year.*

That is, even during the winter, when manure is not available *(Rav from Gem.* 74b).

רַבִּי יוֹסֵי אוֹמֵר: אֵין פּוֹסְקִין עַל־הַזֶּבֶל, אֶלָּא אִם־ כֵּן הָיָה לוֹ זֶבֶל בָּאַשְׁפָּה; — *R' Yose says: A price may not be fixed on manure, unless he had manure in the dung heap,*

R' Yose does not differentiate between winter and summer. He does, however, require that the seller have manure in his dung heap at the time of the agreement *(Rav; Rashi* to *Gem.* ibid.).

וַחֲכָמִים מַתִּירִין. — *the Sages, however, permit [it].*

The Sages do not require that the

וּפוֹסֵק עִמּוֹ כְּשַׁעַר הַגָּבוֹהַּ. רַבִּי יְהוּדָה אוֹמֵר:
אַף־עַל־פִּי שֶׁלֹּא פָסַק עִמּוֹ כַּשַּׁעַר הַגָּבוֹהַּ, יָכוֹל
הוּא לוֹמַר: "תֶּן־לִי כָזֶה, אוֹ תֶּן־לִי מָעוֹתָי."

[ח] **מַלְוֶה** אָדָם אֶת־אֲרִיסָיו חִטִּין בְּחִטִּין —
לְזֶרַע, אֲבָל לֹא לֶאֱכֹל. שֶׁהָיָה רַבָּן

יד אברהם

seller have manure in his dung heap at the time, but they permit fixing a price on manure only during the summer, when it is available, since it has been trodden and has decayed over the winter. Therefore, even if he does not have any, we rely on the fact that others certainly do (ibid.).

The halachah follows the view of the Sages (Rav; Rosh). Rambam (Hil. Malveh 9:1) and Meiri, however, rule in accordance with the opinion of the first, anonymous Tanna.

וּפוֹסֵק עִמּוֹ כְּשַׁעַר הַגָּבוֹהַּ. — He may fix a price with him at the best rate.

That is, the cheapest rate. The Tanna uses the word הַגָּבוֹהַּ [lit., the highest] to indicate that the buyer is getting a large amount of produce for little money (Rav; Rashi).

This sentence refers back to the statement above יָצָא הַשַּׁעַר, פּוֹסְקִין, When the market price is known, a price may be fixed. Although as stated in the commentary (ad loc.) some editions do not have that reading, according to them, the Tanna is referring to the ruling that is deduced from the mishnah's first statement, as explained there (Tos. Yom Tov from Rambam loc. cit. §5 and Tur Yoreh Deah 175).

The intention is that once the market price is known, the buyer may stipulate that if the price subsequently goes down, the seller will supply him with

the merchandise at the lower price (Rav; Rashi), but if it stays the same, or rises, he will give it to him for the price at the time of this agreement (Tif. Yis.; see Meiri).

רַבִּי יְהוּדָה אוֹמֵר: אַף־עַל־פִּי שֶׁלֹּא פָסַק עִמּוֹ — כַּשַּׁעַר הַגָּבוֹהַּ, יָכוֹל הוּא לוֹמַר: "תֶּן־לִי כָזֶה, R' Yehudah says: Although he did not stipulate with him at the best rate, he may say: 'Give me at such [a price],

[R' Yehudah maintains that although it had not been initially stipulated that should the price fall, the seller will give the item at the lower price, if the price does fall, the buyer may insist that the seller either do so or return his money to him.] R' Yehudah reasons that every buyer's intention is to receive the item at the best rate possible, even if he does not specify this (Meiri).

אוֹ תֶּן־לִי מָעוֹתָי." — or give me my money.'

Since the buyer did not perform an act of acquisition, he may still retract. In such a case, he is not subject to the Rabbinic curse mentioned above; since he gave the money with the intention of receiving the item only at a later time, rather than immediately, it is assumed that he intended to receive the item at the lower price in the event the price falls (Rav; Rashi).

The halachah is not in accordance with the view of R' Yehudah (Rav; Rambam Commentary).

8.

⋑§ Lending a seah for a seah

The following two mishnayos deal with the Rabbinic prohibition of lending 'a seah for a seah' — that is, lending a certain amount of produce or merchandise with

5
8

He may fix a price with him at the best rate. R'
Yehudah says: Although he did not stipulate with
him at the best rate, he may say: 'Give me at such [a
price], or give me my money.'

8. **A** person may lend his sharecroppers wheat for
wheat — for sowing, but not for eating. For

YAD AVRAHAM

the intention of being repaid with the same amount of that item. It is forbidden
because if the item gains in value, the creditor would be receiving more than he lent,
which would constitute Rabbinically prohibited interest. In some instances,
however, the Sages permitted this practice; namely, if the market price is known, or
if the debtor has any of this item in his possession. The reason these instances
would be permitted is that since this type of produce is available to the debtor, and
he can pay his debt with it, it is as though the creditor has already acquired it, and it
is the latter's item that has gained in value. Even if, for example, the debtor has only
one *seah* of this type of produce, he may borrow many *se'in* against it. This is
because when he borrows the first *seah*, it is as though he has two *se'in* — the
original one and the borrowed one — against which he can borrow two more *se'in*.
Once he does that, it is as if he owns four *se'in*, against which he can borrow
another four *se'in*, and so on. If, however, the debtor does not have any produce,
and the market price is not known, he may not borrow a *seah* for a *seah*; rather, the
value of the item must be assessed at the time it is borrowed, and that amount of
money is paid to the creditor upon the termination of the loan.

If the item was borrowed without being assessed, and the price has dropped, the
debt may be repaid with produce; if the price has risen, however, the monetary
value of the item at the time of the loan must be paid.

According to *Rambam (Hil. Malveh 10:2)*, even if the market price is known and
the debtor has such merchandise in his possession, such a loan is permitted only if it
was made without specifying the time of payment. Should the time have been
specified, the loan is prohibited in all instances. *Maggid Mishneh* explains that since
the lender and borrower set a date for the payment of the loan, their intention was
that if the price would rise, the debtor should pay the higher amount, which would
constitute Rabbinically prohibited interest. *Ravad* and *Rashba* disagree,
maintaining that it makes no difference whether or not the time of payment was
specified.

The following mishnah deals with lending seeds to an אָרִיס, *sharecropper* — i.e., a
worker who contracts to plow a field and seed it, receiving a portion of the crop as
his pay.

מַלְוֶה אָדָם אֶת־אֲרִיסָיו חִטִּין בְּחִטִּין — *A*
person may lend his sharecroppers
wheat for wheat —

Although one may not lend a *seah* for
a *seah* [as explained in the preface], he
may lend his sharecroppers wheat, and
have them repay the debt with wheat,
even if the price rises *(Meiri; Tif. Yis.)*.

לִזְרַע, — *for sowing,*

That is, the above is true if the owner

of the field gives the sharecroppers the
seeds for the purpose of sowing the
field. The Gemara (74b) qualifies the
mishnah as referring to places where it
is customary that the sharecropper supplies the seeds. Since the sharecroppers
in this case have no seeds, the owner
may dismiss them, even if they have
already entered the field and plowed it.
If, instead, he chooses to supply them
with seeds, it is tantamount to making a

בבא
מציעא
ה/ט

גַּמְלִיאֵל מַלְוֶה אֶת־אֲרִיסָיו חִטִּין בְּחִטִּין לְזֶרַע,
בִּיקֵּר וְהוֹזְלוּ, אוֹ בְזֹל וְהוּקְרוּ, נוֹטֵל מֵהֶן כְּשַׁעַר
הַזֹּל — וְלֹא מִפְּנֵי שֶׁהֲלָכָה כֵן, אֶלָּא שֶׁרָצָה
לְהַחֲמִיר עַל־עַצְמוֹ.

[ט] **לֹא יֹאמַר** אָדָם לַחֲבֵרוֹ: ,,הַלְוֵנִי כוֹר
חִטִּים וַאֲנִי אֶתֵּן לְךָ לַגֹּרֶן.''
אֲבָל אוֹמֵר לוֹ: ,,הַלְוֵנִי עַד שֶׁיָּבֹא בְנִי,'' אוֹ: ,,עַד
שֶׁאֶמְצָא מַפְתֵּחַ.'' וְהִלֵּל אוֹסֵר. וְכֵן הָיָה הִלֵּל

יד אברהם

new agreement, stipulating that the seeds will be deducted from their share. Consequently, when the sharecropper returns the seeds, he is not repaying a loan, but is rather deducting this amount from his usual share of the crops and no prohibition would be involved even if the wheat had gained in value (*Rav; Rashi* to *Gem.* 74b).

In places where the custom is that the owner supplies the seeds, however, he may lend the sharecroppers seeds only before they enter the field by stipulating that — contrary to the local custom — he wants them to provide the seeds. Thus, when they return the seeds, they are merely deducting from their share, as in the case above. Once the sharecroppers enter the field, however, the landlord no longer has the right to dismiss them. Therefore, the custom that the owner must provide the seeds prevails. If the sharecroppers then agree to supply the seeds, it would be a completely new agreement. If the landlord lends them the seeds, it would be a regular loan, just as if he would lend seeds to a stranger. Therefore, should the price rise, the sharecroppers would not be allowed to pay back the same amount of seeds (*Gem.*).

אֲבָל לֹא לֶאֱכֹל — *but not for eating.*
[Lending wheat to one's sharecroppers for food is no different than lending to strangers. It is not related to

the stipulation made regarding sharing the crops.]

שֶׁהָיָה רַבָּן גַּמְלִיאֵל מַלְוֶה אֶת־אֲרִיסָיו חִטִּין בְּחִטִּין לְזֶרַע, — *For Rabban Gamliel would lend his sharecroppers wheat for wheat for sowing,*
It was necessary for the *Tanna* to teach us that the above practice is permitted, since Rabban Gamliel would lend his sharecroppers wheat for wheat for sowing, and if the price would change after the original agreement, he would accept wheat in return only according to the lesser of the two prices, as explained below (*Rav; Rashi*).

בִּיקֵּר וְהוֹזְלוּ, — *[and if he lent them] at a high price and it became cheap,*
He lent them the wheat when it was expensive [and it became cheap when the debt became due].

אוֹ בְזֹל וְהוּקְרוּ, — *or [if he lent them] at a cheap price and it became expensive,*
[The wheat was cheap at the time of the loan, but its price rose prior to the time of payment.]

נוֹטֵל מֵהֶן כְּשַׁעַר הַזֹּל— — *he would take from them at the cheap price —*
If, for example, wheat had been expensive at the time of the loan, a *seah* costing two *selaim*, and then the price fell and a *seah* costed one *sela*, Rabban Gamliel would accept only one *seah*, the amount of grain he had lent them, as

מִשְׁנָיוֹת / בבא מציעא — פרק ה: איזהו נשך [146]

Rabban Gamliel would lend his sharecroppers wheat for wheat for sowing, [and if he lent them] at a high price and it became cheap, or [if he lent them] at a cheap price and it became expensive, he would take from them at the cheap price — not because the law is so, but because he wished to be stringent with himself.

9. A person may not say to another: 'Lend me a *kor* of wheat and I will pay you at threshing time.' But he may say to him: 'Lend me until my son comes,' or 'until I find the key.' Hillel, however,

YAD AVRAHAM

payment. Should wheat have been cheap at the time of the loan — e.g., one *seah* costing a *sela* — and then it became more expensive, one *seah* costing two *selaim*, he would accept only half a *seah*, the value he gave them at the time of the loan, as payment (*Tos. Yom Tov*).

וְלֹא מִפְּנֵי שֶׁהֲלָכָה כֵן, אֶלָּא שֶׁרָצָה לְהַחֲמִיר עַל־עַצְמוֹ. — *not because the law is so, but because he wished to be stringent with himself.*

[Rabban Gamliel did not maintain that the halachah dictated that he must do this, but merely acted stringently.]

9.

The following mishnah continues the discussion of the prohibition of lending a *seah* for a *seah*.

לֹא יֹאמַר אָדָם לַחֲבֵרוֹ: "הַלְוֵנִי כּוֹר חִטִּים וַאֲנִי אֶתֵּן לְךָ לַגֹּרֶן." — *A person may not say to another: 'Lend me a kor of wheat and I will pay you at threshing time.'*

Although the price of wheat seldom rises during this time, the Rabbis prohibited such a loan in the event that the price does rise, and the creditor would thereby receive more value than he had given (*Tos. Yom Tov* from *Tos.* 75a).

Rambam (*Hil. Malveh* 10:1,2) deduces from here that if the lender and borrower set a certain time for repaying the loan, even if the market price is known, and the borrower has produce of this type in his possession, such a loan is prohibited. [Other authorities disagree, as discussed in the preface to mishnah 8.]

אֲבָל אוֹמֵר לוֹ: — *But he may say to him:*
[A person may make the following

agreement with another.]

"הַלְוֵנִי עַד שֶׁיָּבֹא בְּנִי," אוֹ: "עַד שֶׁאֶמְצָא מַפְתֵּחַ." — *'Lend me until my son comes,' or 'until I find the key.'*

[In other words, he has such produce in his possession, but cannot get to it without his son or without finding the key.]

According to this anonymous *Tanna* — who shall be referred to as 'the Sages' — the Rabbis prohibited lending a *seah* for a *seah* only if the borrower does not have in his possession the type of item being lent, as explained above.

Although, in our case, he does not presently have access to the wheat, it is nevertheless sufficient to permit such a loan. Should he have even one *seah* of the produce, he may borrow many *se'in* against it. *Rashi* explains that when he borrows the second *seah*, the first *seah*

בבא אוֹמֵר: לֹא תַלְוֶה אִשָּׁה כִּכָּר לַחֲבֶרְתָּהּ עַד
מציעא שֶׁתַּעֲשֶׂנּוּ דָמִים, שֶׁמָּא יוֹקִירוּ חִטִּים, וְנִמְצְאוּ
ה/י בָּאוֹת לִידֵי רִבִּית.

[י] אוֹמֵר אָדָם לַחֲבֵרוֹ: ,,נַכֵּשׁ עִמִּי וַאֲנַכֵּשׁ
עִמָּךְ,'' ,,עֲדֹר עִמִּי וְאֶעְדֹּר עִמָּךְ'';
וְלֹא יֹאמַר לוֹ: ,,נַכֵּשׁ עִמִּי וְאֶעְדֹּר עִמָּךְ,'' ,,עֲדֹר

יד אברהם

he borrowed may be returned by purchasing other produce. As long as, at the time of the loan, he borrowed the *seah* against the *seah* he had in his possession, it does not matter that it no longer stands as collateral for that loan. It is analogous to eating the *seah* after the loan, which he is permitted to do. Therefore, that one *seah* can serve as collateral for the second, third, or fourth *seah*, ad infinitum. *Maggid Mishneh* explains, as mentioned above, that when he borrows one *seah*, it is regarded as if he has two *se'in*, against which he already can borrow two more *se'in*, and so on (*Tos. Yom Tov*).

וְהֵלֵל אוֹסֵר. — *Hillel, however, prohibits* [*it*].

The halachah is in accordance with the Sages — i.e., the first, anonymous *Tanna* (*Rav*).

וְכֵן הָיָה הִלֵּל אוֹמֵר: לֹא תַלְוֶה אִשָּׁה כִּכָּר לַחֲבֶרְתָּהּ עַד שֶׁתַּעֲשֶׂנּוּ דָמִים, — *And so Hillel used to say: A woman may not lend another a loaf until she assesses its price,*

At the time of the loan, she must determine the price of the loaf, and if the price subsequently rises, the borrower must pay her no more than the price of the loaf that had been borrowed (*Meiri*).

Tiferes Yisrael conjectures that this stringent ruling of Hillel may apply only to women, who are usually parsimonious even with small amounts of food, as mentioned in the *Gemara* (87a).

Men, however, are not particular about such small amounts, and may, therefore, lend others bread without assessing it.

שֶׁמָּא יוֹקִירוּ חִטִּים, וְנִמְצְאוּ בָּאוֹת לִידֵי רִבִּית. — *for perhaps wheat will become expensive, and they will come to [a transgression of] interest.*

[If the loaf is not assessed at the time of the loan, and the price subsequently rises, and the borrower repays the lender with a similar loaf, she will be paying Rabbinically prohibited interest.]

The Sages, however, rule that one may lend a loaf to another without having it assessed, and the latter may repay the debt with a similar loaf (*Rav* from *Gem.* 75a).

Beis Yosef (162) gives two reasons why it is necessary for the mishnah — after stating that Hillel prohibits a case of 'a *seah* for a *seah*' even if the borrower has such produce in his possession — to add that he prohibits also a case of 'a loaf for a loaf' without assessing it:

(1) In addition to permitting the loan of 'a *seah* for a *seah*,' if the borrower has produce of that type, the Sages permitted lending 'a loaf for a loaf' even if the borrower does not have one and the market price is not known, because a small article, such as a loaf of bread, is readily available, and it is considered as though the market price of it is known. Another reason is that people are usually not particular concerning such a

prohibits [it]. And so Hillel used to say: A woman may not lend another a loaf until she assesses its price, for perhaps wheat will become expensive, and they will come to [a transgression of] interest.

10. **A** person may say to another: 'Weed with me and I will weed with you,' [or] 'Hoe with me and I will hoe with you'; but he may not say to him: 'Weed with me and I will hoe with you,' [or] 'Hoe

small item. Hillel differs with the Sages on both rulings and rules that even a loaf of bread must be assessed before lending it.

(2) Alternatively, the Sages did not permit lending a loaf of bread unless the borrower has at least one more in his possession, or the market price is known, because they do not differentiate between 'a *seah* for a *seah*' and 'a loaf for a loaf.' Accordingly, although Hillel had made a statement regarding 'a loaf for a loaf' only, the *Tanna* deduces that the same applies to 'a *seah* for a *seah*.' The mishnah therefore states: *Hillel, however, prohibits it; and so* [i.e., since] *Hillel used to say: A woman may*

not lend another a loaf ... (Tos. Yom Tov).

Meiri, apparently agreeing with the first explanation given by *Beis Yosef*, adds two more reasons for ruling more leniently in the case of loaves than in the case of grain. One is that since a loaf of bread is a small item, it is usually lent out for only a day or two, and in such a short period of time, it is unusual for the price to change. Another reason is that even if the debtor has only flour, since only two steps are required to make it into bread (kneading and baking), it is regarded as if he has bread, as discussed above in the commentary to mishnah 7, s.v. מִשֶּׁקְעוּ.

10.

This mishnah deals with the following types of interest:

(1) *Interest paid by work* — for example, one person says to another: 'Work for me today, and I will repay you tomorrow by doing even more work for you';

(2) *Interest paid in advance, and interest paid afterward;*

(3) רִבִּית דְּבָרִים, *interest with words.*

אוֹמֵר אָדָם לַחֲבֵרוֹ: ,,נַכֵּשׁ עִמִּי וַאֲנַכֵּשׁ עִמָּךְ,"
A person may say to another: 'Weed with me and I will weed with you,'

The translation of the word נַכֵּשׁ as *weed* follows *Rav, Rashi,* and *Aruch. Rambam (Commentary)* renders: *Dig at the roots of the trees.*

The intention is that, for example, Reuven may say to Shimon: 'Weed with me in my field, and I will weed with you at a later date in your field.' We do not fear that weeding at the later date may prove more difficult, that workers'

wages may rise, or that perhaps the day of the repayment is longer than the day of the initial work, so that the work given in repayment by Reuven will be worth more than that initially done by Shimon *(Meiri).*

,,עֲדֹר עִמִּי וְאֶעְדֹר עִמָּךְ," — [or] *'Hoe with me and I will hoe with you';*

'Hoe my field with me today, and I will hoe your field with you at a later date' *(Tif. Yis.).*

וְלֹא יֹאמַר לוֹ: ,,נַכֵּשׁ עִמִּי וְאֶעְדֹר עִמָּךְ," ,,עֲדֹר

עֲמִי וַאֲנַכֵּשׁ עִמָּךְ."

כָּל־יְמֵי גָרִיד אֶחָד, כָּל־יְמֵי רְבִיעָה אֶחָד. לֹא
יֹאמַר לוֹ: „חֲרֹשׁ עִמִּי בַגָּרִיד, וַאֲנִי אֶחֱרֹשׁ עִמָּךְ
בָּרְבִיעָה." רַבָּן גַּמְלִיאֵל אוֹמֵר: יֵשׁ רִבִּית מֻקְדֶּמֶת,
וְיֵשׁ רִבִּית מְאֻחֶרֶת. כֵּיצַד? נָתַן עֵינָיו לִלְווֹת הֵימֶנּוּ,
וְהָיָה מְשַׁלֵּחַ לוֹ וְאוֹמֵר: „בִּשְׁבִיל שֶׁתַּלְוֵנִי" — זוֹ

יד אברהם

עֲמִי וַאֲנַכֵּשׁ עִמָּךְ." — *but he may not say to him: 'Weed with me and I will hoe with you,' [or] 'Hoe with me and I will weed with you.'*

Reuven, for example, may not ask Shimon to do one of these tasks with him on one day, and then repay Shimon by doing the other type of work with him at a later date. We fear that since the two types of labor are different, one may be more difficult than the other. It is therefore very possible that Reuven will be repaying Shimon with more valuable work than he had received from Shimon. Shimon is gaining this extra work because he allows Reuven to pay at a later date, which constitutes Rabbinically prohibited interest (*Rav; Rashi; Tos. Yom Tov; Meiri*).

כָּל־יְמֵי גָרִיד אֶחָד, — *All the days of the dry season are alike,*

That is, we are not concerned that on one day the work will be harder than on another day in the same season or that one day may be longer than the other, since people are not particular about these small differences. Therefore, a person may say to another on a summer day: 'Weed with me today, and I will weed with you on another day later in the summer' (*Rav; Rashi*).

כָּל־יְמֵי רְבִיעָה אֶחָד. — *[and] all the days of the rainy season are alike.*

Likewise, all the days of the winter are alike, and one may say to another on a winter day, 'Weed with me today, and I will weed with you later in the winter' (*Rav*).

לֹא יֹאמַר לוֹ: „חֲרֹשׁ עִמִּי בַגָּרִיד, וַאֲנִי אֶחֱרֹשׁ עִמָּךְ בָּרְבִיעָה." — *[However] he may not say to him: 'Plow with me during the dry season, and I will plow with you during the rainy season.'*

Working in the field in the summer, when the weather is dry, is easier than working in the field during the winter, when the weather is rainy. *Rambam (Commentary)* explains that during the summer the terrain is cleaner and the day is longer (*Tos. Yom Tov*).

If, for example, the agreement was that Shimon would plow Reuven's entire field in the summer, and that Reuven would repay Shimon by plowing his entire field in the winter, this is considered interest. Since plowing in the winter is more difficult and the day is shorter, Reuven will have to work harder and more days to complete his job than Shimon did. He is therefore paying Shimon interest, because the latter gave him time to repay the debt. However, should the agreement be that Reuven will do a day's work for Shimon in return, he would be obliged to accomplish only what he can during the shorter day, also taking into consideration that the work is more difficult; hence, there would be no interest involved (*Shoshannim LeDavid*).

רַבָּן גַּמְלִיאֵל אוֹמֵר: יֵשׁ רִבִּית מֻקְדֶּמֶת, — *Rabban Gamliel says: There is interest paid in advance,*

[That is, even if the interest for a loan is paid before the item is borrowed, it is

5

10

with me and I will weed with you.'

All the days of the dry season are alike, [and] all the days of the rainy season are alike. [However] he may not say to him: 'Plow with me during the dry season, and I will plow with you during the rainy season.'

Rabban Gamliel says: There is interest paid in advance, and there is interest paid afterward. How? [If] he decided to borrow from him, and he sent to him and said: '[I am doing so] in order that you lend

prohibited.]

וְיֵשׁ רִבִּית מֵאַחֶרֶת. — *and there is interest paid afterward.*

Interest may not be paid even some time after the loan has been paid. Both of the above are Rabbinically prohibited (*Tos. Yom Tov* from *Rambam, Hil. Malveh* 5:11).

Although *Rambam*, in his *Commentary* — with regard to these types of interest — states merely that it is proper to distance oneself from such types of interest, *Tos. Yom Tov* construes this as meaning that there is no Biblical prohibition on these types of interest; they are forbidden only Rabbinically.

[It is, however, possible that *Rambam* alludes to the ruling of *Rashba* — quoted by *Beis Yosef* 161 (*Yoreh Deah*) and *Rama* (ibid. §2) that, whereas other types of Rabbinically prohibited interest should be returned in order to fulfill one's duty to Heaven, interest paid in advance or afterward need not be returned. In other words, if one is repenting for his sins and wishes to return the interest he received for loans, he need not return interest paid in advance or afterward. Other types of Rabbinically prohibited interest, on the other hand, must be returned, although the court cannot compel him to do so. If he took Biblically prohibited interest, however, the court can compel him to return it.

This may be what *Rambam* means: it

is proper to distance oneself from these types of interest, but if one already took them, they need not be returned (see *Beur HaGra* ad loc.).]

כֵּיצַד נָתַן עֵינָיו לִלְוֹת הֵימֶנּוּ, — *How? [If] he decided (lit., set his eyes) to borrow from him,*

[One person decided to request a loan from another.]

וְהָיָה מְשַׁלֵּחַ לוֹ וְאוֹמֵר: ,,בִּשְׁבִיל שֶׁתַּלְוֵנִי'' — *and he sent to him and said: '[I am doing so] in order that you lend me' —*

[The prospective borrower sent the person from whom he wished to lend a gift, stating that he was doing so to encourage the latter to grant him a loan.]

This is the reading of most editions of the mishnah. Accordingly, such a loan is prohibited only if the one who intends to borrow states explicitly that he is giving the gift with that intention. It would be permitted, however, to give a gift without stating that his intention is to borrow money (*Tur, Yoreh Deah* 160; *Rama* ibid. §6). Should he give him a large gift, it would be prohibited even if he does not specify his intentions, since it is obvious that he is doing so in order that he lend him money (*Tur* from *Rosh; Maggid Mishneh* from *Rashi; Rama* from *Semag*).

Other editions read: בִּשְׁבִיל שֶׁיַּלְוֵנִי, *in order that he lend me* — that is, his intention is that the person should lend him money, but he does not say this explicitly; nevertheless, it is prohibited.

הִיא רִבִּית מֻקְדֶּמֶת. לָוָה הֵימֶנּוּ, וְהֶחֱזִיר לוֹ אֶת־
מְעוֹתָיו, וְהָיָה מְשַׁלֵּחַ לוֹ, וְאָמַר: ,,בִּשְׁבִיל מָעוֹתֶיךָ
שֶׁהָיוּ בְטֵלוֹת אֶצְלִי״ — זוֹ הִיא רִבִּית מְאֻחֶרֶת.
רַבִּי שִׁמְעוֹן אוֹמֵר: יֵשׁ רִבִּית דְּבָרִים — לֹא יֹאמַר
לוֹ: ,,דַּע כִּי בָא אִישׁ פְּלוֹנִי מִמָּקוֹם פְּלוֹנִי.״

[יא] וְאֵלּוּ עוֹבְרִין בְּלֹא תַעֲשֶׂה: הַמַּלְוֶה,
וְהַלֹּוֶה, וְהֶעָרֵב, וְהָעֵדִים. וַחֲכָמִים
אוֹמְרִים: אַף הַסּוֹפֵר. עוֹבְרִים מִשּׁוּם: ,,לֹא־תִתֵּן,״

יד אברהם

This is the view of *Rambam* (Hil.
Malveh 5:11, according to *Tur Shulchan Aruch* ibid.). According to this
ruling, it is possible that should he state
his intention to the lender, it is deemed
רִבִּית קְצוּצָה, *stipulated interest,* which is
Biblically prohibited (*Beis Yosef* ibid.;
see *Shinuyei Nuschaos, Meleches
Shlomo*).

זוֹ הִיא רִבִּית מֻקְדֶּמֶת. — *this is interest paid
in advance.*
[This is interest that is paid prior to
receiving the loan. As stated above, this
is Rabbinically prohibited.]

לָוָה הֵימֶנּוּ, וְהֶחֱזִיר לוֹ אֶת־מְעוֹתָיו, וְהָיָה מְשַׁלֵּחַ
לוֹ, — *[If] he borrowed from him, and
returned his money to him, and sent to
him,*
After the loan had been made, and the
money returned, the borrower sent the
lender a gift (*Rambam, Hil. Malveh
5:11; Meiri*).

וְאָמַר: ,,בִּשְׁבִיל מָעוֹתֶיךָ שֶׁהָיוּ בְטֵלוֹת אֶצְלִי״ —
— *and said: '[This is] because of your
money that was lying idle with me' —*
Here, too, the intention is that such a
loan is prohibited only if the borrower
states explicitly that he is giving him the
gift in appreciation of the loan he granted him (*Tur Yoreh Deah* 160). Rambam's reading is: וְהָיָה מְשַׁלֵּחַ לוֹ
בִּשְׁבִיל מָעוֹתָיו, *he sent him gifts because*

of his money — i.e., he is doing so for
the money, but does not necessarily
state his intention; nevertheless, it is
prohibited (*Rambam* loc. cit.; *Tur*).

זוֹ הִיא רִבִּית מְאֻחֶרֶת. — *this is interest paid
afterwards.*
As explained above, this is prohibited
Rabbinically (*Rambam*).

רַבִּי שִׁמְעוֹן אוֹמֵר: יֵשׁ רִבִּית דְּבָרִים — *R'
Shimon says: There is interest with
words —*
[In certain instances, if a borrower
merely tells the lender something, it is
considered giving him interest on his
loan.]

לֹא יֹאמַר לוֹ: ,,דַּע כִּי בָא אִישׁ פְּלוֹנִי מִמָּקוֹם
פְּלוֹנִי.״ — *he may not say to him: 'Be
informed that so-and-so has come from
such-and-such a place.'*
The borrower may not say this to the
lender (*Tos. Yom Tov*). [He may not
inform the lender that a certain person
in whom the latter is interested has come
from a certain place, because the borrower is thereby benefiting the lender,
and that would be interest with words.]

Tur, whose version apparently read:
,,דַּע אִם בָּא ...״, construes the mishnah as
meaning that the lender is the speaker,
and he is telling the borrower: 'Find out
if So-and-so has come ...' It would be
prohibited for the borrower to give the

me' — this is interest paid in advance. [If] he borrowed from him, and returned his money to him, and sent to him, and said: '[This is] because of your money that was lying idle with me' — this is interest paid afterwards.

R' Shimon says: There is interest with words — he may not say to him: 'Be informed that so-and-so has come from such-and-such a place.'

11. The following transgress a negative commandment: the lender, the borrower, the guarantor, and the witnesses. And the Sages say: Even the scribe. They transgress: *You shall not give*

YAD AVRAHAM

lender this information because he would thereby be giving him interest with words.

Rambam, whose version also uses the word *if*, understands the mishnah as meaning that the lender may not tell the borrower: 'Find out if So-and-so has come from such-and-such a place, and if he has, honor him and give him food and drink.'

Beis Yosef [160] asks that *Rambam's* case would not be one of interest with words, but with money, since the borrower is giving the other person food and drink. He concludes that according

to *Rambam*, R' Shimon teaches us two laws: (1) There is interest with words — for example, as the *Gemara* (75b) states, if the borrower did not usually greet the lender prior to the loan, he may not greet him after the loan; (2) The lender may not tell the borrower to honor a certain person and give him food and drink if and when he comes from a certain place. Had R' Shimon not told us that the latter is prohibited, we might have thought that it is permissible, since the borrower derives no direct benefit from the food being served to the guest (*Tos. Yom Tov*).

11.

This mishnah teaches us that all parties involved in a transaction of lending money with interest are guilty of transgressing one or more negative commandments.

וְאֵלוּ עוֹבְרִין בְּלֹא תַעֲשֶׂה: הַמַּלְוֶה, וְהַלֹּוֶה, וְהָעֵרֵב, וְהָעֵדִים. — *The following transgress a negative commandment: the lender, the borrower, the guarantor, and the witnesses.*

[That is, the witnesses who testify concerning the loan.]

The lender transgresses all of the prohibitions listed below in the mishnah (*Rav* from *Gem.*). [The others transgress one or more of them, as well as

some interdicts not mentioned by the *Tanna*, as will be explained.]

וַחֲכָמִים אוֹמְרִים: אַף הַסּוֹפֵר. — *And the Sages say: Even the scribe.*

[That is, the scribe who writes the loan contract.]

עוֹבְרִים מִשּׁוּם: "לֹא־תִתֵּן,, — *They transgress: 'You shall not give'* (*Leviticus 25:37*),

The lender transgresses the two

בבא
מציעא
ה/יא

וּמִשּׁוּם ,,בַּל תִּקַּח מֵאִתּוֹ,'' וּמִשּׁוּם ,,לֹא תִהְיֶה־לוֹ
כְנֹשֶׁה,'' וּמִשּׁוּם ,,לֹא־תְשִׂימוּן עָלָיו נֶשֶׁךְ,'' וּמִשּׁוּם
,,וְלִפְנֵי עִוֵּר לֹא תִתֵּן מִכְשֹׁל וְיָרֵאתָ מֵאֱלֹהֶיךָ אֲנִי
יהוה.''

יד אברהם

negative commandments in that verse:
אֶת־כַּסְפְּךָ לֹא־תִתֵּן לוֹ בְּנֶשֶׁךְ וּבְמַרְבִּית לֹא־תִתֵּן
אָכְלֶךָ, *Your money you shall not give
him with interest, nor shall you give
your food with increase* (Rambam, Hil.
Malveh 4:1,2). [As explained in the
preface to this chapter, נֶשֶׁךְ, *interest*, and
מַרְבִּית, *increase*, are synonymous; the
Torah mentions both to denote that the
lender transgresses two negative commandments.]

וּמִשּׁוּם ,,בַּל תִּקַּח מֵאִתּוֹ,'' — 'You shall not
take from him' (ibid. v. 36),
When the lender collects the interest,
he transgresses the negative command-
ment אַל־תִּקַּח מֵאִתּוֹ נֶשֶׁךְ וְתַרְבִּית, *You shall
take from him neither interest nor
increase* (Rashi to Gem. 75b; Tos. Yom
Tov).
[In Talmudic literature the word בַּל, *not*, is
frequently substituted for the words אַל and
לֹא — which have the same meaning — when
they are used in Biblical verse in connection
with a prohibition — e.g., בַּל יֵרָאֶה וּבַל יִמָּצֵא, *it
shall not be seen* and *it shall not be found*
(Pesachim 3:3).]
Although this verse precedes the one
cited above, the *Tanna* chose to state
them in this order, since the lender
transgresses the two commandments
mentioned above immediately upon
stipulating with the borrower that
interest will be paid, even if he
subsequently does not collect it. In
contrast, he does not transgress the
prohibition of ... אַל תִּקַּח, *You shall take
... neither ...* until he actually collects
the interest *(Tif. Yis.)*.

וּמִשּׁוּם ,,לֹא תִהְיֶה־לוֹ כְנֹשֶׁה,'' — 'You shall
not be to him as a creditor' (Exodus
22:24),
When the lender presses the borrower
for the money, he transgresses this

negative commandment *(Rashi). Tos.
Yom Tov* questions *Rashi's* explanation, since it applies only if the lender
actually presses the borrower to pay,
whereas the mishnah makes an unqualified statement that the lender
always transgresses this commandment.
He therefore prefers *Maggid Mishneh's*
interpretation, that the verse includes
any usual practice of creditors. Since a
creditor usually does not lend his money
gratis, the very act of lending with
interest is included in this negative
commandment. Since it is customary for
creditors to press the debtors when the
loan is due, pressing the debtor is
included in this precept as well. *Maggid
Mishneh* adds that although the
prohibition of interest applies even to a
rich borrower, that of pressing a
borrower to pay applies only if the latter
is poor.
Although the prohibition of pressing
a borrower to pay applies even to one
who lends without interest, the mishnah
mentions it with regard to one who
lends with interest, since the latter is
more likely to press for payment. This is
because one who borrows without interest would probably not act so ungrate-
fully as to delay payment beyond the
stipulated time. On the other hand, one
who borrowed with interest probably
did so out of desperation and finds it
difficult to repay the loan. He also
reasons that there is nothing wrong with
procrastinating the payment, since the
lender is earning more interest for the
extra time. In addition, if the borrower
is indeed poor, the lender fears that he
will lose not only the interest, but the
principal as well, and will certainly
press for payment.
Alternatively, it is possible that one

(Leviticus 25:37), *You shall not take from him* (ibid. v. 36), *You shall not be to him as a creditor* (Exodus 22:24), *You shall not impose interest upon him* (ibid.), and *And before a blind man you shall not place a stumbling block, and you shall fear your God; I am* HASHEM (Leviticus 19:14).

YAD AVRAHAM

who lends with interest transgresses this commandment even if he does not press for payment, since the borrower is under pressure to pay, so as not to allow too much interest to accrue (*Tif. Yis.*).

וּמְשׁוּם ,,לֹא־תְשִׂימוּן עָלָיו נֶשֶׁךְ,, — *'You shall not impose interest upon him' (ibid.),*

The lender obviously transgresses this negative commandment when he lends the money. Also, the guarantor and the witnesses, as well as the scribe [according to the Sages] who is instrumental in drawing up such a loan contract, are all guilty of this transgression (*Rav, Tos. Yom Tov* from *Rambam Commentary*).

וּמְשׁוּם ,,וְלִפְנֵי עִוֵּר לֹא תִתֵּן מִכְשֹׁל, — *and 'And before a blind man you shall not place a stumbling block,*

This negative commandment applies to anyone who makes it possible for someone else to commit a sin. In the words of *Rambam* (*Commentary to Sheviis* 5:6): Do not assist one whose eyes are shut by his lust and temptation by adding to his blindness and causing him to stray further from the proper behavior. In our case, the borrower — who makes it possible for the lender to take interest from him, and to transgress all the aforementioned negative commandments — is guilty of violating this prohibition.

Although not mentioned in the mishnah, the borrower is guilty also of transgressing לֹא־תַשִּׁיךְ לְאָחִיךָ, *You shall not cause your brother to take interest* (*Deut.* 23:20) and וּלְאָחִיךָ לֹא תַשִּׁיךְ, *but your brother you shall not cause to take interest* (ibid. v. 21). Therefore, when

the lender accepts interest from the borrower, he causes the latter to transgress these prohibitions, and is consequently guilty of the negative precept of וְלִפְנֵי עִוֵּר ..., *And before a blind man ...* (*Rashi*). Likewise, the guarantor and the witnesses violate the latter precept if the lender would not have given the loan without them (*Tos.*). The same applies to the scribe [even according to the first, anonymous *Tanna*] if the lender insists on a contract, since without him the sin would not have been committed (*Tos. Yom Tov*).

In summary, the lender transgresses all the negative precepts listed in the mishnah, numbering six. The borrower transgresses three negative precepts. The guarantor, the witnesses, and the scribe transgress only *You shall not impose ...* Should the lender grant the loan only if they participate, they transgress *And before a blind man ...* as well (*Gem.* 75b, *Tos.* s.v. ערב).

Surprisingly, the mishnah does not mention the negative precepts that apply to the borrower. The reason for this is that the *Tanna's* intention was to list only those prohibitions pertaining to the lender. Since some of these apply to the borrower, the guarantor, the witnesses, and the scribe, he mentions those individuals as well (*Tif. Yis.; Ravad,* quoted by *Shitah Mekubetzes*).

וְיָרֵאתָ מֵאֱלֹהֶיךָ אֲנִי ה׳.,, — *and you shall fear your God; I am* HASHEM.'

This concluding clause of the verse cited above is added here, although it is not relevant to the rest of the mishnah, in order to conclude the chapter on a positive note (*Tif. Yis*).

[א] **הַשּׂוֹכֵר** אֶת־הָאֻמָּנִין, וְהִטְעוּ זֶה אֶת־זֶה,
אֵין לָהֶם זֶה עַל־זֶה אֶלָּא
תַּרְעֹמֶת.
שָׂכַר אֶת־הַחַמָּר וְאֶת־הַקַּדָּר לְהָבִיא פְּרְיָפָרִין
וַחֲלִילִים, לְכַלָּה אוֹ לְמֵת, וּפוֹעֲלִין לְהַעֲלוֹת

יד אברהם

Chapter 6

1.

הַשּׂוֹכֵר אֶת־הָאֻמָּנִין, — *[If] one hires
craftsmen,*

The term *craftsmen* here applies to
contractors who undertake to do a
certain job, as well as laborers who are
hired by the day. Chapter 7, however,
deals only with laborers who are hired
per diem (*Tos. Yom Tov* from *Tos.*).

Tiferes Yisrael explains that there are
three types of unskilled workers:
(1) שְׂכִיר יוֹם, *a worker hired per diem,*
who does any work that may prove
necessary during that day; (2) פּוֹעֵל, *a
laborer,* hired by the day to do a
particular type of work during that day;
(3) קַבְּלָן, *a contractor,* one who is hired
to do a certain job in its entirety. These
three types, which include such workers
as wood choppers and water drawers,
usually accomplish their work through
physical strength. Those who perform
tasks requiring knowledge and skill —
such as a carpenter, a shoemaker, or a
tailor — are called אֻמָּנִין, *craftsmen.*
Although the mishnah speaks here of
craftsmen, the same ruling applies to
unskilled workers.

וְהִטְעוּ זֶה אֶת־זֶה, אֵין לָהֶם זֶה עַל־זֶה אֶלָּא
תַּרְעֹמֶת. — *and they mislead one another,
they have nothing but resentment
against one another.*

That is, if a person instructed his
worker to hire other workers for him at
the rate of four *dinars* a day, and
instead, the worker offered them only
three *dinars* a day, the employer need
pay them only three *dinars* a day, since
the worker has agreed to work for that

amount. They may, however, have
resentment against the worker who
hired them, since he had the opportunity to benefit them and did not do so.

They can tell him: אַל־תִּמְנַע־טוֹב מִבְּעָלָיו,
*Do not withhold good from whom it is
due* [*Proverbs 3:27*] (*Rav* from *Gem.*
76a; *Rambam, Hil. Sechirus* 9:3; *Ritva,*
quoted in *Shitah Mekubetzes*).

Another explanation offered by the
Gemara does not involve one worker
hiring others. Rather, a person hired
workers, and either they misled the hirer
by refusing to appear for work, or the
hirer misled them by refusing to accept
them for work in the morning, before
they went to work (*Rav* from *Gem.*
76b). [In either case, the wronged party
cannot legally force the other party to
adhere to the agreement.]

By choosing a negative expression —
they have nothing but resentment— the
Tanna implies that the guilty party has
absolutely no obligation to pay, even if
he wishes to fulfill his duty to Heaven
(*Tif. Yis.*)

This refers to a place where
employment is not available for the
workers; hence, the hirer did not cause
them to lose some other job by engaging
them and then reneging. As *Rav* notes,
this applies only if they have not begun
doing the work. Once they start the job,
however, it is considered a binding
agreement, and the hirer must pay them
their wages, albeit only as idle workers,
since, in fact, they did no work. He
must, therefore, pay them what they
would expect to get for neglecting their

1. **[I**f] one hires craftsmen, and they mislead one another, they have nothing but resentment against one another.

[If] he hired a donkey driver or a wagoner to bring wood for a litter or flutes, for a bride or for a dead person, or laborers to remove his flax from the

YAD AVRAHAM

work and sitting idle. Should they have been able to find other employment prior to being hired by this person, but now find that all positions are filled, the hirer must pay them their full wages, since he caused them this loss. This is called דִּינָא דְגַרְמֵי, *the law of indirect cause,* for which the perpetrator is liable. If they can still find other employment, however, even if they already arrived to work for this hirer, he can tell them to find work elsewhere. The workers can have resentment against him in such a case, since they had bothered themselves unnecessarily (*Tos. R' Akiva* from *Tos.* 76b).

[The hirer, too, can have *nothing but resentment* against the workers only if their retraction caused him no loss. If it did, however, the hirer may take action, as the mishnah will now explain.]

שָׂכַר אֶת־הַחַמָּר — [*If*] *he hired a donkey driver*

[A person hired someone who carries loads on his donkey.]

וְאֶת־הַקַּדָּר — *or a wagoner* (lit., *a potter*)

It was customary for potters to have wagons. Many editions read: הַקָּרָר, *a wagoner,* from the word קָרוֹן, *a wagon* (*Rav; Tos.; Tos. Yom Tov*). *Tiferes Yisrael* prefers the second reading, which he associates with the German *karre,* a wheelbarrow. *Aruch Hashalem* compares it to the Latin *carrator carrarius* [perhaps related to the English *car* or *cart*].

לְהָבִיא פְּרְיָפָרִין — *to bring wood for a litter*

The translation follows the interpretations of *Rav* and *Rashi,* who explain this term to mean planed wood to make a litter — i.e., a bed or a couch

suspended between poles that are used to carry it. *Aruch* construes the word פְּרְיָפָרִין as the litter itself. *Musaf HeAruch* defines it as a curved trumpet. *Shiltei HaGibborim* (*Hashir Shebamikdash,* p. 51) describes it as a type of flute, which was used in the Temple for the שִׂמְחַת בֵּית הַשּׁוֹאֵבָה, *The Rejoicing of the Place of the Water Drawing* which took place on *Sukkos.*

וַחֲלִילִים, — *or flutes,*

[All agree that this was one of the instruments used in the Temple. For particulars, see *Shiltei HaGibborim* ibid.]

לְכַלָּה — *for a bride*

That is, to play at a wedding and bring joy to the groom and bride (*Tos. Yom Tov* from *Rashi*).

אוֹ לְמֵת, — *or for a dead person,*

[In those days it was customary to play the flute at funerals during the eulogy (see *Kesubos* 4:4 and commentary there).]

Were these items not to arrive for the wedding or funeral [although no monetary loss is involved (*Tif. Yis.*)], it is considered an irretrievable loss, since they are useful only at the time of the ceremony, not later (*Tos. Yom Tov* from *Tos.*).

וּפוֹעֲלִין — *or laborers*

This is another case: a person hired laborers (*Meiri*).

לְהַעֲלוֹת פִּשְׁתָּנוֹ מִן־הַמִּשְׁרָה, — *to remove his flax from the steeping water,*

The capsules of the flax are soaked until they become soft, then dried in an oven, and then beaten to be made into linen fibers. If they are left in the steeping water too long, they will decay.

פִּשְׁתָּנוֹ מִן־הַמִּשְׁרָה, וְכָל־דָּבָר שֶׁאָבֵד, וְחָזְרוּ בָהֶן
— מָקוֹם שֶׁאֵין שָׁם אָדָם, שׂוֹכֵר עֲלֵיהֶן, אוֹ מַטְעָן.

[ב] **הַשּׂוֹכֵר** אֶת־הָאֻמָּנִין וְחָזְרוּ בָהֶן, יָדָן עַל
הַתַּחְתּוֹנָה; אִם בַּעַל הַבַּיִת חוֹזֵר
בּוֹ, יָדוֹ עַל הַתַּחְתּוֹנָה.

יד אברהם

Although any person can remove the flax from the water, if one expected others to do it for him, and they do not, it is considered an irretrievable loss (*Tif. Yis.*).

[This is because most people are not accustomed to such work and will therefore find difficulty in doing it (see *Terumas Hadeshen* 329).]

וְכָל־דָּבָר שֶׁאָבֵד, — *or anything which may cause a loss,*

That is, a person hired workers to do a type of job which, should they retract from the agreement, would cause him an irretrievable loss (*Meiri*).

וְחָזְרוּ בָהֶן — *and they retracted—*

The workers retracted before they commenced their work (*Tos. Yom Tov from Rosh*, quoting *Ravad*).

מָקוֹם שֶׁאֵין שָׁם אָדָם, — *in a place where there are no people,*

That is, the hirer is in a place where no workers are presently available at the rate he agreed to pay these workers (*Tif. Yis.*).

The mishnah must be dealing with a case in which other workers were available at that rate at the time he hired these workers. Otherwise, the latter would not have caused him any loss, since he could not find others at that rate, even if these workers had not accepted the job (*Tos. Yom Tov* from *Maggid Mishneh, Hil. Sechirus* 9:4, quoting *Rashba*).

שׂוֹכֵר עֲלֵיהֶן, — *he may hire [other workers] in addition to them,*

If, by retraction from this agreement, the workers will cause the hirer an

irreparable loss, because the job will not get done, he may hire other workers for as much as double the wages he had agreed to pay the first workers. The latter must reimburse him for this extra amount, since they expected to pay this much of a penalty for causing the employer a loss by retracting (*Tos. Yom Tov* from *Rosh, Tur* 333).

According to *Rashi*, the intention is that if the workers had already done part of the work before they quit, and the employer had not yet paid them, he may take the money he owes them and use it toward the extra amount it costs him when he hires other workers for the remainder of the work.

Should the workers have left their tools with their employer, he may keep the tools to pay the extra amount it costs him to hire other workers. The *Gemara* (78a) states that he may pay up to forty or fifty *zuz* from the workers' property. *Ramban* and *Nimmukei Yosef* explain that this is the amount a person would be willing to spend above the normal rate of pay to have his work done in case of loss (see *Beis Yosef* 333, *Sma* ibid. §26).

If the loss caused by the workers is not a monetary one — for example, they are teachers who retract from the agreement and do not teach — they must pay only if the hirer spent extra money to engage other workers; if he did not engage other workers, the first workers do not have to pay the hirer for the loss. Should it be a monetary loss, however, *Rama* (ibid. §6) rules that the workers must pay for it. *Shach* (§39) disagrees, construing *Nimmukei Yosef* as not steeping water, or anything which may cause a loss, and they retracted — in a place where there are no people, he may hire [other workers] in addition to them, or trick them.

2. [If] one hires craftsmen and they retract, they are at a disadvantage; if the hirer retracts, he is at a disadvantage.

YAD AVRAHAM

differentiating between the two types of loss, maintaining instead that the workers are not liable in either case.

אוֹ מַטְעָן — *or trick them.*
An alternative plan for the hirer to avoid the loss is by promising the workers who wish to retract more than he had originally agreed with them and then, when they return and do the work, he need not give them the extra amount *(Rav from Gem. 76b).*

2.

הַשּׂוֹכֵר אֶת־הָאֻמָּנִין — *[If] one hires craftsmen*
He hires them to do a certain job for a certain amount of money *(Rav; Rashi).*

וְחָזְרוּ בָּהֶן, — *and they retract,*
After doing a certain amount of the work, the workers leave the job *(Rav; Rashi).*
The mishnah is dealing with a case in which there is no loss involved *(Tif. Yis.).*

יָדָן עַל הַתַּחְתּוֹנָה; — *they are at a disadvantage;*
Should the rate of pay for workers rise — thereby necessitating the hirer to pay more for the workers who will complete the job — he may deduct the extra amount from the pay of the first workers in order to compensate for the difference. Should the rate of pay go down, and the hirer finds that he can have the work completed by other workers for less than he had agreed with the first workers, the amount of work the first workers did is assessed according to the previous rate of pay, and he pays them that amount. They cannot claim that the second workers are completing the work as substitutes for them, and that they should therefore receive their full wage as had been agreed, less the amount given the second workers *(Rav; Rashi).*

As stated above, this ruling applies only to workers who contract to do a job. Those who are hired by the day, however, may quit the job whenever they wish, and yet have the advantage that no deduction is made from their wages to pay the workers who continue their job. This is based on the verse *(Lev. 25:55)*: כִּי־לִי בְנֵי־יִשְׂרָאֵל עֲבָדִים עֲבָדַי הֵם, *for the Children of Israel are servants to Me; they are My servants,* intimating that they cannot be enslaved by anyone else, but are free to quit their employment whenever they wish. This verse applies only to workers hired per diem, who are in the employ of the hirer. Contractors, however, are self-employed, and are therefore servants to themselves, rather than to the employers for whom they are working. However, even those working by the day who cause a loss to the hirer are governed by the ruling delineated in the mishnah *(Tos. Yom Tov from Gem. 77b).*

אִם בַּעַל הַבַּיִת חוֹזֵר בּוֹ, יָדוֹ עַל הַתַּחְתּוֹנָה. — *if the hirer (lit., householder) retracts, he is at a disadvantage.*

כָּל־הַמְשַׁנֶּה יָדוֹ עַל הַתַּחְתּוֹנָה, וְכָל־הַחוֹזֵר בּוֹ
יָדוֹ עַל הַתַּחְתּוֹנָה.

[ג] **הַשּׂוֹכֵר** אֶת־הַחֲמוֹר לְהוֹלִיכָהּ בָּהָר,
וְהוֹלִיכָהּ בַּבִּקְעָה, בַּבִּקְעָה,
וְהוֹלִיכָהּ בָּהָר — אֲפִלּוּ זוֹ עֶשֶׂר מִילִין וְזוֹ עֶשֶׂר
מִילִין — וָמֵתָה, חַיָּב.

יד אברהם

If the hirer discharges them in the midst of the job, he must pay them for what they have already done. If the rate of pay for workers has gone down, and he hires new workers, he must pay the first workers for the complete job, less the wage of the second workers, who receive the lower rate of pay (Rav; Rashi).

Should the rate of pay have risen, however, the workers need not be paid according to the present higher rate for the work they have already done, since they are not losing by having been discharged. On the contrary, they are now free to accept employment at the higher rate (Tos. Yom Tov from Tos. 76a).

כָּל־הַמְשַׁנֶּה — Whoever deviates

[This refers to any worker who deviates from the instructions given him by his employer.] For example, the dyer who dyes black what he was ordered to dye red, or vice versa (Rav from Gem. 77b).

יָדוֹ עַל הַתַּחְתּוֹנָה, — is at a disadvantage,

In the case of the dyer, for example, if the amount that the material was improved by being dyed exceeds the expenses and the labor put into it, the dyer receives payment only for the labor and the expenses. Should the labor and expenses exceed the improvement resulting therefrom, he is paid only for

the improvement (Rav). This ruling is in accordance with R' Yehudah [Bava Kamma 9:4] (Tos. Yom Tov from Gem. 77b). [R' Meir (Bava Kamma ibid.) maintains that a worker who deviates from his employer's instructions is tantamount to a thief, and — as is the law regarding all thieves — he acquires the item given him if it undergoes a change while in his possession (see preface to ArtScroll Bava Kamma 9:1).] In our case, the dyer aquires the material with the change he performed by dyeing it, and he therefore can keep the finished product and pay only the price of the undyed material.

וְכָל־הַחוֹזֵר בּוֹ יָדוֹ עַל הַתַּחְתּוֹנָה. — and whoever retracts is at a disadvantage.

Although this rule is obvious from the first part of the mishnah, the Tanna makes this statement in order to include the case of one who sells a field for one thousand zuz, and the buyer makes a down payment of two hundred zuz. Should the seller retract from the agreement, the buyer has the advantage — he may insist that the seller return his money or, if he prefers, that he give him land corresponding to the payment. If the buyer retracts, the seller may insist that the buyer take back his money, or, if he prefers, that he take land corresponding to the down payment (Rav from Gem. ibid).

3.

The next three mishnayos deal with a donkey rented to be used in a certain

manner, which was then used in a manner other than the one stipulated.

Whoever deviates is at a disadvantage, and whoever retracts is at a disadvantage.

3. [I[f] one rents a donkey to drive it on the mountains, and he drives it in a valley, [or] in a valley, and he drives it on the mountains — even if this is ten *mil* and this is ten *mil* — and it dies, he is liable.

YAD AVRAHAM

הַשּׂוֹכֵר אֶת־הַחֲמוֹר לְהוֹלִיכָה בָּהָר, — *[If] one rents a donkey to drive it on the mountains,*

[It was agreed that the animal would be driven only on mountains.]

וְהוֹלִיכָה בַּבִּקְעָה, — *and he drives it in a valley,*

[Instead of driving the donkey only on the mountains as stipulated, the renter[1] drives it in a valley.]

בַּבִּקְעָה, וְהוֹלִיכָה בָּהָר — *[or] in a valley, and he drives it on the mountains —*

[Instead of driving as stipulated, he drove it on the mountains.]

אֲפִלּוּ זוֹ עֶשֶׂר מִילִין וְזוֹ עֶשֶׂר מִילִין — *even if this is ten mil and this is ten mil —*

[That is, although the paths in the valley and the mountains are of the same length, and hence, the renter did not drive it on a longer path than had been stipulated.]

Other editions read: עֲשֶׂרֶת מִילִין or עֲשָׂרָה מִילִין, taking מִיל as masculine. According to our edition, it is feminine.

In fact, even if the renter drove the animal a shorter distance than had been stipulated, he is liable; the *Tanna*, however, did not feel it necessary to elaborate and say this explicitly *(Tos. Yom Tov from Tos.).*

וָמֵתָה, חַיָּב. — *and it dies, he is liable.*

Although the donkey did not slip on the mountain or die of heat in the valley, but rather died a natural death, since the renter did not comply with the agreement, the animal's death is attributed to the change of air — perhaps it had been accustomed to mountain air or valley air and suffered because of the change. Accordingly, the *Tanna* does not differentiate between cases of the animal slipping and those in which it dies because of the heat, as he does below *(Gem.* 78a, according to *Rav, Rashi).*

Tos. Yom Tov challenges the above interpretation of the *Gemara,* since donkeys are usually taught to traverse both hill and dale. He prefers the explanation of *Tosafos,* that the renter knew that the air on the mountain or in the valley — wherever he was not supposed to ride the donkey — was undesirable for the animal because of snow or rain. Thus, the renter's deviation from the stipulation made at the time of the rental constitutes negligence, and he is therefore liable for the animal's death. The mishnah does not state that he stipulated to drive the donkey on one mountain or valley, but instead drove it on another mountain or valley, since it is unusual for the weather to differ from one mountain to another, or from one valley to another.

Meiri follows R' Yochanan's attribution of the mishnah to R' Meir, who

---

1. [Since the terms *renter* and *hirer* have various — sometimes conflicting — definitions, we will define how these terms are used throughout these chapters. *Renter* refers to one who holds property by payment of rent; the party he rents from is called the *owner. Hirer* refers to one who engages the services of a worker.]

הַשּׂוֹכֵר אֶת־הַחֲמוֹר, וְהִבְרִיקָה אוֹ שֶׁנַּעֲשֵׂית אַנְגַּרְיָא, אוֹמֵר לוֹ: ,,הֲרֵי שֶׁלְּךָ לְפָנֶיךָ.'' מֵתָה אוֹ נִשְׁבְּרָה, חַיָּב לְהַעֲמִיד לוֹ חֲמוֹר.

יד אברהם

rules that if one deviates from the owner's orders, he is deemed a robber [see commentary to mishnah 2, s.v. יָדוֹ], and is therefore liable for accidents. In our case, since the owner specified that the donkey be driven either in the valley or on the mountains, and the renter did not comply with the agreement, he is deemed a robber and is liable for any accidents that befall the donkey.

◈§ The following section of the mishnah discusses under what circumstances an owner is obligated to provide the renter with another animal. *Rav* explains this section after the following one, indicating that in his edition, this section appeared at the end of the mishnah. The same is true of the edition of the mishnah printed with the *Gemara*. Our editions, however, concur in this instance with the sequence of the mishnah printed with *Yerushalmi* (*Tos. Yom Tov*).

הַשּׂוֹכֵר אֶת־הַחֲמוֹר, וְהִבְרִיקָה — *If one rents a donkey, and it becomes blind*

Rav comments that the donkey became blinded by a skin growing over the eye. *Tos. Yom Tov* explains that *Rav's* version reads וְהִבְדִּיקָה, from דּוֹק, a skin. According to our reading, וְהִבְרִיקָה, the word is derived from בָּרָק, *lightning*, a euphemism for blindness.

Others suggest that *Rav*, too, had our reading, but explains that the blindness came about through a skin growing over the eye (footnote in *Yachin U'Boaz* ed. of the Mishnah).

Another interpretation is that the donkey's legs became wormy (*Rav* from *Gem.* 78b).

Based on these interpretations, *Rambam* (*Hil. Sechirus* 5:1) refers to our case as one in which the donkey took sick.

אוֹ שֶׁנַּעֲשֵׂית אַנְגַּרְיָא, — *or is seized for public service,*

[In those times, it was not uncommon for the king's officers to seize animals and use them for public service.]

אוֹמֵר לוֹ: ,,הֲרֵי שֶׁלְּךָ לְפָנֶיךָ.'' — *he may say to him: 'That which is yours is before you.'*

[The owner may tell the renter that he is not responsible for what occurred to the donkey; hence, he need not provide him with another animal in its stead,

and the renter must pay the full rental fee despite what happened.] In the case of the donkey becoming blind or sick, this is because it is still possible to use the animal to some extent — albeit with difficulty (*Rambam*, as explained by *Maggid Mishneh*, *Hil. Sechirus* 5:1). In the case of the donkey being seized for public service, since the officers do not go searching in houses, but take only animals which are on the road, the owner can claim that it was the renter's misfortune that the donkey happened to be on the road precisely when the officers came (ibid.; *Tos. Yom Tov* from *Tos.* 78b). Indeed, should the animal be seized while it is in the house, the owner is required to provide the renter with another animal (*Tos. Yom Tov* from *Tos.* 78b).

According to *Rashi*, the *Gemara* (ibid.) explains that if the officers appropriate the donkey to drive it in the same direction in which the renter is headed, the latter should rent another animal until the officers seize the donkey of a second victim and return the first one to him, since it was partially due to his misfortune that the donkey was taken. [Should they be taking it in another direction, however, the owner must provide another donkey.]

These interpretations follow the view

6
3

If one rents a donkey, and it becomes blind or is seized for public service, he may say to him: 'That which is yours is before you.' [If] it dies or breaks a leg, he is obligated to provide him with [another] donkey.

of Shmuel, whose opinion the halachah always follows in monetary matters. According to Rav [the *Amora*], however, the mishnah is qualified as referring to a case in which the officers are taking the donkey with the intention of returning it after they are finished with it. In that case, the renter must wait until the animal is returned, although this causes him some delay. Should they take the donkey with the intention of not returning it, the owner must provide another animal, since this is tantamount to the mishnah's next case, in which the donkey breaks its leg *(Gem.)*.

In the case of the donkey becoming blind or ill, the owner is exempt from providing another animal only if he had specified that he was renting out this particular donkey, and only if the rental was for the purpose of carrying packs. If, however, no particular animal had been specified — regardless of the purpose of the rental — the owner must provide another donkey [since the renter can always demand an animal that is more fit for work]. Likewise, if the purpose of the rental was to use the animal for riding, even if this particular donkey had been specified, another animal must be provided in its stead *(Rav; Rambam Commentary)*. This is because the blind or sick donkey is not considered suitable for riding, since it may fall beneath him on a bridge, or throw him into a pit *(Rav)*. *Rambam* in *Mishneh Torah*[1] *(Hil. Sechirus* 5:1), however, as well as *Rosh* and *Tur* (301) do not differentiate between cases in which a particular donkey had been specified and those in which it had not.

In the case of the donkey being seized for public service, it makes no difference for what purpose the animal had been rented *(Tos. Yom Tov* from *Maggid Mishneh* ad loc.).

Should the donkey have been rented for the purpose of carrying glass [or other fragile items], it is equivalent to having rented it for riding, and the owner must provide another animal *(Gem.* 79a; *Tur, Rambam* ibid.). In the cases in which the owner must provide another donkey, the intention is that he must do so if he wishes to collect the entire rental fee that had been originally stipulated. Otherwise, the renter pays him only for the portion of the way he was able to ride the animal or use it to carry his glass *(Rav; Rambam* ibid.).

According to other authorities, even in cases in which the owner is not obligated to provide another animal, the renter need not pay the complete rental fee, since he could not use the donkey properly. They maintain also that in those cases regarding which the mishnah required the owner to provide another donkey, he must do so even if he is willing to forego part of the rental fee *(Maggid Mishneh)*.

מֵתָה אוֹ נִשְׁבְּרָה, — [If] it dies or breaks a leg,

The donkey thereby becomes unfit for the work for which the renter needs it *(Meiri)*.

חַיָּב לְהַעֲמִיד לוֹ חֲמוֹר. — he is obligated to provide him with [another] donkey.

The owner must sell the hide, and the carcass for dog food, and add money in order to purchase another donkey so

---

1. See footnote to 1:2.

הַשּׂוֹכֵר אֶת־הַחֲמוֹר לְהוֹלִיכָהּ בָּהָר, וְהוֹלִיכָהּ
בַּבִּקְעָה — אִם הֶחֱלִיקָה, פָּטוּר; וְאִם־הוּחַמָּה,
חַיָּב. לְהוֹלִיכָהּ בַּבִּקְעָה, וְהוֹלִיכָהּ בָּהָר — אִם
הֶחֱלִיקָה, חַיָּב; וְאִם הוּחַמָּה, פָּטוּר; אִם מֵחֲמַת
הַמַּעֲלָה, חַיָּב.

[ה] **הַשּׂוֹכֵר** אֶת־הַפָּרָה לַחֲרשׁ בָּהָר, וְחָרַשׁ
בַּבִּקְעָה — אִם נִשְׁבַּר הַקַּנְקַן,

יד אברהם

that the renter can reach his intended
destination. This applies only if the
owner had not stipulated that he was
renting him this particular donkey.
Should he have done so, he need not add
money, but must purchase another
donkey from the proceeds of the sale of
the carcass and the hide. If the proceeds
do not suffice to purchase even a
smaller donkey, he must rent a donkey
from the proceeds, so that the renter can
reach his intended destination (*Choshen
Mishpat* 310:1, *Sma* ad loc. from *Gem.*
79a, following the view of Shmuel).

If the money does not suffice even to
rent another donkey, the renter must
pay only for having used the animal
until that point. Even this amount need
be paid only if he accomplished something by traveling to that point — e.g.,
he can sell his merchandise there (*Meiri;
Choshen Mishpat* loc. cit. §2).

Rambam (*Hil. Sechirus* 5:2) rules that
if the owner had stipulated that he was
renting him this particular donkey, and
the donkey died in middle of the way,
the owner is obligated to sell the carcass
and the hide in order to rent another
animal only if the rental had been for
the purpose of riding the animal or
using it to transport glass. Should the
rental have been for the purpose of
transporting regular merchandise, however, the owner is not obligated to rent
another animal, and the renter must pay
him a part of the rental fee for having

used the donkey until it died (see *Sma*
§9).

הַשּׂוֹכֵר אֶת־הַחֲמוֹר לְהוֹלִיכָהּ בָּהָר, וְהוֹלִיכָהּ
בַּבִּקְעָה — אִם הֶחֱלִיקָה, — [*If*] *one rents a
donkey to drive it on the mountains,
and he drives it in the valley — if it slips,*

[The animal slipped and was killed or
broke its leg.]

פָּטוּר; — *he is exempt;*

The renter is exempt from paying for
the donkey, since it would more likely
have slipped on the steep sides of the
mountains had he led it there as
stipulated (*Rav; Rashi*).

Although he committed an act of
negligence by leading the donkey in the
valley — a place where it could very well
die of the heat — he is nevertheless
exempt when it dies by slipping, since
the accident that actually occurred was
not due to his negligence (*Tos. Yom Tov*
from *Tos.* 78a).

וְאִם־הוּחַמָּה, — *but if it dies from the
heat,*

[It dies from the warm air of the
valley.]

The valley is usually warm, since it is
surrounded by mountains, and the cool
air does not penetrate into it (*Rav;
Rashi*).

חַיָּב. — *he is liable.*

[This is considered negligence on the
part of the renter, since he violated the
agreement to ride the donkey only on

[If] one rents a donkey to drive it on the mountains, and he drives it in the valley — if it slips, he is exempt; but if it dies from the heat, he is liable. [If he rents it] to drive it in the valley, and he drives it on the mountains — if it slips, he is liable; but if it dies from the heat, he is exempt; if [it dies] because of the ascent, he is liable.

4. [If] one rents a cow to plow on the mountains, and he plows in the valley — if the colter breaks, he is exempt. [If he rents it to plow] in the

the mountains.]

לְהוֹלִיכָה בַּבִּקְעָה, וְהוֹלִיכָה בָּהָר—אִם הֶחֱלִיקָה, חַיָּב; — [If he rents it] to drive it in the valley, and he drives it on the mountains — if it slips, he is liable;

[The renter is liable for the accident, since he committed an act of negligence by driving it on the steep mountains instead of in the valley, as had been stipulated.]

וְאִם הוּחַמָּה, פָּטוּר; — but if it dies from the heat, he is exempt;

[Since the mountain air is cooler than the valley air, the animal would surely have died had he driven it in the valley.]

אִם מֵחֲמַת הַמַּעֲלָה, — if [it dies] because of the ascent,

The animal became overheated because of the climb up the mountain (Rav; Rashi).

חַיָּב. — he is liable.

Since he hired it on condition that he drive it in the valley, and he deviated from the agreement, this is regarded as an act of negligence (ibid.).

The preceding case — for which the renter is exempt when the donkey dies of the heat after having been driven on the mountain — refers to an instance in which the donkey climbed the mountain without effort and walked a considerable distance without sweating; only later did it become heated and die. In such a case, it is obvious that the heat had not been caused by the ascent (Tos. Yom Tov from Tos. 79a).

4.

הַשּׂוֹכֵר אֶת־הַפָּרָה לַחֲרשׁ בָּהָר, — [If] one rents a cow to plow on the mountains,

He rented the cow along with all its trappings. He would have two workers going along with it, one to hold the goad to guide the cow, and the other one to walk behind the plow and press the colter deeply enough into the soil in order to plow it (Rav, Rashi, Tos. Yom Tov).

[The renter has two fields — one on a mountain and one in a valley — and he hires this cow with its trappings to plow his field on the mountain.]

וְחָרַשׁ בַּבִּקְעָה — and he plows in the valley —

[Instead, he instructs his workers to plow his field in the valley.]

אִם נִשְׁבַּר הַקַּנְקָן, פָּטוּר. — if the colter breaks, he is exempt.

The renter is exempt from paying the owner for the plowshare, since the blade would surely have broken had he plowed his field on the mountain as stipulated [the mountainous terrain being harder and more rocky than that of the valley] (Meiri).

פָּטוּר. בַּבִּקְעָה, וְחָרַשׁ בָּהָר — אִם נִשְׁבַּר הַקַּנְקָן,
חַיָּב; לָדוּשׁ בַּקִּטְנִית, וְדָשׁ בַּתְּבוּאָה, פָּטוּר; לָדוּשׁ
בַּתְּבוּאָה, וְדָשׁ בַּקִּטְנִית, חַיָּב, מִפְּנֵי שֶׁהַקִּטְנִית
מַחֲלֶקֶת.

[ה] **הַשּׂוֹכֵר** אֶת־הַחֲמוֹר לְהָבִיא עָלֶיהָ חִטִּים,
וְהֵבִיא עָלֶיהָ שְׂעוֹרִים, חַיָּב;
תְּבוּאָה, וְהֵבִיא עָלֶיהָ תֶּבֶן, חַיָּב, מִפְּנֵי שֶׁהַנֶּפַח
קָשֶׁה לַמַּשּׂאוּי. לְהָבִיא לֶתֶךְ חִטִּים, וְהֵבִיא לֶתֶךְ
שְׂעוֹרִים, פָּטוּר, וְאִם הוֹסִיף עַל־מַשָּׂאוֹ, חַיָּב.

יד אברהם

Instead, the worker who held the plowshare is liable and must pay for the damage, since he pressed it into the soil too deeply (*Rambam Commentary*, *Rashi* to *Gem.* 80a).

Nimmukei Yosef disagrees, maintaining that even the workers are not liable for the mishap. According to *Tos. Yom Tov* the case is one in which the workers are the young sons of the one who rented the cow; since they are minors, they are not responsible (see *Lechem Shamayim*).

בַּבִּקְעָה, וְחָרַשׁ בָּהָר — אִם נִשְׁבַּר הַקַּנְקָן, חַיָּב;
— [*If he rents it to plow*] *in the valley, and he plows on the mountains — if the colter breaks, he is liable;*

The renter is considered negligent, since it is harder to plow the rocky mountainous terrain than to plow the valley (*Rav; Rashi*).

Although the mishnah states that the renter is liable, that is with regard to the owner of the cow. The renter himself may, however, in turn sue the worker, who was not careful when holding the plow and allowed it to penetrate into the ground too deeply (*Tif. Yis.* from *Rambam, Hil. Sechirus* 4:1; *Choshen Mishpat* 309:4). Should the workers have been hired by the owner of the cow, some authorities rule that they

may claim that they never undertook to watch the plowshare on mountainous terrain, but only in a valley. Had they been instructed to plow in a valley, the colter would not have broken (*Rama* from *Tur* quoting *Rosh; Tos.* 80a).

לָדוּשׁ בַּקִּטְנִית, — *to thresh beans,*
[One rented a cow with the understanding that he will use it to thresh beans.]

וְדָשׁ בַּתְּבוּאָה, — *and he threshes grain,*
[Instead of threshing beans, he threshes grain.]

פָּטוּר; — *he is exempt;*
If the cow slips on the grain and breaks its leg, he is exempt (*Rav; Rashi*).

לָדוּשׁ בַּתְּבוּאָה, — *to thresh grain,*
[One rented a cow to use it to thresh grain.]

וְדָשׁ בַּקִּטְנִית, — *and he threshes beans,*
[Instead, he threshes beans with it.]

חַיָּב, — *he is liable,*
The renter is liable if the cow slips (*Meiri; Tif. Yis.*).

מִפְּנֵי שֶׁהַקִּטְנִית מַחֲלֶקֶת. — *because beans are slippery.*
[Consequently, his deviation from the agreement caused the injury to the cow.]

valley, and he plows on the mountains — if the colter breaks, he is liable; to thresh beans, and he threshes grain, he is exempt; to thresh grain, and he threshes beans, he is liable, because beans are slippery.

5. [If] one rents a donkey on which to bring wheat, and he brings barley on it, he is liable; grain, and he brings straw on it, he is liable, because the added bulk is difficult to carry. [If he rents it] to bring a *lesech* of wheat, and he brings a *lesech* of barley, he is exempt; but if he added to its load, he is liable.

YAD AVRAHAM

5.

הַשּׂוֹכֵר אֶת־הַחֲמוֹר לְהָבִיא עָלֶיהָ חִטִּים, — [If] one rents a donkey on which to bring wheat,

And he specifies that he will use it to carry a certain weight of wheat (*Tif. Yis.*).

וְהֵבִיא עָלֶיהָ שְׂעוֹרִים, — and he brings barley on it,

Instead of wheat, he brings barley, which is lighter than wheat (*Rav; Rashi*), but he brings a larger amount, so that it has the same weight as the wheat he had stipulated to bring (*Tif. Yis.*).

חַיָּב; — he is liable;

If the animal is injured thereby, the renter is liable, for — although the barley weighed no more than the wheat would have — its extra bulkiness caused the injury (ibid.).

תְּבוּאָה, וְהֵבִיא עָלֶיהָ תֶבֶן, — grain, and he brings straw on it,

[He rented the donkey to carry a certain amount of grain, and instead he loads it with straw.]

חַיָּב, — he is liable,

[The renter is responsible for any injury thereby caused to the donkey.]

מִפְּנֵי שֶׁהַנֶּפַח קָשֶׁה לַמַּשּׂאוּי. — because the added bulk is difficult to carry.

[This applies to both of the above

cases.] If the weight of the load he actually brings equals that of the load he had stipulated, but is bulkier, it is considered an added strain on the animal (*Gem.*, according to Rava's version of the mishnah).

Tiferes Yisrael suggests that the mishnah gives the additional example regarding the straw to teach us that although straw is very bulky, if the renter brought it instead of the grain he had stipulated, he is liable only if he loads enough straw on the animal so that the weight of the straw equals the weight of the stipulated grain (*Tif. Yis.*).

לְהָבִיא לֶתֶךְ חִטִּים, — [If he rents it] to bring a *lesech* of wheat,

A *lesech* is a dry measure, equaling fifteen *se'in* or one half of a *kor* (*Tif. Yis.*). [See table in preface to 3:7.]

וְהֵבִיא לֶתֶךְ שְׂעוֹרִים, — and he brings a *lesech* of barley,

[Instead of loading the donkey with a *lesech* of wheat, he loaded it with a *lesech* of barley, and the donkey was thereby injured.]

פָּטוּר; — he is exempt;

Since a *lesech* of barley is lighter than a *lesech* of wheat, and not more bulky than it, the renter is exempt for the injury to the donkey. In fact, even if he adds to the load, as long as it does not

וְכַמָּה יוֹסִיף עַל־מַשָּׂאוֹ וִיהֵא חַיָּב? סוּמְכוֹס אוֹמֵר
מִשּׁוּם רַבִּי מֵאִיר: סְאָה לְגָמָל, שְׁלֹשָׁה קַבִּין
לַחֲמוֹר.

[ו] **כָּל־הָאֻמָּנִין** שׁוֹמְרֵי שָׂכָר הֵן, וְכֻלָּן
שֶׁאָמְרוּ: ,,טֹל אֶת־שֶׁלְּךָ
וְהָבֵא מָעוֹת'' שׁוֹמֵר חִנָּם. ,,שְׁמֹר לִי וְאֶשְׁמֹר לָךְ,''

יד אברהם

equal the weight of a *lesech* of wheat, he is exempt, as explained below (*Tif. Yis.*).

וְאִם הוֹסִיף עַל־מַשָּׂאוֹ, — *but if he added to its load,*

He added a *seah*, causing the load of barley to equal the weight of a *lesech* of wheat (ibid. from *Gem.* 80a, according to Rava's interpretation). [The renter has now placed a bulkier load on the animal than had been stipulated.]

חַיָּב. — *he is liable.*

The renter is liable for any injury to the donkey caused by the extra bulk he loaded on its back (ibid.; *Meiri*).

וְכַמָּה יוֹסִיף עַל־מַשָּׂאוֹ וִיהֵא חַיָּב? — *How much must he add to its load to be liable?*

How much more of a load must a renter put on to an animal to be liable for any injury caused to it thereby if he loads it with the same material as had been agreed upon (ibid.)?

סוּמְכוֹס אוֹמֵר מִשּׁוּם רַבִּי מֵאִיר: סְאָה לְגָמָל, — *Sumchos says in the name of R' Meir: A seah for a camel,*

If the rented animal was a camel, the renter must have added one-fifteenth more than he had stipulated, in order to be liable for the injury. Using the example of our mishnah, in which the renter had agreed to carry a *lesech* — which equals fifteen *se'in* — he would have had to add an additional *seah* (*Tif. Yis.* from *Choshen Mishpat* 308:5).

שְׁלֹשָׁה קַבִּין לַחֲמוֹר. — *three kavs for a donkey.*

If the rented animal is a donkey, he

must overload it with one-thirtieth more than he had stipulated in order to be liable (ibid.). [In the mishnah's case, the excess amount would be three *kavs*, since a *lesech* equals ninety *kavs*.]

Heretofore, we have explained the mishnah according to the version of most editions: מִפְּנֵי שֶׁהַנֶּפַח קָשֶׁה לַמַּשָּׂאוּי, *because the added bulk is difficult to carry.* This reading — which is followed by *Meiri, Rambam (Commentary)* and *Tiferes Yisrael* — is in accordance with the version of Rava, who maintains that extra bulk can have no dire consequences unless the extra, bulky load weighs as much as that which the renter should have loaded on the donkey. Should the load be lighter than the stipulated load, even if it is bulkier, the renter is exempt from any injury thereby caused to the animal. Rava therefore construes the beginning of the mishnah as meaning that the renter brought barley weighing as much as a *lesech* of wheat.

Rav, Rashi, and *Nimmukei Yosef* have the reading: מִפְּנֵי שֶׁהַנֶּפַח קָשֶׁה בַּמַּשָּׂאוּי, *because the bulk is as difficult as the load,* meaning that equal bulk is as difficult to carry as equal weight. This follows the version of Abaye, who explains the beginning of the mishnah as meaning that if one rented a donkey to carry a certain amount of wheat, and instead he used it to carry an even larger — albeit lighter — amount of barley, he is liable if the extra amount of barley is not less than the amounts mentioned at the conclusion of the mishnah — a *seah* for a camel, three *kavs* for a donkey. Accordingly, Abaye interprets the

6
6
How much must he add to its load to be liable?
Sumchos says in the name of R' Meir: A *seah* for a
camel, three *kavs* for a donkey.

6. **A**ll craftsmen are regarded as paid *shomerim*,
and any of them who says: 'Take your
[article] and bring money' is an unpaid *shomer*. [If
one says:] 'Watch for me and I will watch for you,'

conclusion of the mishnah as being an
explanation of the beginning *(Tos. Yom
Tov* from *Tos.* 80a).

The halachah is in accordance with
Rava, as is the rule in almost all disputes
between Abaye and Rava *(Rif).*

6.

כָּל־הָאֻמָּנִין — *All craftsmen*
This refers to all craftsmen who
undertake to do work in their own
establishments, such as a dyer or a tailor
(Rav; Rashi; Meiri).

שׁוֹמְרֵי שָׂכָר הֵן, — *are regarded as paid
shomerim,*
That is, they are liable for the theft or
loss of the articles in their trust. [See
preface to chapter 3.] The craftsmen are
considered paid *shomerim* since they
have the article in their possession and,
if necessary, are able to hold it against
their pay. This benefit is considered
their remuneration for watching the
item *(Rav* from *Gem.* 80b).
Tos. R' Akiva notes that the halachah
follows the anonymous mishnah in
Shevuos 8:1, which equates a renter
with a paid *shomer* — his 'pay' being the
mere fact that the article is presently in
his possession for his benefit *(Gem.,
Rashi* ad loc.). Accordingly, a craftsman
is deemed a paid *shomer* for the same
reason, even were it not for the reason
mentioned by *Rav.*

וְכֻלָּן שֶׁאָמְרוּ: ,,טֹל אֶת־שֶׁלְּךָ וְהָבֵא מָעוֹת'' שׁוֹמֵר
חִנָּם. — *and any of them who says: 'Take
your [article] and bring money' is an
unpaid shomer.*
A craftsman who tells the owner of
the article: 'Take it, for I have finished it
and am not holding it against my pay;
after you have taken it you will pay me'

is considered an unpaid *shomer (Rav;
Rashi).*
From the very fact that the craftsman
first says, 'Take it' and then says, 'bring
money,' he implies thereby that he is not
holding it against his pay; therefore, he
no longer has the benefit which made
him a paid *shomer (Meiri).*
Rav and *Rashi,* too, do not mean that
he must state specifically that he is not
holding it against his pay, but rather
that this is implied by the order in which
he gave instructions to the owner. Indeed, if the craftsman instructs the
owner in the reverse order by saying,
'Bring money and take your article,' he
remains in the status of a paid *shomer*
until he receives his pay *(Tos. Yom Tov*
from *Gem.* 81a).
Even if he merely says: 'I have
finished it,' it is sufficient indication
that he no longer wishes to hold it
against his pay, and he becomes an
unpaid *shomer (Gem.;* see *Tos. Yom
Tov, Tos. R' Akiva).*
Should he state explicitly: 'I will
watch it no longer,' he does not have the
responsibility of a *shomer* — even an
unpaid one — and is exempt even if an
accident occurred to the item as a result
of his negligence *(Tif. Yis.* from
Choshen Mishpat 306:1).

,,שְׁמֹר לִי וְאֶשְׁמֹר לָךְ'', — *[If one says:]
'Watch for me and I will watch for you,'*

שׁוֹמֵר שָׂכָר. "שְׁמֹר לִי," וְאָמַר לוֹ: "הַנַּח לְפָנַי,"
שׁוֹמֵר חִנָּם.

[ז] **הִלְוָהוּ** עַל־הַמַּשְׁכּוֹן, שׁוֹמֵר שָׂכָר. רַבִּי
יְהוּדָה אוֹמֵר: הִלְוָהוּ מָעוֹת, שׁוֹמֵר
חִנָּם; הִלְוָהוּ פֵּרוֹת, שׁוֹמֵר שָׂכָר. אַבָּא שָׁאוּל

יד אברהם

One person says to another: 'Watch my things for me today, and I will watch your things for you tomorrow' (Rav from Gem. 81a).

The same applies if he says: 'Watch my things in the morning, and I will watch yours in the afternoon' (Tif. Yis.).

שׁוֹמֵר שָׂכָר. — he is a paid shomer.

Each one is considered a paid shomer for the other person's item, since each of them is watching for the other in payment for the other's watching for him (Meiri).

Should he say: 'Watch this for me now, and I will watch your things for you at the same time,' both of them are exempt from paying for the items even if they are lost or stolen, since this is an instance of the owner being employed by the shomer while he has the item in his possession (Rav). In such a case, Scripture (Exodus 22:14) states that a borrower is exempt if an accident occurs to the item [see 8:1 and commentary ad loc.], and the Gemara (95a) deduces that this applies not only to a borrower, but also to a paid shomer exempting him for theft and loss (Tos. Yom Tov). According to some, this exemption applies also to an unpaid shomer even if an accident results from his negligence (Gem. ibid., Rashi ad loc., s.v. פשיעה).

"שְׁמֹר לִי," וְאָמַר לוֹ: "הַנַּח לְפָנַי," — [If one says:] 'Watch for me,' and he replies: 'Put it down before me,'

[One person asks another to watch an article for him, and the latter tells him to put down the article in front of him.]

שׁוֹמֵר חִנָּם. — he is an unpaid shomer.

The Gemara (81b) explains that the mishnah's ruling applies even if the person who was asked to watch the item was standing in the street. Although an act of acquisition is necessary for one to assume responsibility as a shomer, since the owner places the article within four cubits of the other person, this is regarded as an act of acquisition, because one can acquire ownerless objects lying within that area around him, as discussed in the commentary to 1:4. Alternatively, the mishnah is dealing with an animal which the shomer struck, causing it to run, which is an act of acquisition (Nimmukei Yosef quoting Ravad and Rashba).

If, unlike the mishnah's case, when the person asked the other to watch the item, the latter replied: 'Put it down in front of yourself' or merely 'Put it down,' he does not have the responsibility of a shomer — even an unpaid one — since he indicated he does not wish to undertake any such obligation (Rav from Gem. 81b).

7.

הִלְוָהוּ עַל־הַמַּשְׁכּוֹן, שׁוֹמֵר שָׂכָר. — [If] he lent him on security, he is a paid shomer.

[If one person lends something to another, and an item is taken from the

borrower as security for the loan, the lender is considered a paid shomer with regard to the pledge, as explained below.]

The Gemara (82a) discusses two

he is a paid *shomer*. [If one says:] 'Watch for me,' and he replies: 'Put it down before me,' he is an unpaid *shomer*.

7. [I f] he lent him on security, he is a paid *shomer*. R' Yehudah says: [If] he lent him money, he is an unpaid *shomer*; [if] he lent him produce, he is a

YAD AVRAHAM

types of securities: one taken at the time of the loan, and one taken when the loan is due and is not being paid. An article taken at the time of the loan is obviously taken as security — the lender does not gain any ownership of it, nor does the borrower lose any ownership. One taken when the loan is due and the borrower cannot yet meet his obligation, on the other hand, is taken as a form of collection (pending the repayment of the debt) and to a degree, the lender does gain ownership of the security — certainly to the extent that he assumes the responsibility of a paid *shomer*, who is liable if the item is stolen or lost. This is true if before the lender takes the security, he receives permission from the court, as required [see 9:13]. Should he transgress the law and take something from the borrower without court sanction, he is deemed a robber and is responsible even for accidents and even for the amount that the security is worth over the amount of the loan (*Tif. Yis.*).

The mishnah, however, deals also with a lender who takes a security at the time of the loan, as implied by the expression *he lent him on security*. In such an instance, the lender gains nothing by taking the security over not having granted the loan at all, and is therefore unlike the craftsman in mishnah 6, who gains by holding the item against his pay (*Tos.* 80b). Nevertheless, explains the *Gemara*, he is considered a paid *shomer*, because he performs a *mitzvah* by lending out his money, and one who performs a *mitzvah* is exempt from performing other *mitzvos* at that time, including

giving charity to any poor person who approaches him. This potential monetary gain that he receives from the loan is deemed a benefit and makes him a paid *shomer* on the security. Although this benefit is only at the time the transaction is taking place [since later he is no longer *performing* the *mitzvah*], he remains a paid *shomer* as long as the security is in his possession, just as one becomes a paid *shomer* for a long period of time by dint of the payment he receives at the inception of the period or at its conclusion (ibid.; *Tos. Yom Tov* from *Nimmukei Yosef*).

— רַבִּי יְהוּדָה אוֹמֵר: הִלְוָהוּ מָעוֹת, שׁוֹמֵר חִנָּם; *R' Yehudah says: [If] he lent him money, he is an unpaid shomer;*

The first, anonymous *Tanna* does not differentiate between loans of money and those of produce. R' Yehudah, however, disagrees, maintaining that the benefit gained by performing a *mitzvah* is not sufficient to make one a paid *shomer* (*Rav; Rashi*).

The *Gemara*, however, advances a different explanation, concluding that R' Yehudah and the first *Tanna* agree that the benefit gained by the *mitzvah* is enough to make him a paid *shomer*. They disagree only with regard to a case in which the lender needs the security for his own purposes and deducts from the debt accordingly. R' Yehudah holds that such a loan is not a *mitzvah*; the first *Tanna* contends that it is.

הִלְוָהוּ פֵּרוֹת, שׁוֹמֵר שָׂכָר. — *[if] he lent him produce, he is a paid shomer.*

Since produce is likely to rot, the lender gains by lending out what he has now, and receiving fresh produce in its

אוֹמֵר: מֻתָּר אָדָם לְהַשְׂכִּיר מַשְׁכּוֹנוֹ שֶׁל־עָנִי,
לִהְיוֹת פּוֹסֵק עָלָיו וְהוֹלֵךְ, מִפְּנֵי שֶׁהוּא כְמֵשִׁיב
אֲבֵדָה.

[ח] **הַמַּעֲבִיר** חָבִית מִמָּקוֹם לְמָקוֹם וּשְׁבָרָהּ,
בֵּין שׁוֹמֵר חִנָּם בֵּין שׁוֹמֵר שָׂכָר,
יִשָּׁבַע. רַבִּי אֱלִיעֶזֶר אוֹמֵר: זֶה וְזֶה יִשָּׁבַע, וְתָמֵהַּ
אֲנִי אִם יְכוֹלִין זֶה וָזֶה לִשָּׁבַע.

יד אברהם

stead at the time of payment. This gain
is considered his reward, making him a
paid *shomer* (*Rav; Meiri; Tif. Yis.*).

The halachah follows the first *Tanna*
(*Rav; Rambam Commentary*).

אַבָּא שָׁאוּל אוֹמֵר: מֻתָּר אָדָם לְהַשְׂכִּיר מַשְׁכּוֹנוֹ
שֶׁל־עָנִי, לִהְיוֹת פּוֹסֵק עָלָיו וְהוֹלֵךְ, — *Abba
Shaul says: A person may rent out a
poor man's security, fixing a price and
progressively [diminishing the debt],*

If one lent money to another and
received a security from him, he may
rent out that security to others, fixing a
price for the rental of the security (*Rav;
Rashi*), and then progressively deduct
the rental fee from the debt (*Meiri*).

However, one may not rent out a rich
man's security (*Tosefta 7:10*).

The intention of *Rav* and *Rashi* is
that the lender may not rent it himself
for his own use; he may only rent it out
to others. *Tur* (72) explains that if he
uses it himself, he will be suspected of
doing so without deducting the rental
fee from the debt (*Tos. Yom Tov; Sma
72:3*) or renting it to himself at a rate
below the usual price (*Beur HaGra*). He
may therefore rent it out only to others,
not to himself, in order to avoid such
suspicion. This ruling is based on *Bava
Basra 8b*, where the *Gemara* states that
if charity collectors found no needy

people to whom to distribute the money
they had collected, they should change
the copper coins for silver ones, since
the latter will not corrode, but they
should do this only with other people.
They may not exchange the money with
their own coins, however, lest people
suspect them of taking more copper
coins than they should (*Tos. Yom Tov*).
For varying opinions, see *Bach* (loc.
cit.).

Should the lender stipulate at the time
of the loan that he can use the security,
it is permissible (*Beis Yosef* ad loc.;
Rama 72:1).

מִפְּנֵי שֶׁהוּא כְמֵשִׁיב אֲבֵדָה. — *because he is
as one who returns a lost article.*

[The lender may rent out the security,
because he thereby enables the borrower
to redeem his debt.]

This ruling applies only to articles
that depreciate only slightly and can be
rented out for a high fee — e.g., a shovel,
a plane, an axe, and the like (*Rav* from
Gem. 82b). This is intimated by the
expression: מַשְׁכּוֹנוֹ שֶׁל־עָנִי, *a poor man's
pledge*, since these implements are
usually pledged by the poor
(*Shoshannim LeDavid*).

The halachah is in accordance with
the view of Abba Shaul (*Rav, Rambam
Commentary* from *Gem. 82b*).

8.

הַמַּעֲבִיר חָבִית מִמָּקוֹם לְמָקוֹם וּשְׁבָרָהּ, בֵּין שׁוֹמֵר
חִנָּם בֵּין שׁוֹמֵר שָׂכָר, — *[If] one moves a
cask from one place to another and*

*breaks it, whether he is an unpaid
shomer or a paid shomer,*

[That is, whether he is being paid for

paid *shomer*. Abba Shaul says: A person may rent out a poor man's security, fixing a price and progressively [diminishing the debt], because he is as one who returns a lost article.

8. [I]f] one moves a cask from one place to another and breaks it, whether he is an unpaid *shomer* or a paid *shomer*, he must swear. R' Eliezer says: [Indeed] both must swear, but I wonder whether both can swear.

YAD AVRAHAM

moving the cask or not.]

יִשָּׁבַע. — *he must swear.*

The one who moved the cask must swear that he did not do so negligently (*Rav; Rashi*).

רַבִּי אֱלִיעֶזֶר אוֹמֵר: זֶה וְזֶה יִשָּׁבֵעַ, — *R' Eliezer says: [Indeed] both must swear,*

R' Eliezer adds that he, too, heard from his mentors that both of the above must swear (*Rav; Rashi*).

Rishon LeTzion maintains that the correct reading is רַבִּי אֶלְעָזָר, *R' Elazar,* rather than *R' Eliezer.* He proves this from the fact that the first, anonymous *Tanna* — in reply to whom the above statement was made — is R' Meir, as implied by the *Gemara,* and R' Eliezer preceded R' Meir by two generations, for R' Akiva — R' Meir's teacher — was a disciple of R' Eliezer. He cites *Rosh* whose reading is R' Elazar. [Our editions of Rosh, however, read: *R' Eliezer.*] *Meleches Shlomo* states that the mishnah is referring to R' Elazar ben Shammua, a contemporary of R' Meir.

וְתָמַהּ אֲנִי אִם יְכוֹלִין זֶה וְזֶה לִשָּׁבַע. — *but I wonder whether both can swear.*

He wonders how the one who broke the cask can exempt himself from payment by merely swearing that he was not negligent. This may be the case regarding the one who is not paid for moving the cask and is considered an unpaid *shomer*; he is therefore exempt for any mishap occurring to the item, except one involving negligence on his

part. But this should not apply to the one who is paid for the job and is considered a paid *shomer*. He is liable for theft and loss, and since what occurred was not completely an accident, it fits into the latter category. Moreover, even an unpaid *shomer* can exempt himself only if the cask was broken on sloping ground, since it can be attributed to an accident. If it was broken on flat ground, however, it was surely due to negligence, and even an unpaid *shomer* cannot exempt himself with an oath.

Indeed, R' Meir agrees that there is no basis for exempting the one who broke the cask if he merely swears that he had not been negligent. Rather, he maintains that this is a different type of oath. The Rabbis realized that it is common for one to break a cask while moving it, and if a worker would be required to pay for such breakage every time he moved a cask, no one would be willing to undertake such jobs. They therefore enacted that if the mover swears that he did not break the cask intentionally, he is exempt (*Rav from Gem.* 83a; cf. *Ritva,* quoted in *Shitah Mekubetzes*).

This reasoning follows only according to R' Meir, who rules that if one stumbles, it is deemed negligence (see *Bava Kamma* 3:1 and commentary ad loc.). Accordingly, even an unpaid *shomer* would be liable if he stumbled on flat ground, were it not that he could swear that he had not broken it intentionally and be exempt. According

[א] **הַשּׂוֹכֵר** אֶת־הַפּוֹעֲלִים וְאָמַר לָהֶם
לְהַשְׁכִּים וּלְהַעֲרִיב — מְקוֹם
שֶׁנָּהֲגוּ שֶׁלֹּא לְהַשְׁכִּים וְשֶׁלֹּא לְהַעֲרִיב, אֵינוֹ רַשַּׁאי
לְכוֹפָן.

מְקוֹם שֶׁנָּהֲגוּ לָזוּן, יָזוּן; לְסַפֵּק בִּמְתִיקָה, יְסַפֵּק;
הַכֹּל כְּמִנְהַג הַמְּדִינָה.

מַעֲשֶׂה בְּרַבִּי יוֹחָנָן בֶּן־מַתְיָא שֶׁאָמַר לִבְנוֹ: ,,צֵא
שְׂכֹר לָנוּ פוֹעֲלִים." הָלַךְ, וּפָסַק לָהֶם מְזוֹנוֹת.

יד אברהם

to R' Yehudah whose view is followed by the halachah, however, stumbling is not caused by negligence; rather, it is considered an accident. Consequently, an unpaid *shomer* can merely swear that he had not been negligent and be exempt. A paid *shomer*, too, was granted the right to exempt himself by swearing that he was not negligent (*Tos. Yom Tov* from *Rif.* and *Rosh*).

Chapter 7

1.

If one hires workers on a per diem basis, he may make any stipulations he wishes, even regarding practices that are not customary in that locality. Should he hire them without any stipulation, however, he is bound by local custom.

הַשּׂוֹכֵר אֶת־הַפּוֹעֲלִים — [*If*] *one hired laborers*

[As mentioned above, this chapter refers to workers hired on a day-to-day basis.]

The intention is that he hired them without making any specific stipulations (*Tos. Yom Tov* from *Tos.* 83a; *Meiri*; *Choshen Mishpat* 294:1).

וְאָמַר לָהֶם לְהַשְׁכִּים וּלְהַעֲרִיב — *and ordered them to work early and late* —

Subsequently, the employer ordered the laborers to report for work before sunrise and remain after sunset (*Tos. Yom Tov* from *Tos., Meiri*).

מְקוֹם שֶׁנָּהֲגוּ שֶׁלֹּא לְהַשְׁכִּים וְשֶׁלֹּא לְהַעֲרִיב, אֵינוֹ רַשַּׁאי לְכוֹפָן. — [*in*] *a place where it is customary not to work early or not to work late, he has no right to compel them.*

Although the employer pays these workers more than the current wage, he cannot claim that he had intended that

they should work longer hours by coming before sunrise and leaving sometime after sunset. The workers may reply that they had accepted the higher wage with the intention of doing exceptionally good work, which they did (*Rav, Tos. Yom Tov* from *Gem.* 83a; see *Sma* 331:1).

Should they neglect to do exceptional work, some authorities rule that the employer may deduct from the additional wages he had promised them. Others explain that the intention is that they should do their work diligently to the best of their ability and not be lazy; hence, if the workers claim that they did their best, the employer cannot deduct from the additional wages (*Meiri; Turei Zahav* loc. cit.).

As mentioned above, should the employer have stipulated at the time of hiring that the workers must come early and stay late, they are obliged to do so (*Meiri; Nimmukei Yosef; Shulchan*

1. [If] one hired laborers and ordered them to work early and late — [in] a place where it is customary not to work early or not to work late, he has no right to compel them.

[In] a place where it is customary to give [the workers] food, he must give [them] food; to provide relish, he must provide relish; everything [must be done] according to the local custom.

It once happened that R' Yochanan ben Massia said to his son: 'Go out [and] hire laborers for us.' He

YAD AVRAHAM

Aruch ibid.).

מְקוֹם שֶׁנָּהֲגוּ לָזוּן, יָזוּן; — [In] *a place where it is customary to give [the workers] food, he must give [them] food;*

This refers to adequate meals (*Meiri*).

לְסַפֵּק בְּמְתִיקָה, יְסַפֵּק; — *to provide relish, he must provide relish;*

Rav and *Rashi* explain that wherever it is customary for employers to provide their workers with relish in which to dip their bread, he must do so. [Apparently, this means that in addition to providing food, the custom is to provide relish as well.]

Rambam (Hil. Sechirus 9:1) construes the term מְתִיקָה as meaning figs, dates, or the like. *Tif. Yis.* — citing *Choshen Mishpat* 331:1, which follows *Rambam's* translation — equates this with serving whiskey in our times. According to him, the employer supplied these refreshments in addition to the regular meals. *Meiri*, however, explains the mishnah to mean that in some places the employers are stingy with food and provide only figs, dates, or other sweets, but not regular meals.

הַכֹּל בְּמִנְהַג הַמְּדִינָה. — *everything [must be done] according to the local custom.*

This ruling includes places where the workers usually eat and drink at their employer's house in the morning before going to their place of work. Should the

employer tell them to go out early to work in the field, and that he will bring them their breakfast there, they may reply that they wish to eat in his house before going out to the field, as is the local custom (*Rav* from *Gem.* 86a).

If the breakfast is not ready, the workers may insist on waiting in the house until it is ready and go out to the field only after they have eaten (*Tos. Yom Tov* from *Tos.* ad loc.)

Since the following incident mentioned by the mishnah appears to contradict the aforementioned principle that *everything must be done according to the local custom*, the *Gemara* explains that the text is defective[1] and that the following statement should be inserted at this point: *But if he stipulates to give them food, he has added food for them.* That is, in a place where the local custom dictates that food must be provided for workers, if the employer stipulates that he will give them food, he is certainly not referring to the usual amount of food given the workers, since they are entitled to that according to the local custom. Rather, we interpret his words as meaning that he will give them more than the customary amount of food. To prove this, the *Tanna* cites a precedent — the incident below (*Rav*).

מַעֲשֶׂה בְּרַבִּי יוֹחָנָן בֶּן־מַתְיָא שֶׁאָמַר לִבְנוֹ: "צֵא שְׂכֹר לָנוּ פוֹעֲלִים." הָלַךְ, — *It once*

1. [For a discussion regarding corrections and additions to the text of the Mishnah, see ArtScroll commentary to *Nedarim* 1:1, p. 8.]

וּכְשֶׁבָּא אֵצֶל אָבִיו, אָמַר לוֹ: ,,בְּנִי, אֲפִלּוּ אַתָּה
עוֹשֶׂה לָהֶם כִּסְעָדַת שְׁלֹמֹה בִּשְׁעָתוֹ, לֹא יָצָאתָ יְדֵי
חוֹבָתְךָ עִמָּהֶן, שֶׁהֵן בְּנֵי אַבְרָהָם, יִצְחָק, וְיַעֲקֹב.
אֶלָּא, עַד שֶׁלֹּא יַתְחִילוּ בַמְּלָאכָה, צֵא וֶאֱמֹר לָהֶם:
,,עַל־מְנָת שֶׁאֵין לָכֶם עָלַי אֶלָּא פַת וְקִטְנִית
בִּלְבָד.'' רַבָּן שִׁמְעוֹן בֶּן־גַּמְלִיאֵל אוֹמֵר: לֹא הָיָה
צָרִיךְ לוֹמַר; הַכֹּל כְּמִנְהַג הַמְּדִינָה.

יד אברהם

happened that R' Yochanan ben Massia
said to his son: 'Go out [and] hire
laborers for us.' He went,

[He went and hired them.]

וּפָסַק לָהֶם מְזוֹנוֹת. וּכְשֶׁבָּא אֵצֶל אָבִיו, אָמַר לוֹ:
,,בְּנִי, אֲפִלּוּ אַתָּה עוֹשֶׂה לָהֶם כִּסְעָדַת שְׁלֹמֹה
בִּשְׁעָתוֹ, — and agreed to give them food.
When he came to his father, he said to
him: 'My son, even if you prepare for
them [a meal] like Solomon's banquet in
his time,

That is, at the time he reigned. [As
described in I Kings 5:2,3, Solomon
would provide a lavish feast each day
for all who came to eat with him (see
Metzudas David ad loc.).] In his later
years, however, Solomon was deposed
[by Ashmadai] (Rav; Rashi), as related
in Gittin 68b (Tif. Yis.).

Meleches Shlomo explains that even
according to those who maintain that
Solomon's kingdom was ultimately
restored to him, it did not equal the
glory of his first kingdom. Accordingly,
R' Yochanan ben Massia is saying to his
son that not only if he gives the laborers
a meal like that given by Solomon after
his return to the throne has he not
discharged his duty to them, but even if
he gives them a meal like those served
by Solomon before he was deposed
from his throne, he has still not fulfilled
his obligation.

לֹא יָצָאתָ יְדֵי חוֹבָתְךָ עִמָּהֶן, שֶׁהֵן בְּנֵי אַבְרָהָם,
יִצְחָק, וְיַעֲקֹב. — you have not discharged
your duty toward them, for they are
children of Abraham, Isaac, and Jacob.

The Gemara (86b) relates that the
meals served by Abraham were more
elaborate and sumptuous than
Solomon's. This is based on Genesis
18:7, וַיִּקַּח בֶּן־בָּקָר רַךְ וָטוֹב, and he took a
calf, tender and good, which the Rabbis
interpret exegetically to mean that there
were three calves which Abraham
served his three guests — one for each of
them. Regarding Solomon's banquet,
however, Scripture (I Kings 4:20) states
that it was attended by: יְהוּדָה וְיִשְׂרָאֵל
רַבִּים כַּחוֹל אֲשֶׁר־עַל־הַיָּם, Judah and Israel
were many, as the sand on the seashore
(Rav, Tos. Yom Tov from Gem). [That
is, although Solomon served much more
at his banquet, since there was such a
multitude in attendance, each partici-
pant received a smaller portion than
those who dined with Abraham.]
Although the mishnah derives this from
verses regarding Abraham, it mentions
Isaac and Jacob, as well, to indicate that
only their descendants are entitled to
these privileges, since they are considered Abraham's heirs, and not
Ishmael and Esau. The Rabbis derive
this from Genesis 21:12: כִּי בְיִצְחָק יִקָּרֵא
לְךָ זָרַע, for in Isaac shall offspring be
considered yours. Scripture states:
בְיִצְחָק, in Isaac, intimating that only part
of Isaac's offspring will be counted as
Abraham's seed — Jacob, but not Esau
(Tos. Yom Tov).

[Thus, we see from the incident of R'
Yochanan ben Massia that although the
local custom was to provide workers
with merely bread and beans, as implied

went, and agreed to give them food. When he came to his father, he said to him: 'My son, even if you prepare for them [a meal] like Solomon's banquet in his time, you have not discharged your duty toward them, for they are children of Abraham, Isaac, and Jacob. Rather, before they start work, go out and say to them: 'On condition that you have no claim upon me other than bread and beans.' Rabban Shimon ben Gamliel says: He did not have to say [it]; everything is according to the local custom.

YAD AVRAHAM

below, since it was stipulated that they would receive food, this is construed as meaning that they would get more than dictated by the local custom.]

אֶלָּא, עַד שֶׁלֹּא יַתְחִילוּ בִמְלָאכָה, — *Rather, before they start work,*

Since they have not yet begun working, the agreement with them is merely a verbal one, and he can still retract and give them less. After they start work, however, he can no longer renege (*Rav; Rashi*).

צֵא וֶאֱמֹר לָהֶם: "עַל־מְנָת שֶׁאֵין לָכֶם עָלַי אֶלָּא פַּת וְקִטְנִית בִּלְבָד." — *go out and say to them: 'On condition that you have no claim upon me other than bread and beans.'*

'Tell them that you meant that you will provide them with only bread and beans, as is customary in our locality' (*Kehati*).

רַבָּן שִׁמְעוֹן בֶּן־גַּמְלִיאֵל אוֹמֵר: לֹא הָיָה צָרִיךְ לוֹמַר; הַכֹּל כְּמִנְהַג הַמְּדִינָה. — *Rabban Shimon ben Gamliel says: He did not have to say [it]; everything is according*

to the local custom.

[Despite the fact that he had promised them food, he did not have to specify that he was giving them only bread and beans, since that was customary in his locality. We do not assume that by stipulating to provide the workers with food, he intended to give a greater amount than that stipulated by local custom.]

The word *everything* is meant to include the case of an employer who promises his worker that he will pay him like one or two of the townspeople: Rabban Shimon ben Gamliel rules that he must pay him like an average wage-earner in the town. *Rashi* explains this as meaning that he is paid as much as an average worker receives. *Ramah*, however, construes this to mean that we determine the highest wage and the lowest wage that are paid for workers in the town, and this worker then receives the amount exactly between them, although the average worker may be paid more or less than this sum (*Tos. Yom Tov* from *Tur* 331).

2.

After stating in the preceding mishnah that laborers are given their meals by virtue of local custom or by virtue of a promise by their employer, the *Tanna* now proceeds to tell us that some workers may eat of the produce with which they are working, even without any promise or local custom. They are given this privilege by the Torah itself (*Tos. Yom Tov* from *Tur* 87a). This ruling is based on *Deuteronomy* 23:25,26: כִּי תָבֹא בְּכֶרֶם רֵעֶךָ וְאָכַלְתָּ עֲנָבִים כְּנַפְשְׁךָ שָׂבְעֶךָ וְאֶל־כֶּלְיְךָ לֹא תִתֵּן.

[ב] **וְאֵלּוּ** אוֹכְלִין מִן־הַתּוֹרָה: הָעוֹשֶׂה בִמְחֻבָּר
לַקַּרְקַע, בִּשְׁעַת גְּמַר מְלָאכָה,
וּבְתָלוּשׁ מִן־הַקַּרְקַע, עַד שֶׁלֹּא נִגְמְרָה
מְלַאכְתּוֹ—בְּדָבָר שֶׁגִּדּוּלוֹ מִן־הָאָרֶץ.
וְאֵלּוּ שֶׁאֵינָן אוֹכְלִין: הָעוֹשֶׂה בִמְחֻבָּר לַקַּרְקַע,
בְּשָׁעָה שֶׁאֵין גְּמַר מְלָאכָה; וּבְתָלוּשׁ מִן־הַקַּרְקַע,
מֵאַחַר שֶׁנִּגְמְרָה מְלַאכְתּוֹ; וּבְדָבָר שֶׁאֵין גִּדּוּלוֹ מִן־
הָאָרֶץ.

יד אברהם

כִּי תָבֹא בְּקָמַת רֵעֶךָ וְקָטַפְתָּ מְלִילֹת בְּיָדְךָ וְחֶרְמֵשׁ לֹא תָנִיף עַל קָמַת רֵעֶךָ, *When you come into another's vineyard, you may eat grapes according to your desire, to your satiety, but you shall not put any in your vessel. When you come into another's standing grain, you may pluck ears with your hand, but you may not raise a sickle upon the standing grain of the other person.*

The *Gemara* (87b) construes these verses as referring to a worker.

וְאֵלּוּ אוֹכְלִין — *These may eat*

These laborers may eat of the produce with which they are working (*Rav; Rashi*).

מִן־הַתּוֹרָה: — *by virtue of [the law of] the Torah:*

That is, even without any stipulation or local custom (*Tos. Yom Tov*).

הָעוֹשֶׂה בִמְחֻבָּר לַקַּרְקַע, בִּשְׁעַת גְּמַר מְלָאכָה, — *One who works with [produce] attached to the ground, at the time of the completion of the work,*

One who works with produce that is still attached to the ground may eat of it when it is being picked. This is derived from (loc. cit., v. 25): וְאֶל־כֶּלְיְךָ לֹא תִתֵּן, *but you shall not put any in your vessel,* implying that when the worker puts the produce into the owner's vessel — i.e., when he picks it — he may partake thereof (*Rav from Gem.* 87b).

The expression *completion of the work* refers to the ripening of the produce, when it no longer requires the soil and may be picked. This excludes the worker who is hired to weed out stunted onions or garlic to give the large ones room to spread out. Since the produce is not yet ripe, the worker does not have the privilege of eating it (*Rav*

from *Gem.* 89a). Although he puts these vegetables into the owner's vessel, the Torah's intention is that he may eat only when he puts ripe produce into the vessel (*Rabbenu Yehonasan*, quoted in *Shitah Mekubetzes*).

Rambam (*Hil. Sechirus* 12:2) rules that the picker may eat only after he has filled the owner's basket. *Meiri* differs.

וּבְתָלוּשׁ מִן־הַקַּרְקַע, — *or with [produce] detached from the ground,*

That is, he works with produce already detached from the ground (*Rav*).

עַד שֶׁלֹּא נִגְמְרָה מְלַאכְתּוֹ — *when its work is not yet completed —*

If it is a species that requires the separation of *terumah* [the portion of the crop given to the *Kohen*] and tithes, the laborer may eat of it if he works on it before the completion of the work, which makes the produce liable for these separations. [See *Rav.*] Should he be working with grain, which, after being ground and kneaded, will require separation of *challah* [the portion of the dough given to the *Kohen*], he may partake of the grain prior to that time. However, if he is kneading dough, or rolling it and smoothing its surface, or

2. These may eat by virtue of [the law of] the Torah: One who works with [produce] attached to the ground, at the time of the completion of the work, or with [produce] detached from the ground, when its work is not yet completed — with something that grows from the ground.

These do not eat: one who works with [produce] attached to the ground, when the work is not completed; or with [produce] detached from the ground, after its work has been completed; or with something that does not grow from the ground.

YAD AVRAHAM

baking it, he may not eat of the dough, since it is already liable for *challah*. Should he have been hired to remove pebbles from flour or to grind wheat into flour, since it is not yet liable for *challah*, he may partake of it *(Rambam, Hil. Sechirus 12:5)*. The underlying principle is that the laborer may eat of the produce until it becomes liable for the performance of the last *mitzvah* which must be done with it *(Tif. Yis.; Rashi 89a)*.

In the case of flour mentioned above, *Ravad (Hil. Sechirus 9:5)* contends that since the grain already became liable for tithing, the worker may not partake of the flour.

Excluded by the mishnah, for example, is a worker hired to separate figs or dates that are stuck together. He may not eat them, since they already have the requirement of separating tithes from them *(Rav from Gem. 89a)*. *Ravad* (quoted by *Shitah Mekubetzes*) explains that they would separate figs and dates that had been pressed together and were beginning to become moldy.

בְּדָבָר שֶׁגִּדּוּלוֹ מִן־הָאָרֶץ. — *with something that grows from the ground.*

[The worker may eat from that with which he is working only if they are things that grow from the ground (see *Rav*).]

וְאֵלּוּ שֶׁאֵינָן אוֹכְלִין: — *These do not eat:*

The following workers eat neither by virtue of Torah law nor by virtue of general custom *(Tos. Yom Tov from Gem. 93a).*

הָעוֹשֶׂה בִמְחֻבָּר לַקַּרְקַע, בְּשָׁעָה שֶׁאֵין גְּמַר מְלָאכָה; — *one who works with [produce] attached to the ground, when the work is not completed;*

[For example, he weeds onions or garlic, as discussed above.]

וּבְתָלוּשׁ מִן־הַקַּרְקַע, מֵאַחַר שֶׁנִּגְמְרָה מְלַאכְתּוֹ; — *or with [produce] detached from the ground, after its work has been completed;*

[E.g., separating figs or dates, kneading or rolling dough, or baking bread. As explained above, the worker may not eat these, since they are already liable for tithes or *challah*.]

וּבְדָבָר שֶׁאֵין גִּדּוּלוֹ מִן־הָאָרֶץ. — *or with something that does not grow from the ground.*

This excludes dairy workers, such as those engaged in milking, pressing thick milk, or cheese making *(Rav from Gem. 89a).*

Although it is obvious from the first half of the mishnah that all those listed in this sentence are precluded from eating, since they are not included in the categories mentioned above, the *Tanna* wishes to exclude these workers from eating even by virtue of general custom *(Gem. 93a).*

[ג] הָיָה עוֹשֶׂה בְּיָדָיו, אֲבָל לֹא בְּרַגְלָיו; בְּרַגְלָיו,
אֲבָל לֹא בְּיָדָיו; אֲפִלּוּ בִּכְתֵפוֹ, הֲרֵי זֶה
אוֹכֵל. רַבִּי יוֹסֵי בְּרַבִּי יְהוּדָה אוֹמֵר: עַד שֶׁיַּעֲשֶׂה
בְּיָדָיו וּבְרַגְלָיו.

[ד] הָיָה עוֹשֶׂה בַּתְּאֵנִים, לֹא יֹאכַל בָּעֲנָבִים;
בָּעֲנָבִים, לֹא יֹאכַל בַּתְּאֵנִים; אֲבָל
מוֹנֵעַ אֶת־עַצְמוֹ עַד שֶׁמַּגִּיעַ לִמְקוֹם הַיָּפוֹת וְאוֹכֵל.
וְכֻלָּן, לֹא אָמְרוּ אֶלָּא בִּשְׁעַת מְלָאכָה; אֲבָל מִשּׁוּם
הָשֵׁב אֲבֵדָה לַבְּעָלִים, אָמְרוּ: פּוֹעֲלִין אוֹכְלִין
בַּהֲלִיכָתָן מֵאוּמָן לְאוּמָן, וּבַחֲזִירָתָן מִן־הַגַּת.

3.

This is a continuation of the preceding mishnah. The *Tanna* discusses more details of the rules concerning the laborers' privilege to eat from the produce.

הָיָה עוֹשֶׂה בְּיָדָיו, אֲבָל לֹא בְּרַגְלָיו; — [If] one was working with his hands, but not with his feet;

For example, he works with a reaper or a picker (*Meiri*).

בְּרַגְלָיו, אֲבָל לֹא בְּיָדָיו; — with his feet, but not with his hands;

E.g., he threshes the grain with his feet, or treads the grapes (ibid.).

אֲפִלּוּ בִּכְתֵפוֹ, — [or] even with his shoulder,

That is, even if he does not move his hands or feet (*Tos. Yom Tov* from *Rashi*). For example, one who is hired to carry grapes on his shoulder to the winepress (*Meiri*).

הֲרֵי זֶה אוֹכֵל. — he may eat.

The Torah grants him the privilege of eating from the produce with which he works (ibid.).

רַבִּי יוֹסֵי בְּרַבִּי יְהוּדָה אוֹמֵר: עַד שֶׁיַּעֲשֶׂה בְּיָדָיו וּבְרַגְלָיו. — R' Yose, the son of R' Yehudah, says: [He may not eat] unless he works with his hands and his feet.

R' Yose maintains that the worker may eat the produce only if he works with both his hands and feet, because he is then like an ox, which may not be muzzled while it is threshing [*Deut.* 25:4] (*Rav* from *Gem.* 91b). The first, anonymous *Tanna*, however, contends that Scripture [ibid. 23:25] states: ... כִּי תָבֹא בְּכֶרֶם רֵעֶךָ וְאָכַלְתָּ, When you come into another's vineyard, you may eat ..., implying that he may do so when he does any type of work. It does not specify: When you come to pick (*Tos. Yom Tov* from *Gem.*).

The halachah is in accordance with the first *Tanna* (*Rav; Rambam Commentary*).

4.

This mishnah continues to discuss laws of workers eating in the vineyard; they may eat only when they are working, and only of the species with which they are working at the time.

3. [If] one was working with his hands, but not with his feet; with his feet, but not with his hands; [or] even with his shoulder, he may eat. R' Yose, the son of R' Yehudah, says: [He may not eat] unless he works with his hands and his feet.

4. [If] he was working with the figs, he may not partake of the grapes; with the grapes, he may not partake of the figs; but he may abstain until he reaches the place of the best [fruits] and eat.

Concerning all of these, [the Rabbis] said [they may eat] only at the time of work; but in order to avoid a loss to its owner, they said: The laborers may eat while walking from row to row, and when they

YAD AVRAHAM

הָיָה עוֹשֶׂה בַתְּאֵנִים, לֹא יֹאכַל בָּעֲנָבִים; בָּעֲנָבִים, לֹא יֹאכַל בַּתְּאֵנִים; — [If] he was working with the figs, he may not partake of the grapes; with the grapes, he may not partake of the figs;

Since the Torah (loc. cit.) specifies that *When you come into another's vineyard, you may eat grapes,* it is construed as meaning that when you work in his vineyard, you may eat grapes, but not figs. In addition, you may eat grapes only when you work in his vineyard, not when you work on his fig trees (*Tos. Yom Tov* from *Rambam, Hil. Sechirus* 12:10; *Sifre* loc. cit.; *Yerushalmi, Maasros* 2:8). Others derive it from the end of the verse: *but you shall not put any in your vessels,* implying that you may eat only of the species you are putting into the owner's vessel, not another species (*Tos. Yom Tov* from *Sma* 337:22).

Even if the laborer is hired to work on both grapes and figs, he may partake only of the species with which he is working at the time (ibid. from *Tur* 337).

אֲבָל מוֹנֵעַ אֶת־עַצְמוֹ עַד שֶׁמַּגִּיעַ לִמְקוֹם הַיָּפוֹת וְאוֹכֵל. — *but he may abstain until he reaches the place of the best [fruits] and*

eat.

[The worker may abstain from eating the inferior fruits until he works in the place where the better fruits grow, and eat to satiety there.]

וְכֻלָּן, לֹא אָמְרוּ אֶלָּא בִשְׁעַת מְלָאכָה; — *Concerning all of these, [the Rabbis] said [they may eat] only at the time of work;*

Concerning all of these laborers, the Rabbis said that they may eat of the produce only while they are working. Although they may have refrained from eating until they have finished, they may not sit down then and eat (*Tos. Yom Tov* from *Rashi*).

אֲבָל מִשּׁוּם הָשֵׁב אֲבֵדָה לַבְּעָלִים — *but in order to avoid* (lit., *return*) *a loss to its owner,*

That is, lest the workers neglect their work in order to eat (*Rav; Rashi*).

אָמְרוּ: — *they said:*

In other words, they enacted (*Tos. Yom Tov* from *Nimmukei Yosef*).

פּוֹעֲלִין אוֹכְלִין בַּהֲלִיכָתָן מֵאוֹמָן לְאוֹמָן, — *The laborers may eat while walking from row to row,*

After the workers finish one row and

וּבַחֲמוֹר, כְּשֶׁהִיא פּוֹרֶקֶת.

[ה] **אוֹכֵל** פּוֹעֵל קִשּׁוּת אֲפִלּוּ בְדִינָר, וְכוֹתֶבֶת אֲפִלּוּ בְדִינָר. רַבִּי אֶלְעָזָר חִסְמָא אוֹמֵר: לֹא יֹאכַל פּוֹעֵל יָתֵר עַל־שְׂכָרוֹ. וַחֲכָמִים מַתִּירִין, אֲבָל מְלַמְּדִין אֶת־הָאָדָם שֶׁלֹּא יְהֵא רַעַבְתָן, וִיהֵא סוֹתֵם אֶת־הַפֶּתַח בְּפָנָיו.

[ו] **קוֹצֵץ** אָדָם עַל־יְדֵי עַצְמוֹ, עַל־יְדֵי בְּנוֹ וּבִתּוֹ הַגְּדוֹלִים, עַל־יְדֵי עַבְדּוֹ וְשִׁפְחָתוֹ הַגְּדוֹלִים, עַל־יְדֵי אִשְׁתּוֹ, מִפְּנֵי שֶׁיֵּשׁ בָּהֶן דָּעַת.

יד אברהם

are walking to the next row to begin working on it, they may eat. Although they are not actually working at that time, the employer is pleased with such an arrangement, since they thereby do not take off time from work *(Rav; Rashi; Meiri)*.

וּבַחֲזִירָתָן מִן־הַגַּת. — *and when they return from the winepress.*

The workers may eat when they have placed their load of grapes in the winepress and are going for the next load *(Meiri)*.

וּבַחֲמוֹר, כְּשֶׁהִיא פּוֹרֶקֶת. — *Concerning a donkey, [it may eat] when it is being unloaded.*

The intention is that the donkey may

eat from the load on its back *until it is unloaded (Rav from Gem. 92a).*

The mishnah cannot mean literally that it may eat when it is being unloaded, because the entire load is taken off at once, and there is no time for it to eat. *Tosafos* explain that had the mishnah not told us this, we would have thought that the prohibition of restraining an animal from eating the produce that it is working with [*Deut.* 25:4; see *Sefer HaChinuch* §596] does not apply in cases that it does not see the produce, such as when the animal is carrying it on its back — although the reason for the prohibition is not that the animal is pained by being unable to eat what it can see *(Tos. Yom Tov).*

5.

אוֹכֵל פּוֹעֵל קִשּׁוּת אֲפִלּוּ בְדִינָר, וְכוֹתֶבֶת אֲפִלּוּ בְדִינָר. — *A laborer may eat a cucumber even [if it is worth] a dinar, or a date even [if it is worth] a dinar.*

While he is working, he may eat the produce he is working with, even if it is worth a *dinar (Rav; Rashi)*, although all he is being paid for the work is one-sixth of a *dinar (Meiri)*. [In other words, he may eat as much as he wishes, even if the fruit is expensive, regardless of the wages he is receiving.]

רַבִּי אֶלְעָזָר חִסְמָא אוֹמֵר: לֹא יֹאכַל פּוֹעֵל יָתֵר עַל־שְׂכָרוֹ. — *R' Elazar Chisma says: A laborer may not eat in excess of his wages.*

R' Elazar Chisma bases his view on the verse *(Deut.* 23:25): וְאָכַלְתָּ עֲנָבִים כְּנַפְשְׁךָ, which he translates literally: *You may eat grapes according to your soul.* This alludes to the laborer's wages, for which he risks his life by going up on ramps and hanging from trees. Hence, Scripture says: You may eat according

return from the winepress. Concerning a donkey, [it may eat] when it is being unloaded.

5. A laborer may eat a cucumber even [if it is worth] a *dinar*, or a date even [if it is worth] a *dinar*. R' Elazar Chisma says: A laborer may not eat in excess of his wages. The Sages permit [it], but [maintain that] we should teach a person not to be a glutton, lest he shut the door in his face.

6. A person may stipulate for himself, for his son and daughter who are of age, for his male slave and female slave who are of age, [and] for his wife, because they have understanding. But he may

to your wages (*Rav* from *Gem.* 92a).

וַחֲכָמִים מַתִּירִין, — *The Sages permit* [*it*],
The Sages, like the first, anonymous *Tanna*, permit the laborer to eat produce worth even more than his wages. They derive their view from the next word in the verse quoted above, שָׂבְעֶךָ, *your satiety,* meaning that the laborer may eat until he is satisfied (*Tos. Yom Tov* from *Sifre* loc. cit and *Rambam, Hil. Sechirus* 12:11).

From this same word the Sages deduce also that although the laborer may eat until he is satiated, he may not overeat (*Gem.* 87b).

אֲבָל מְלַמְּדִין אֶת־הָאָדָם שֶׁלֹּא יְהֵא רַעַבְתָן, וְיִהֵא סוֹתֵם אֶת־הַפֶּתַח בְּפָנָיו. — *but* [*maintain that*] *we should teach a person not to be a glutton, lest he shut the door in his face.*

Those who see the worker (*Meiri*) advise him to limit the amount he eats (*Rav*), so that people will not refrain from hiring him (*Rashi*).

The first *Tanna* disagrees with the Sages in that he does not prescribe admonishing the laborers to limit the amount they eat (*Rav* from *Gem.* 92a).

The halachah is in accordance with the view of the Sages (*Rav; Rambam Commentary*).

6.

This mishnah discusses instances in which a laborer may relinquish his privilege of eating produce while working.

קוֹצֵץ אָדָם — *A person may stipulate*
That is, a laborer may agree to accept money for relinquishing his rights to eat the produce (*Rav; Tif. Yis.*).

[This is not a contradiction to the statement in mishnah 11 that [*If*] *anyone stipulates contrary to Biblical law, his stipulation is void,* since — as *Meiri* comments there — that rule does not apply to monetary matters.]

עַל־יְדֵי עַצְמוֹ, — *for himself,*

He may make such a stipulation on his own behalf (*Rav*).

עַל־יְדֵי בְנוֹ וּבִתּוֹ הַגְּדוֹלִים, עַל־יְדֵי עַבְדּוֹ וְשִׁפְחָתוֹ הַגְּדוֹלִים, עַל־יְדֵי אִשְׁתּוֹ, — *for his son and daughter who are of age, for his male slave and female slave who are of age,* [*and*] *for his wife,*
If one hires himself out along with his children and slaves who are of age [the males are above the age of thirteen; the females, above twelve] and his wife, and

אֲבָל אֵינוֹ קוֹצֵץ עַל־יְדֵי בְּנוֹ וּבִתּוֹ הַקְּטַנִּים, וְלֹא
עַל־יְדֵי עַבְדּוֹ וְשִׁפְחָתוֹ הַקְּטַנִּים, וְלֹא עַל־יְדֵי
בְּהֶמְתּוֹ, מִפְּנֵי שֶׁאֵין בָּהֶן דָּעַת.

[ז] **הַשּׂוֹכֵר** אֶת־הַפּוֹעֲלִים לַעֲשׂוֹת בְּנֶטַע
רְבָעִי שֶׁלּוֹ, הֲרֵי אֵלּוּ לֹא יֹאכְלוּ.
אִם לֹא הוֹדִיעָן, פּוֹדֶה וּמַאֲכִילָן.
נִתְפָּרְסוּ עִגּוּלָיו נִתְפַּתְּחוּ חָבִיּוֹתָיו, הֲרֵי אֵלּוּ לֹא
יֹאכְלוּ. אִם לֹא הוֹדִיעָן, מְעַשֵּׂר וּמַאֲכִילָן.

יד אברהם

stipulates that he should receive wages, and that his family and servants will not eat of the produce, the stipulation is valid (Rambam, Hil. Sechirus 12:14).

The slaves referred to are gentiles (Tos. Yom Tov from Maggid Mishneh, loc. cit.).

Such a stipulation may be made only with the consent of these individuals (ibid. from Tur 337).

מִפְּנֵי שֶׁיֵּשׁ בָּהֶן דָּעַת. — because they have understanding.

They understand that if they agree to the stipulation, they are foregoing the privilege to partake of the produce (Rav).

אֲבָל אֵינוֹ קוֹצֵץ עַל־יְדֵי בְּנוֹ וּבִתּוֹ הַקְּטַנִּים, וְלֹא עַל־יְדֵי עַבְדּוֹ וְשִׁפְחָתוֹ הַקְּטַנִּים, וְלֹא עַל־יְדֵי בְּהֶמְתּוֹ, מִפְּנֵי שֶׁאֵין בָּהֶן דָּעַת. — But he may

not stipulate for his son and daughter who are minors, nor for his male slave and female slave who are minors, nor for his animal, since they have no understanding.

He may not agree to accept money for relinquishing their right to eat of the produce, because they do not have the understanding necessary to relinquish their rights (Tif. Yis.).

The Gemara (92b) explains that the right to eat of the produce is a gift of Heaven, similar to other gifts to which the Torah entitles the poor. Therefore, it does not belong to the worker until he puts it into his mouth. Hence, the owner of the slaves or the animal never acquires any rights to it and can therefore not relinquish it in exchange for a higher wage (Tos. Yom Tov).

7.

הַשּׂוֹכֵר אֶת־הַפּוֹעֲלִים לַעֲשׂוֹת בְּנֶטַע רְבָעִי שֶׁלּוֹ, — [If] one hires laborers to work in his revai plantings,

[In Leviticus 19:23,24 Scripture states that if one plants a tree, it is forbidden to derive any benefit during the first three years, during which time it is known as עָרְלָה, orlah ('closed up').] The fruit that grows during the fourth year is called רְבָעִי, revai; it must be brought to Jerusalem and eaten there, or be redeemed and the proceeds taken to

Jerusalem [where food is purchased with it and eaten there] (Rav).

[The mishnah deals with someone who hired laborers to work on his trees that are in their fourth year of growth, and the laborers were aware of the tree's status.]

הֲרֵי אֵלּוּ לֹא יֹאכְלוּ. — they may not eat.

Although it is obvious that they may not eat the produce outside Jerusalem, the mishnah is telling us that they also

not stipulate for his son and daughter who are minors, nor for his male slave and female slave who are minors, nor for his animal, since they have no understanding.

7. [If] one hires laborers to work in his *revai* plantings, they may not eat. If he did not notify them, he must redeem [the fruit] and give them to eat.

[If] his fig cakes separated [or] his casks opened, they may not eat. If he did not notify them, he must tithe [the fruit] and give them to eat.

YAD AVRAHAM

cannot claim that they had thought the owner would redeem the fruit so that they should be able to eat of it. On the contrary, since they made no such stipulation with him, they may not eat, because it is assumed that they accepted the job without the privilege of eating from the fruits (*Tos. Yom Tov* from *Nimmukei Yosef*).

אָם לֹא הוֹדִיעָן, — *If he did not notify them,*

This is a new case in which one hired workers to pick the grapes in his vineyard and did not notify them that the vineyard was in its fourth year of growth (ibid. from *Maggid Mishneh, Hil. Sechirus* 12:7).

פּוֹדֶה וּמַאֲכִילָן. — *he must redeem [the fruit] and give them to eat.*

It is assumed that had they known that the fruit was *revai*, they would not have accepted the job. It is therefore deemed a מֶקַח טָעוּת, *mistaken transaction,* and the owner must redeem the fruit so that the laborers should be able to eat it. However, if the owner had hired them without specifying what work they would be doing, they have no claim, since they were given no indication that they would receive the privilege of eating produce (ibid.).

נִתְפָּרְסוּ עִגּוּלָיו — *[If] his fig cakes separated*

One's cakes of dried figs became separated, and he hired workers to press them together (*Rav*).

נִתְפַּתְּחוּ חָבִיּוֹתָיו, — *[or] his casks opened,*

His casks of wine opened, and he hired workers to reseal them (ibid.).

הֲרֵי אֵלּוּ לֹא יֹאכְלוּ. — *they may not eat.*

Since the work involved in the preparation of the wine or the figs is already completed, and they are now liable for tithing, they may not be eaten until they are tithed (ibid.). [As in the first case of the mishnah, since the workers were aware of this when they undertook the job, it is assumed that they thereby agreed to forgo the privilege to eat of the produce.]

אִם לֹא הוֹדִיעָן, — *If he did not notify them,*

He hired the workers to seal the wine casks or to press the figs together, but did not inform them that they were already subject to tithes (*Tif. Yis.*).

מְעַשֵּׂר וּמַאֲכִילָן. — *he must tithe [the fruit] and give them to eat.*

Since they were under the impression that they would be able to eat of the wine or figs, because they were not yet liable for tithes, it is considered a mistaken transaction and the owner must tithe the produce and let the workers eat them (*Tif. Yis.*).

בבא [ח] שׁוֹמְרֵי פֵּרוֹת אוֹכְלִין מֵהִלְכוֹת מְדִינָה,
אֲבָל לֹא מִן־הַתּוֹרָה.
אַרְבָּעָה שׁוֹמְרִין הֵן: שׁוֹמֵר חִנָּם, וְהַשּׁוֹאֵל,
נוֹשֵׂא שָׂכָר, וְהַשּׂוֹכֵר. שׁוֹמֵר חִנָּם נִשְׁבָּע עַל־הַכֹּל;
וְהַשּׁוֹאֵל מְשַׁלֵּם אֶת־הַכֹּל. וְנוֹשֵׂא שָׂכָר וְהַשּׂוֹכֵר
נִשְׁבָּעִים עַל־הַשְּׁבוּרָה, וְעַל־הַשְּׁבוּיָה, וְעַל־הַמֵּתָה,

יד אברהם

The difference between the two cases discussed in this mishnah is that the first case deals with produce that is still attached to the ground, while the second deals with produce that is already detached (*Tos. Yom Tov*).

8

This mishnah completes the laws of laborers who may eat produce during their work, and begins discussing the laws of the four *shomerim*.

שׁוֹמְרֵי פֵּרוֹת — *Shomerim of produce*

This refers to those who watch wine presses, stacks of grain, or detached fruits (*Rav*).

אוֹכְלִין מֵהִלְכוֹת מְדִינָה, — *may eat by virtue of common custom* (lit., *the laws of the land*),

They may eat of the produce, because it has become the generally accepted practice to do so (ibid.; *Rashi*).

אֲבָל לֹא מִן־הַתּוֹרָה. — *but not by virtue of Biblical law.*

Although this produce has not yet been completed to make it liable for tithing, the *shomerim* do not have the Scripturally ordained privilege of eating

it, since watching is not regarded as active work. Should they be employed to watch orchards or gardens containing attached produce, they have no privilege to eat at all, even by virtue of common custom (*Rav* from *Gem.* 93a, following the view of Shmuel).

According to Rav [the *Amora*] those who watch stacks of grain and winepresses may eat of the produce by virtue of Biblical law — since he deems watching as active work — and *shomerim* of orchards and gardens may eat by virtue of common custom. The halachah is in accordance with the view of Shmuel, as is the rule in all laws involving monetary matters (*Rosh*).

⊷§ The Four Shomerim (Guardians)

The following segment of the mishnah is based on the passage of the Torah dealing with *shomerim* (Exodus 22:6-14), which consists of three paragraphs. The first (vs. 6-8) states that if the *shomer* claims that the article he had been entrusted with was stolen from him, he should swear to that effect, and he is exempt, unless it is proven through witnesses that he stole the article himself, in which case he pays twofold. The Rabbis qualify this paragraph as dealing with a שׁוֹמֵר חִנָּם, *unpaid shomer* — since he receives no remuneration for his services, he is not liable for any mishaps occurring to the article in his care unless he was negligent or actually caused the loss himself.

The second paragraph (vs. 9-12) states that the *shomer* is liable if the item is taken and that if he claims that an unavoidable accident occurred to it, and there are no witnesses to substantiate his claim, he must swear to that effect. The Rabbis construe this paragraph as referring to a שׁוֹמֵר שָׂכָר, *paid shomer*. Since he is remunerated for his services, he has additional liabilities.

The third paragraph (vs. 13,14) teaches us that if one borrows an animal and it

8. **S**homerim of produce may eat by virtue of common custom, but not by virtue of Biblical law. There are four [types of] shomerim: an unpaid shomer, a borrower, a paid shomer, and a renter. An unpaid shomer swears for everything; a borrower pays for everything. A paid shomer and a renter swear concerning an animal that broke a limb, an animal that was captured, and an animal that died,

YAD AVRAHAM

dies a natural death or breaks a limb, he is liable. Since he has full use of the animal or the article without paying for it — his only obligation is that he must feed the animal — he is liable for any mishap that occurs to it, even an unavoidable accident.

The renter, too, is mentioned in this paragraph, but Scripture is not explicit concerning his liabilities. Consequently, there is a dispute whether he has the liabilities of the unpaid shomer or the paid shomer, as discussed below.

אַרְבָּעָה שׁוֹמְרִין הֵן: — There are four [types of] shomerim:

Nevertheless, the laws governing them can be divided into three categories, because — as explained below — the liabilities of the paid shomer and those of the renter are the same (Tos. Yom Tov).

שׁוֹמֵר חִנָּם, — an unpaid shomer,

[That is, one who agrees to watch money, utensils, or anything else, without receiving remuneration.]

וְהַשׁוֹאֵל, — a borrower,

[This refers to one who borrows something without paying for its use.]

נוֹשֵׂא שָׂכָר, — a paid shomer,

Mishnah often uses the term נוֹשֵׂא שָׂכָר, [lit., one who receives payment], instead of the more explicit שׁוֹמֵר שָׂכָר, paid shomer, to indicate that even if one accepts an article merely as a broker — who earns a commission only if he can sell it — he has the same responsibility to watch the article as a paid shomer, because of the benefit he expects to derive from it (Tif. Yis.).

וְהַשׂוֹכֵר. — and a renter.

[That is, one who pays for the use of an article.]

שׁוֹמֵר חִנָּם נִשְׁבָּע עַל־הַכֹּל; — An unpaid shomer swears for everything;

He is exempt from all liabilities mentioned in conjunction with the other types of shomerim [except negligence, for which case all shomerim are liable] (Tos. Yom Tov from Tos. 94b). In order to prove his claim, however, he must swear (Rav; Rashi). The Sages deduce this from the words וְנִקְרַב בַּעַל־הַבַּיִת אֶל־הָאֱלֹהִים, and the householder shall come near to the judges (Ex. 22:7), which means that he shall come to the judges to swear that the article has been stolen, as he claims (Gem. 41b).

וְהַשׁוֹאֵל מְשַׁלֵּם אֶת־הַכֹּל. — a borrower pays for everything.

This includes all the occurrences mentioned in the section dealing with shomerim — theft, loss, natural death, capture, and fractured limbs. Not included is death due to normal work, for which the borrower is exempt, since he is permitted to work with the animals [and the lender thus assumed this risk by lending it] (Tos. Yom Tov from Gem., Tos. 94b).

This ruling is derived from Exodus 22:13: וְכִי־יִשְׁאַל אִישׁ מֵעִם רֵעֵהוּ וְנִשְׁבָּר אוֹ־מֵת ... שַׁלֵּם יְשַׁלֵּם, If a man borrows from another, and it breaks a leg or dies ... he shall surely pay.

וְנוֹשֵׂא שָׂכָר וְהַשּׂוֹכֵר נִשְׁבָּעִים עַל־הַשְּׁבוּרָה, וְעַל־הַשְּׁבוּיָה, וְעַל־הַמֵּתָה, — A paid shomer

ומְשַׁלְּמִין אֶת־הָאֲבֵדָה וְאֶת־הַגְּנֵבָה.

[ט] זְאֵב אֶחָד אֵינוֹ אֹנֶס; שְׁנֵי זְאֵבִים אֹנֶס. רַבִּי
יְהוּדָה אוֹמֵר: בִּשְׁעַת מִשְׁלַחַת זְאֵבִים,
אַף זְאֵב אֶחָד אֹנֶס. שְׁנֵי כְלָבִים אֵינוֹ אֹנֶס. יַדּוּעַ
הַבַּבְלִי אוֹמֵר מִשּׁוּם רַבִּי מֵאִיר: מֵרוּחַ אַחַת, אֵינוֹ

יד אברהם

and a renter swear concerning an animal
that broke a limb, an animal that was
captured, and an animal that died,

As explained above, the second
paragraph in the passage concerning
shomerim deals with the paid shomer. It
begins: כִּי־יִתֵּן אִישׁ אֶל־רֵעֵהוּ חֲמוֹר
אוֹ־שׁוֹר אוֹ־שֶׂה וְכָל־בְּהֵמָה לִשְׁמֹר וּמֵת אוֹ־
נִשְׁבָּר אוֹ־נִשְׁבָּה אֵין רֹאֶה. שְׁבֻעַת ה' תִּהְיֶה בֵּין
שְׁנֵיהֶם ... וְלָקַח בְּעָלָיו וְלֹא יְשַׁלֵּם — If a man
gives another a donkey, a bull, a lamb,
or any animal to watch, and it dies,
breaks a leg, or is captured, with no one
seeing it, an oath of God shall be
between them both ... and the owner
shall accept [it] and he shall not pay.

Captured means that it is taken by an
armed brigand (Tif. Yis.).

The renter, too, is exempt from
paying for these mishaps, since he does
not have the complete benefit from the
rented animal, in that he must pay for
its use (Rav).

This is unlike the borrower, who does
not pay for the use of the item, and in
some cases — e.g., all articles other than
animals — not even for feed (Tos. Yom

Tov from Gem. 94b).

These two shomerim are exempt also
if the animal or object is consumed by
fire (Tif. Yis.).

ומְשַׁלְּמִין אֶת־הָאֲבֵדָה וְאֶת־הַגְּנֵבָה. — and they
pay for loss and theft.

Scripture (Ex. 22:11) states: וְאִם־גָּנֹב
יִגָּנֵב מֵעִמּוֹ יְשַׁלֵּם לִבְעָלָיו, If it is stolen from
him, he shall pay its owner. Since he
must pay for theft, which is akin to an
unavoidable accident, he must surely
pay for loss, which is akin to negligence
(Rav from Gem. 94b).

The renter, too, has the same
liabilities as the paid shomer. Since the
rented article is in his possession mainly
for his benefit, although he pays for it,
he is adjudged a paid shomer. The fact
that he pays for it only distinguishes
him from the borrower, who has all the
benefits without paying for it. This is R'
Yehudah's view. R' Meir rules that a
renter is judged as an unpaid shomer.
He reasons that the renter pays for his
use of the article, and watches it gratis
(Gem., Rashi 80b).

9.

The Torah, in the section dealing with the paid shomer, delineates those instances
in which he is exempt. In verse 12, it states: אִם־טָרֹף יִטָּרֵף יְבִאֵהוּ עֵד הַטְּרֵפָה לֹא יְשַׁלֵּם, If
it is torn, he shall bring it as evidence; the torn one he shall not pay. Since the Torah
states: הַטְּרֵפָה, the torn one, with the definite article, this implies that not for every
animal torn by another is the paid shomer exempt, but only for certain ones —
namely, if the incident was unavoidable. To explain this, the mishnah discusses
many examples of animals tearing sheep that are considered unavoidable accidents,
and many others that are not. Similarly, the Tanna defines the concept of the animal
being captured, for which Scripture exempts the paid shomer.

זְאֵב אֶחָד — One wolf
[That is, one wolf attacking a flock
and tearing a sheep.]

אֵינוֹ אֹנֶס; — is not an unavoidable
accident;
[It is assumed that the shomer can

and they pay for loss and theft.

9. One wolf is not an unavoidable accident; two wolves is an unavoidable accident. R' Yehudah says: At a time when wolves are sent out, even one wolf is an unavoidable accident. Two dogs is not an unavoidable accident. Yaddua the Babylonian says in the name of R' Meir: From one

YAD AVRAHAM

beat off one wolf.] Therefore, it is not deemed an unavoidable accident, and the paid *shomer* and the renter are held liable for the torn animal *(Rav)*.

Although this is not considered an unavoidable accident to exempt a paid *shomer*, it is nevertheless not deemed negligence to make an unpaid *shomer* liable *(Noda B'Yehudah Vol. I, Choshen Mishpat §36; Ketzos Hachoshen 303:3).*

שְׁנֵי זְאֵבִים — *two wolves*
[That is, two wolves attacking the flock.]

אֹנֶס. — *is an unavoidable accident.*
[Since one shepherd cannot beat off two wolves, a paid *shomer* and a renter are not responsible for such an occurrence.]

רַבִּי יְהוּדָה אוֹמֵר: בִּשְׁעַת מִשְׁלַחַת זְאֵבִים, — *R' Yehudah says: At a time when wolves are sent out,*
That is, when wolves are divinely incited to attack *(Rav; Rashi).*
The word מִשְׁלַחַת means *inciting*, and is derived from *Exodus* 8:17. See *Rashi* ad loc. and *Deuteronomy* 32:24 [see *Targum* ad loc.] *(R' Baruch Yitzchak Lifshitz, son of Tif. Yis.).* *Tiferes Yisrael* interprets it as expressions of *breaking out*, derived from שֶׁלַח, meaning *width*. The intention is that they expand their territory and come nearer to civilization. [The former interpretation appears more accurate and more in conformance with the classical commentaries.]
According to *Aruch Hashalem*, it means: *At the time of a release of wolves.*

אַף זְאֵב אֶחָד אֹנֶס. — *even one wolf is an unavoidable accident.*
In such times, a wolf is known to spring on a man *(Rav; Rashi).*
The halachah is, however, in accordance with the view of the first, anonymous *Tanna Kamma* that, even in such times, an incident involving one wolf is not considered an unavoidable accident *(Rav).*

שְׁנֵי כְלָבִים — *Two dogs*
[That is, two dogs attacking the flock.]

אֵינוֹ אֹנֶס. — *is not an unavoidable accident.*
[The *shomer* should have warded them off.]
If, however, more than two dogs are involved, it does constitute an unavoidable accident *(Rambam, Hil. Sechirus* 3:4). *Rambam* derives this from the fact that the mishnah specifies the number two, implying that it is the maximum number of dogs that does not constitute an unavoidable accident *(Maggid Mishneh ad loc.).*

יַדּוּעַ הַבַּבְלִי אוֹמֵר מִשּׁוּם רַבִּי מֵאִיר: מֵרוּחַ אֶחָת, — *Yaddua the Babylonian says in the name of R' Meir: From one direction,*
[That is, if both dogs came from the same direction.]

אֵינוֹ אֹנֶס; — *it is not an unavoidable accident;*
Since the dogs are afraid to the point that they don't want to separate from each other, the *shomer* can surely protect himself against them. Hence, he

אָנֵס; מִשְׁתֵּי רוּחוֹת, אָנֵס. הַלִּסְטִם הֲרֵי זֶה אָנֵס. הָאֲרִי, וְהַדֹּב, וְהַנָּמֵר, וְהַבַּרְדְּלָס, וְהַנָּחָשׁ הֲרֵי זֶה אָנֵס. אֵימָתַי? בִּזְמַן שֶׁבָּאוּ מֵאֲלֵיהֶן. אֲבָל אִם הוֹלִיכָן לִמְקוֹם גְּדוּדֵי חַיָּה וְלִסְטִים, אֵינוֹ אָנֵס.

[י] **מֵתָה** כְּדַרְכָּהּ, הֲרֵי זֶה אָנֵס; סִגְּפָהּ, וָמֵתָה, אֵינוֹ אָנֵס.

יד אברהם

should not have fled, leaving his flock at their mercy. His doing so is deemed negligence (*Rabbeinu Yehonasan*, cited in *Shitah Mekubetzes*).

מִשְׁתֵּי רוּחוֹת, — *from two directions,*
[That is, if two dogs approach from two different directions.]

אָנֵס. — *it is an unavoidable accident.*
Since the dogs are bold enough to separate from each other, the *shomer* cannot fight them, and it is surely impossible for him to ward them off from two different sides (ibid.).

The halachah follows the view of the first, anonymous *Tanna* that an attack by two dogs — even from two directions — does not constitute an unavoidable accident (*Rav; Rambam Commentary*). *Tur* (*Choshen Mishpat* 303), however, rules in accordance with the view of Yaddua the Babylonian. He construes Yaddua's statement as qualifying that of the first *Tanna* (*Beis Yosef* ad loc.).

הַלִּסְטִם — *A brigand*
[That is, an attack by an armed brigand.]
This spelling is found in the versions of *Rav* and *Rashi*, based on the *Gemara's* statement that the mishnah is dealing with one bandit. [They deem the term לִסְטִים — found in the reading printed with the *Gemara* — to be plural.] *Tishbi*, tracing the origin of the word to the Greek, reads הַלִּסְטֵס, denoting the singular form.

הֲרֵי זֶה אָנֵס. — *is an unavoidable accident.*

The *Gemara* qualifies this as referring only to an armed brigand. Even if the *shomer*, too, is armed, he does not fight with the same courage as the brigand, who comes to be killed or to kill and take money. The *shomer*, however, is not expected to risk his life to that extent. Should the brigand be unarmed, the *shomer* is expected to be able to defend himself (*Tos. Yom Tov* from *Gem.* 93b).

הָאֲרִי, וְהַדֹּב, וְהַנָּמֵר, — *A lion, a bear, a leopard,*
[That is, an attack by any one of these beasts.]
[Although some translate נָמֵר as *tiger* (see *Tif. Yis.* to Bava Kamma 1:4), we have rendered it as leopard, following *Rashi* to Jeremiah 13:23.] *Radak* in *Sefer Hashorashim* identifies it as a spotted beast. *Targum Onkelos* (Gen. 30:32) equates the Hebrew נָקֹד, *spotted*, with the Aramaic נְמוֹר.

וְהַבַּרְדְּלָס, — *a bardelas,*
[Concerning this term there is much controversy and conjecture.] *Rashi* (*Sanhedrin* 15b) and *Be'er Hagolah* (*Choshen Mishpat* 389:30) identify this animal as a skunk. *Tosafos* (loc. cit.) take exception to this definition, since *bardelas* is listed among animals that are much fiercer than the skunk, and that customarily kill humans. Rather, they conjecture that it is a species of the snake. *Aruch* renders this term as a *leopardess*, which is even more ferocious than its male counterpart. Other commentators translate *bardelas*

direction, it is not an unavoidable accident; from two directions, it is an unavoidable accident. A brigand is an unavoidable accident. A lion, a bear, a leopard, a *bardelas*, or a snake is an unavoidable accident. When? When they came of themselves. But if he led them to a place [frequented by] bands of beasts or brigands, it is not an unavoidable accident.

10. [**I**f] it died naturally, it is an unavoidable accident; [if] he afflicted it, and it died, it is not an unavoidable accident.

YAD AVRAHAM

as a *cheetah* and yet others as a *hyena* (*Kafich* to *Bava Kamma* 1:4). See *Aruch Hashalem*.

וְהַנָּחָשׁ הֲרֵי זֶה אֹנֶס. — *or a snake is an unavoidable accident.*

A *shomer* cannot protect his flock against these five beasts — the first four because of their strength; the snake because of its venom (*Rabbeinu Yehonasan*, cited in *Shitah Mekubetzes*).

אֵימָתַי? בִּזְמַן שֶׁבָּאוּ מֵאֲלֵיהֶן. — *When? When they came of themselves.*

[Attacks by brigands or beasts are considered unavoidable accidents only if they came to the place where the flocks had been grazing.]

אֲבָל אִם הוֹלִיכָן לִמְקוֹם גְּדוּדֵי חַיָּה וְלִסְטִים, — *But if he led them to a place [frequented by] bands of beasts or brigands,*

[The *shomer* himself led the flock to such a place.]

אֵינוֹ אֹנֶס. — *it is not an unavoidable accident.*

Rather, this is deemed an act of negligence, and even an unpaid *shomer* would be liable in such a case (*Aruch Hashulchan, Choshen Mishpat* 303:10).

10.

The *Tanna* continues to discuss various types of unavoidable accidents.

מֵתָה כְדַרְכָּהּ, — [*If*] *it died naturally,*
[The animal in the care of a paid *shomer* died a natural death.]

הֲרֵי זֶה אֹנֶס; — *it is an unavoidable accident;*
[The *shomer* is therefore exempt, as stated in *Exodus* 22:9.]

סִגְּפָהּ, — [*if*] *he afflicted it,*
The *shomer* starved it or made it stand in the sun during the summer or in the cold during the winter (*Rav; Rashi*).

Aruch Hashulchan (*Chosen Mishpat* 303:17) states that this includes cases in which the *shomer* did not feed the animal adequately, let it drink con-

taminated water, or fed it food that did not agree with it.

וָמֵתָה, — *and it died,*
The animal died some time later, and there is no definite proof that its death was a result of the *shomer's* afflicting it (*Tos. Yom Tov* from *Tos.* 93b; *Rosh; Maggid Mishneh* from *Rabbeinu Yehonasan*).

אֵינוֹ אֹנֶס. — *it is not an unavoidable accident.*
Although it is possible that the animal did not die from the *shomer's* afflicting it, he is nevertheless liable, since he should not have done so (*Tos.* 93b) — i.e., now that he has afflicted it, he can

עָלְתָה לְרָאשֵׁי צוּקִין וְנָפְלָה, הֲרֵי זֶה אֹנֶס;
הֶעֱלָה לְרָאשֵׁי צוּקִין, וְנָפְלָה וָמֵתָה, אֵינוֹ אֹנֶס.
מַתְנֶה שׁוֹמֵר חִנָּם לִהְיוֹת פָּטוּר מִשְּׁבוּעָה;
וְהַשּׁוֹאֵל, לִהְיוֹת פָּטוּר מִלְּשַׁלֵּם; נוֹשֵׂא שָׂכָר
וְהַשּׂוֹכֵר, לִהְיוֹת פְּטוּרִין מִשְּׁבוּעָה וּמִלְּשַׁלֵּם.

no longer swear that it died a natural death, because it may be that the animal took sick in one of its internal organs on the day of the affliction, and that this was the cause of its eventual death (Bach loc. cit. §10; Maggid Mishneh, Hil. Sechirus 3:a).

The expression, אֵינוֹ אֹנֶס, it is not an unavoidable accident, should not be construed as implying that only a paid shomer is liable because he is exempt only for unavoidable accidents. Rather, since this is deemed an act of negligence, even an unpaid shomer is liable in such a case (Tos. Yom Tov from Maggid Mishneh ibid., see Aruch Hashulchan loc. cit.).

If, however, the animal seemed to be in perfect health and appearance following the affliction, even a paid shomer would be exempt, since we cannot attribute its death to the affliction (Aruch Hashulchan ibid.).

עָלְתָה לְרָאשֵׁי צוּקִין — [If] it ascended steep mountain tops

The animal overpowered him and broke away, running up to the top of a steep mountain (Rav, Tos. Yom Tov from Gem. 36b).

וְנָפְלָה, — and fell,

Again the animal overpowered the shomer and fell from the mountaintop (Gem. ibid.).

הֲרֵי זֶה אֹנֶס; — it is an unavoidable accident;

This applies only to a paid shomer, from whom a superior watching is expected. Therefore, if the animal did not overpower him prior to falling down, he is liable. Even if it overpowers him when it falls down, if it did not

overpower him when it went up, his neglect in preventing it from climbing the mountain is considered the cause of its fall, and the case is deemed one of תְּחִלָּתוֹ בִּפְשִׁיעָה וְסוֹפוֹ בְּאֹנֶס, its beginning was with negligence and its end was with an unavoidable accident, for which the shomer is liable (Tos. Yom Tov from Maggid Mishneh, loc. cit., Nimmukei Yosef).

הֶעֱלָה לְרָאשֵׁי צוּקִין, וְנָפְלָה וָמֵתָה, — [if] he took it up to steep mountain tops, and it fell and died,

That is, either the shomer led the animal up to the mountain tops, or it went up by itself and he could have stopped it, but failed to do so. Then, the animal fell and was killed (Tos. Yom Tov from Rambam, loc. cit.).

אֵינוֹ אֹנֶס. — it is not an unavoidable accident.

The shomer is liable — although he could not prevent the animal from falling — because allowing the animal to go up the mountain was an act of negligence. Hence, he is liable, although the final fall was an unavoidable accident, as explained above (Tos. Yom Tov).

מַתְנֶה שׁוֹמֵר חִנָּם לִהְיוֹת פָּטוּר מִשְּׁבוּעָה; — An unpaid shomer may stipulate to be exempt from an oath;

Upon accepting the article for safekeeping, he may stipulate that he does so only on the condition that should he ever claim that he did not commit an act of negligence with the article entrusted to him, the owner must believe him. Even in such a case, if he confesses or witnesses testify that he had been negligent, he is liable. The

[If] it ascended steep mountain tops and fell, it is an unavoidable accident; [if] he took it up to steep mountain tops, and it fell and died, it is not an unavoidable accident.

An unpaid *shomer* may stipulate to be exempt from an oath; a borrower, to be exempt from paying; [and] a paid *shomer* and a renter, to be exempt from an oath or from paying.

YAD AVRAHAM

shomer may stipulate even that he be exempt for negligence. However, it is unusual for the owner of the item to agree to this *(Meiri; Tif. Yis.* from *Shitah Mekubetzes; Choshen Mishpat* 305:4), since negligence is tantamount to damaging the article, and no one would allow others to damage his property *(Rabbeinu Yehonasan,* cited in *Shitah Mekubetzes).*

Others maintain that since the mishnah does not mention that the unpaid *shomer* may stipulate to be exempt from negligence, he indeed cannot do so *(Hagahos Asheri,* quoted by *Tif. Yis.).*

וְהַשּׁוֹאֵל, לִהְיוֹת פָּטוּר מִלְּשַׁלֵּם; — *a borrower, to be exempt from paying;*

[A borrower may stipulate to be exempt from liability for theft, loss, or unavoidable accidents.] He may stipulate also that if he claims that the animal died because of its work, he will be exempt from swearing *(Meiri).*

נוֹשֵׂא שָׂכָר וְהַשּׂוֹכֵר, — [and] *a paid shomer and a renter,*

[They may make either of the following stipulations.]

לִהְיוֹת פְּטוּרִין מִשְּׁבוּעָה — *to be exempt from an oath*

That is, if they claim that the animal

entrusted to them was the victim of an unavoidable accident, they would be believed without an oath (ibid.).

וּמִלְּשַׁלֵּם. — *or from paying.*

They may stipulate that if the article is stolen or lost, they will be exempt from paying (ibid.). They may stipulate also to be exempt from paying for negligence, as discussed above *(Choshen Mishpat* 305:4).

Although the following mishnah states that *If anyone stipulates contrary to Biblical law, his stipulation is void,* that principle does not apply to the responsibilities of *shomerim.* The *Gemara* (94a) offers several reasons for this exception. One is that this mishnah follows the view of R' Yehudah, who rules that in monetary matters one may stipulate contrary to Biblical law.

The *Gemara* concludes, however, that even R' Meir — who rules that one may not stipulate contrary to Biblical law, even in monetary matters — would concur with the ruling of this mishnah. This is because a person does not become responsible as a *shomer* before he takes the article into his possession and undertakes its responsibilities. Hence, one may stipulate prior to undertaking those responsibilities that he accepts only part of them *(Rav* from *Gem.).*

11.

תְּנָאִים ◆§ / **Stipulations**

In connection with the final statement in the preceding mishnah, this mishnah proceeds to delineate the rules of stipulations. As derived from the classic stipulation regarding the Gadites and the Reuvenites *(Num.* 32:29,30), one has the

[יא] כָּל־הַמַּתְנֶה עַל־מַה־שֶּׁכָּתוּב בַּתּוֹרָה, תְּנָאוֹ בָטֵל. וְכָל־תְּנַאי שֶׁיֵּשׁ מַעֲשֶׂה בִתְחִלָּתוֹ — תְּנָאוֹ בָטֵל. וְכָל־ שֶׁאֶפְשָׁר לוֹ לְקַיְּמוֹ בְסוֹפוֹ, וְהִתְנָה עָלָיו מִתְּחִלָּתוֹ — תְּנָאוֹ קַיָּם.

יד אברהם

power to make the validity of any act contingent on the fulfillment of a condition. The Torah tells us that Moses stipulated: ... אִם־יַעַבְרוּ בְנֵי־גָד וּבְנֵי־רְאוּבֵן אִתְּכֶם אֶת־הַיַּרְדֵּן — *If* וּנְתַתֶּם לָהֶם אֶת־אֶרֶץ הַגִּלְעָד לַאֲחֻזָּה; וְאִם־לֹא יַעַבְרוּ חֲלוּצִים אִתְּכֶם וְנֹאחֲזוּ בְתֹכְכֶם בְּאֶרֶץ כְּנָעַן *the children of Gad and the children of Reuven will cross the Jordan with you ... you shall give them the land of Gilead as an allotment. But if they will not cross armed with you, they shall inherit in your midst in the Land of Canaan.*

Should a stipulation not conform with the rules derived from this precedent, the act remains in force even if the condition is not met. There are also other regulations governing actions contingent upon the fulfillment of a condition, some of which are discussed below. See *Kiddushin* 3:4 and ArtScroll commentary there.

כָּל־הַמַּתְנֶה עַל־מַה־שֶּׁכָּתוּב בַּתּוֹרָה, — [If] *anyone stipulates contrary to Biblical law,*

The classic example is that of a man who performs *erusin* (betrothal; see General Introduction to ArtScroll *Kiddushin*) on condition that the woman agree that he need not provide her with food, clothing, and marital relations, contrary to the Scriptural law [*Ex.* 21:10] which obligates every husband to do so (*Gem.* 94a).

תְּנָאוֹ בָטֵל. — *his stipulation is void.*

In the aforementioned case, the stipulation is void, and the *erusin* is in force with all its usual obligations. This is R' Meir's view. R' Yehudah, however, contends that in monetary matters, one may stipulate contrary to Biblical law. Therefore, in the above case, the stipulation is in force with regard to food and clothing, since these are pecuniary matters. As regards marital relations, however, the stipulation is void, and the husband must fulfill that duty. Although this mishnah follows the view of R' Meir, the halachah is in accordance with R' Yehudah's opinion (*Rav*).

Rambam Commentary explains that the mishnah refers to transactions other

than monetary ones, in which case even R' Yehudah rules that the stipulation is void. This is difficult to understand, since the conclusion of the *Gemara* is that the mishnah follows R' Meir, as evidenced by the next statement, which is generally accepted to be his opinion (*Tos. Yom Tov*; see commentary to ArtScroll *Kesubos* 5:1, pp. 43-45).

וְכָל־תְּנַאי שֶׁיֵּשׁ מַעֲשֶׂה בִתְחִלָּתוֹ — *Any stipulation which is preceded by the action —*

The stipulator stated the action before stating the condition upon which it is contingent; for example: 'I will do this on condition that you do that' (*Rav; Rashi*).

תְּנָאוֹ בָטֵל. — *his stipulation is void.*

The act is in force, and it is not contingent on the condition. This is derived from the classic stipulation involving the Gadites and the Reuvenites, discussed above, in which the condition was stated first and then the action: *If the children of Gad and the children of Reuven will cross ... you shall give.* This teaches us that in order for a stipulation to be valid, it must be stated in such a sequence (ibid.).

Rambam (Hil. Ishus 6:4 and

11. [I]f] anyone stipulates contrary to Biblical law, his stipulation is void. Any stipulation which is preceded by the action — his stipulation is void. Anything that is possible to fulfill at the end, and he stipulated concerning it in the beginning — his stipulation is valid.

YAD AVRAHAM

Commentary) construes the mishnah as meaning that the stipulator actually performed the act and then made the stipulation. For example, he gave a woman money and said, 'You are betrothed to me,' and after she accepted it, he said that the *erusin* should be subject to a certain stipulation. Or, he gave his wife a *get* (bill of divorce), and after saying, 'This is your *get*,' he said that the divorce should be subject to a certain stipulation. In these cases, the divorce and the *erusin* are in force, but they are not contingent on the condition stated after the acts had been performed.

The wording of many mishnayos that state the action before the stipulation convinced *Rambam* that the mishnah is referring to a case in which the stipulation was made after the act had already been performed, and not to one in which the stipulator merely stated the act before the condition (*Tos. Yom Tov* from *Maggid Mishneh*). Since most authorities differ with him, the halachah is not in accordance with the view of

Rambam (Tos. Yom Tov; Tif. Yis.).

וְכָל-שֶׁאֶפְשָׁר לוֹ לְקַיְּמוֹ בְּסוֹפוֹ, — *Anything that is possible to fulfill at the end,*

[That is, any condition that will eventually be possible to fulfill.]

The mishnah is referring to a condition not contrary to Biblical law (*Tif. Yis.* in *Boaz*).

וְהִתְנָה עָלָיו מִתְּחִלָּתוֹ — *and he stipulated concerning it in the beginning —*

He stated the stipulation prior to stating the act, as discussed above (*Rav*).

תְּנָאוֹ קַיָּם. — *his stipulation is valid.*

Should the stipulation be impossible to fulfill, however, the action is in force and the stipulation is void. For example, if one says to his wife, 'This is your *get* on condition that you go up to the sky,' or 'that you go down into the deep,' or 'that you swallow a cane of one hundred cubits,' or 'that you walk across the Mediterranean Sea,' the *get* is valid. His intention was merely to provoke her and to pretend that he did not wish to divorce her (ibid. from *Gem.* 94a).

Chapter 8

We have already explained that a borrower is liable even for unavoidable accidents. The Torah states, however (*Exodus* 22:13,14): בְּעָלָיו אֵין-עִמּוֹ שַׁלֵּם יְשַׁלֵּם. אִם-בְּעָלָיו עִמּוֹ לֹא יְשַׁלֵּם. — [if] *its owner is not with him, he shall surely pay. If its owner is with him, he shall not pay* ... Oral tradition teaches us that the definition of this law is that if the owner was working for the borrower at the time of the loan, even though he was not with him at the time of the accident, he is exempt from payment. If the owner was not working for him at the time of the loan, even if he was working with him at the time of the accident, this exemption does not apply and the borrower is liable. It follows from this that in order for the exemption to apply, the owner of the cow must have entered the employ of the borrower before, or at the latest simultaneous with, the loan of the cow. These laws are discussed in our mishnah.

[א] הַשׁוֹאֵל אֶת־הַפָּרָה וְשָׁאַל בְּעָלֶיהָ עִמָּהּ,
אוֹ שָׂכַר בְּעָלֶיהָ עִמָּהּ, שָׁאַל אֶת
הַבְּעָלִים אוֹ שְׂכָרָן וּלְאַחַר־כָּךְ שָׁאַל אֶת־הַפָּרָה,
וָמֵתָה — פָּטוּר, שֶׁנֶּאֱמַר: ,,אִם־בְּעָלָיו עִמּוֹ לֹא
יְשַׁלֵּם." אֲבָל שָׁאַל אֶת־הַפָּרָה וְאַחַר־כָּךְ שָׁאַל
אֶת־הַבְּעָלִים אוֹ שְׂכָרָן, וָמֵתָה — חַיָּב, שֶׁנֶּאֱמַר:
,,בְּעָלָיו אֵין עִמּוֹ שַׁלֵּם יְשַׁלֵּם."

יד אברהם

1.

הַשׁוֹאֵל אֶת־הַפָּרָה וְשָׁאַל בְּעָלֶיהָ עִמָּהּ, — [*If*]
one borrowed a cow and borrowed [*the service of*] *its owner along with it,*

This case of the mishnah refers to when at the very same time that he borrowed the cow, he borrowed the services of the owner (*Tos. Yom Tov* from *Gem.* 94b). [I.e., the owner of the cow agreed to do some work gratis for the borrower.]

Arranging for these two borrowings to take effect simultaneously presents a technical problem. The rule is that the responsibility devolving on a borrower is effected by means of a *kinyan*, act of acquisition, in the same manner as with a sale (see General Introduction), and the object is not legally borrowed until such a *kinyan* has taken place. Generally, the loan of an animal is effected by the method of *kinyan* known as *meshichah*, pulling the animal into his (in this case the borrower's) possession (see General Introduction). If the lender were to offer the services of himself and his cow to the borrower, with the loan of the cow to be acquired with the customary *kinyan* of *meshichah*, the loan of the owner's services would be effected immediately by his mere speech, since Jews are not suspected of going back on their promise. [Therefore, anyone who promises to give his services is considered 'borrowed' (*Nimmukei Yosef*).] The loan of the cow, however, would not be effected until some point later when the borrower drew the cow into his possession. This would negate the simultaneity of the two borrowings.

Nimmukei Yosef offers two ways out of this predicament. The first is that the cow was in the property of the borrower at the time its owner said, 'My cow and I are on loan to you for your work.' In such a case, the loan of the cow would take effect immediately through the *kinyan* of a courtyard, i.e., by being in the borrower's property [a person's property can acquire on his behalf objects which enter it; see General Introduction], while the loan of the owner's services would be effected simultaneously by his mere speech. The second way would be for the borrower to stipulate that the loan of the owner's services should not take effect until he pulls the cow. [Since the borrower refuses to accept the loan of services until that time, he would not acquire it before then.]

According to *Tos.* and *Rosh*, the owner is not considered 'borrowed' unless he prepares to go to work (*Tos. Yom Tov; Tif. Yis.*). [Thus, he would have to have been in such a state of preparation at the time the loan of the cow took legal effect.]

אוֹ שָׂכַר בְּעָלֶיהָ עִמָּהּ, — *or hired its owner along with it,*

The same law applies if, rather than borrowing his services, he hired the owner of the cow at the time he borrowed the cow, either for the same type of work or for another type of work (*Rav* from *Gem.* 95b).

שָׁאַל אֶת הַבְּעָלִים אוֹ שְׂכָרָן וּלְאַחַר־כָּךְ שָׁאַל
אֶת־הַפָּרָה, — [*or*] *he borrowed* [*the*

1. **[I**f] one borrowed a cow and borrowed [the service of] its owner along with it, or hired its owner along with it, [or] he borrowed [the service of] the owner or hired him and afterwards borrowed the cow, and it died — he is exempt, as it is said (*Exodus* 22:14): 'If its owner is with him, he need not pay.' But [if] he borrowed the cow and afterwards borrowed [the service of] the owner or hired him, and it died — he is liable, as it is said (ibid. 13): '[If] its owner is not with him, he shall surely pay.'

YAD AVRAHAM

of] the owner or hired him and afterwards borrowed the cow,

I.e., he borrowed the cow while the owner was still working for him either as a favor or as a hired worker *(Meiri).*

וָמֵתָה — פָּטוּר, — *and it died — he is exempt,*

[If, after borrowing the cow either simultaneously with the loan or hire of the owner's services or subsequent to obtaining the owner's services, the cow died while in the possession of the borrower, the borrower is exempt from paying for the cow.]

שֶׁנֶּאֱמַר: ,,אִם־בְּעָלָיו עִמּוֹ לֹא יְשַׁלֵּם". — *as it is said (Exodus 22:14): 'If its owner is with him, he need not pay.'*

This is interpreted to mean that if the owner of the animal is with the borrower, doing his work, the borrower is exempt. As mentioned above, this ruling applies even if the owner is helping the borrower with a different type of work in a different place. The *Gemara* (97a) states that even if the owner gives the borrower a drink of water as he lends him the cow, it is considered that he is working with him, and the borrower is exempt *(Tif. Yis.).*

אֲבָל שָׁאַל אֶת־הַפָּרָה וְאַחַר־כָּךְ שָׁאַל אֶת־ הַבְּעָלִים אוֹ שְׂכָרָן, וָמֵתָה — חַיָּב, — *But [if] he borrowed the cow and afterwards borrowed [the service of] the owner or*

hired him, and it died — he is liable,

[If he borrowed the cow before obtaining the services of its owner, then the owner was not in his employ at the time the loan of the cow took effect.] Consequently, if the cow should die in the borrower's possession, the borrower would be liable even if the owner was in the borrower's service at the time of the mishap *(Rav, Rashi from Gem. 95b).*

שֶׁנֶּאֱמַר: ,,בְּעָלָיו אֵין עִמּוֹ שַׁלֵּם יְשַׁלֵּם". — *as it is said (ibid. 13): '[If] its owner is not with him, he shall surely pay.'*

The Oral Law teaches that the intention of the verse is that if the owner is not with the borrower in his work at the time of the borrowing, even though he is with him at the time of the mishap, the borrower is liable *(Rav from Gem. 95b).* Since it is the act of borrowing that obligates the borrower relative to the animal, it is that time that exerts influence upon his future liability, not the time of the mishap. Rav Ashi claims that this ruling is apparent from verse 13: וְכִי־יִשְׁאַל אִישׁ מֵעִם רֵעֵהוּ ... שַׁלֵּם יְשַׁלֵּם, *And should a man borrow from his neighbor ... he shall surely pay.* The Torah is exact in using the word מֵעִם — lit., *from with* — meaning that the owner is no longer with the borrower at the time of borrowing. Should he be with him, helping him in his work, he is exempt *(Tos. Yom Tov from Gem.).*

[כב] **הַשּׁוֹאֵל** אֶת־הַפָּרָה: שָׁאֲלָהּ חֲצִי הַיּוֹם
וּשְׂכָרָהּ חֲצִי הַיּוֹם, שָׁאֲלָהּ הַיּוֹם
וּשְׂכָרָהּ לְמָחָר, שָׂכַר אַחַת וְשָׁאַל אַחַת, וָמֵתָה —
הַמַּשְׁאִיל אוֹמֵר שְׁאוּלָה מֵתָה, בְּיוֹם שֶׁהָיְתָה
שְׁאוּלָה מֵתָה, בְּשָׁעָה שֶׁהָיְתָה שְׁאוּלָה מֵתָה;
וְהַלָּה אוֹמֵר אֵינִי יוֹדֵעַ, חַיָּב. הַשּׂוֹכֵר אוֹמֵר

יד אברהם

2.

הַשּׁוֹאֵל אֶת־הַפָּרָה: — [If] one borrowed a cow,

[As the mishnah will explain, this borrowing was not entirely a loan but a combination of loan and hire, in one of three variations which the mishnah will now list.]

שָׁאֲלָהּ חֲצִי הַיּוֹם וּשְׂכָרָהּ חֲצִי הַיּוֹם, — [and] he [either] borrowed it for half a day and hired it for half a day,

[I.e., if he received a cow for one full day, half the day on loan, and the remaining half day for hire.]

שָׁאֲלָהּ הַיּוֹם וּשְׂכָרָהּ לְמָחָר, — [or] borrowed it for one day [lit., today] and hired it for the next day [lit., tomorrow],

[I.e., he received the cow for two days, for the first as a loan and for the second as a hire.]

שָׂכַר אַחַת וְשָׁאַל אַחַת, — [or] he hired one and borrowed one,

[I.e., he received two cows, one as a hire, and the other as a loan.]

וָמֵתָה — and it died —

[The cow died and it cannot be proven whether it died during the loan period or the rental period. Or, in the last variation, one of the two cows died and there is a question whether it was the borrowed one or the hired one. The relevance of this question is in the law that a renter is not obligated to pay for a hired animal which dies in his possession through no fault of his own (above, 6:3), while a borrower is obligated to pay even for such a death

(Exodus 22:13).]

הַמַּשְׁאִיל אוֹמֵר שְׁאוּלָה מֵתָה, בְּיוֹם שֶׁהָיְתָה שְׁאוּלָה מֵתָה, בְּשָׁעָה שֶׁהָיְתָה שְׁאוּלָה מֵתָה; — the lender claims [that] the borrowed one died, [or that] it died on the day it was borrowed, [or that] it died during the hour that it was borrowed;

I.e., in the case of the two cows the lender claims that the borrowed one died (Rashi) and that the borrower is therefore liable to pay for it even though he was not at fault (Rav). Or in the case in which only one cow was involved, he claims that it died during the day of the loan or during the loan hours (Rashi).

וְהַלָּה אוֹמֵר אֵינִי יוֹדֵעַ, — while the other one says [that] he does not know [lit., I do not know],

The borrower responds that he does not know for sure which one died or during which period it died, and that perhaps the hired one died, or that it died during the period of hire, which would exempt him for paying for the unavoidable death of the animal (Rav).

חַיָּב. — he is liable.

[The borrower must pay.]

This mishnah cannot be explained in its apparent sense since the halachah is that if one puts forth an unsubstantiated claim that another owes him money, and the other replies that he does not know, the defendant is liable only to swear a שְׁבוּעַת הֶיסֵת, shevuas heseis [a post-Mishnaic Rabbinic oath innovated during Amoraic times] that

2. [I[f] one borrowed a cow, [and] he [either] borrowed it for half a day and hired it for half a day, [or] borrowed it for one day and hired it for the next day, [or] he hired one and borrowed one, and it died — the lender claims [that] the borrowed one died, [or that] it died on the day it was borrowed, [or that] it died during the hour that it was borrowed; while the other one says [that] he does not know, he is

YAD AVRAHAM

he does not know, and he is exempt.[1] Accordingly, since in the case of this mishnah the lender has not proven that the borrowed cow died or that the cow died during the period in which it was on loan rather than hired, his claim for reimbursement remains unsubstantiated and he cannot exact any more than an oath from the borrower that he really does not know which or when it died.[2]

Therefore, the *Gemara* (97b, 98a) qualifies the mishnah as referring to a case in which a Biblical oath is involved. The rule for Biblical oaths is that if the defendant cannot swear with certainty that the claim is untrue, he must pay. Such a situation arises where the lender actually gave two cows, both for one half a day, or for one full day, as a loan,

and for the other half or full day as a rental. The lender claims that they both died during the loan period, while the borrower replies that yes, one died during the loan period, but he is unsure when the other one died. In this case, he admits part of the claim [viz., that he is liable to pay for at least one of the animals], and he is therefore liable for a Biblical oath for one who admits to part of a claim, as was taught above in 4:7 [see also, General Introduction]. Since he admits that he does not know when the second animal died, he cannot swear with certainty that he is not also liable for the second cow. Consequently, he must pay for it *(Rav; Tos. Yom Tov).*

[The mishnah explicitly lists only the cow which is in dispute, not the additional cow

1. This follows the view of Rav Nachman and R' Yochanan. The *Gemara* (97b), however, also cites the opposing view of Rav Huna and Rav Yehudah that where the defendant is uncertain, while the plaintiff is definite in his claim, the plaintiff indeed collects even without proof. According to this view, this part of the mishnah is readily understood but another part of the mishnah poses difficulties. The *Gemara* explains the mishnah according to both views, but the commentary here follows the view accepted as halachah — that of Rav Nachman and R' Yochanan (see *Choshen Mishpat* 75:9).

2. According to the view accepted as halachah, only when there was once a definite obligation to pay, and the defendant is uncertain whether or not he paid, is the definite claim of the other sufficient to exact payment *(Bava Kamma* 10:7). This case, however, is analogous to another case in *Bava Kamma* 10:7, where the mishnah states that if one replies, 'I do not know whether I robbed you,' 'whether you lent me', or 'whether you deposited with me,' he is exempt. Since there is doubt as to whether he ever became obligated, he cannot be made to pay for his uncertainty without proof. In this case, too, the borrower was never yet liable until the animal died. Therefore, there is doubt as to whether the borrower ever became obligated to pay the lender *(Tos. Yom Tov* from *Nimmukei Yosef).*

Even according to the *Amoraim* who rule that once someone borrows something, he is obligated for any future damages from the time he takes it (in this case, the animal) into his possession *(Kesubos* 34b), the intention is that when the mishap occurs, he becomes liable retroactively, and his property is pledged from that time. Prior to the mishap, however, even they rule that there is no obligation. Therefore, it is viewed as a question of whether any obligation ever existed, and he is exempt *(Tos. R' Akiva* from *Ritva).*

שְׁכוּרָה מֵתָה, בְּיוֹם שֶׁהָיְתָה שְׁכוּרָה מֵתָה, בְּשָׁעָה
שֶׁהָיְתָה שְׁכוּרָה מֵתָה; וְהַלָּה אוֹמֵר אֵינִי יוֹדֵעַ,
פָּטוּר. זֶה אוֹמֵר שְׁאוּלָה, וְזֶה אוֹמֵר שְׂכוּרָה, יִשָּׁבַע
הַשּׂוֹכֵר שֶׁשְּׂכוּרָה מֵתָה. זֶה אוֹמֵר אֵינִי יוֹדֵעַ, וְזֶה

יד אברהם

which all agree died during the loan period.] Similarly, in the case of the two cows, the *Gemara* explains that there were in reality three cows, two loaned and one rented. Two of these cows died. Since the borrower admits that one of the two cows which died was a borrowed cow (for which he is definitely liable), and he questions only whether the second dead cow was the other borrowed one or the rented one, he admits to part of the lender's claim. Thus, he becomes obligated in a Biblical oath, which, because of his uncertainty, he cannot swear to refute. Consequently, he is obligated to pay for that animal as well (*Gem.* 98a).]

הַשּׂוֹכֵר אוֹמֵר שְׂכוּרָה מֵתָה, בְּיוֹם שֶׁהָיְתָה
שְׂכוּרָה מֵתָה, בְּשָׁעָה שֶׁהָיְתָה שְׁכוּרָה מֵתָה; — [*If*] *the renter claims* [*that*] *the hired one died*, [*or that*] *it died on the day it was hired*, [*or that*] *it died during the hour it was hired;*

[The mishnah now considers the reverse case, where the renter claims definitely to know that the hired animal died and not the borrowed one, or that the animal died during the rental period, not during the loan period; while the owner of the animal states that he has no knowledge of which animal died or when it died.]

Although the mishnah referred to him previously as the borrower, he is here called the renter since he claims that the mishap befell the hired cow (*Tos. Yom Tov*). When he is in doubt, however [and is thus accountable as the holder of a borrowed animal], he is referred to as *the other one* (*Tif. Yis.*).

וְהַלָּה אוֹמֵר אֵינִי יוֹדֵעַ, — *while the other one says* [*that*] *he does not know* [lit., *I do not know*],

[The owner states that he doesn't know, but that perhaps it was the borrowed one that died, or that it died

during the time it was under loan, which would make the user liable.]

פָּטוּר. — *he is exempt.*

The renter/borrower is exempt, even from an oath. Since the claimant puts forth an uncertain claim, there is not even an obligation to swear a *shevuas heseis*. Although any *shomer* must swear concerning the nature of the mishap in order to be exempted (*Shevuos* 7:8), that is because he rationalizes to himself that it seemed to him that the animal died by an unavoidable accident, when in fact it died through his negligence. [The object of the oath, therefore, is to force him to forsake this claim unless he is really sure of it.] In this case, however, since the borrower knows definitely whether the cow was borrowed or hired, there is no way for him to rationalize to himself that it was the other animal which died. Therefore, there is no need for an oath (*Nimmukei Yosef*).

There is a rule that once a person is obligated to respond to another person's claim with an oath, the claimant may attach additional oaths to that basic oath concerning other claims for which he otherwise could not extract an oath (see below; *Sotah* 2:5; *Kiddushin* 1:5, 27b). Nevertheless, although in the case under discussion in this mishnah the borrower can at least be obligated by the owner to swear that the cow died a natural death (as any *shomer* could be), he cannot attach to this oath a further oath that it was indeed the hired one that died. In such cases, when the claimant is uncertain, an oath may be attached only when there is reason to doubt a defendant's denial. Since here we have no inherent reason to doubt his claim that it was the hired one that died, no oath may be attached (*Tos. Yom Tov* from *Tos.* and *Rosh; Choshen Mishpat* 94:2).

זֶה אוֹמֵר שְׁאוּלָה, וְזֶה אוֹמֵר שְׂכוּרָה, — [*If*] *this*

8
2
liable. [If] the renter claims [that] the hired one died, [or that] it died on the day it was hired, [or that] it died during the hour it was hired; while the other one says [that] he does not know, he is exempt. [If] this one claims [it was] the borrowed one, and this one claims [it was] the hired one, the renter swears that the hired one died. [If] this one says he does not

YAD AVRAHAM

one claims [it was] the borrowed one, and this one claims [it was] the hired one,

[I.e., both claim their positions with certainty — the lender that the borrowed one died, making the borrower liable, and the borrower/renter that the hired one died, leaving him exempt.]

יִשָּׁבַע הַשּׂוֹכֵר שֶׁשְּׂכוּרָה מֵתָה. — *the renter swears that the hired one died.*

[The borrower/renter must swear to his claim that it was the hired cow that died (or that it died during the hire period).]

Seemingly, there is no reason for the renter to swear in this case, since he totally denies any liability and the plaintiff has no proof of his claim.[1] We must, therefore, qualify the mishnah as referring to the case that the plaintiff demands that the defendant swear that the cow died a natural death, something which the depositor may demand of any *shomer*. Having obligated the borrower in this oath, the lender may proceed to attach an additional oath that it was the borrowed one that died *(Rav; Rambam Comm.* from *Gem.* 98b). [As explained above (s.v. פטור), oaths which could normally not be exacted can be attached to oaths which are required by law.]

This is indeed the answer cited by the *Gemara.* However, *Rashi* and *Nimmukei Yosef* assert that it follows only one of the interpretations given by the *Gemara* for the earlier part of the mishnah. However, according to the view which qualifies the first part of the mishnah as referring to the case that there is a Biblical oath involved (the view noted above, s.v. חיב), it is unnecessary to qualify this segment as referring to a case in which the plaintiff attaches an oath. Rather, it can be explained in the same vein as the earlier part of the mishnah, viz. as referring to the case in which the lender claims two borrowed cows, and the borrower admits to one having died through negligence, while denying that he ever borrowed the second one. This makes him liable for the Biblical oath of one who admits part of a claim.

Rambam, however, in *Hil. She'eilah* 3:3, qualifies the first part of the mishnah as referring to the case of two cows, and explains this part of the mishnah as referring to an attached oath. *Kesef Mishneh* states that *Rambam* holds that even those who explain the beginning of the mishnah as referring to two cows, in which there is a Biblical oath involved, explain this part of the mishnah as referring to an attached oath. He does not explain why this is necessary. *Tos. Yom Tov* and *Lechem Mishneh* explain that, indeed, it is not necessary to explain the mishnah in this manner, but that it is the more apparent meaning of the mishnah. For this reason, *Rav,* too, adopts this explanation.

1. This is not considered the equivalent of admitting to part of a claim, which mandates a Biblical oath as explained above, since that rule applies only to an admission which is of the same variety as the claim. In this case, however, since the plaintiff claims that the borrowed cow died and the defendant admits that the hired cow died, there is no oath. This is analogous to one claiming wheat and the other admitting barley [see *Shevuos* 6:3] *(Rav* from *Gem.* 98b).

In Amoraic times, the Rabbis enacted that even if the defendant denies the claim completely, he must take a Rabbinic oath, known as *shevuas heseis.* Therefore, in this case, the renter/borrower would be liable to such an oath. The mishnah, however, cannot be referring to this oath, since it had not yet been instituted in Mishnaic times.

אוֹמֵר אֵינִי יוֹדֵעַ, יַחֲלֹקוּ.

[ג] **הַשּׁוֹאֵל** אֶת־הַפָּרָה וְשִׁלְחָהּ לוֹ בְּיַד בְּנוֹ,
בְּיַד עַבְדּוֹ, בְּיַד שְׁלוּחוֹ, אוֹ בְּיַד
בְּנוֹ, בְּיַד עַבְדּוֹ, בְּיַד שְׁלוּחוֹ שֶׁל־שׁוֹאֵל, וָמֵתָה —
פָּטוּר. אָמַר לוֹ הַשּׁוֹאֵל: ,,שַׁלְחָהּ לִי בְּיַד בְּנִי,"
,,בְּיַד עַבְדִּי," ,,בְּיַד שְׁלוּחִי," אוֹ ,,בְּיַד בִּנְךָ," ,,בְּיַד
עַבְדְּךָ," ,,בְּיַד שְׁלוּחָךְ;" אוֹ שֶׁאָמַר לוֹ הַמַּשְׁאִיל:

יד אברהם

[*If*] — זֶה אוֹמֵר אֵינִי יוֹדֵעַ, וְזֶה אוֹמֵר אֵינִי יוֹדֵעַ,
*this one says he does not know, and this
one says he does not know,*

[I.e., neither the lender nor the
borrower claims to know whether it was
the borrowed one that died or the hired
one.]

יַחֲלֹקוּ. — *they divide.*

The *Gemara* (98b) attributes this last
ruling of the mishnah to the *Tanna*
Sumchos, who holds that מָמוֹן הַמֻּטָּל
בְּסָפֵק חוֹלְקִין, *money that lies in doubt is*

divided. The Sages, however, rule that
in such cases, הַמּוֹצִיא מֵחֲבֵרוֹ עָלָיו הָרְאָיָה,
*the burden of proof lies on the one
seeking to exact payment,* in this case
the lender.[1] The halachah is in
accordance with the Sages. Therefore,
since the lender cannot prove that it was
the borrowed cow that died (or that it
died during the loan period), he cannot
collect. He can only exact the post-
Mishnaic *shevuas heseis* oath from the
defendant that he does not know (*Rav;
Ros. Yom Tov from Rambam Comm.*).

3.

הַשּׁוֹאֵל אֶת־הַפָּרָה וְשִׁלְחָהּ לוֹ בְּיַד בְּנוֹ, בְּיַד
עַבְדּוֹ, בְּיַד שְׁלוּחוֹ — [*If*] *one borrowed a
cow and he sent it to him through his
son, through his slave, through his
agent,*

The lender sent the cow over to the
borrower through his (the lender's) son,
slave, or agent (*Rav; Rashi*).

אוֹ בְּיַד בְּנוֹ, בְּיַד עַבְדּוֹ, בְּיַד שְׁלוּחוֹ שֶׁל־שׁוֹאֵל,

— וָמֵתָה — *or through the son, slave, or
agent of the borrower, and it died —*

The cow died in transit (*Rav; Rashi*).

פָּטוּר. — *he is exempt.*

[The borrower is exempt from paying
for the cow because the cow died before
the borrower received it. Although the
lender had sent the cow to the borrower
through a representative, the borrower

1. Sumchos also accepts this rule but does not consider it applicable to cases in which the
doubt confronting us is inherent in the situation, not an outgrowth of conflicting claims (*Tos.*
97b, s.v. לימא תהוי תיובתא). I.e., even if we were to set aside their claims, there would still be a
question as to whom the money belongs. For example, in this case all agree that the cow was
partially borrowed and partially rented, or that the one cow was borrowed while the other was
rented. Thus, when one dies, there is an obvious question — apart from any claims by the
parties involved — whether the borrowed cow died or the rented one died (*Maharam*). Since
this question does not arise from their conflicting claims — neither one, in fact, claims to know
the truth — Sumchos feels that the proper procedure is to divide the sum in question. The
Sages, however, are of the opinion that in order to collect anything, one must be able to prove
that the money is coming to him. Otherwise, the doubt is resolved by leaving the property (in
this case, the reimbursement money for the dead cow) where it is. [See below, mishnah 6, fn. to
s.v. יחלקו]

know, and this one says he does not know, they divide.

3. [If] one borrowed a cow and he sent it to him through his son, through his slave, through his agent, or through the son, slave, or agent of the borrower, and it died — he is exempt. [If] the borrower said to him: 'Send it to me through my son,' 'through my slave,' 'through my agent,' or 'through your son,' 'through your slave,' [or] 'through your agent'; or the lender said to him: 'I am

YAD AVRAHAM

did not instruct him to do so and thus did not accept responsibility with the representative's reception of the cow.]

The *Gemara (Bava Kamma* 104a) cites a dispute between Rabbah and Rav Chisda whether this ruling of the mishnah refers even to a duly appointed agent. Rav Chisda maintains that the case of the borrower's agent refers only to his worker or lodger who lives with him. Since he works for him or lives with him as a companion, no witnesses are required to verify the fact that he acts on his behalf. He is not, however, a duly appointed agent. Should he send it with an agent who was duly appointed by the borrower in the presence of witnesses,[1] he represents the borrower, who assumes liability when the agent receives the cow. Rabbah, however, rules that even if the borrower appointed the agent in the presence of witnesses, the borrower does not mean to assume liability with the agent's reception of the cow. His appointment

is merely meant to convey to the lender the message that the agent is a reliable person but is not meant to grant him the legal right to act on his behalf (*Rav, Rashi* from *Bava Kamma* 104a).

The halachah is in accordance with Rav Chisda's view (*Choshen Mishpat* 121:2).

אָמַר לוֹ הַשּׁוֹאֵל: ,,שָׁלְחָה לִי בְּיַד בְּנִי,'' ,,בְּיַד עַבְדִּי,'' ,,בְּיַד שְׁלוּחִי,'' — [If] the borrower said to him: 'Send it to me through my son,' 'through my slave,' 'through my agent,'

[Unlike the previous case of the mishnah, in which the lender, on his own initiative, sent one of these people to deliver the cow, in this case the borrower instructed the lender to send him the cow with his (the borrower's) son, slave or agent.]

— אוֹ ,,בְּיַד בִּנְךָ,'' ,,בְּיַד עַבְדְּךָ,'' ,,בְּיַד שְׁלוּחֲךָ''; or 'through your son,' 'through your slave,' [or] 'through your agent';

[I.e., the borrower instructed the

1. Some authorities rule that it is not necessary to appoint the agent in the presence of witnesses. The witnesses are required only in the event that the borrower denies the appointment. Should he admit that he appointed the agent, however, he becomes liable as soon as the cow reaches the agent's hands (*Tos. Yom Tov* based on *Tos.* and *Rosh*). Others see this as a prerequisite for the borrower's liability. The fact that he went to the trouble of appointing the agent before witnesses indicates that he wished this agent to represent him in accepting the cow. Therefore, he is liable only if the appointment was performed in the presence of witnesses. Otherwise, he was merely suggesting that the lender send it through his agent, but not accepting responsibility until the cow comes into his possession (*Nimmukei Yosef; Sma* 121:6).

Should the borrower instruct the agent to tell the lender to send the cow with him, many

„הֲרֵינִי מְשַׁלְּחָה לְךָ בְּיַד בְּנִי,‟ „בְּיַד עַבְדִּי,‟ „בְּיַד
שְׁלוּחִי,‟ אוֹ „בְּיַד בִּנְךָ,‟ „בְּיַד עַבְדְּךָ,‟ „בְּיַד
שְׁלוּחֶךָ,‟ וְאָמַר לוֹ הַשּׁוֹאֵל: „שַׁלַּח,‟ וְשִׁלְּחָהּ
וָמֵתָה — חַיָּב. וְכֵן בְּשָׁעָה שֶׁמַּחֲזִירָהּ.

[ז] הַמַּחֲלִיף פָּרָה בַּחֲמוֹר וְיָלְדָה; וְכֵן

יד אברהם

lender to send it through the lender's son, slave, or agent.]

The slave mentioned here is a Jewish bondman (עֶבֶד עִבְרִי) [i.e., a Jew indentured to another Jew], who is not legally treated as the property of his master. However, in the case of a gentile slave (עֶבֶד כְּנַעֲנִי) [i.e., a non-Jewish slave owned by a Jew], who is legally viewed as his master's property, placing the cow in his hands would be tantamount to leaving it in the owner's hands. Consequently, the borrower could in no way be considered to have received the cow (Rav from Gem. 99a).

אוֹ שֶׁאָמַר לוֹ הַמַּשְׁאִיל: „הֲרֵינִי מְשַׁלְּחָה לְךָ בְּיַד בְּנִי,‟ „בְּיַד עַבְדִּי,‟ „בְּיַד שְׁלוּחִי,‟ אוֹ „בְּיַד בִּנְךָ,‟ „בְּיַד עַבְדְּךָ,‟ „בְּיַד שְׁלוּחֶךָ,‟ וְאָמַר לוֹ הַשּׁוֹאֵל: שַׁלַּח. — or the lender said to him: 'I am sending it to you through my son,' [or] 'through my slave,' or 'through your son,' 'through your slave,' [or] 'through your agent,' and the borrower replied: 'Send [it],'

[Even if the proposal to send the cow over to the borrower through one of these people did not originate with the borrower but with the lender, if the borrower replied to the lender's suggestion affirmatively and told him to send it with them, it is the same as if the borrower had issued the instruction himself.]

וְשִׁלְּחָהּ וָמֵתָה — and he sent it and died [I.e., it died in transit before reaching the borrower.]

חַיָּב. — he is liable.

[The borrower is liable for the cow because it is considered to have entered his possession with its reception by his designated representative.]

וְכֵן בְּשָׁעָה שֶׁמַּחֲזִירָהּ. — So [it is] at the time he returns it.

I.e., if the borrower sent it through his son, slave, or agent, or through the son, slave, or agent of the lender, it does not leave the possession of the borrower until it reaches the lender. Therefore, if it dies in transit, the borrower is liable. However, should the lender instruct the borrower to send it with one of these people, or affirm the borrower's suggestion that he do so, if the animal should die in transit the borrower would be exempt. [In this case, handing over the animal to the lender's designated representative is tantamount to returning it to the lender himself.]

The mishnah refers only to a case in which the cow is returned during the term of the loan, when the borrower is still liable for unavoidable accidents. Should the borrower return it after the expiration of the loan period, the borrower would no longer be liable for unavoidable accidents. Although he must still guard the animal until it is returned to the lender, once the loan has expired he is no longer deemed a borrower but is adjudged a paid shomer [because of the benefit he derived from the cow during the term of borrowing] (Rav from Gem. 81a).

authorities rule that he becomes liable even though the appointment was not witnessed (Sma ad loc.; Nesivos Hamishpat, Mishpat HaUrim #3).

sending it to you through my son,' 'through my slave,' [or] 'through my agent,' or 'through your son,' 'through your slave,' [or] 'through your agent,' and the borrower replied: 'Send [it],' and he sent it and died — he is liable. So [it is] at the time he returns it.

4. **[**If**]** one exchanges a cow for a donkey and it

YAD AVRAHAM

4.

After completing the laws of borrowing, the *Tanna* proceeds to the laws concerning disputes between buyers and sellers. These are included here because they bear a similarity to the issues discussed in mishnah 2 in regard to disputes between borrowers and lenders *(Meiri)*.

The mishnah deals with חֲלִיפִין, *chalifin*. *Chalifin* — exchange — is a method of acquisition derived from the verse *(Ruth 4:7): Formerly, this was done in Israel in cases of redemption and exchange transactions to validate all matters; one would remove his shoe and give it to another (Bava Metzia 47a).*

There are two categories of *chalifin*: one is an even exchange of two objects, in which each serves in place of payment for the other, as well as its means of acquisition. This is referred to in the verse by the word *exchange transactions*. The other, more familiar type is uneven exchange [often referred to as קִנְיָן סוּדָר, lit., *acquisition by handkerchief*], in which the article given as the means of acquisition is not being used in place of payment and is generally returned (see *Nedarim* 48b). This is derived from the words *to validate all matters (Tos. to Bava Metzia 47a, s.v. גאולה).*

This mishnah deals with the first category of *chalifin*. When *chalifin* is used as the medium of transfer, it is not necessary for both objects to be physically transferred. Once it has been agreed that one object is to be exchanged for the other, the transfer of one object suffices to complete the transaction and the second object is then automatically acquired by its new owner as well. It follows from this that the second object need not even be present when this exchange is formalized. This in turn may lead to various uncertainties concerning the second object, which the mishnah will now treat.

הַמַּחֲלִיף פָּרָה בַּחֲמוֹר — [If] one exchanges a cow for a donkey

I.e., Reuven has a cow and Shimon has a donkey, which they agree to exchange. Reuven effects the exchange by performing *meshichah* [the act of acquisition most commonly performed on animals; see General Introduction] on the donkey. Since animals can also be acquired through *chalifin*, once Reuven acquires the donkey by *meshichah*, Shimon automatically gains ownership of the cow although it is still in Reuven's possession *(Tif. Yis.).*

וְיָלְדָה — and it calves;

The cow calved before Shimon took physical possession of it, and it is not known whether it calved prior to the act of acquisition of the donkey (in which case the calf would belong to Reuven, having been born while the cow was still his), or following it (in which case it would belong to Shimon, having been born after he acquired the cow).

This doubt is possible only in the case of exchange. Should the cow be sold for money, the sale would not be final until *meshichah* was performed (as above,

הַמּוֹכֵר שִׁפְחָתוֹ וְיָלְדָה — זֶה אוֹמֵר: ,,עַד שֶׁלֹּא
מָכַרְתִּי,'' וְזֶה אוֹמֵר: ,,מִשֶּׁלָּקַחְתִּי,'' יַחֲלֹקוּ. הָיוּ לוֹ
שְׁנֵי עֲבָדִים, אֶחָד גָּדוֹל וְאֶחָד קָטָן; וְכֵן שְׁתֵּי
שָׂדוֹת, אַחַת גְּדוֹלָה וְאַחַת קְטַנָּה; הַלּוֹקֵחַ אוֹמֵר
גָּדוֹל לָקַחְתִּי, וְהַלָּה אוֹמֵר אֵינִי יוֹדֵעַ, זָכָה בַּגָּדוֹל.

יד אברהם

4:2); i.e., until the buyer drew the cow
into his possession. That being the case,
it would be clear whether the cow had
calved before or after the sale (Rashi;
Rav).

וְכֵן הַמּוֹכֵר שִׁפְחָתוֹ וְיָלְדָה — and similarly
[if] one sells his maidservant and she
gives birth —

[This case does not refer to chalifin
but to a straightforward sale.] Gentile
slaves, the type to which the mishnah
refers, can be acquired with money,
since slaves are generally governed by
the rules relating to real estate, not
movables (see Kiddushin 1:3). Thus, it
is possible to purchase a slave without
the slave being physically present at the
transaction. Consequently, as soon as
Shimon, the buyer, gives the money to
Reuven, the seller, the ownership of the
slave is transferred to Shimon (Rav;
Rashi).

The slave in question was a woman
who gave birth around the time of the
sale, before reaching Shimon's physical
possession. It is therefore not clear
whether she gave birth prior to the sale
[which would leave the child the
property of the seller] or following it
[making the child the property of the
buyer] (Rav; Rashi).

זֶה אוֹמֵר: ,,עַד שֶׁלֹּא מָכַרְתִּי,'' וְזֶה אוֹמֵר:
,,מִשֶּׁלָּקַחְתִּי,'' — this one says: '[It
happened] before I sold,' while this one

says: '[It happened] after I bought,'
Reuven, the seller, claims that the
cow or the slavewoman gave birth
before being exchanged or sold, and that
the offspring therefore belongs to him.
Shimon, the buyer, however, claims that
the cow or the slavewoman gave birth
after the exchange or purchase, making
the offspring his (Tif. Yis.).

יַחֲלֹקוּ. — they divide.
[I.e., they divide the value of the calf
or slave child.]

As above at the end of mishnah 2,
this mishnah is attributed to the Tanna
Sumchos, who rules that money which
lies in doubt is divided, even though
each litigant makes a definite claim that
it is his. This is so, however, only if
neither is in physical possession of the
article. Thus, the mishnah must refer to
a case in which the cow was in a public
meadow and the slavewoman was in the
street. Otherwise, the offspring would
belong to the one in whose possession it
was found, and it would be up to the
other one to prove that it was his.[1] The
halachah is, however, not in accordance
with Sumchos, but with the Sages, who
rule that even in such a case we apply
the principle: הַמּוֹצִיא מֵחֲבֵרוֹ עָלָיו הָרְאָיָה,
whoever wishes to exact money from
another must bring the proof.

Since the cow or the slavewoman was
originally in the seller's possession, they

1. Above, at the end of mishnah 2 (s.v. יחלקו), the mishnah ruled that if neither the lender nor
borrower claims to be sure whether the borrowed cow died or the rented one, they divide. This
was explained there to follow the opinion of Sumchos that money that lies in doubt (viz., the
reimbursement for the dead cow) is divided. Yet in that case, the money in question clearly lies
in the possession of the defendant — and he must nevertheless pay half to the plaintiff!
Tos. (100a) explain that if the one holding physical possession of the money in question
claims with certainty that it is his, even Sumchos agrees that nothing can be taken from him
without proof. However, in the case of mishnah 2, the borrower does not claim that he is

calves; and similarly [if] one sells his maidservant and she gives birth — this one says: '[It happened] before I sold,' while this one says: '[It happened] after I bought,' they divide. [If] he had two slaves, one large and one small; and similarly, [if he had] two fields, one large and one small; the buyer claims he bought the large one, while the other one says [that] he does not know, he receives the large one. [If the

YAD AVRAHAM

rule that in this context the buyer is always adjudged the claimant even if the cow and the slavewoman are not presently in the seller's property but in a meadow or in the street. This is known as חֶזְקַת מָרֵיהּ קַמָּא, *the possession of the first owner*. This holds true even when the buyer makes a definite claim while the seller puts forth a doubtful claim, admitting that he doesn't know.

Although the seller is considered the holder, in the view of the Sages, and the buyer the claimant, in the case of the cow the seller must swear an oath that the calf is his. Since the buyer comes to court demanding both the cow and the calf, and the seller admits to owing the cow but denies that the calf belongs to the buyer, he is liable to the Biblical oath for one who admits part of a claim. In the case of the slavewoman, however, he would not be liable to such an oath since slaves are treated as real estate, and matters of real estate are excluded from Biblical oaths (אֵין נִשְׁבָּעִין עַל הַקַּרְקָעוֹת). He must, therefore, swear only a *shevuas heseis*, a post-mishnaic oath (which applies even to real estate).

Should the buyer have obtained possession, however, the seller is considered the claimant and the buyer keeps it unless the seller can prove his claim. He can only demand of the buyer a *shevuas heseis* and even that only when the seller claims to know with certainty that the birth preceded the sale.

If both admit they don't know for sure, and it is in the possession of neither of them, the seller is regarded as in possession, and the calf or the young slave belongs to him. According to some authorities, however, they

divide (*Tif. Yis.* from *Shulchan Aruch* 223:2).

[*If*] — הָיוּ לוֹ שְׁנֵי עֲבָדִים, אֶחָד גָּדוֹל וְאֶחָד קָטָן; *he had two slaves, one large and one small;*

[If the seller sold a slave but did not specify which of his two slaves he was selling. One of the slaves was a big man, while the other was small, making one worth more than the other.]

— וְכֵן שְׁתֵּי שָׂדוֹת, אַחַת גְּדוֹלָה וְאַחַת קְטַנָּה; *and similarly, [if he had] two fields, one large and one small;*

[He sold one of his two fields without specifying which of the two he was selling.]

הַלּוֹקֵחַ אוֹמֵר גָּדוֹל לָקַחְתִּי, וְהַלָּה אוֹמֵר אֵינִי יוֹדֵעַ, — *the buyer claims he bought the large one, while the other one says [that] he does not know,*

[The buyer claims to be certain that they had agreed on the sale of the larger slave or field, while the seller says that he is not certain which one they agreed upon and that perhaps it was the smaller one.]

זָכָה בַגָּדוֹל. — *he receives the large one.*

[The buyer receives the large slave or field. This ruling presents problems. Since the seller is still in possession of the objects of the sale, it should be up to the buyer to *prove* his contention, not just win on his unsupported claim. Now there is an opinion which holds that בָּרֵי וְשֶׁמָּא בָּרֵי עָדִיף, *When a certain claim*

definitely exempt; rather he agrees that he does not know. Consequently, Sumchos' view is that his physical possession of the questionable money does not avail him and they divide the amount in question.

הַמּוֹכֵר אוֹמֵר קָטָן מָכַרְתִּי, וְהַלָּה אוֹמֵר אֵינִי יוֹדֵעַ,
אֵין לוֹ אֶלָּא קָטָן. זֶה אוֹמֵר גָּדוֹל, וְזֶה אוֹמֵר קָטָן,
יִשָּׁבַע הַמּוֹכֵר שֶׁהַקָּטָן מָכַר. זֶה אוֹמֵר אֵינִי יוֹדֵעַ
וְזֶה אוֹמֵר אֵינִי יוֹדֵעַ, יַחֲלֹקוּ.

יד אברהם

confronts an uncertain claim, the certain claim prevails [lit., certain and uncertain — certain is stronger], and that the certain claim prevails even to the extent of extracting money from the uncertain holder of the money (see above, mishnah 2, s.v. חיב). According to this view, the mishnah is readily understood. The halachah is, however, not in accordance with this view, but with the view that money cannot be extracted from the person in possession of it merely because he is uncertain in his claim while the plaintiff claims certainty. Only proof is sufficient to take money from its holder, not merely a more positive claim (see *Gem.* 97a). Therefore, the commentators seek other explanations for this ruling.]

Tos. Yom Tov prefers the explanation that the dispute does not concern an actual field or slave, but the worth of a field or slave, i.e., money given for a purchase of one of these which never materialized. The buyer now demands a refund claiming that he had given for this failed purchase the value of a large field or slave, while the seller replies that he is not certain, but he may have received only the worth of a small slave. This sets up a situation involving an oath, since should the seller state definitely that he owes him only the worth of a small slave, he must swear the Biblical oath for one who admits to part of a claim while denying the rest of it. Since he states that he does not know definitely that it was only the worth of a small slave, he cannot take that oath, and since he cannot swear to rebut the buyer's claim, he must pay (as explained above in mishnah 2).

[This explanation cannot work if the issue involves an actual field or slave since, among other reasons, Biblical

oaths do not apply to matters of real estate and slaves. The *Gemara*, in fact, explains the end of the mishnah in such a manner, and *Tos. Yom Tov* is merely extending that explanation to this case as well. This will be explained at length at the end of the mishnah.]

הַמּוֹכֵר אוֹמֵר קָטָן מָכַרְתִּי, וְהַלָּה אוֹמֵר אֵינִי יוֹדֵעַ, אֵין לוֹ אֶלָּא קָטָן. — [If] the seller says he sold the small one, while the other one claims he does not know, he receives only the small one.

[In this case the seller is definite in his claim while the buyer — the claimant — is unsure.] Consequently, the seller is not even required to swear in reply to the buyer's uncertain claim (*Tif. Yis.*).

זֶה אוֹמֵר גָּדוֹל, וְזֶה אוֹמֵר קָטָן, יִשָּׁבַע הַמּוֹכֵר שֶׁהַקָּטָן מָכַר. — [If] this one claims [it was] the large one, while this one claims [it was] the small one, the seller must swear that he sold the small one.

[If the buyer claims definitely that he bought the large field or slave while the seller states with certainty that he took money only for the small one, the seller must swear that he sold the small one. The obvious intention is that the seller must take a Biblical oath that he sold the small slave or field, since he has admitted part of the buyer's claim, viz. that he owes him at least the small slave or field. The *Gemara* (100a) points out, however, that this ruling is untenable on three counts: (a) The seller did not admit a part of the buyer's claim, but something else. The buyer claimed a large slave or field, while the seller admitted selling him a completely different slave or field. (b) By admitting that he is holding a tangible asset of the plaintiff, that asset is immediately established as the legal property of the plaintiff wherever it

seller says he sold the small one, while the other one claims he does not know, he receives only the small one. [If] this one claims [it was] the large one, while this one claims [it was] the small one, the seller must swear that he sold the small one. [If] both say they do not know, they divide.

YAD AVRAHAM

may be, and is thereby removed from the realm of a claim. [Thus, in regard to the only matter outstanding, the seller denies everything, for which there is no Biblical oath.] This is known as the rule of הֵילָךְ, lit., *here it is*. This is not considered an admission to make one liable for the Biblical oath for the partial admission of a claim.[1] (c) There are no Biblical oaths for litigation concerning real estate or slaves.

To resolve all these questions, the *Amora* Rav therefore explains the mishnah as referring to one who claims the *worth* of a large slave or field, not the slave or field itself, while the defendant admits owing the *worth* of a small slave or field. Since the dispute is over money, the defendant's admission is of the same variety as the plaintiff's claim. And, since even after this admission the money does not immediately become the plaintiff's but remains a debt owed him by the defendant, it remains part of the overall claim and the admission constitutes an admission of part of that claim. Again, since the claim does not concern slaves or real estate but money, it is amenable to an oath *(Rav* from *Gem.* 100a).

Since the mishnah talks of a slave or field, however, it is clear that the money in question must relate in some fashion to the purchase of a slave or field. *Rashi* explains the case to mean that Reuven gave Shimon money to purchase a slave or a field for him, and when Shimon failed to execute his errand, Reuven demanded that he return the money.

Reuven claimed that he gave him a sum of money sufficient to buy a large slave or field, while Shimon maintained that he received only the amount sufficient to purchase a small slave or field. He must therefore swear that he received only that amount.

Tosafos object to this interpretation on the grounds that the mishnah refers to the litigants as buyer and seller, not as principal and agent. They therefore explain the mishnah to refer to a case in which the buyer paid for a slave or field, but did not yet draw up a deed. This took place in a locale in which deeds are always drawn up for transfers of real estate (slaves being considered real estate), and he may therefore retract until the deed is written. [Alternatively, they stipulated that they should be able to retract even after paying.] In the event, one of them did retract and the buyer now asks for his money back, claiming that he paid for a large field or slave. The seller, on the other hand, replies that he was given only enough for a small field or slave. He must, therefore, swear that he received only the smaller amount.

As mentioned above, *Tos. Yom Tov* explains the earlier part of the mishnah in this same manner. In that segment of the mishnah, since the seller maintains that he does not know, he cannot swear, and must consequently pay. For other explanations of both parts of the mishnah, see *Tos. Yom Tov.*

זֶה אוֹמֵר אֵינִי יוֹדֵעַ וְזֶה אוֹמֵר אֵינִי יוֹדֵעַ, יַחֲלֹקוּ. — [If] *both say they do not know* [lit.,

---

1. The *Gemara* (4a) actually cites a dispute whether this exempts from the Biblical oath for the admission of part of a claim but *Tosafos* (ibid.) prove from the *Gemara's* question here that the halachah follows the view that it does exempt. See also *Rambam, Hil. To'ein* 1:3 and *Choshen Mishpat* 87:1, 75:6.

[ה] הַמּוֹכֵר

[ה] **הַמּוֹכֵר** זֵיתָיו לָעֵצִים, וְעָשׂוּ פָחוֹת מֵרְבִיעִית לַסְאָה, הֲרֵי אֵלוּ שֶׁל־בַּעַל הַזֵּיתִים. עָשׂוּ רְבִיעִית לַסְאָה, זֶה אוֹמֵר: "זֵיתַי גְּדֵלוּ," וְזֶה אוֹמֵר: "אַרְצִי גְדֵלָה," יַחֲלֹקוּ. שָׁטַף נָהָר זֵיתָיו וּנְתָנָם לְתוֹךְ שְׂדֵה חֲבֵרוֹ, זֶה אוֹמֵר: "זֵיתַי גְּדֵלוּ," וְזֶה אוֹמֵר: "אַרְצִי גְדֵלָה,"

יד אברהם

this one says ... and this one says ...], they divide.

This, too, is in accordance with Sumchos (see above, s.v. יחלקו). The Sages, however, rule that the burden of proof lies on the buyer (Meiri; Nimmukei Yosef). However, if the article in question is in no one's possession, even the Sages rule that it be divided (Nimmukei Yosef).

5.

הַמּוֹכֵר זֵיתָיו לָעֵצִים, — [If] one sells his olive trees for the wood,

I.e., the trees produce little, so the owner therefore sells them to be chopped down for their wood.[1] He did not, however, stipulate with the buyer how long he may keep them there before chopping them down (Rav, Meiri from Gem. 100b).

וְעָשׂוּ פָחוֹת מֵרְבִיעִית לַסְאָה, — and they produced less than a quarter-log per seah,

The buyer left them growing until they produced olives, but the trees were so inferior that they yielded olives which produce less than a quarter-log (reviis) of oil per seah of olives (Rav; Rashi).[2] This is reckoned after deducting the cost of picking and pressing (ibid.).

Others explain this to mean that all the olives growing in an area fit for planting a seah of barley (an area of 50 x 50 cubits) produce only a quarter-log of oil (Rabbeinu Chananel; Rabbeinu Yehonasan, Meiri).

הֲרֵי אֵלוּ שֶׁל־בַּעַל הַזֵּיתִים. — these belong to the owner of the olive trees.

Although the land contributed to the growth of the olives as well (and the land beneath the trees was not sold), the owner of the trees does not receive any payment for them because people are not particular about such a small amount (Rav from Gem. 100b).

Should the seller stipulate that the buyer may leave the trees there indefinitely, the owner of the trees may keep them there even if they produce a quarter-log or more (Rav from Gem. 100b). This is tantamount to granting him the rights to the products of the trees that grow in his land.

Should he stipulate that the buyer cut down the trees immediately, even if they produce less than a quarter-log per seah, the olives belong to the owner of the land (Rav; Rambam Comm. and Hil. Shecheinim 4:11; Shulchan Aruch 168:2), since they derived their sustenance from his land (Sma ibid. 6). Since he is strict about cutting down the trees, he is obviously particular even about less than a quarter-log. Rashba, however, rules that they share the produce, as in the case discussed further in the mishnah (Nimmukei Yosef; Maggid Mishneh, Hil. Shecheinim 4:11).

עָשׂוּ רְבִיעִית לַסְאָה, — [If] they produced a quarter-log per seah,

If the olives yielded a quarter-log of

1. Although the Torah forbids cutting down fruit trees (Deut. 20:19), it is permissible if the trees produce so little that their wood is worth more than their fruit (Bava Kamma 92a).

2. The conversion of these measures into contemporary measurements is a matter of controversy. According to the various measures, the quarter-log ranges from 3 to 5.3 ounces. The seah ranges from about 2.25 — 4 gallons.

5. **[I**f] one sells his olive trees for the wood, and they produced less than a quarter-*log* per *seah*, these belong to the owner of the olive trees. [If] they produced a quarter-*log* per *seah*, [and] this one claims: 'My olive trees produced [it],' while this one claims: 'My land produced [it],' they divide. [If] a river washed away his olive trees and placed them in the midst of his neighbor's field, [and] this one claims: 'My olive trees produced [them],' while this

YAD AVRAHAM

oil per *seah*, and surely if they produced more *(Tos. Yom Tov)*.

זֶה אוֹמֵר: "זֵיתַי גְדְלוּ," וְזֶה אוֹמֵר: "אַרְצִי גְדְלָה," — [and] this one claims: 'My olive trees produced [it],' while this one claims: 'My land produced [it],'

[The buyer claims that the olives are the result of the trees and therefore rightfully belong to him, while the seller, who still owns the land, maintains that their nourishment is derived from his ground and they should therefore belong to him.]

יַחֲלֹקוּ. — *they divide.*

[Since, in fact, both were instrumental in the production of the olives, both share.] This holds true according to all opinions, not only Sumchos, and is indeed the halachah *(Rambam, Shecheinim 4:11)*.

שָׁטַף נָהָר זֵיתָיו וּנְתָנָם לְתוֹךְ שְׂדֵה חֲבֵרוֹ, — [If] a river washed away his olive trees and placed them in the midst of his neighbor's field,

This is not a continuation of the previous case, but a new case dealing with a man who had good olive trees in his own field *(Meiri)*. A river overflowed its banks and inundated this man's field, washing away his olive trees and depositing them in the neighboring field. These trees were uprooted together with the clods of earth in which they were rooted, and these clods were large enough to sustain the trees, if need be *(Rav from Gem. 101a)*. However,

they eventually took root on their own in the neighboring field *(Meiri, and see Rambam, Hil. Shecheinim 4:10)* and produced fruit. Since they were uprooted with clods of earth sufficient to sustain them, they maintain their legal status of 'old trees.' This is relevant to the laws of *orlah*, the Torah's *(Lev. 19:23)* commandment that the fruit of new trees be forbidden for the first three years of the tree's growth. Had they been uprooted without the earth surrounding their roots, they would be legally classified as new trees and the fruit of the first three years would be subject to the *orlah* prohibition. See above, 7:7 *(Rav from Gem. 101a)*.

Should the owner of the trees wish to remove them from his neighbor's field, he is not permitted to do so. The Sages enacted this so that *Eretz Yisrael* should be well cultivated *(Gem. 101a)*. Since there is no reason to believe that the owner of the field in which the trees have now taken root will plant new ones if these are removed (having failed to do so before the flood), while there is every reason to assume that the previous owner of the trees *will* plant new ones to replace those washed away by the flood, by decreeing that the trees must remain in their new location the Rabbis were increasing the level of cultivation of *Eretz Yisrael* *(Beis Yosef 168)*.

זֶה אוֹמֵר: "זֵיתַי גְדְלוּ," וְזֶה אוֹמֵר: "אַרְצִי גְדְלָה," — [and] this one claims: 'My olive trees produced [them],' while this one

בבא מציעא ח/ו

בָּבָא יַחֲלֹקוּ.

[ו] **הַמַּשְׂכִּיר** בַּיִת לַחֲבֵרוֹ, בִּימוֹת הַגְּשָׁמִים אֵינוֹ יָכוֹל לְהוֹצִיאוֹ, מִן־הֶחָג וְעַד הַפֶּסַח, בִּימוֹת הַחַמָּה, שְׁלֹשִׁים יוֹם. וּבַכְּרַכִּים, אֶחָד יְמוֹת הַחַמָּה וְאֶחָד יְמוֹת הַגְּשָׁמִים, שְׁנֵים

יד אברהם

claims: 'My land produced [them],'

[The owner of the trees claims the olives as the produce of his trees, while the owner of the field into which they were transplanted claims them as the produce of his land.] Although the trees took root with their original clods, the clods alone could only keep the tree alive but could not produce the fruit without the soil of the new field (Tos. Yom Tov from Maggid Mishneh, Hil. Shecheinim).

יַחֲלֹקוּ. — they divide.

The owner of the olive trees divides the fruit with the owner of the field for the first three years of their transplanted existence. Since these trees, because of their clods of earth, produce fruit that is not orlah, and therefore permissible, the owner of the field into which they were transplanted benefits from them. Had he planted his own trees, he would not have had usable fruit for these three years, since any such fruit would be orlah. Therefore, the owner of the trees deserves a share of the fruit. After three years, however, the owner of the field may claim that had he planted his own trees, he would now be permitted to eat the fruit in any case. Therefore, the owner of the trees no longer has any claim (Rav from Gem. 101a).

Although the owner of the field benefited by being able to use the fruit within the first three years, this does not entitle the owner of the trees to any permanent share, since the owner of the field also lost something by having these mature trees growing in his field. Had he planted young trees, they would have been thin, with few branches, and he would have also been able to plant vegetables beneath them during those years (Gem. 101a). Therefore, transplanting the older trees was only worth his while if their produce reverts entirely to him after three years (Tos.).

Tos. and Rosh state that the present owner of the trees must nevertheless remunerate the previous owner for his trees by paying him the price of olive trees which are sold for transplanting. It does not suffice to pay merely the price of trees sold for wood, since these trees were cultivated for planting (Tos. Yom Tov).

Similarly, should the olive trees become uprooted without their clods — in which case they immediately become the property of the field in which they have taken root (Rambam, Hil. Shecheinim 4:10) — the owner of that field must pay the original owner of the trees the value of trees sold for transplanting (Ravad ibid.).

Rambam, however, mentions nothing about a requirement to pay for the trees. Maggid Mishneh explains that if the trees are uprooted without clods, the owner despairs of them, just as he despairs of anything washed away by the river or the sea (see introduction to chapter 2). Additionally, if the trees are uprooted without clods of earth clinging to their roots, the river carries them farther off, and this makes it even more probable that he despairs of ever finding them. If they are uprooted with clods, however, they cannot be carried far, and he hopes to recover them. Indeed, he would recover them were it not for the mitzvah of cultivating Eretz Yisrael.

Kesef Mishneh objects to the first solution, since, were that so, even if they were uprooted with their clods, the owner would despair of recovering them, and the owner of the field would keep them gratis. He there-one claims: 'My land produced [them],' they divide.

6. **[I**f] one rents a house to his neighbor, he cannot evict him in the winter, from Succos until Pesach, [unless he gives him notice] in the summer, thirty days. In big cities, both in summer and winter, [he must give] twelve-months [notice]. With stores,

YAD AVRAHAM

fore prefers the second solution, adding that this ruling applies only in *Eretz Yisrael*. In the Diaspora, however, he may remove his trees. He suggests further that perhaps *Rambam* actually concurs with *Ravad* concerning compensation, though he does not state so explicitly (see further *Sma* 168:4).

Since the mishnah does not specify, we understand it to mean that even if the olives yield less than a quarter-*log* per *seah*, they must be divided. Also, the mishnah applies only if the owner of the field agrees to keep the trees. Should he refuse to do so, he may tell the owner of the trees to take out his trees, either within the three-year period or after it *(Tos. Yom Tov* citing *Nimmukei Yosef* from *Ritva).*

6.

From here to the end of the chapter, the mishnah deals with renting houses and stores.

הַמַּשְׂכִּיר בַּיִת לַחֲבֵרוֹ, — *[If] one rents a house to his neighbor,*

The mishnah refers to one who rents a house without a definite term *(Rav from Gem.* 101b). The tenant pays either a monthly or yearly rental, without being told when he will be asked to leave *(Tos. Yom Tov* from *Nimmukei Yosef; Maggid Mishneh* to *Hil. Sechirus* 6:7).

בִּימוֹת הַגְּשָׁמִים אֵינוֹ יָכוֹל לְהוֹצִיאוֹ, מֵן הֶחָג וְעַד הַפֶּסַח, — *he cannot evict him in the winter* [lit., *in the days of rain], from Succos until Pesach;*

The owner cannot evict the tenant from his house at any time during the winter [from Succos, which marks the beginning of the rainy season through Pesach, which marks its conclusion], since few dwellings are available at that time *(Gem.* 101b).

בִּימוֹת הַחַמָּה, שְׁלֹשִׁים יוֹם. — *[unless he gives him notice] in the summer, thirty days.*

I.e., he cannot evict him during the winter unless he gives him thirty-days

notice during the summer. Thus, if he wishes to evict him after Succos, he must give him notice on the fifteenth of Elul, thirty days before the first day of Succos. Should he fail to give him notice on that date, he cannot evict him until Pesach. By the same token, we learn from this that if one wishes to evict a tenant who has no lease at any time during the summer, he must give him thirty-days notice *(Rav from Gem.* 101b).

וּבַכְּרַכִּים, — *In big cities,*

I.e., in heavily populated metropolises, where there is a housing shortage *(Rav; Rashi).*

אֶחָד יְמוֹת הַחַמָּה וְאֶחָד יְמוֹת הַגְּשָׁמִים, שְׁנֵים עָשָׂר חֹדֶשׁ. — *both in summer and winter, [he must give] twelve-months [notice].*

Whether he wishes to evict him in the summer or in the winter, he must give him twelve-months notice *(Rav from Gem.* 101b).

Just as the landlord must give notice to evict the tenant, so the tenant must give notice that he is moving — thirty days in

עֶשֶׂר חֹדֶשׁ. וּבַחֲנוּיּוֹת, אֶחָד עֲיָרוֹת וְאֶחָד כְּרַכִּים,
שְׁנֵים עָשָׂר חֹדֶשׁ. רַבָּן שִׁמְעוֹן בֶּן־גַּמְלִיאֵל אוֹמֵר:
חֲנוּת שֶׁל־נַחְתּוֹמִים וְשֶׁל־צַבָּעִים, שָׁלֹשׁ שָׁנִים.

[ז] **הַמַּשְׂכִּיר** בַּיִת לַחֲבֵרוֹ, הַמַּשְׂכִּיר חַיָּב
בְּדֶלֶת, בַּנֶּגֶר, וּבַמַּנְעוּל, וּבְכָל־
דָּבָר שֶׁהוּא מַעֲשֵׂה אֻמָּן. אֲבָל דָּבָר שֶׁאֵינוֹ מַעֲשֵׂה
אֻמָּן, הַשּׂוֹכֵר עוֹשֵׂהוּ.

יד אברהם

town, and twelve months in big cities. Should he fail to give notice, he may not move out unless he pays the rent (Rav from Gem. 101b).

Should he find another tenant as respectable as he, whose household members do not exceed his, he may place him in the house in his stead. Should the landlord live together with his tenant in the house, however, he may object to this new tenant (Tif. Yis. from Shulchan Aruch 312:7, 316:1, Sma ibid.:1).

וּבַחֲנוּיּוֹת, אֶחָד עֲיָרוֹת וְאֶחָד כְּרַכִּים, שְׁנֵים עָשָׂר חֹדֶשׁ. — With stores, both in towns and cities, [he must give] twelve-months [notice].

Twelve-months notice is required for the eviction of a rented store because a storekeeper sells to many people on credit, and they pay only over a long period of time. Should he have to vacate suddenly, he would lose some of these debts because not all his customers would know where to locate him (Tos. Yom Tov from Rashi).

Just as the landlord must give the storekeeper twelve-months notice, so the storekeeper must give the landlord similar notice. This is because the landlord will not find anyone to give up his old location unless the latter has twelve months to collect his outstanding debts, and to give his landlord notice that he is moving (Tos. Yom Tov from Beis Yosef 312).

רַבָּן שִׁמְעוֹן בֶּן־גַּמְלִיאֵל אוֹמֵר: חֲנוּת שֶׁל־נַחְתּוֹמִים וְשֶׁל־צַבָּעִים, שָׁלֹשׁ שָׁנִים. — Rabban Shimon ben Gamliel says: [With] bakeries or dye shops, [he must give] three-years [notice].

These types of shops grant very long-term credit. Therefore, they must have longer to collect their debts (Rav; Rashi from Gem. 101b).

Meiri questions this interpretation on the grounds that he sees no apparent reason for bakers and dyers to grant credit for longer terms than other merchants. He therefore explains that bakers and dyers find it more difficult to move, since they must find a building suitable for keeping their huge utensils and for keeping a fire burning constantly (see, e.g., Bava Basra 2:3). This appears to be Rambam's interpretation as well. See Rambam Commentary.

The halachah is in accordance with Rabban Shimon ben Gamliel (Rav; Tos. Yom Tov from Rif, Rosh, Rambam Comm.). Rambam in Hil. Sechirus 6:7, however, does not decide the halachah in favor of Rabban Shimon ben Gamliel, and neither does the Baal Halttur (Maggid Mishneh ad loc.). Shulchan Aruch 312:6 follows this latter view of Rambam. Rama follows other authorities, deciding in favor of Rabban Shimon ben Gamliel.

7.

הַמַּשְׂכִּיר בַּיִת לַחֲבֵרוֹ, הַמַּשְׂכִּיר חַיָּב בְּדֶלֶת, — [If] one rents a house to another, the

landlord must provide the door, I.e., if the tenant did not see the house

8
7
both in towns and cities, [he must give] twelve-months [notice]. Rabban Shimon ben Gamliel says: [With] bakeries or dye shops, [he must give] three-years [notice].

7. **[I**f] one rents a house to another, the landlord must provide the door, the bolt, the lock, and everything that is the work of a craftsman. But anything that is not the work of a craftsman, the tenant must make [for himself].

YAD AVRAHAM

before he rented it and did not stipulate with the landlord concerning the type of facilities he must provide, the contract is assumed to require the landlord to provide the following items, the first of which are proper doors *(Meiri)*.

Should everything be in order at the time the tenant takes over the house but deteriorate in the course of time, *Meiri* rules that the landlord is responsible to replace those things for which he was responsible initially. *Nimmukei Yosef*, however, differentiates based on the terms of the original contract. If the rental agreement called for providing the tenant with a house, but no particular house was stipulated, the landlord is indeed responsible to replace any deterioration. If the contract called for a specific house, however, he is only required to provide the proper repairs at the onset of the rental. After that, he is no longer responsible for deterioriation, since this house is no longer intact *(Tif. Yis.* from *Rama, Choshen Mishpat* 314:1). Since the contract was for a specific house, the owner did not undertake to provide him with housing for the duration of the lease, but only to let him have the use of this particular house. If the house deteriorated, it is as though this house is no longer standing, in which case he is not obligated to provide him with another house, as will be explained in mishnah 9 *(Sma* 314:7).

בַּנֶּגֶר, — *the bolt,*
This they would use to lock the door from the inside by thrusting it into the hole in the threshold *(Rav; Rashi; Meiri; Nimmukei Yosef).*

וּבַמַּנְעוּל, — *the lock,*
Nimmukei Yosef defines this as a padlock, with which the tenant may lock the door when he leaves the premises.

וּבְכָל־דָּבָר שֶׁהוּא מַעֲשֵׂה אֻמָּן. — *and everything that is the work of a craftsman.*
The landlord must construct or repair any item fundamental to living in a house and courtyard which requires a craftsman to build or fix *(Tos. Yom Tov* from *Rambam, Hil. Sechirus* 6:3). For example: windows and beams *(Gem.* 101b).

אֲבָל דָּבָר שֶׁאֵינוֹ מַעֲשֵׂה אֻמָּן, הַשּׂוֹכֵר עוֹשֵׂהוּ. — *But anything that is not the work of a craftsman, the tenant must make [for himself].*
For example, a parapet or a ladder *(Gem.* 101b). Any item which an ordinary person can be expected to make for himself, the tenant must make out of his own expense *(Rambam, Hil. Sechirus* 6:3). In all these matters, however, we follow the prevailing local custom *(Choshen Mishpat* 314:2).

הַזֶּבֶל שֶׁל־בַּעַל הַבַּיִת, וְאֵין לַשּׂוֹכֵר אֶלָּא הַיּוֹצֵא
מִן־הַתַּנּוּר וּמִן־הַכִּירַיִם בִּלְבָד.

[ח] **הַמַּשְׂכִּיר** בַּיִת לַחֲבֵרוֹ לַשָּׁנָה, נִתְעַבְּרָה
הַשָּׁנָה, נִתְעַבְּרָה לַשּׂוֹכֵר.
הִשְׂכִּיר לוֹ לֶחֳדָשִׁים, נִתְעַבְּרָה הַשָּׁנָה, נִתְעַבְּרָה

יד אברהם

הַזֶּבֶל שֶׁל־בַּעַל הַבַּיִת, — *Manure belongs to the landlord,*

In earlier times, it was customary to save animal manure and compost for use as fertilizer. It was also the architectural style of those days to build houses around a large courtyard, and those who would rent the houses would make much use of it. Villagers who would come to the city on market day would also arrange to feed their cattle in a courtyard. The excess straw and stubble would be crushed under the cattle's feet and would become fertilizer. Ordinarily, this would be abandoned in the courtyard in addition to the fee paid for the use of the yard (*Meiri*). This manure, the mishnah teaches, belongs to the owner of the courtyard, not the tenant. Manure produced by the tenant's cattle, however, belongs to the tenant (*Rav* from *Gem.* 102a).

Many authorities rule that this applies only if the courtyard is not itself rented to the tenant of the house. Then, manure produced by cattle coming from outside belongs to the landlord since the courtyard is his, and it acquires for him anything found in it (see above 1:4). Should the courtyard be rented by the tenant, however, it is treated as his courtyard, and the manure found in it belongs to him (*Rashi* 102a; *Ravad, Hil. Sechirus* 6:5).

Rambam (*Sechirus* 6:5), however, rules that one's courtyard acquires property for him even though it is rented to others. He concludes, therefore, that the manure produced by cattle that came from the outside belongs to the owner of the yard in any

case. This view is accepted by *Shulchan Aruch* 313:3, by *Tos. Yom Tov,* by *Shach* (ibid. 1) and others; see below.

וְאֵין לַשּׂוֹכֵר אֶלָּא הַיּוֹצֵא מִן־הַתַּנּוּר וּמִן־הַכִּירַיִם בִּלְבָד. — *and the tenant has nothing but the refuse of the oven or the double stove.*

[The tenant who rents the house retains nothing found in the yard except the ashes of the stoves and ovens which can also be used in fertilizer (*Rav; Rashi*). [For a description of the ovens and double stoves of mishnaic times, see ArtScroll *Shabbos* 3:1.]

The reason for the ashes belonging to the tenant requires some explanation. *Tur* (*Choshen Mishpat* 313), quoting *Ramah,* qualifies the mishnah as referring to an oven and stove situated in the courtyard [as was often the case; see *Bava Basra* 3:5] and rented by the tenant. The mishnah teaches us that, even if strangers come and cook and bake in these stoves, their ashes belong to the tenant, since the stove is his rented property.

It follows from this that there is no fundamental difference between manure and ashes, since had the tenant rented the yard, the manure would also belong to him, in the view of many authorities (*Rashi; Ravad*), as explained above. The mishnah distinguishes between them only because it was customary to rent the courtyard stove to the tenant, but not the courtyard itself (*Tos. Yom Tov*).

As noted, this follows the view of *Rashi* and *Ravad,* who rule that a rented yard acquires property for the tenant. According to *Rambam,* however, who rules that a rented courtyard acquires property on behalf of its owner, not tenant, we encounter a problem. Why should the tenant gain ownership of the ashes produced by others, since the stove belongs to the landlord and, according to *Rambam,* acquires property for him not-

Manure belongs to the landlord, and the tenant has nothing but the refuse of the oven or the double stove.

8. [**I**f] one rented a house for the year, [and] a leap year was declared, it was declared for the tenant. [If] he rented it to him by the month, [and] a leap year was declared, it was declared for the

YAD AVRAHAM

withstanding the fact that it is rented to the tenant? *Sma* (313:7) suggests that since the tenant cooks and bakes in this oven, and his ashes become mingled with the ashes produced by the strangers, the landlord waives his right to the small amount of ashes he could obtain from the strangers.

Tos. Yom Tov, however, interprets the mishnah to mean, according to *Rambam*, that

only the ashes produced by the tenant belong to him. The ashes produced by the strangers, however, indeed belong to the landlord. For this reason, he explains, *Rambam* does not state this halachah; since it deals only with the ashes produced by the tenant, it is self-evident from the previously stated rule of the manure produced by the tenant's cattle, which belongs to the tenant.[1]

8.

הַמַּשְׂכִּיר בַּיִת לַחֲבֵרוֹ לְשָׁנָה, — [*If*] *one rented a house for the year,*

I.e., he rented him a house for the current year, or for a particular year (*Tos. Yom Tov* from *Nimmukei Yosef*, quoting *Ritva*).

נִתְעַבְּרָה הַשָּׁנָה, — [*and*] *a leap year was declared,*

[In ancient times, leap years were not determined by a fixed calendar. During the period when the Sanhedrin consecrated the months, they decided on a year-to-year basis whether it was necessary to add an extra month. This thirteenth month was called אֲדָר שֵׁנִי, *Second Adar*. Nowadays, we rely on the permanent calendar computed by Hillel the Second in 4119 (359 C.E.). The commentary will discuss below the relevance of the mishnah's ruling in

light of our fixed calendar.]

נִתְעַבְּרָה לַשׂוֹכֵר. — *it was declared for the tenant.*

I.e., the added month goes to the tenant, who need not pay any additional rent for it; it is included in the yearly rental (*Rav; Rashi*).

[Now that the calendar is fixed, the length of the year is known in advance, and this ruling would be self-evident.]

Even today, however, should the landlord claim that he was unaware that the current year was a leap year, he must nevertheless allow the tenant to stay there for the same yearly rental. He has no more rights than the landlord of mishnaic times, who was surely unaware that the year would be a leap year, since the Sanhedrin had not yet convened to proclaim it a leap year (responsum of *Rif*, quoted by *Shitah Mekubetzes*, and by *Ketzos HaChoshen* 312:4).

1. *Ketzos HaChoshen* (313:1) asserts that *Rambam* is really also of the opinion that a rented courtyard acquires property for the tenant rather than for the landlord, and that it is only in the case concerning manure that *Rambam* rules that it belongs to the landlord. That is because since he does not rent out the stable, he indicates that he reserves rights to whatever comes to him through the stable, viz., manure. Since he reserves those rights, he does not rent out the yard with the right of acquiring manure, but reserves that right in the courtyard for himself. The ashes in the stove, however, belong to the tenant since he rents the stove without any reservation by the landlord.

לַמַּשְׂכִּיר. מַעֲשֶׂה בְּצִפּוֹרִי בְּאֶחָד שֶׁשָּׂכַר מֶרְחָץ
מֵחֲבֵרוֹ ,,בִּשְׁנֵים עָשָׂר זָהָב לַשָּׁנָה, מִדִּינַר זָהָב
לַחֹדֶשׁ.'' וּבָא מַעֲשֶׂה לִפְנֵי רַבָּן שִׁמְעוֹן בֶּן־גַּמְלִיאֵל
וְלִפְנֵי רַבִּי יוֹסֵי, וְאָמְרוּ: יַחֲלְקוּ אֶת־חֹדֶשׁ הָעִבּוּר.

[ט] **הַמַּשְׂכִּיר** בַּיִת לַחֲבֵרוֹ וְנָפַל, חַיָּב
לְהַעֲמִיד לוֹ בַּיִת. הָיָה קָטָן, לֹא

יד אברהם

According to some authorities, the ruling of the mishnah applies only if the transaction took place at the beginning of the year, and the landlord stipulated that he was renting the house to the tenant for *this* year. In that case, he rented it to him for the duration of the year regardless of whether it is twelve months or thirteen. Should he state that he is renting it to him for 'a year,' a conventional year would be meant, and the tenant would be entitled to live in the house for twelve months only (*Tos. Yom Tov* from *Nimmukei Yosef*, quoting *Ritva*; *Maggid Mishneh, Hil. Sechirus* 7:2).

Rambam, however, does not appear to make this distinction, and the *Shulchan Aruch* does not record this view (*Shulchan Aruch* 312:15). *Sma*, however, accepts *Ritva's* ruling (*Tos. Yom Tov*).

הִשְׂכִּיר לוֹ לֶחֳדָשִׁים, — [If] he rented it to him by the month,

I.e., if they arranged for the tenant to live in it at the rate of a *sela* per month, for example (*Meiri*).

נִתְעַבְּרָה הַשָּׁנָה, נִתְעַבְּרָה לַמַּשְׂכִּיר. — [and] a leap year was declared, it was declared for the landlord.

[I.e., the added month is for the benefit of the landlord, and the tenant must pay him an extra month's rent for it.]

This ruling seems to be self-evident. Since the landlord rented the house to the tenant by the month, the latter is obviously required to pay for thirteen months. According to *Rambam* cited above (s.v. נתעברה לשוכר), the mishnah teaches us that only if the house is rented by the month does the tenant pay for the thirteenth month. Should it be rented by the year, even if the agreement was to rent it for 'a year,' the thirteenth month is included

in the yearly rental. According to *Ritva* and *Rashba* (ibid.), however, since the tenant in any case must pay for the thirteenth month if the landlord rented it to him for 'a year,' this sentence appears superfluous. *Nimmukei Yosef*, therefore, explains that it is indeed superfluous, but that the mishnah states the various laws involved in this matter for the sake of completeness.

Sma (312:24) suggests two other solutions: (1) That this law is stated to highlight the case discussed at the end of the mishnah (see below). (2) Since the thirteenth month added in the leap year is to even the lunar year with the solar year, it could be argued that the extra month should be counted in a twelve-month rental (*Tos. Yom Tov*).

מַעֲשֶׂה בְּצִפּוֹרִי — It happened in Tzippori [Sepphoris]

The *Gemara* notes that the story which follows seems, if anything, to negate the ruling just given. This contravenes the mishnah's customary practice to cite case histories to support previously given rulings. Consequently, the *Gemara* explains that another clause must be inserted here: *If he* [the landlord] *said to him, '… for twelve golden dinars per year, at the rate of one golden dinar per month,'* they divide. It happened … (*Rav* from *Gem.* 102b).

בְּאֶחָד שֶׁשָּׂכַר מֶרְחָץ מֵחֲבֵרוֹ ,,בִּשְׁנֵים עָשָׂר זָהָב לַשָּׁנָה, מִדִּינַר זָהָב לַחֹדֶשׁ.'' — that one rented a bathhouse from another for 'twelve gold [dinars] for a year, at [the rate of] one gold dinar per month.'

[I.e., the lease stipulated both the yearly and monthly rates. The year was then declared a leap year, so that a month was added to the year.]

landlord. It happened in Tzippori that one rented a bathhouse from another for 'twelve gold [*dinars*] for a year, at [the rate of] one gold *dinar* per month.' The incident was brought before Rabban Shimon ben Gamliel and before R' Yose, and they said: Let them divide the additional month.

9. [I]f] one rented a house to another, and it collapsed, he is required to provide him with a

YAD AVRAHAM

וּבָא מַעֲשֶׂה לִפְנֵי רַבָּן שִׁמְעוֹן בֶּן־גַּמְלִיאֵל וְלִפְנֵי רַבִּי יוֹסֵי, וְאָמְרוּ: יַחֲלְקוּ אֶת־חֹדֶשׁ הָעִבּוּר. — *The incident was brought before Rabban Shimon ben Gamliel and before R' Yose, and they said: Let them divide the additional month.*

[The terms of the lease are contradictory, since a yearly rate includes the extra month if one is added, whereas the monthly rate requires additional payment for the leap month should one be added.] Since we do not know whether to regard the first expression as primary or the second, they divide the amount in question.

Should the two expressions not contradict one another, R' Yose (and Rabban Shimon ben Gamliel) rules that both expressions are regarded (see, e.g., *Temurah* 5:4). Should the second expression explain the first expression, we follow the second one (even where it negates the effect of the first; see, e.g., *Nazir* 9a and *Menachos* 103a). In this case, however, since the two expressions contradict each other, we cannot regard both (*Tos.* 102b).

If the second expression does not follow the first immediately, we assume that the second represents a retraction of the first. In this case, however, since

one expression immediately follows the other, they are contradictory, and we cannot follow both. Rabban Shimon ben Gamliel and R' Yose are in doubt whether he still wishes to follow his first expression or whether he wishes to retract it in favor of the second expression, and they therefore rule that the money should be divided (*Tos. Yom Tov* and *Tif. Yis.*).

The halachah, however, is not in accordance with Rabban Shimon ben Gamliel and R' Yose, but with the view cited in the *Gemara* (102b) that we always follow the lesser of the two expressions. Therefore, since land is always considered to be in its owner's possession, the tenant may not use it without proof that he has the right to it. Consequently, he may not use the house during the thirteenth month without paying rent (*Rav; Rambam Comm.*).

Even if the case should not come before the court until after the thirteenth month ended with the tenant occupying the house, the renter's possession of the house during the thirteenth month gives him no power. Since from the very beginning it was doubtful whether the tenant had the right to live there rent free, he was not allowed to use it without first establishing his right (*Rashi* 102b).

9.

הַמַּשְׂכִּיר בַּיִת לַחֲבֵרוֹ וְנָפַל, — *[If] one rented a house to another, and it collapsed,*

[The house collapsed during the time it was rented by the tenant.] The same applies if it burned down (*Tif. Yis.* from *Choshen Mishpat* 312:17).

חַיָּב לְהַעֲמִיד לוֹ בַּיִת. — *he is required to provide him with a house.*

The landlord is required to provide the tenant with another house for the duration of his lease (*Tos. Yom Tov* from *Rashi*). When the tenant takes

יַעֲשֶׂנּוּ גָדוֹל; גָדוֹל, לֹא יַעֲשֶׂנּוּ קָטָן; אֶחָד, לֹא
יַעֲשֶׂנּוּ שְׁנַיִם; שְׁנַיִם, לֹא יַעֲשֶׂנּוּ אֶחָד; לֹא יִפְחֹת
מֵהַחַלּוֹנוֹת, וְלֹא יוֹסִיף עֲלֵיהֶן — אֶלָּא מִדַּעַת
שְׁנֵיהֶם.

יד אברהם

possession, the landlord's property becomes pledged to the obligation to provide the tenant with a house (*Tos. Yom Tov* from *Tur* 312).

This ruling applies only if the lease called for renting a house without specifying this house. Should the lease specify a particular house, however, and it collapses, the landlord has no responsibility to provide the tenant with another house (*Rav* from *Gem.* 103a). The collapse is assigned to the tenant's misfortune (*Rashi*), and the landlord is freed from all further obligations while the tenant must pay the rent for the period he occupied the house (*Choshen Mishpat* 312:17).

Above in mishnah 6:3, it was explained that if one rented a specific donkey and it died during the term of the lease, if the carcass is worth enough to purchase another donkey, the owner must sell the carcass, buy another donkey and give it to the renter to complete his rental. Even if the carcass is only worth enough to hire another donkey, he must sell the carcass, hire another donkey and provide it to the renter. In the case of our mishnah, however, if the lease called for a specific house and it collapsed, we do not require the landlord to sell the stones and purchase another house or rebuild the house to complete the terms of the rental.

A number of different suggestions have been put forth to account for the difference. (1) It was customary to sell a donkey's carcass. Therefore, when the owner hires out the donkey, it is understood that should the animal die, he must sell the carcass to make good his commitment. In the case of the house, however, it is not customary to sell the stones of a house that has collapsed and thus no such requirement was implied by the rental agreement. (2) A house cannot be

rebuilt on the money realized from the sale of its stones. Thus, even if the stones were sold, the landlord would have to supplement his own money to rebuild the house, and he is not required to do so (*Tos. Yom Tov* from *Maggid Mishneh, Hil. Sechirus* 5:6; *Nimmukei Yosef; Tos.* 79a). (3) A dead donkey is still a donkey, and its carcass is therefore still pledged to the renter. Thus, it must be sold to provide him with a substitute. A house that has fallen, however, is no longer considered a house, merely a pile of rubble. Therefore, its stones are not pledged to the tenant (*Tos. R' Akiva* from *Shitah Mekubetzes*, quoting *Ran*).

Accordingly, if the house is still standing, but it has deteriorated to the extent that its occupancy is dangerous, since it is customary to repair it, and it is still considered a house, the landlord is required to restore it for the tenant (*Tos. Yom Tov; Tif. Yis.* from *Choshen Mishpat* 312:17).[1]

הָיָה קָטָן, לֹא יַעֲשֶׂנּוּ גָדוֹל; — [*If*] *it was small, he may not make it large;*

This refers to a case in which the landlord had pointed out a small house to the renter and said that he would rent him 'a house like this one.' If the house provided collapsed, so that the landlord is now required to provide the tenant with another house (since the lease was not for any specific house but only for a small house), he may not force the tenant to accept a large one. The tenant may object that he does not want such a large house (*Rashi*).

Should the lease have specified the precise dimensions of the house it would be self-evident that he cannot give him a house that is larger or smaller than the one originally rented to him. The mishnah tells us that even if he

---

1. This seems to contradict the ruling of *Rama* (*Choshen Mishpat* 314:1) cited above in mishnah 7 (s.v. המשכיר בית לחבירו), that if the door or bolt breaks during the term of the lease, the landlord is not required to replace it. See *Ketzos HaChoshen* 314:1.

house. [If] it was small, he may not make it large; [if it was] large, he may not make it small; [if it was] one, he may not make it two; [if it was] two, he may not make it one; [and] he may not decrease the [number of] windows, nor may he add to them — except by common agreement.

YAD AVRAHAM

said, 'I am renting you a house like this one,' he cannot later claim that he was not referring to its size but to some other feature, such as its location near the river or near the market, for example. Rather, he must give him a house with the same dimensions as the one he showed him (Tos. Yom Tov from Gem. 103a).

Whether the new house must also have the same conveniences as the original one is a point of dispute between the authorities. Rashi's view is that these conveniences (such as location) are also required, that the original intention is understood to have been for both the dimensions and the location. Ritva and Rambam, however, rule that the house need not be in the same location with the same conveniences, but must have only the same dimensions. Neither must the new house be as beautiful as the original one (Nimmukei Yosef; Choshen Mishpat 12:17).

גָּדוֹל, לֹא יַעֲשֶׂנּוּ קָטָן; — [if it was] large, he may not make it small;

If the original house was large, he may not force him to take a small one in its stead, since some are particular about a large house (Tos. Yom Tov).

Should the original lease have called merely for a house, he may give him any size house, either large or small, as long as it can be called a house (Rav; Ram-

bam Comm. from Gem. 103a).

אֶחָד, לֹא יַעֲשֶׂנּוּ שְׁנַיִם; — [if it was] one, he may not make it two;

[I.e., if the original house was a single unit, he may not replace it with one consisting of two units.] Aruch Ha-Shulchan (312:35) states: If it was one room, he shall not make it two.

שְׁנַיִם, לֹא יַעֲשֶׂנּוּ אֶחָד; — [if it was] two, he may not make it one;

[If he originally rented him two houses he may not replace it with one consisting of those dimensions built into one house.] Here, too, Aruch HaShul-chan explains it to mean that if he originally had rented him two rooms, he may not substitute one large room for them.

לֹא יִפְחֹת מֵהַחַלּוֹנוֹת, — [and] he may not decrease the [number of] windows,

[I.e., he may not give him a house with fewer windows than the house that fell down.]

וְלֹא יוֹסִיף עֲלֵיהֶן — nor may he add to them —

[By the same token, he may not give him a house with more windows than the house that collapsed.]

אֶלָּא מִדַּעַת שְׁנֵיהֶם. — except by common agreement.

[All of the above may not be altered unless the tenant agrees to the changes proposed by the landlord.]

Chapter 9

The major portion of chapter nine deals with leased fields and the tenant farmers' rights and responsibilities regarding those fields.

There are basically two arrangements under which a field may be leased: (a) אֲרִיסוּת, arisus, sharecropping [also referred to as קַבְּלָנוּת, kablanus], a type of lease

[א] הַמְקַבֵּל שָׂדֶה מֵחֲבֵרוֹ — מְקוֹם שֶׁנָּהֲגוּ לִקְצֹר, יִקְצֹר; לַעֲקֹר, יַעֲקֹר; לַחֲרֹשׁ אַחֲרָיו, יַחֲרֹשׁ; הַכֹּל כְּמִנְהַג הַמְּדִינָה. כְּשֵׁם שֶׁחוֹלְקִין בַּתְּבוּאָה, כָּךְ חוֹלְקִין בַּתֶּבֶן וּבַקַּשׁ; כְּשֵׁם

יד אברהם

under which the sharecropper [אָרִיס, *aris*, or קַבְּלָן, *kablan*] must pay the land owner a fixed percentage of the crop, e.g., a half, a third, or a fourth[1]; or (b) a fixed rental. This latter arrangement can in turn be made in one of two ways — either for a fixed fee to be paid in produce, an arrangement called חֲכִירוּת, *chachirus*, in which the farmer is called a חוֹכֵר, *chocher*; or for a fixed fee to be paid in money, a type of lease known as שְׂכִירוּת, *sechirus*, in which the farmer is called a שׂוֹכֵר, *socher*[2] (*Rav; Tos. Yom Tov; Tif. Yis.*).

Some of the mishnayos that follow are applicable to both *arisus* and *chachirus*; others are relevant to one or the other. The commentary at the beginning of each mishnah will point out the leasing arrangement to which the mishnah refers.

1.

הַמְקַבֵּל שָׂדֶה מֵחֲבֵרוֹ — — *[If] one leases a field from another* —

The rule to be stated here applies whether he leases it as an *aris* (sharecropper), who pays the owner a percentage of the crop, or as a *chocher* (tenant farmer), who pays a fixed annual fee of produce (*Rav; Rashi* from *Gem.* 104a).

מְקוֹם שֶׁנָּהֲגוּ לִקְצֹר, יִקְצֹר; — *where it is customary to cut [the crops], he must cut;*

Grain may be reaped in either of two ways: it may be cut [e.g., with a sickle] or uprooted. Each method has its unique advantages. Cutting the grain is less strenuous than uprooting it and leaves the stubble in the ground to rot and fertilize the field. Uprooting cleans the field more completely and allows the stubble to be used as animal feed. The mishnah teaches that when the landowner and tenant farmer disagree on which method to use, local practice

determines which one to follow. Thus, in a locale where grain is customarily cut, the farmer cannot insist upon uprooting the grain; the landlord may prevent him from doing so by claiming that he wishes the stubble to remain in the ground to fertilize his soil. On the other hand, should the landlord demand that the *aris* uproot the grain, the latter may refuse on the grounds that uprooting is more difficult than cutting (*Tos. Yom Tov* from *Gem.* 103b).

לַעֲקֹר, יַעֲקֹר; — *to uproot, he must uproot;*

Conversely, in an area where the grain is usually uprooted, but the tenant would rather cut the grain, the landlord may object on the grounds that he wishes to clean his field. Should the landlord insist that the tenant cut the grain, the latter may object that he wishes to feed the stubble to his livestock (*Tos. Yom Tov* from *Gem.* 103b).

The rule that unspecified agreements are to

---

1. Although most commentaries use the words *arisus* and *kablanus* interchangeably, *Meiri* distinguishes between the two, explaining *kablanus* as a general term for sharecropping, while *arisus* usually specifies a fifty-fifty division of the crop.

2. There is no legal distinction between *chachirus* and *sechirus* except according to R' Yehudah (below, mishnah 6) whose opinion is not accepted as halachah (*Tos. Yom Tov* citing *Rambam, Hil. Sechirus* 5:5; *Tur Choshen Mishpat* 320).

1. **[I**f] one leases a field from another — where it is customary to cut [the crops], he must cut; to uproot, he must uproot; to plow afterwards, he must plow; all according to local practice. Just as they share the grain, so they share the stubble and the

YAD AVRAHAM

be interpreted following local custom is found many times throughout the Talmud, yet the *Gemara* usually does not try to defend its application. *Nimmukei Yosef* wonders why the *Gemara* here finds it necessary to discuss the tenant's and landowner's respective reasons for insisting that local practice be followed.

Tos. Yom Tov explains that the reason is because the rationale for insisting upon following local custom is not as obvious here as it is in other instances. Should there be no valid reason whatsoever underlying the local practice, however, such a practice would be adjudged a custom of Sodom and would not be binding on either of the parties involved.

לַחֲרֹשׁ אַחֲרָיו, יַחֲרֹשׁ; — *to plow afterwards, he must plow;*

In some places it is customary to plow the field after cutting the grain or uprooting it, in order to destroy any weeds in the field and prevent them from sprouting again *(Rav; Rashi).*

This portion of the mishnah seems to be obvious and therefore should not have been included. The *Gemara* explains that the mishnah refers even to a place where it is not customary to weed the fields, yet the tenant voluntarily weeded his field. He cannot subsequently claim that he weeded it in lieu of plowing it over after the harvest and that he should therefore be exempt from that plowing. This claim is only valid if it was stipulated at the inception of the lease *(Tos. Yom Tov from Gem. 103b).*

הַכּל כְּמִנְהַג הַמְּדִינָה. — *all according to local practice.*

The *Gemara* teaches that this seemingly redundant phrase alludes to a place where it is customary to include any fruit trees growing in the field in the lease although they yield fruit without any effort on the part of the *aris*. Should

the prevailing custom be for the landlord to take one-third of the crop, and he agreed instead to take only one-fourth of the crop, he cannot claim that he accepted a lower rental because he excluded the produce of the trees from the sharecropping agreement. Had he meant such an arrangement, he should have stipulated so from the onset *(Tos. Yom Tov from Gem. 103b).*

By the same token, in places where it is customary to exclude the trees from the lease (since they yield fruit without any effort on the part of the *aris*), should the prevailing custom be for the landlord to take one-quarter of the crop, and the *aris* agreed to give him one-third of the crop, he cannot claim that he consented to a higher rental in order to share in the fruit of the trees. In this case, too, in order to effect such an arrangement, he should have stipulated so from the onset *(Gem. 103b).*

כְּשֵׁם שֶׁחוֹלְקִין בַּתְּבוּאָה, כָּךְ חוֹלְקִין בַּתֶּבֶן וּבַקַּשׁ; — *Just as they share the grain, so they share the stubble and the straw;*

[The accepted percentage of the crop to be paid the landowner also applies to the stubble and straw.]

This section of the mishnah applies only to *arisus*. In the case of a flat-fee lease *(chachirus* or cash-lease *sechirus;* see prefatory notes to this chapter), however, sharing is obviously inapplicable *(Tos. Yom Tov from Rashi).*

The translations of תֶּבֶן as *stubble* and קַשׁ as *straw* follows *Rashi* (to *Shabbos* 20:3 and *Exodus* 5:7,12), who defines קַשׁ as the straw that is cut from the ground together with the grain, while תֶּבֶן, *stubble,* is the straw left in the ground after the grain has been cut. *Tosafos* (ibid.) explain these terms in the reverse manner *(Tos. Yom Tov).*

שֶׁחוֹלְקִין בַּיַּיִן, כָּךְ חוֹלְקִין בַּזְּמוֹרוֹת וּבַקָּנִים;
וּשְׁנֵיהֶם מְסַפְּקִין אֶת־הַקָּנִים.

[ב] הַמְקַבֵּל שָׂדֶה מֵחֲבֵרוֹ, וְהִיא בֵּית הַשְּׁלָחִין
אוֹ בֵּית הָאִילָן — יָבֵשׁ הַמַּעְיָן
וְנִקְצַץ הָאִילָן, אֵינוֹ מְנַכֶּה לוֹ מִן־חֲכוֹרוֹ. אִם אָמַר
לוֹ: "חֲכֹר לִי שְׂדֵה בֵית הַשְּׁלָחִין זֶה," אוֹ "שָׂדֶה
בֵית הָאִילָן זֶה," יָבֵשׁ הַמַּעְיָן וְנִקְצַץ הָאִילָן, מְנַכֶּה
לוֹ מִן־חֲכוֹרוֹ.

יד אברהם

כְּשֵׁם שֶׁחוֹלְקִין בַּיַּיִן, כָּךְ חוֹלְקִין בַּזְּמוֹרוֹת וּבַקָּנִים;
— *just as they share the wine, so they share the branches and the canes;*

[Where the lease involved a vineyard, the same percentage used to divide the wine produced by this vineyard is used to divide the branches cut off.] By the same token, once they are no longer needed, they share the canes used for props to support the vines (*Rashi; Rav*).

These were used to prevent the vines from sagging on the ground and becoming soiled (*Meiri*).

וּשְׁנֵיהֶם מְסַפְּקִין אֶת־הַקָּנִים. — *and both of them provide the canes.*

The *aris* is solely obligated to provide the labor necessary to work and guard the field. The responsibility to supply the canes, however, falls on both the tenant and the landowner equally.

This last statement of the mishnah is by way of an explanation of the previous one. The mishnah tells us that they share the canes because they both shared the expense of providing them (*Rav* from *Gem.* 104a). Should one or the other have provided the canes, however, he takes them all back (*Rambam, Hil. Sechirus* 8:10, see *Maggid Mishneh; Choshen Mishpat* 327:2).

2.

הַמְקַבֵּל שָׂדֶה מֵחֲבֵרוֹ, — *[If] one leases a field from another,*

This refers to either an *aris* or a *chocher* (*Tif. Yis.* from *Gem.* 104a).

וְהִיא בֵּית הַשְּׁלָחִין — *and it is an irrigated field*

The field consisted of land that could not subsist on rainfall alone (*Rav*), but required irrigation. The area was served by a small river (see below), but this particular field also contained a spring from which the *aris* could easily water it (*Tif. Yis.*).

בֵּית הַשְּׁלָחִין is literally a *tired* or *thirsty* field. The *Targum* of עָיֵף, *tired,* (Deut. 25:18) is שְׁלָהֵי (=שלהי=שלחין) (*Tos. Yom*

Tov from *Moed Katan* 2a with *Rashi*).

אוֹ בֵּית הָאִילָן — *or a field containing a tree —*

[I.e., in addition to the area to be seeded, the field also contained fruit trees.] Such a field is very desirable for an *aris* since he receives a share of the fruit without working for it (*Rav; Rashi*). However, neither in the case of the tree nor of the irrigation spring did the renter specify that he wanted a field with a tree or spring (*Sma* 321:1).

יָבֵשׁ הַמַּעְיָן — *[if] the spring dried up*

I.e., the spring within the field from which it is watered dried up (*Rav*). This

straw; just as they share the wine, so they share the branches and the canes; and both of them provide the canes.

2. **[**I**f]** one leases a field from another, and it is an irrigated field or a field containing a tree — [if] the spring dried up or the tree was felled, he may not deduct from his rent. If he said to him: 'Lease me this irrigated field,' or 'this field containing a tree,' [then if] the spring dried up or the tree was cut down, he may deduct from his rent.

YAD AVRAHAM

spring was a branch of a river that watered the entire region *(Tos. Yom Tov* from *Gem.* 103b). Though water may be drawn from this river, it requires a great deal more effort.

Should the large river that watered the entire region dry up, however, this is adjudged a widespread plague, and the rule of mishnah 6 would apply *(Tos. Yom Tov* from *Gem.* 103b).

וְנִקְצַץ הָאִילָן, — *or the tree was felled,*

[As a result of the loss of the tree or spring, the tenant demands a reduction of his rental, claiming that he agreed to a higher rent only because of the presence of the spring or tree.]

אֵינוֹ מְנַכֶּה לוֹ מִן־חֲכוֹרוֹ. — *he may not deduct from his rent.*

In either case, he may not deduct from the rental fee since he did not specify at the time of the rental that he was accepting this rental because the field contained a tree or spring *(Rav, Rashi).* Though the irrigated field now lacks a water source, it is still arable since the tenant can irrigate the field with water drawn from the river *(Gem.* 104a).

This ruling applies to *arisus* as well — the sharecropper may not deduct from the percentage of the crop due the landowner according to their agreement *(Tos. Yom Tov* from *Gem.* 104a).

However, according to some authorities, if this resulted from a widespread calamity he may deduct from his rental, but only in the case of *chachirus.* In the case of *arisus,* though, he may not deduct from the percentage of the crops due the landlord even in this case *(Tos. Yom Tov).*

אִם אָמַר לוֹ: — *If he said to him:*

If the tenant stipulated to the landowner when he first leased the field *(Rav, Rashi).*

Others explain this to mean that the landowner said this to the tenant when he offered him the field for rent — 'Lease from me this irrigated field ...' *(Rif; Rambam, Sechirus* 8:4). Actually, both these interpretations are offered by the *Gemara* (104a); see below.

"חַכֹר לִי שְׂדֵה בֵית הַשְּׁלָחִין זֶה," אוֹ "שְׂדֵה בֵית הָאִילָן זֶה," — *'Lease me this irrigated field,' or 'this field containing a tree,'*

In this case, the tenant indicates that he desires this particular field because it is irrigated or because it is stocked with trees, and it is for this reason that he is paying this rental *(Rav).*

יָבֵשׁ הַמַּעְיָן וְנִקְצַץ הָאִילָן, מְנַכֶּה לוֹ מִן־חֲכוֹרוֹ. — *[then if] the spring dried up or the tree was cut down, he may deduct from his rent.*

[Since the tenant made clear that he was renting the field because of the spring or tree, their loss entitles him to a reduction of his rent.]

The commentary to this point has followed *Rav* and *Rashi,* who seem to

[ג] הַמְקַבֵּל שָׂדֶה מֵחֲבֵרוֹ, וְהוֹבִירָהּ — שָׁמִין
אוֹתָהּ כַּמָּה רְאוּיָה לַעֲשׂוֹת, וְנוֹתֵן
לוֹ. שֶׁכָּךְ כּוֹתֵב לוֹ: ,,אִם אוֹבִיר וְלֹא אַעֲבִיד,
אֲשַׁלֵּם בְּמֵיטָבָא.''

[ד] הַמְקַבֵּל שָׂדֶה מֵחֲבֵרוֹ וְלֹא רָצָה לְנַכֵּשׁ,
וְאָמַר לוֹ: ,,מָה אִכְפַּת לָךְ, הוֹאִיל

יד אברהם

have followed the explanation of the
Amora Shmuel (*Gem.* 104a). The
Gemara there, however, cites another
explanation of the mishnah, that of
Ravina, who explains even the second
case of the mishnah to refer to the lease
proposal offered by the landowner (not
that asked for by the tenant). According
to this view, this latter case differs from
the earlier one in that the language of
the offer indicates that the spring or tree
are being offered as a component of this
rental. As the *Gemara* explains, the
pronoun *this* implies that they are
standing in the field. Therefore, it was
not necessary to specify 'this *irrigated
field*,' and the fact that he did so
indicates that he is guaranteeing it to be
irrigated throughout the term of the
lease just as it is at the present time.

Accordingly, he need not specify 'this
irrigated field.' *Rif* and *Rambam* (*Hil.
Sechirus* 8:4), however, rule that he must

say, *this*, in order to demonstrate that it
should be as it is at the present time (*Tos.
Yom Tov*).

The commentators assume this
second explanation to be the *Gemara's*
conclusion.[1] Thus, in the view of
Tosafos, whether the landowner makes
this offer to the tenant or the tenant
makes the offer to the landowner, rent is
only deducted for the loss of the spring
or tree if the rental agreement was made
while standing in the field and
stipulated that '*this irrigated field*' was
being rented. According to many
authorities, however, if the tenant
makes this statement to the landowner,
he need mention only 'irrigated field' to
make clear his insistence on the
inclusion of a spring. He need not say,
'this,' nor need he be standing in the
field (*Rama* 321:2, quoting *Ramah*,
Maggid Mishneh to *Hil. Sechirus* 8:9,
Nimmukei Yosef).

3.

הַמְקַבֵּל שָׂדֶה מֵחֲבֵרוֹ, — [If] one leased a
field from another,

As will be obvious from the case
described, the rule set forth in this
mishnah applies only to *arisus*,
sharecropping, but not to *chachirus*
(*Rav; Rashi*).

וְהוֹבִירָהּ — and left it fallow —

He failed to plow it or sow it. The
ruling below is applicable even if he
neglected only part of the field (*Tif. Yis.*
from *Gem.* 104b).

שָׁמִין אוֹתָהּ כַּמָּה רְאוּיָה לַעֲשׂוֹת, — we assess
how much it was fit to yield,

[The *beis din* assesses how much the
field was fit to yield had it been

1. [*Rav's* and *Rashi's* understanding may have been that Ravina does not dispute Shmuel but
merely contends that the mishnah can also be explained on the basis of the landowner making
this statement rather than the tenant. Since there is no dispute, and since the simplest meaning
of the words follows Shmuel's interpretation, *Rav* and *Rashi* chose this alternative to offer as
the explanation of the mishnah.]

3. **[I**f] one leased a field from another and left it fallow — we assess how much it was fit to yield, and he [must] give [it] to him. For so he writes to him: 'If I leave it fallow or do not till it, I will pay of the best.'

4. **[I**f] one leased a field from another and he did not wish to weed [it], and he says to him:

YAD AVRAHAM

cultivated properly.]

וְנוֹתֵן לוֹ. — *and he [must] give [it] to him.*
Based on this estimate, the tenant pays the landowner his share *(Rambam Comm.; Meiri).*
This obviously applies only to *arisus* (sharecropping). In the case of *chachirus* (fixed rental), however, there is no reason to assess the field, since the tenant must pay his fixed rent regardless of the yield *(Tos. Yom Tov from Rashi).*

שֶׁכָּךְ כּוֹתֵב לוֹ: — *For so he writes to him:*
The *aris* customarily includes the following clause in the sharecropping agreement which he signs. Therefore, even if he does not write it, it is understood to be included and is binding. If he had, in fact, written it, it would be self evident that he must comply with the stipulation and the mishnah would not have to state this *(Tos. Yom Tov from Tos. 74a; Rosh).*

„אִם אוֹבִיר וְלֹא אֲעֲבִיד, — *'If I leave it fallow or do not till it,*
I.e., if I do not till it as much as necessary *(Rav; Rashi).*

אֲשַׁלֵם בְּמֵיטָבָא.". — *I will pay of the best.'*
I will pay you your share of what the field should have produced had it been worked properly *(Rav; Rashi).*
However, should he write, 'I will pay one thousand *zuz*,' the agreement would not be binding. Since he agrees to pay more than the potential damage he may cause, his statement is a mere exaggeration and it is assumed that he meant merely to gain credibility for his promise to till the field. This is known as *asmachta* and is not binding *(Gem. 104b); see above, 5:3, s.v.* אסמכתא*, An Insincere Transaction.*
Even in this case, however, he is obligated to pay the share due the landowner, since he would have been obligated to pay that amount even without his written agreement *(Tos. R' Akiva from Rashi; Sma 328:3).*

4.

הַמְקַבֵּל שָׂדֶה מֵחֲבֵרוֹ — *[If] one leased a field from another*
[This mishnah applies only to a *chachir* paying a fixed rental, but not to an *aris*, sharecropper, as will be evident further.]

וְלֹא רָצָה לְנַבֵּשׁ, — *and he did not wish to weed [it],*
This refers to a place where there is no definite custom regarding weeding the fields. Should there be such a custom, however, the matter would be

resolved on the basis of the custom. Thus, if the custom of that place was not to weed, the tenant would not be obligated to do so *(Maggid Mishneh, Hil. Sechirus 8:8; Tos. Yom Tov).* On the other hand, should there be a definite custom for farmers to weed, it would be self evident that the tenant is obligated to do so *(Lechem Mishneh ad loc.).*

וְאָמַר לוֹ: — *and he says to him:*
[The tenant says to the landowner.]

וַאֲנִי נוֹתֵן לְךָ חֲכוֹרָהּ?״ אֵין שׁוֹמְעִין לוֹ, מִפְּנֵי
שֶׁיָּכוֹל לוֹמַר לוֹ: ,,לְמָחָר אַתָּה יוֹצֵא מִמֶּנָּה,
וּמַעֲלָה לְפָנַי עֲשָׂבִים.״

[ה] הַמְקַבֵּל שָׂדֶה מֵחֲבֵרוֹ וְלֹא עָשְׂתָה — אִם
יֵשׁ בָּהּ כְּדֵי לְהַעֲמִיד כְּרִי, חַיָּב
לְטַפֵּל בָּהּ. אָמַר רַבִּי יְהוּדָה: מַה־קִּצְבָה בַּכְּרִי?
אֶלָּא, אִם יֵשׁ בָּהּ כְּדֵי נְפִילָה.

[ו] הַמְקַבֵּל שָׂדֶה מֵחֲבֵרוֹ, וַאֲכָלָהּ חָגָב אוֹ
נִשְׁדָּפָה — אִם מַכַּת מְדִינָה הִיא,

יד אברהם

,,מָה אִכְפַּת לָךְ, הוֹאִיל וַאֲנִי נוֹתֵן לְךָ חֲכוֹרָה?״ —
*'What concern is it of yours, since I am
paying you its rental?'*
What concern is it of yours that I do
not weed, since it is only my share that
is diminished, not your rental.
Although it is true that the growth of
weeds in a field reduces the crop yield,
as long as I pay you the amount
contracted, you lose nothing by my
failure to weed (*Rav; Rashi*).
The literal meaning of this phrase is: 'Who
forces or binds this matter upon you?'
(*Aruch*). Rambam (*Comm.* and *Hil. Sechirus*
8:8) renders: 'What loss do you suffer?'
Obviously, this claim has no validity
except in the case of *chachirus*, where
the contract calls for a fixed rental. In
the case of *arisus* (sharecropping),
however, the landlord indeed suffers by
the field's reduced yield, since he

receives only a percentage of the crop
(*Tos. Yom Tov* from *Rashi*).

אֵין שׁוֹמְעִין לוֹ, מִפְּנֵי שֶׁיָּכוֹל לוֹמַר לוֹ: ,,לְמָחָר
אַתָּה יוֹצֵא מִמֶּנָּה, וּמַעֲלָה לְפָנַי עֲשָׂבִים.״ — *We
do not listen to him, since he can say to
him: 'Tomorrow you will withdraw
from it, and it will grow weeds for me.'*
[Nevertheless, we do not heed the
tenant's argument because the landlord
may legitimately claim that since the
tenant may decide not to renew the lease
when it expires, he (the owner) will be
left with a field full of weeds.
Even if he offers to plow the field
after the harvest and thereby destroy
the weeds, the owner may object on the
grounds that in the meantime weed
seeds will fall into the earth and take
root again the following year (*Tos. Yom
Tov* from *Gem.* 105a, *Rashi* ad loc.).

5.

הַמְקַבֵּל שָׂדֶה מֵחֲבֵרוֹ — *[If] one leased a
field from another*
This mishnah speaks of an *aris* (*Rav;
Rashi*). In similar circumstances a
chocher would have to pay the entire
fixed rental (*Tif. Yis.*).

וְלֹא עָשְׂתָה — *and it did not produce* —
Something grew, but the yield is not

enough to make it worth the tenant
farmer's while, and he wishes,
therefore, to terminate his lease (*Rav;
Rashi*).

אִם יֵשׁ בָּהּ כְּדֵי לְהַעֲמִיד כְּרִי, — *if there is
enough in it to put up a heap,*
The field must yield enough grain to
put up a heap into which the

'What concern is it of yours, since I am paying you its rental?' We do not listen to him, since he can say to him: 'Tomorrow you will withdraw from it, and it will grow weeds for me.'

5. **[**I**f]** one leased a field from another and it did not produce — if there is enough in it to put up a heap, he is obligated to cultivate it. Said R' Yehudah: What kind of measure is a heap? Rather, if there is as much as was sown.

6. **[**I**f]** one leased a field from another, and locusts devoured it or it was swept by storm — if it is a

YAD AVRAHAM

winnowing fan can be thrust and remain upright [in the manner in which a shovel is thrust into a pile of dirt and left standing]. This amounts to two *seah* of grain after deducting for expenses (*Rav; Tif. Yis.* from *Gem.* 105a).

[After grain is threshed to separate the kernels from the chaff, the kernels are piled into heaps or mounds.]

חַיָּב לְטַפֵּל בָּהּ. — *he is obligated to cultivate it.*

The *aris* is obligated to live up to the terms of the sharecropping agreement. This obligation is based on the wording of the standard contract drawn up between the landlord and the *aris*, in which the latter writes, 'I will stand and plow and sow and reap and bind and thresh and winnow and put up a heap' (*Gem.* 105a). The *aris* is obligated to do these labors regardless of whether the contract is committed to writing or not (*Tos. Yom Tov*).

This applies only to *arisus*, not to *chachirus*, since in the latter case, the landowner receives a fixed rental from the tenant and thus can have no objection if the *chocher* neglects the field (*Tos. Yom Tov* from *Rashi*).

אָמַר רַבִּי יְהוּדָה: מַה־קִצְבָה בִכְרִי? — *Said R' Yehudah: What kind of measure is a heap?*

It is not proper for both a large field and a small field to have the same measure, since the labor involved in cultivating a large field is much more than that involved in cultivating a small one (*Rav; Rashi*).

אֶלָּא, אִם יֵשׁ בָּהּ כְּדֵי נְפִילָה. — *Rather, if there is as much as was sown.*

I.e., if it produces at least as much seed as was sown, the *aris* is obligated to cultivate it. Otherwise, he is not. The halachah is decided in favor of the first *Tanna* (*Rav; Choshen Mishpat* 328:1).

6.

הַמְקַבֵּל שָׂדֶה מֵחֲבֵרוֹ, — *[If] one leased a field from his another,*

This mishnah refers to *chachirus*, a fixed-rental lease, as is evident further in the mishnah (*Rav; Rashi*).

וַאֲכָלָהּ חָגָב אוֹ נִשְׁדָּפָה — *and locusts devoured it or it was swept by storm —*

The field was swept by a storm whose high winds caused the kernels to fall out of the ears of the grain (*Tif. Yis.*).

אִם מַכַּת מְדִינָה הִיא, — *if it is a widespread calamity,*

I.e., if the locust plague or the storm devastated a wide area — i.e., most of the

מְנַכֶּה לּוֹ מִן־חֲכוֹרוֹ; אִם אֵינָהּ מַכַּת מְדִינָה, אֵין
מְנַכֶּה לוֹ מִן חֲכוֹרוֹ. רַבִּי יְהוּדָה אוֹמֵר: אִם קִבְּלָהּ
הֵימֶנּוּ בְּמָעוֹת, בֵּין כָּךְ וּבֵין כָּךְ, אֵינוֹ מְנַכֶּה לוֹ
מֵחֲכוֹרוֹ.

[ז] הַמְקַבֵּל שָׂדֶה מֵחֲבֵרוֹ בַּעֲשֶׂרֶת כּוֹר חִטִּים
לַשָּׁנָה, לָקְתָה, נוֹתֵן לוֹ מִתּוֹכָהּ.
הָיוּ חִטֶּיהָ יָפוֹת, לֹא יֹאמַר לוֹ: ,,הֲרֵינִי לוֹקֵחַ מִן־
הַשּׁוּק,׳׳ אֶלָּא נוֹתֵן לוֹ מִתּוֹכָהּ.

[ח] הַמְקַבֵּל שָׂדֶה מֵחֲבֵרוֹ לְזָרְעָהּ שְׂעוֹרִים,
לֹא יִזְרָעֶנָּה חִטִּים; חִטִּים —

יד אברהם

fields of that province or valley were hit
(Rav).

Tos. Yom Tov explains that these two
examples represent two variant readings in
the Gemara (105b). Rashi's reading is most of
the valley, while Rambam, as explained by
Maggid Mishneh (Hil. Sechirus 8:5), had the
reading most of the valleys. Rambam,
therefore, states: most of the fields of that
city, defining מְדִינָה as city. Rav states both
readings to indicate that we judge leniently
with the chocher, allowing him to deduct
from his rental in either case.

מְנַכֶּה לוֹ מִן־חֲכוֹרוֹ; — he may deduct from
his rent;

He may deduct according to the loss
he suffered (Rambam, Hil. Sechirus
8:5). The adjustment must be based on a
calculation of the actual loss suffered in
this field, and not on the average loss of
the area as a whole (Tos. Yom Tov from
Sma 322:3).

אִם אֵינָהּ מַכַּת מְדִינָה, אֵין מְנַכֶּה לוֹ מִן חֲכוֹרוֹ. —
if it is not a widespread calamity, he
may not deduct from his rental.

If the devastation affected only a few
of the fields in the area the landowner
may claim that it is the tenant's ill
fortune which is to blame for the loss,
and he need not suffer because of it

(Rav; Rashi).

— רַבִּי יְהוּדָה אוֹמֵר: אִם קִבְּלָהּ הֵימֶנּוּ בְּמָעוֹת,
R' Yehudah says: If he leased it from
him for money,

[I.e., the rent was to be paid in
money, not produce.]

בֵּין כָּךְ וּבֵין כָּךְ, אֵינוֹ מְנַכֶּה לוֹ מֵחֲכוֹרוֹ. — in
either case, he may not deduct from his
rent.

Whether the devastation was a
widespread calamity or restricted just to
this field, no adjustment is made. Since
the Divine decree inflicting the loss was
not directed against the money of this
area's inhabitants, but against their
crops, and the rental agreement called
for payment in cash and not crops, the
tenant cannot shift the burden of loss
onto the landowner by deducting from
the rental he owes (Rav; Rashi).

The halachah follows the first view
(Rambam, Sechirus 8:5; Choshen
Mishpat 322:1).

Obviously, this ruling of this
mishnah applies only to chachirus, as
mentioned above. In the case of arisus,
however, in which the landowner is
paid with a percentage of the yield, they
share whatever crops actually grow
(Tos. Yom Tov from Rashi).

widespread calamity, he may deduct from his rent; if it is not a widespread calamity, he may not deduct from his rental. R' Yehudah says: If he leased it from him for money, in either case, he may not deduct from his rent.

7. **[**I**f]** one leased a field from another for ten *kors* of wheat per year, [and] it was struck, he may pay him out of it. [If] its wheat was superior, he may not say to him: 'I will buy from the market,' but he must give him out of it.

8. **[**I**f]** one leased a field from another to sow barley in it, he may not sow it [with] wheat; wheat —

YAD AVRAHAM

7.

הַמְקַבֵּל שָׂדֶה מֵחֲבֵרוֹ בַּעֲשֶׂרֶת כּוֹר חִטִּים לַשָׁנָה, — [If] one leased a field from another for ten kors of wheat per year,

[I.e., for a fixed rental of ten *kors* of wheat per annum, for example.]

לָקְתָה, — [and] it was struck,

The wheat was struck by a storm or some other calamity, which weakened the plants and reduced the quality of the crop (Rav; Rashi).

נוֹתֵן לוֹ מִתּוֹכָהּ. — he may pay him out of it.

He may pay the landowner from the wind-blasted wheat and the owner may not demand better wheat (Rav). [It is understood that the payment of grain stipulated in the contract is to come out of the field's yield.]

הָיוּ חִטֶּיהָ יָפוֹת, — [If] its wheat was superior,

[If the wheat the field yielded was superior to the average sold in the market.]

לֹא יֹאמַר לוֹ: "הֲרֵינִי לוֹקֵחַ מִן-הַשּׁוּק," אֶלָּא נוֹתֵן לוֹ מִתּוֹכָהּ. — he may not say to him: 'I will buy from the market,' but he must give him out of it.

[When paying his rent, the tenant may not substitute average wheat purchased in the market for the superior wheat yielded by this field.]

This mishnah deals with *chachirus*. In the case of *arisus*, it is self-evident that each one receives his share of the crop, regardless of their quality (Tos. Yom Tov from Rashi).

8.

הַמְקַבֵּל שָׂדֶה מֵחֲבֵרוֹ — [If] one leased a field from another

This mishnah refers to one who leased a field as a *chocher*, contracting to pay a certain amount of grain or money per year (Rav). [However, see below for a dissenting view.]

לְזָרְעָהּ שְׂעוֹרִים, — to sow barley in it,

[At the time he rented the field, the tenant indicated to the landowner that his intention was to sow it with barley.]

לֹא יְזָרְעֶנָּה חִטִּים; — he may not sow it [with] wheat;

The tenant may not subsequently change his mind and sow the field with wheat, because wheat exhausts the soil

יִזְרָעֶנָּה שְׂעוֹרִים. רַבָּן שִׁמְעוֹן בֶּן־גַּמְלִיאֵל אוֹסֵר.
תְּבוּאָה — לֹא יִזְרָעֶנָּה קִטְנִית; קִטְנִית — יִזְרָעֶנָּה
תְּבוּאָה. רַבָּן שִׁמְעוֹן בֶּן־גַּמְלִיאֵל אוֹסֵר.

[ט] **הַמְקַבֵּל** שָׂדֶה מֵחֲבֵרוֹ לְשָׁנִים מֻעָטוֹת,
לֹא יִזְרָעֶנָּה פִּשְׁתָּן, וְאֵין לוֹ

יד אברהם

more than barley (Rav; Rashi). [Thus, he is using the field to a greater degree than the rental agreement called for, which he may not do without the owner's permission. Since no benefit accrues to the owner as a result of this increased use, his agreement cannot be assumed.]

The rulings of this mishnah apply only to chachirus. In the case of arisus, however, when the owner takes a percentage of the yield, he may deviate from the agreement [even without the owner's agreement]. Since the deviation will bring the landowner a greater profit as well, his agreement can be assumed. This may be seen from the folk maxim, 'Let the land become exhausted, but let the owner not become exhausted' (Gem. 104b). As Nimmukei Yosef explains, a person would rather have the profit go into his pocket than have it remain in the land.

Ramban (quoted by Maggid Mishneh, Hil. Sechirus 8:9), however, differs, ruling that in the case of arisus the owner's agreement to a deviation from the initial agreement cannot be assumed. Since his share is a percentage of the crop, it is possible that he needs barley and not wheat. Thus, even though wheat may have greater market value, it is not what the landowner needs.

יִזְרָעֶנָּה שְׂעוֹרִים. — wheat — he may sow it [with] barley.

[If the tenant stipulated that he was going to grow wheat, he may change his mind and grow barley instead. Since barley exhausts the soil less than wheat, the owner loses nothing by this change

and in fact benefits by receiving the same rental at less cost to his field.]

רַבָּן שִׁמְעוֹן בֶּן־גַּמְלִיאֵל אוֹסֵר. — Rabban Shimon ben Gamliel prohibits [it].

Rabban Shimon ben Gamliel believes that the land becomes exhausted by alternating the crops from year to year (Rav). Therefore, even if the landowner agreed to sowing wheat, we cannot assume that he would also agree to the sowing of barley, since it may be that he had sown wheat the previous year, and by sowing barley, the tenant will further exhaust the soil (Tos. Yom Tov from Rashi).

Rashbam, however, claims that on the contrary, rotating the crops is beneficial for the soil. The intention is quite the opposite. The tenant may not deviate from wheat to barley because the owner may have sown barley the previous year and wishes to sow wheat this year to replace the nutrients extracted from the soil by last year's barley crop (Tos. 107a).

The halachah is that, based on local soil conditions, the tenant may not sow a crop that exhausts the field more than the one for which he contracted. He may, however, sow a crop that exhausts the soil to a lesser degree (Rav). This determination must be made in consultation with agricultural experts (Rambam Comm.).

תְּבוּאָה — לֹא יִזְרָעֶנָּה קִטְנִית; — Grain — he may not sow it [with] beans;

If he contracted to sow grain, he may not change to beans, because beans exhaust the soil more than grain (Tos. Yom Tov from Rashi).

קִטְנִית — יִזְרָעֶנָּה תְּבוּאָה. — beans — he may

he may sow it [with] barley. Rabban Shimon ben Gamliel prohibits [it]. Grain — he may not sow it [with] beans; beans — he may sow [it] with grain. Rabban Shimon ben Gamliel prohibits [it].

9. [If] one leased a field from another for a few years, he may not sow it [with] flax, and he has

YAD AVRAHAM

sow [it] with grain.

[If he contracted to sow beans he may change to grain, because grain exhausts the soil to a lesser degree than beans, and the owner would thus not object to the change.]

This ruling applies to *Eretz Yisrael*, which is a mountainous land, and exhausting the land has disastrous effects. In Babylonia, however, where the land is flat and well watered, this consideration does not apply and one may therefore change from grain to beans (*Gem.* 107a as explained by *Rashi*).

The mishnah printed in *Yerushalmi*, as well as that found in many editions of *Rif* and in the Naples edition of *Mishnayos*, reads the opposite of our edition. According to this reading, the mishnah states that if the contract called for planting beans he may *not* change to grain, but that if it stipulated sowing grain, he may change to beans. Accordingly, the *Gemara's* distinction between *Eretz Yisrael* and Babylonia is also reversed. *Rambam* (Hil. Sechirus 8:9) follows this latter reading and thus rules that in Babylonia, if he contracted to sow grain, he may not sow beans. See *Shulchan Aruch* 324.

Sma questions how the authorities could disagree on a fact that could easily be determined by consulting agronomists. *Tos. Yom Tov* conjectures that since this ruling applies to *Eretz Yisrael*, the nature of whose soil was unknown to the *Rishonim* of both Europe and North Africa, each followed the reading of the editions available to him. [*Imrei Daas*, however, points out from *Rambam Comm.* on *Bechoros* 4:4 that *Rambam* had indeed visited *Eretz Yisrael*.]

Derishah explains that *Rif* and *Rambam* do not differ with *Rashi* regarding *chachirus*. They, too, agree that grain exhausts the soil to a lesser degree than beans. Therefore, the tenant may deviate from beans to grain, but not from grain to beans. They interpret this segment of the mishnah as referring to *arisus*, in which case the *aris* may deviate to sow the more profitable crop although it exhausts the soil more than that contracted. Therefore, the *aris* may deviate from barley to wheat, the opposite of *chachirus*. For this same reason, he may deviate from grain to beans although the latter exhausts the soil to a greater degree. He may not, however, deviate from beans to grain since it is not as profitable.

רַבָּן שִׁמְעוֹן בֶּן־גַּמְלִיאֵל אוֹסֵר. — *Rabban Shimon ben Gamliel prohibits [it].*

As explained above (s.v. רבן שמעון בן גמליאל), Rabban Shimon ben Gamliel considers the possibility that the owner may either wish (*Rashbam*) or object (*Rashi*) to having the crops in his field rotated, to avoid straining the field.

According to *Derishah*, Rabban Shimon ben Gamliel's view is stated twice since the mishnah deals first with *chachirus* and then with *arisus*. According to *Rashi* and *Rosh*, it is not clear why Rabban Shimon ben Gamliel's view is repeated when it could have been stated at the end of the mishnah in reference to both instances.

9.

הַמְקַבֵּל שָׂדֶה מֵחֲבֵרוֹ — *[If] one leased a field from another*

The mishnah refers now to one who leased by *chachirus*, for a fixed rental (*Tos. Yom Tov* from *Rashi*).

לְשָׁנִים מֻעָטוֹת, — *for a few years,*

I.e., for fewer than seven years; see below (*Rav; Rashi*).

לֹא יִזְרָעֶנָּה פִשְׁתָּן, — *he may not sow it [with] flax,*

Flax depletes the soil excessively (*Rav*), and it takes up to seven years for

בְּקוֹרַת שִׁקְמָה. קִבְּלָהּ הֵימֶנּוּ לְשֶׁבַע שָׁנִים, שָׁנָה רִאשׁוֹנָה יִזְרָעֶנָּה פִּשְׁתָּן, וְיֵשׁ לוֹ בְּקוֹרַת שִׁקְמָה.

[יז] **הַמְקַבֵּל** שָׂדֶה מֵחֲבֵרוֹ לְשָׁבוּעַ אֶחָד בְּשֶׁבַע מֵאוֹת זוּז, הַשְּׁבִיעִית מִן־הַמִּנְיָן. קִבְּלָהּ הֵימֶנּוּ שֶׁבַע שָׁנִים בְּשֶׁבַע מֵאוֹת זוּז, אֵין הַשְּׁבִיעִית מִן־הַמִּנְיָן.

יד אברהם

it to fully recover *(Rashi)*. Furthermore, the roots remain in the ground for up to seven years [making it harder to plow the following year] *(Rav; Rambam Comm.).* Thus, unless the owner expressly agreed to allow the tenant to sow flax, he may not do so.

In contrast to the previous mishnah, this mishnah makes no reference to which crop they had originally agreed to sow in this field. Accordingly, *Aruch HaShulchan* (325:) suggests that, unlike the previous mishnah, this mishnah deals with a case in which nothing was stipulated. The tenant may, therefore, sow the field with anything but flax because it causes severe damage. [However, from *Ramban* quoted below by *Maggid Mishneh*, it seems that *Ramban* understood the lease of this mishnah to have originally been for grain.]

He suggests further that the previous mishnah, which in contrast to this mishnah makes no mention of the duration of the lease, deals only with a one-year lease. Should the tenant lease the field for two years, in the first year he may deviate, since it takes no longer than a year for the field to recover. He may not, however, sow the field with flax unless he leases it for at least seven years, since it takes that long for the soil to fully recover.

Rashi concludes that the mishnah deals only with *chachirus* (fixed rent). In the case of *arisus* (sharecropping), however, there is no restriction on what the *aris* may sow, because wherever the landlord shares in the more profitable crop, he is assumed to agree to a more intense use of the field, as stated above in mishnah 8.

However, as noted above, *Ramban* (quoted by *Maggid Mishneh, Hil. Sechirus* 8:3) explains that on the contrary, in the case of *arisus*, one may never sow any crop but that contracted for with the landowner. Since the owner's rental is a share of the crop, he may insist on receiving the crop he contracted for, in this case grain, not flax (see above mishnah 8, s.v. לא יזרענה). Nevertheless, he too concludes from the next part of the mishnah that the mishnah must be referring to *chachirus*.

Since the mishnah states further that if he leased it for seven years, he *may* sow flax, it must definitely refer to *Chachirus*, not *arisus (Tos. Yom tov).*

Rambam (ibid.) interprets the mishnah as referring to both instances *(Tos. Yom Tov).*

וְאֵין לוֹ בְּקוֹרַת שִׁקְמָה. — *and he has no right to the beams of the sycamore.*

This is a non-fruit bearing tree, whose branches are cut off for beams, after which they grow back. Since it takes seven years for them to grow back, one who leases a field for less than seven years without expressly leasing the right to cut the sycamore standing in it may not cut off the branches of the sycamore *(Rashi).*

קִבְּלָהּ הֵימֶנּוּ לְשֶׁבַע שָׁנִים, שָׁנָה רִאשׁוֹנָה יִזְרָעֶנָּה פִּשְׁתָּן, — *[If] he leased it from him for seven years, the first year he may sow it [with] flax,*

[If the tenant leased the field for seven years or more, then he is permitted to sow flax during the first year of the lease. Since the field will regain its vitality by the end of the seven-year period when the tenant leaves it, the owner loses nothing.]

no right to the beams of the sycamore. [If] he leased it from him for seven years, the first year he may sow it [with] flax, and he has rights to the beams of the sycamore.

10. [If] one leased a field from another for one septenary for seven hundred *zuz*, the *Shemittah* year is counted. [If] he leased it from him for seven years for seven hundred *zuz*, the *Shemittah* year is not counted.

YAD AVRAHAM

וְיֵשׁ לוֹ בְּקוֹרַת שִׁקְמָה. — *and he has rights to the beams of the sycamore.*

I.e., in places where the trees are leased along with the field, the tenant may cut off the branches during the first year of his lease since they will grow back by the time the lease terminates (*Meiri*). [I.e., since at the end of the lease the owner will receive back as much as he leased, the use of the tree is considered one of the benefits included in the lease.]

10.

הַמְקַבֵּל שָׂדֶה מֵחֲבֵרוֹ לְשָׁבוּעַ אֶחָד בְּשֶׁבַע מֵאוֹת זוּז, — *[If] one leased a field from another for one septenary for seven hundred zuz,*

[The field was leased for a fixed fee to be paid in cash. This is a form of *chachirus* known as *sechirus*, as explained in the preface to this chapter. This form of rental, as well as the particular sum mentioned, are chosen by the *Tanna* of the mishnah merely because they offer a simple illustration of the mishnah's ruling.] The same would apply, however, if he leased it as an *aris* or a *chocher* (*Rambam, Hil. Sechirus* 8:3, *Maggid Mishneh* ad loc.).

[A septenary is a unit of seven years. By taking a lease for the entire septenary, he has perforce included the *Shemittah* (Sabbatical) year, during which it is forbidden to work the field (if it is located in Eretz Yisrael) (*Lev.* 25:4).]

הַשְּׁבִיעִית מִן הַמִּנְיָן. — *the Shemittah year is counted.*

He need not leave the land in his possession for another year to compen-

sate for the *Shemittah* year, when the tenant could not work and did not profit from the field (*Meiri*). Furthermore, since the rental agreement fixed the seven hundred *zuz* fee for one septenary, rather than for seven years, the owner need not deduct a seventh of the rental for the *Shemittah* year (100 *zuz*) even though the tenant cannot till the field that year (*Tos. Yom Tov* from *Nimmukei Yosef*). [I.e., there is no implication that the fee was based on a calculation of 100 *zuz* per year. Rather, 700 *zuz* was the fee for the entire period, which is understood to include only six working years.]

קִבְּלָהּ הֵימֶנּוּ שֶׁבַע שָׁנִים בְּשֶׁבַע מֵאוֹת זוּז, אֵין הַשְּׁבִיעִית מִן הַמִּנְיָן. — *[If] he leased it from him for seven years for seven hundred zuz, the Shemittah year is not counted.*

If the rental agreement stipulated *seven years* (rather than one septenary) *for seven hundred zuz,* the implication is that the owner must leave it in the tenant's possession for another year in lieu of the *Shemittah* year when he could not work (*Meiri*).

בבא
מציעא
ט/יא

[יא] שָׂכִיר יוֹם גּוֹבֶה כָּל־הַלַּיְלָה. שְׂכִיר לַיְלָה
גּוֹבֶה כָּל־הַיּוֹם. שְׂכִיר שָׁעוֹת גּוֹבֶה
כָּל־הַלַּיְלָה וְכָל־הַיּוֹם. שְׂכִיר שַׁבָּת, שְׂכִיר חֹדֶשׁ,
שְׂכִיר שָׁנָה, שְׂכִיר שָׁבוּעַ — יָצָא בַיּוֹם, גּוֹבֶה כָּל־

יד אברהם

11.

The following two mishnayos deal with the law of paying a hired worker on time. The Torah declares one positive and two negative precepts in this regard: *Deut.* (24:15) states: בְּיוֹמוֹ תִתֵּן שְׂכָרוֹ, *During his day you shall give his wage.* This verse also adds to this command the injunction: וְלֹא־תָבוֹא עָלָיו הַשֶּׁמֶשׁ, *and the sun shall not set upon it* (ibid.). In *Leviticus* (19:13) the Torah also enjoins: לֹא־תָלִין פְּעֻלַּת שָׂכִיר אִתְּךָ עַד־בֹּקֶר, *the wage of a hired worker shall not stay over with you until morning.* The following mishnayos delineate the times different workers must be paid and to what instances these precepts apply.

שְׂכִיר יוֹם — *One who is hired for the day*
I.e., a worker who is hired for one day's work. The mishnah refers specifically to one who works for the entire day and completes his work at evening (*Rashi*).

גּוֹבֶה כָּל־הַלַּיְלָה. — *collects [his wages] all night.*
I.e., the entire night constitutes the payment time of this worker, and if the employer pays the worker within this time, he has not violated the Torah's command to pay on time. Also, within this time, the worker is believed under oath should he claim that he has not yet been paid his wages [as will be explained below, mishnah 12] (*Rashi*). This is derived from the verse (*Lev.* 19:13): לֹא־תָלִין פְּעֻלַּת שָׂכִיר אִתְּךָ עַד־בֹּקֶר, *The wage of a hired worker shall not stay over with you until morning.* Since wages are first due once the employment has terminated,[1] the verse forbidding the employer to keep the wage until morning (implying that it was due even before then) cannot be referring to the wage of a worker hired for the night since the obligation to pay him does not commence until morning.

Consequently, it must refer to a day worker whose wage became due at nightfall. The verse thus teaches that the employer is allowed an entire night's grace to pay his day worker (*Rav* from Gem. 110b).

Workers who do not work until sunset, however, but terminate their employment before the end of the day, must be paid before sunset (*Nimmukei Yosef; Tif. Yis.* from *Rama* 339:3).

שְׂכִיר לַיְלָה — *One who is hired for the night*
I.e., one who terminates his employment at dawn (*Rashi*).

גּוֹבֶה כָּל־הַיּוֹם. — *collects all day.*
His payment period is the entire following day, and the employer does not transgress the prohibition on withholding wages as long as he pays the worker on that day (*Rashi*).
The Torah states: וְלֹא־תָבוֹא עָלָיו הַשֶּׁמֶשׁ, *and the sun shall not set upon it* [the wage]. This refers to a worker who is hired for the night, to whom the employer becomes obligated in the morning when his employment terminates (*Rav* from Gem. 110b). [As

1. This is derived from the verse (*Lev.* 25:53): כִּשְׂכִיר שָׁנָה בְּשָׁנָה, *as a hired worker for a year in a year,* meaning that the wages for this year are paid at the beginning of the next year (*Gem.* 65a).

11. One who is hired for the day collects [his wages] all night. One who is hired for the night collects all day. One hired for [several] hours collects all night or all day. One hired for a week, a month, a year, [or] a septenary — [if] he departs by

YAD AVRAHAM

explained above, a wage is not due until the employment is terminated.]

Nor does the employer transgress the prohibition forbidding him from keeping wages overnight, since that prohibition applies only to the wages of day workers, as explained above. Similarly, a night worker is believed all the next day if he claims under oath that he has not yet been paid [see mishnah 12] (Rashi).

שָׂכִיר שָׁעוֹת — *One hired for [several] hours*

[I.e., a worker who is not hired for an entire day or night but only for several hours.]

גּוֹבֶה כָּל־הַלַּיְלָה — *collects all night*

I.e., if he is hired for several hours of the night, he must be paid before morning. If the employer delays past dawn, he transgresses the prohibition on keeping the wages overnight (Rav; Rambam Comm. from Gem. 111a).

וְכָל־הַיּוֹם. — *or all day.*

I.e., a worker hired for several hours of the day must be paid before the end of the day. If the sun should set without his having been paid, the employer has transgressed two precepts: the positive command to pay the worker during his day, and the negative precept not to allow the sun to set upon the wage. Since his employment terminates during the day, the employer becomes obligated to pay him at that time, and he therefore transgresses at the end of the day (Rav from Gem. 111a, Rashi).

The above represents the interpretation of the Amora Rav. The Gemara (111a), however, also records the dissenting view of Shmuel. Although

Shmuel concurs with Rav as regards the worker hired for several hours during the day, in his opinion, the worker hired for several hours of the night may be paid his wages throughout the remainder of the night and all the following day. He reasons that since in Torah law the day follows the night, the employer has the entire 'day' in which to pay the worker. He explains the entire last sentence of the mishnah as referring to a single worker — one hired for several hours of the night. The mishnah thus rules that such a worker *may collect all [the rest of the] night and all day*. Rif, Rosh and Rambam (Hil. Sechirus 11:2) decide the halachah in accordance with Rav. Semag (Negative Precept 181), however, decides in favor of Shmuel. The Shulchan Aruch (339:4) accepts the former ruling.

שָׂכִיר שַׁבָּת, שָׂכִיר חֹדֶשׁ, שָׂכִיר שָׁנָה, שָׂכִיר שָׁבוּעַ — *One hired for a week, a month, a year, [or] a septenary —*

[The rulings stated previously in the mishnah were for workers hired for a day or less. The mishnah now defines the law for workers hired for longer periods of time, who need not be paid each day.]

יָצָא בַיּוֹם, — *[if] he departs by day,*

I.e., if his employment terminates at dawn or anytime during the day (Rav).

גּוֹבֶה כָּל־הַיּוֹם; — *he collects all [that] day;*

He must be paid before sunset of the day his employment concludes. If he fails to do so, the employer transgresses the commandment to pay the worker during his day and the commandment not to allow the sun to set on the worker's wage (Rav).

הַיּוֹם; יָצָא בַלַּיְלָה, גּוֹבֶה כָּל־הַלַּיְלָה וְכָל־הַיּוֹם.

[יב] אֶחָד שְׂכַר אָדָם, וְאֶחָד שְׂכַר בְּהֵמָה, וְאֶחָד שְׂכַר כֵּלִים, יֶשׁ בּוֹ מִשּׁוּם „בְּיוֹמוֹ תִתֵּן שְׂכָרוֹ,״ וְיֶשׁ בּוֹ מִשּׁוּם „לֹא־תָלִין פְּעֻלַּת שָׂכִיר אִתְּךָ עַד־בֹּקֶר.״ אֵימָתַי? בִּזְמַן שֶׁתְּבָעוֹ; לֹא תְבָעוֹ, אֵינוֹ עוֹבֵר עָלָיו. הִמְחָהוּ אֵצֶל חֶנְוָנִי אוֹ אֵצֶל שֻׁלְחָנִי, אֵינוֹ עוֹבֵר עָלָיו.

יד אברהם

יָצָא בַלַּיְלָה, — [if] he departs at night,
I.e., if his employment terminates at night (Rav).

גּוֹבֶה כָּל־הַלַּיְלָה וְכָל־הַיּוֹם. — he collects all night and [the following] day.
Since his employment extended into the night, he is adjudged as one hired for the night, and the employer therefore has the remainder of the night and all the next day to pay (Rav).

This contradicts the Amora Rav's interpretation of the mishnah's previous ruling that a worker who finishes working during the night must be paid before the end of that night, and supports the view of Shmuel, that one hired for several hours of the night may be paid all night and all the following day. To explain the view of Rav, the Gemara (111a) attributes this final ruling of the mishnah to R' Shimon, who differs with R' Yehudah on this point, as may be seen from a baraisa cited by the Gemara. Rav decides in favor of R' Yehudah, to whom he attributes the earlier ruling of the mishnah, not according to R' Shimon, since the halachah is always in accordance with R' Yehudah when he differs with R' Shimon (Tos. Yom Tov). [As noted above (s.v. וכל היום) most authorities follow the ruling of Rav in this matter.]

12.

The law prohibiting the withholding of wages applies not only to the hire of workers, but to the hire of any object, as the mishnah will now explain.

אֶחָד שְׂכַר אָדָם, — Whether it be the hire of a man,
[I.e., whether it be the wages due a man for his labor.]

וְאֶחָד שְׂכַר בְּהֵמָה, — the hire of a beast,
[The hire one owes for renting an animal.]

וְאֶחָד שְׂכַר כֵּלִים, — or the hire of utensils,
[The hire one owes for renting tools or the like.]

יֶשׁ בּוֹ מִשּׁוּם „בְּיוֹמוֹ תִתֵּן שְׂכָרוֹ, — [the law:] 'On his day you shall give his wages' (Deut. 24:15) applies,

I.e., if the hirer does not pay on time, he transgresses this positive precept. Furthermore, he also transgresses the negative precept of that verse, and the sun shall not set upon it (Tos. Yom Tov; Rambam, Hil. Sechirus 11:1; see Gem. 111b for derivation).

[As above, this applies to articles hired at night, for which the hirer may pay throughout the following day.]

וְיֶשׁ בּוֹ מִשּׁוּם „לֹא־תָלִין פְּעֻלַּת שָׂכִיר אִתְּךָ עַד־בֹּקֶר.״ — as well as [the law:] 'The wage of a hired worker shall not stay over with you until morning' (Lev.

day, he collects all [that] day; [if] he departs at night, he collects all [that] night and [the following] day.

12. Whether it be the hire of a man, the hire of a beast, or the hire of utensils, [the law:] *'On his day you shall give his wages'* (Deut. 24:15) applies, as well as [the law:] *'The wage of a hired worker shall not stay over with you until morning'* (Lev. 19:13). When? When he claimed it; [but if] he did not claim it, he does not transgress it. [If] he gave him a draft on a storekeeper or a moneychanger, he does not transgress it.

YAD AVRAHAM

19:13).

[As above, this applies to the articles hired for the day, for which the hirer may pay throughout the night.]

אִימָתַי — *When?*

[Under what circumstances is the hirer guilty of these transgressions?]

בִּזְמַן שֶׁתְּבָעוֹ; — *When he claimed it;*

I.e., the hired party claimed his hire and the hirer did not give it to him (Rambam, Hil. Sechirus 11:4).

לֹא תְבָעוֹ, אֵינוֹ עוֹבֵר עָלָיו. — *[but if] he did not claim it, he does not transgress it.*

[If he did not ask for his wage, the hirer has not violated the transgression by withholding payment.] This ruling is derived from the verse (Lev. 19:13): *The wage of a hired worker shall not stay over with you until morning.* The word אִתְּךָ, *with you,* indicates by your [the employer's] decision, not by his [the worker's]. Should he neglect to demand it, the delay in payment is partially due to his decision as well (Rav from Gem. 112a).

הִמְחָהוּ אֵצֶל חֶנְוָנִי אוֹ אֵצֶל שֻׁלְחָנִי, — *[If] he gave him a draft on a storekeeper or a moneychanger,*

I.e., the employer transferred the debt from himself to a storekeeper or

moneychanger by arranging an account with them from which his workers draw food or money for their wages (Rav; Rashi). The workers agreed to this arrangement (Choshen Mishpat 339:10), as did the storekeeper or moneychanger (Rambam, Hil. Sechirus 11:4, Kesef Mishneh ad loc. Tur and Choshen Mishpat loc. cit.).

The etymology of the word הִמְחָהוּ is obscure. Several derivations are proposed. Kol HaRemez theorizes that the root is מחה, *erase.* The intention is that the hirer erases the debt from his account and places it on the account of the storekeeper or moneychanger. Tos. Yom Tov associates it with Num. 34:11: וּמָחָה, *and it shall reach.* Thus, he renders: and he made it reach a storekeeper or a moneychanger. Mussaf HeAruch renders: he placed it with a storekeeper, based on the Aramaic.

אֵינוֹ עוֹבֵר עָלָיו. — *he does not transgress it.*

[I.e., if the storekeeper or the moneychanger did not pay the worker during the prescribed period, the hirer does not transgress the Torah's prohibition on delaying payment.] This, too, is based on the word אִתְּךָ, *with you,* which means that the debt is on the employer's account, not on the account of a storekeeper or a moneychanger (Rav from Gem. 112a).

שָׂכִיר — בִּזְמַנּוּ, נִשְׁבָּע וְנוֹטֵל; עָבַר זְמַנּוֹ, אֵינוֹ נִשְׁבָּע וְנוֹטֵל. אִם יֵשׁ עֵדִים שֶׁתְּבָעוֹ, הֲרֵי זֶה נִשְׁבָּע וְנוֹטֵל.

גֵּר תּוֹשָׁב — יֵשׁ בּוֹ מִשּׁוּם ,,בְּיוֹמוֹ תִתֵּן שְׂכָרוֹ,,

יד אברהם

שָׂכִיר — בִּזְמַנּוּ, נִשְׁבָּע וְנוֹטֵל; — [If] a hired worker [claims his wage] when it is due [lit., a hired worker: in his time], he may swear and take [it];

If a worker claims his wage when it becomes due [i.e., whenever he finishes his work and for the rest of that day or night (mishnah 11, s.v. גובה כל הלילה)] and the employer claims to have already paid (Meiri), the worker may come before the court and swear that he has not yet received his wages and collect from the employer.

This is a Rabbinic institution based on the fact that an employer is often preoccupied with his workers and will sometimes think that he has paid a particular worker his wages although, in fact, he has not. Consequently, the Rabbis transferred the oath which should normally have applied here (see below) from the employer to the worker (Rav from Gem. 112b).

This is not to be taken literally, to be applied only to a case in which the employer has many workers. Even if this is his only worker, the same ruling applies. The intention is that an employer is preoccupied with his affairs and may think that he has already paid his worker although he has not (Nimmukei Yosef from Yerushalmi; Tos., Shevuos 45a).

The nature of this oath which should have normally applied to the employer is not clearly identified by the Gemara. Should the mishnah refer to a case in which the employer admits part of the claim, he would be obligated to swear a Biblical oath to exempt himself from the part of the claim which he denies (see 4:7). This oath, then, was transferred by the Rabbis from the employer to the worker, who swears that he is owed the

money denied by the employer and collects. Should the mishnah refer as well to a case in which the employer claims that he paid the entire wage, thereby denying the claim completely (so that there is no basis for a Biblical oath), the intention is that, although it would have been fitting for the Rabbis to institute an oath for such a case and place it on the employer (the defendant),[1] because of the aforementioned reason it was transferred to the worker (Tos. Yom Tov from Tos. 112b). See above 4:7.

Should the employer dispute the amount stipulated, e.g., if the worker claims that the employer promised to pay him two dinars and the employer claims that he promised him only one, the employer must swear, since he always remembers the amount stipulated. Thus there is no reason to reverse the usual procedure of oath (Gem. 112b).

Rosh (see also Tos. 112b), quoting Shevuos 45b, rules that this entire halachah applies only when there are witnesses that the worker had been hired by this employer. In the absence of such proof, the employer is believed with a miggo that he never hired him. [I.e., if the employer is dishonest, he could have negated the claim entirely by denying having anything to do with this worker. Since he instead admits having hired him, we are forced to consider his counterclaim of having paid as plausible.] This halachah is also cited both in Rambam (Hil. Sechirus 11:6) and Choshen Mishpat (89:3).

עָבַר זְמַנּוֹ, אֵינוֹ נִשְׁבָּע וְנוֹטֵל. — [if] his time has passed, he may not swear and take [it].

Once the time granted the employer

---

1. The general procedure for cases requiring an oath is for the oath to be sworn by the defendant to exempt himself from the claim.

[If] a hired worker [claims his wage] when it is due, he may swear and take [it]; [if] his time has passed, he may not swear and take [it]. If there are witnesses that he demanded [it] of him, he may swear and take [it].

[As for] a resident alien — [the law:] *'On his day*

YAD AVRAHAM

to pay his workers has passed, the worker is no longer believed on the basis of his oath that he has not been paid. The Rabbis assumed that an employer would not wish to transgress the Biblical prohibition against delaying the payment of wages, and they were therefore confident that even though he might temporarily forget as a result of his preoccupations, he would remind himself of his debt before the expiration of the time granted to pay the workers (*Rav* from *Gem.* 113a). [Thus, the Rabbis did not institute the worker's oath past that time, and the worker must prove his claim through witnesses to collect.]

[Although it is possible that the employer is lying, the worker has no proof of this and it is equally possible that *he* is lying. Consequently, the worker cannot exact money from the employer merely on the basis of his oath. The most he can exact is a *shevuas heseis* (post-Mishnaic Rabbinical oath) to the effect that the employer has paid. The reversal of oaths cited above was never instituted to protect against a dishonest employer (whom we have no reason to suspect more than the worker), only against a forgetful one. Since in the estimation of the Rabbis such a lapse was not likely to persist past the deadline, there was no reason to institute a reversal of oath for such a situation and the basic law therefore remains in effect.]

אם יֵשׁ עֵדִים שֶׁתְּבָעוֹ, — *If there are witnesses that he demanded* [*it*] *of him,*

If there are witnesses that the worker demanded his wages of the employer up to the termination of the time granted to pay — e.g., they witnessed him demand payment and be rebuffed at the very end of the day on which his payment was due (*Tos. Yom Tov* from *Gem.*

113a, as explained by *Rosh*).

הֲרֵי זֶה נִשְׁבַּע וְנוֹטֵל. — *he may swear and take* [*it*].

The worker may go to court anytime during the following day and swear and collect his wages. Although this claim is being pressed past the payment deadline, when such an oath is generally no longer effective, the fact that witnesses attest to the claim being pressed and rejected by the employer before and up to the deadline makes it clear that the employer did not remind himself (if he indeed forgot). Thus, the worker may still swear and collect.

This delayed oath, however, is effective only the following day. Thereafter, the worker is no longer believed with an oath that his employer has not yet paid him since it would be highly unusual for a worker to leave his wages uncollected and refrain from demanding them beyond this time. The burden of proof, therefore, reverts back to him (*Tos. Yom Tov* from *Gem.* 113a, *Rosh*). Others rule that as long as he continues to demand his wages, he is granted a day after he discontinues his demands. E.g., if he continued to demand for a day after the wages were due, he is allowed another day, etc. *Rambam* (*Hil. Sechirus* 11:6) subscribes to this view, but grants him only the following day or the following night, not a complete twenty-four hour period. Afterwards, we assume that the worker is busy with his affairs and has perhaps forgotten that he has collected his pay.

גֵּר תּוֹשָׁב — [*As for*] *a resident alien* —

I.e., one who undertook to refrain from idolatry, but who continues to eat נְבֵלוֹת, *nevelos*, animals which died

וְאֵין בּוֹ מִשּׁוּם ,,לֹא-תָלִין פְּעֻלַּת שָׂכִיר אִתְּךָ עַד-
בֹּקֶר.''

[יג] הַמַּלְוֶה אֶת-חֲבֵרוֹ לֹא יְמַשְׁכְּנֶנּוּ אֶלָּא
בְּבֵית דִּין; וְלֹא יִכָּנֵס לְבֵיתוֹ לִטּוֹל
מַשְׁכּוֹנוֹ, שֶׁנֶּאֱמַר: ,,בַּחוּץ תַּעֲמֹד.'' הָיוּ לוֹ שְׁנֵי

יד אברהם

without being slaughtered according to
the laws of *shechitah*, and טְרֵפוֹת, *treifos*,
animals suffering from terminal injuries
or ailments, although slaughtered
according to halachah (*Rav; Rashi*).

Surprisingly, *Rav* and *Rashi* here combine
the views of two *Tannaim*. The *Gemara*
(*Avodah Zarah* 64b) quotes a *baraisa*, which
states that R' Meir considers one who
refrains from idolatry a *ger toshav*, resident
alien. The Sages, however, consider only one
who undertakes to keep all seven Noachide
commandments a *ger toshav*. Others
consider only one who undertakes to keep all
the *mitzvos* save the interdict against eating
nevelos. Hence, *Rashi* combines R' Meir's
view with that of others (*Vavei Ha'Am-
mudim, Sefer Yereim 264*). See above 5:6.

יֵשׁ בּוֹ מִשּׁוּם ,,בְּיוֹמוֹ תִתֵּן שְׂכָרוֹ,''
— [the law:] *'On his day you shall give his wages'
applies to him*,

[Although he is not Jewish, and many
of the Torah's laws govern only
relations between fellow Jews, the
prohibition against delaying payment of
wages applies to the employer of a *ger
toshav* (resident alien) as well. This is
derived from the introductory verse of
the section containing these laws in
Deuteronomy 24:14: לֹא-תַעֲשֹׁק שָׂכִיר
בִּשְׁעָרֶיךָ ... , *You shall not oppress a
hired worker ... in your cities.* The
apparently redundant word בִּשְׁעָרֶיךָ, *in*

your cities, is taken by the *Gemara*
(111b) as an allusion teaching the
inclusion of the resident alien in the list
of workers protected by these laws.

The intention would seem to be that
the negative commandment, *and the sun
shall not set upon it*, which appears in
the same verse, also applies to the
resident alien (see above, s.v. יֵשׁ בּוֹ
מִשּׁוּם).

Rambam (*Hil. Sechirus* 11:1),
however, states that if the employer of a
ger toshav does not pay before the end
of the day, he does not transgress the
negative commandment, only the
positive one. *Chinnuch* 588 follows this
view as well (*Tos. R' Akiva*).

וְאֵין בּוֹ מִשּׁוּם ,,לֹא-תָלִין פְּעֻלַּת שָׂכִיר אִתְּךָ
עַד-בֹּקֶר.'' — *but [the law:] 'The wage of a
hired worker shall not stay over with
you until morning' does not apply to
him.*

We learn this from the word רֵעֲךָ,
your fellow, used in the introductory
verse of the *Leviticus* (19:13) section on
this law. This excludes the *ger toshav*,
who is not a member of the Jewish
people (*Rav*). [I.e., the *ger toshav* hired
to work by day need not be paid before
dawn of the night following his day of
work but may be paid throughout the
following day.]

13.

The final mishnah of this chapter deals with the various laws relating to a creditor
who wishes to exact security from a debtor who is delinquent in repaying his loan.
These laws are dealt with by the Torah in *Deuteronomy* chapter 24.

The first of these laws taken up by this mishnah is given in verses 10-13:
כִּי-תַשֶּׁה בְרֵעֲךָ מַשַּׁאת מְאוּמָה לֹא-תָבֹא אֶל-בֵּיתוֹ לַעֲבֹט עֲבֹטוֹ. בַּחוּץ תַּעֲמֹד וְהָאִישׁ אֲשֶׁר אַתָּה נֹשֶׁה
בוֹ יוֹצִיא אֵלֶיךָ אֶת-הָעֲבוֹט הַחוּצָה: וְאִם-אִישׁ עָנִי הוּא לֹא תִשְׁכַּב בַּעֲבֹטוֹ: הָשֵׁב תָּשִׁיב לוֹ אֶת-הָעֲבוֹט
כְּבוֹא הַשֶּׁמֶשׁ וְשָׁכַב בְּשַׂלְמָתוֹ וּבֵרֲכֶךָּ וּלְךָ תִּהְיֶה צְדָקָה לִפְנֵי ה' אֱלֹהֶיךָ.

you shall give his wages' applies to him, but [the law:] *'The wage of a hired worker shall not stay over with you until morning'* does not apply to him.

13. **O**ne who lends his neighbor may not exact security from him except in court; nor may he enter his house to take his security, as it is said (Deut. 24:11): *'You shall stand outside.'* [If] he has

YAD AVRAHAM

10 *When you make any kind of loan to your fellowman, you shall not enter his house to exact his security.* 11 *You shall stand outside, and the man who is indebted to you shall bring the security out to you.* 12 *And if he is a poor man, you shall not retire with his security.* 13 *You shall return the security to him when the sun sets, and he shall lie in his garment and bless you, and it shall be deemed a merit before* HASHEM *your God.*

There is another, related law stated by the Torah in v. 17: וְלֹא תַחֲבֹל בֶּגֶד אַלְמָנָה, *and you shall not take as security the garment of a widow.*

Finally, there is the law stated earlier in that chapter (v. 6): לֹא־יַחֲבֹל רֵחַיִם וָרָכֶב, כִּי־נֶפֶשׁ הוּא חֹבֵל, *He shall not take a lower millstone or an upper millstone as security for he is taking a life as security.* This is the final topic of our mishnah, which, as will be seen below, is extended to mean any implement used to prepare food for human consumption.

הַמַּלְוֶה אֶת־חֲבֵרוֹ לֹא יְמַשְׁכְּנֶנּוּ אֶלָּא בְּבֵית דִּין; — *One who lends his neighbor may not exact security from him except in court;*

The mishnah refers to a case in which the loan fell due but the borrower was unable to meet his obligations. The lender now wishes to seize property as security until the loan is paid. The mishnah teaches that he may not seize such property from the borrower forcibly. Rather, he must apply to the court and have the property exacted by an agent of the *beis din* with the consent of the *beis din* (*Rav; Rashi*).

[Should the lender demand collateral at the time of the loan, he need not apply to the court, but may take whatever they agree upon.]

As taught by the verse cited in the preface, there is a Biblical prohibition to enter the borrower's house to obtain an article for security. The ruling requiring the lender to obtain security through the courts, therefore, applies even to articles taken from the borrower in the street (*Rav; Rashi*). *Rabbeinu Yitzchak (Ri)* holds this requirement to be a

Rabbinical one designed to safeguard against the lender's entering the debtor's house, which is prohibited by the Torah (*Tos.* 113a). *Nimmukei Yosef*, too, subscribes to this view. *Sma* (97:7), however, points out that *Rambam (Hil. Malveh* 3:4) and *Tur* (97) consider the prohibition on the lender to exact security forcibly from the borrower to be a Biblical one. Although the Torah states: *You shall not enter his house,* the same applies to seizing his belongings in the street, and perhaps, even more so. It is only the agent of the *beis din* who may seize the debtor's belongings when he meets him in the street. But, as will be seen below, even he may not enter the borrower's house to take them for a pledge (*Tos. Yom Tov*).

Should the agent of *beis din* meet the debtor in the street, he may take his belongings by force and even strike him if he refuses to give them (*Tif. Yis.* from *Shulchan Aruch* 97:6, *Sma* ibid. 9).

וְלֹא יָבֹא לְבֵיתוֹ לִטוֹל מַשְׁכּוֹנוֹ, שֶׁנֶּאֱמַר: ,,בַּחוּץ תַּעֲמֹד." — *nor may he enter his house to*

כֵּלִים, נוֹטֵל אֶחָד וּמַנִּיחַ אֶחָד; וּמַחֲזִיר אֶת־הַכַּר
בַּלַּיְלָה וְאֶת־הַמַּחֲרֵשָׁה בַּיּוֹם. וְאִם מֵת, אֵינוֹ מַחֲזִיר
לְיוֹרְשָׁיו. רַבָּן שִׁמְעוֹן בֶּן־גַּמְלִיאֵל אוֹמֵר: אַף
לְעַצְמוֹ אֵינוֹ מַחֲזִיר אֶלָּא עַד שְׁלֹשִׁים יוֹם.

יד אברהם

take his security, as it is said (Deut. 24:11), 'You shall stand outside.'

I.e., even the agent of the beis din is barred from entering the debtor's house, and certainly the creditor (Rav from Gem. 113).

Rabbeinu Tam explains that this ruling applies only if the creditor wishes to take an object as security for the eventual repayment of his money. Should he wish to take it as payment of his overdue debt, the agent of the beis din may even enter the debtor's house. Otherwise, a debtor could escape collection of his loan by never taking any valuables with him when he goes out into the street (Tos. Yom Tov from Rosh).

הָיוּ לוֹ שְׁנֵי כֵלִים, נוֹטֵל אֶחָד וּמַנִּיחַ אֶחָד; — [If] he has two utensils, he may take one and leave one;

Verses 12 and 13 of the passage cited in the preface state that if one takes an article from a poor man as security and it is something that the debtor needs to live with, it must be returned to him to use each time he needs it following its use, and it may again be held until the next time it is needed (Rambam, Malveh 3:5). [Although the verses refer by way of example to sleepwear, the law applies to all utensils.] The mishnah now teaches that if the debtor has two utensils which together equal the amount of the loan, and the lender took them both as security, he must return each one to the debtor as he needs it while holding on to the other. The mishnah proceeds to illustrate this rule (Rav; Rashi).

According to our reading, the word וּמַנִּיחַ, leaves, is interpreted as returns. In many editions, we find the word וּמַחֲזִיר, returns,

explicitly. This is the reading of Yerushalmi, Rif, and Rosh (Tos. Yom Tov). [Surprisingly, Tos. Yom Tov neglects to mention that Rashi, too, has that reading.]

וּמַחֲזִיר אֶת־הַכַּר בַּלַּיְלָה וְאֶת־הַמַּחֲרֵשָׁה בַּיּוֹם. — and he must return the pillow by night and the plowshare by day.

I.e., if he took a pillow and a plowshare from a poor debtor as security, he must return the pillow at night, when he may take the plowshare, and the plowshare by day, when he may take the pillow (Meiri).

Many commentators question the permissibility of taking a plowshare as security at any time. As mentioned in the preface to this mishnah, the Torah forbids taking as security any implement used in the preparation of food for human consumption. Since the plowshare is used to prepare the earth for planting grain and other edibles, it should fall under this prohibition.

Many solutions have been offered for this difficulty. One is that at night, when the plowshare is not used, that prohibition does not apply (Maggid Mishneh, Hil. Malveh 3:5).

Another solution is that the mishnah refers to one who transgressed the law of the Torah and took the plowshare for a pledge. He must, nevertheless, return it when it is needed (Tos. Yom Tov from Nimmukei Yosef).

This view assumes that once one has transgressed the law of the Torah and taken an implement used in the preparation of food, it is a fait accompli, and he is not forced to return it. [Thus, only the need consideration still applies, not the prohibition on taking an article used to prepare food.] This does not conform with Rambam, Hil. Malveh 3:2. Tos. R' Akiva discusses this matter at length; see also Rashba in Shitah

two utensils, he may take one and leave one; and he must return the pillow by night and the plowshare by day. If he dies, he need not return [it] to the heirs. Rabban Shimon ben Gamliel says: Even to [the debtor] himself he need only return [it] up to thirty

YAD AVRAHAM

Mekubetzes.

Others rule that since a plowshare is not used directly in the preparation of food, but in the preparation of the soil for growing the food, it is not considered an implement used to prepare food *(Rabbeinu Tam).*

Rabbeinu Tam ventures further to define מַחֲרֵשָׁה not as a plowshare but as a back-scratcher, used in the bathhouse. This is obviously not used in the preparation of food.

Baal HaMaor and *Meiri* qualify the mishnah as referring to a case in which the debtor gave the security of his own free will.

וְאָם מֵת, אֵינוֹ מַחֲזִיר לְיוֹרְשָׁיו. — *If he dies, he need not return [it] to the heirs.*

If the debtor dies, there is no obligation for the lender to return the utensil taken as security to his heirs [even if they need it]. The Torah expressly states (v. 13): *You shall return the security 'to him,'* indicating that the obligation to return it is only to him [the borrower], not to his heirs *(Rav; Rashi).* Rather, the creditor may immediately sell the security and collect the debt from the proceeds *(Rashi).* During the debtor's lifetime, however, the creditor must always return it *(Tos. Yom Tov).* If the creditor wishes to collect the debt, he must return the security when the debtor does not need it, e.g., the plowshare at night or the pillow by day, thus relinquishing it as security. Then, he can collect it as payment of the debt *(Rosh; Maggid Mishneh 3:6; Tur* and *Shulchan Aruch Choshen Mishpat*

97:22).

The *Gemara* (114b, 115a) cites a *baraisa* in which R' Meir asks why, in view of the law that the security must be returned to the poor man whenever he needs it, should the lender bother to take it at all? He replies that by establishing the article as security for the loan, the lender benefits by having the loan exempted from the cancellation of debts decreed by the Torah every seventh year as part of the *Shemittah* (Sabbatical year) observance *(Deut. 15:2).* As stated by the mishnah in *Sheviis* 10:2, loans secured by collateral are exempted from the law of cancellation. Additionally, the lender benefits in case the debtor should die. The law is that a debtor's movable property, once he dies, is not subject to collection from his heirs.[1] Articles which have been taken as security, however, are not subject to this rule, and it is thus to the creditor's benefit to secure the articles as collateral.

This, however, does not explain the benefit to the lender in continually taking back the article of security after every time the borrower needs it. In response to this, *Rabbeinu Elchanan* (quoted by *Tos.* 115a) replies that by the creditor's keeping the security, the debtor will be unable to deny his indebtedness. Additionally, it puts pressure on him to repay the loan as soon as possible, since he is ashamed to have his utensil returned to him daily *(Tos. Yom Tov* from *Tos.* 115a).

רַבָּן שִׁמְעוֹן בֶּן־גַּמְלִיאֵל אוֹמֵר: אַף לְעַצְמוֹ אֵינוֹ מַחֲזִיר אֶלָּא עַד שְׁלֹשִׁים יוֹם. — *Rabban Shimon ben Gamliel says: Even to [the debtor] himself he need only return [it] up to thirty days.*

This is the time customarily granted by *beis din (Rav; Rashi)* for executing its orders, e.g., to eliminate dangerous

---

1. This was the law throughout Talmudic times. However, the *Geonim* subsequently instituted that even a debtor's movable property may be collected from his heirs *(Rambam, Hil. Malveh 11:11; Choshen Mishpat 107:1).*

וּמְשַׁלְּשִׁים יוֹם וּלְהַלָּן מוֹכְרָן בְּבֵית דִּין.
אַלְמָנָה, בֵּין שֶׁהִיא עֲנִיָּה בֵּין שֶׁהִיא עֲשִׁירָה, אֵין
מְמַשְׁכְּנִין אוֹתָהּ, שֶׁנֶּאֱמַר: ,,וְלֹא תַחֲבֹל בֶּגֶד
אַלְמָנָה.''
הַחוֹבֵל אֶת־הָרֵחַיִם עוֹבֵר בְּלֹא תַעֲשֶׂה; וְחַיָּב
מִשּׁוּם שְׁנֵי כֵלִים, שֶׁנֶּאֱמַר: ,,לֹא יַחֲבֹל רֵחַיִם

יד אברהם

conditions such as a tree overhanging
the street or a wall ready to collapse (see
below, 10:4). The same period is
granted to pay debts (Tos. Yom Tov).

וּמְשַׁלְּשִׁים יוֹם וּלְהַלָּן מוֹכְרָן בְּבֵית דִּין. — After
thirty days, he sells them in court.

[I.e., after thirty days, he may sell the
articles he took as security and collect
his debt.] The halachah is not in
accordance with Rabban Shimon ben
Gamliel, but in accordance with the
Tanna Kamma (Rav; Choshen Mishpat
97:18).

As explained above, this ruling does
not deal with foreclosures. Should he
wish to foreclose, he may take anything,
leaving him only his bare essentials (see
Choshen Mishpat 97:23). We are
discussing only the case in which the
lender wishes to give the debtor a
chance to raise the money and not lose
his household articles. Also, it is
possible that a person wishes to seize
articles that he would not be permitted
to keep should he seize them in payment
(see Choshen Mishpat ibid.). As
security, however, he may hold them
either by day or at night.

אַלְמָנָה, בֵּין שֶׁהִיא עֲנִיָּה בֵּין שֶׁהִיא עֲשִׁירָה, אֵין
מְמַשְׁכְּנִין אוֹתָהּ, — We may not exact
security [from] a widow, whether she be
poor or rich,

The Torah (Deut. 24:17) expressly
forbids taking security from a widow.
The Gemara (115a) notes the opinion of
R' Shimon, that this prohibition applies
only to a poor widow, to whom the
creditor would have to return the article
daily. Since by frequenting her house,
he would bring her to disrepute among

her neighbors (who would not
necessarily be aware of the purpose of
his visits), the Torah prohibited taking
security from her. It follows from this
that one should be permitted to take
security from a rich widow, since in that
case he would not have to return it to
her each day. This is indeed R' Shimon's
ruling, based upon his principle of דְּקְרָא
דָּרְשִׁינָן טַעֲמָא, we expound the reason for
Scripture [i.e., that our understanding
of the rationale of a Torah law can, in
certain well-defined cases, be used to
define its limits]. The Tanna of the
mishnah, however, rules that the
rationale of a Scriptural commandment
cannot be used to expound the law.
Thus, the verse must be taken at face
value to teach that we may not take
security from any widow, whether rich
or poor (Rav).

שֶׁנֶּאֱמַר: ,,וְלֹא תַחֲבֹל בֶּגֶד אַלְמָנָה.'' — as it is
said (ibid. 17): 'And you shall not take
as security the garment of a widow.'

This unqualified commandment includes both a poor widow and a rich
one, since we do not expound the
rationale of Scripture (Rav from Gem.
115a).

Although it is prohibited to enter
anyone's house to take security, if one
enters a widow's house to do so he has
transgressed two negative precepts, the
one including all persons and the
additional one prohibiting entering the
house of a widow to take her security
(Rashba). Nimmukei Yosef, however,
deduces from Rambam (Hil. Malveh
3:1) that one may not take from a
widow even if he meets her outside, and

days. After thirty days, he sells them in court.

We may not exact security [from] a widow, whether she be poor or rich, as it is said (ibid:17): *'And you shall not take as security the garment of a widow.'*

One who takes a mill as security transgresses a negative commandment; and he is guilty of [taking] two utensils, as it is said (ibid:6): *'He shall not take a lower millstone or an upper millstone as security.'*

YAD AVRAHAM

even if the agent of the *beis din* takes it for him. See also *Tos. HaRosh.*

Rambam (Hil. Malveh 3:1) rules that one may not take security from a widow even at the time of the loan. This is difficult, however, since that is analogous to a sale — since she gives him the security of her own free will — and it should be permissible. *Ravad,* too, criticizes him for that (*Tos. Yom Tov* from *Nimmikei Yosef*). *Shulchan Aruch* (*Choshen Mishpat* 97:4) decides against *Rambam.*

According to *Shach,* the mishnah's ruling includes only a widow, since she is heartbroken and an unfortunate. One would, however, be permitted to take security from a divorcee. According to *Sma,* the law includes a divorcee as well, since she has no husband to watch over her and she is out of her father's jurisdiction, but not a virgin who is still under her father's jurisdiction. *Taz,* however, includes even a virgin in this ruling (*Tos. R' Akiva; Tif. Yis.*).[1]

הַחוֹבֵל אֶת־הָרֵחַיִם עוֹבֵר בְּלֹא תַעֲשֶׂה; — *One who takes a mill as security transgresses a negative commandment;*

[The Torah expressly forbids taking a mill as security, as the mishnah will quote below.]

The mishnah must refer here to a handmill. Since such a mill is portable, it is deemed movable property and is therefore

subject to being taken as security. Watermills, however, are regarded as real estate and cannot be taken as security, only as payment (*Tos. Yom Tov* from *Tur Choshen Mishpat* 97). However, as *Tos. Yom Tov* points out, there is a discrepancy in *Tur's* ruling since in *Choshen Mishpat* 107 he rules that *beis din* may take land for security (just as they may collect the debt from it) if it is to the benefit of the debtor, by affording him the opportunity to redeem it. *Lechem Shamayim* resolves the difficulty by explaining *Tur* 97 to mean that though land may be taken as security, it is not subject to the various Torah laws governing securities described above. Since the Torah formulates these prohibitions only in terms of utensils that a person can bring out of his house, they apply only to movable property, not real estate. Thus, the obligation to return it is not relevant and neither is the negative precept involved.

וְחַיָּב מִשׁוּם שְׁנֵי כֵלִים, שֶׁנֶּאֱמַר: ,,לֹא יַחֲבֹל רֵחַיִם וָרָכֶב." — *and he is guilty of [taking] two utensils, as it is said (ibid:6): 'He shall not take a lower millstone or an upper millstone as security.'*

I.e., he is guilty of taking the lower millstone and the upper one (*Rav; Rashi*). Since the Torah mentions each millstone specifically, he is guilty of two transgressions although both stones work together as part of a single

1. [Although these authorities are, in a way, expounding the rationale of Scripture, it appears that this may be done if the verse itself is not qualified thereby. Thus, since the verse specifically bars only a widow, these reasons may be used to limit the *extension* of the Scriptural prohibition to other women. R' Shimon, however, expounds the reason of Scripture even to the extent of qualifying the verse itself, in this case excluding a rich widow. According to all views, there is no reason to prohibit taking security from a married woman, since she is not an unfortunate and there is no reason to suspect the creditor of immoral acts with her since her husband is there.]

וָרָכֶב." וְלֹא רֵחַיִם וָרֶכֶב בִּלְבַד אָמְרוּ, אֶלָּא כָל־
דָּבָר שֶׁעוֹשִׂין בּוֹ אֹכֶל נֶפֶשׁ, שֶׁנֶּאֱמַר: ,,כִּי נֶפֶשׁ הוּא
חֹבֵל."

[א] **הַבַּיִת** וְהָעֲלִיָּה שֶׁל־שְׁנַיִם שֶׁנָּפְלוּ, שְׁנֵיהֶם
חוֹלְקִים בָּעֵצִים וּבָאֲבָנִים וּבֶעָפָר;
וְרוֹאִים אֵלוּ אֲבָנִים הָרְאוּיוֹת לְהִשְׁתַּבֵּר. אִם הָיָה
אֶחָד מֵהֶן מַכִּיר מִקְצָת אֲבָנָיו, נוֹטְלָן וְעוֹלוֹת לוֹ

יד אברהם

operation (Meiri). Accordingly, he is
punished by being dealt twice forty
lashes, although he is warned only once
for taking as a security the lower
millstone and the upper millstone.
Should he be warned twice, he is given
two series of lashes even if he takes two
upper millstones or two lower ones
(Tos. Yom Tov from Tos. 115a).

This applies only if the creditor took the
millstones as a pledge after the debtor
neglected to pay the loan. Should he take
them at the time of the loan, the prohibition
against taking millstones as security does not
apply, according to most authorities. Only
Rambam rules that it applies in that case as
well (Tos. Yom Tov from Nimmukei Yosef).

וְלֹא רֵחַיִם וָרֶכֶב בִּלְבַד אָמְרוּ, — They did not
speak only of the lower millstone and
the upper millstone,

I.e., the Sages did not mean that only
in the case of taking the two millstones
as security is one liable separately for
taking two utensils which are used for a
single function (Tos. Yom Tov).

אֶלָּא כָל־דָּבָר שֶׁעוֹשִׂין בּוֹ אֹכֶל נֶפֶשׁ, — but [of]
anything with which food for human
consumption is prepared,

I.e., any utensil used for the
preparation of food for human consumption which is composed of two
components renders one liable for two
transgressions if he takes them both as
security. E.g., a scissors used to cut
vegetables or a yoke used in plowing
(Tos. Yom Tov from Gem. 116a).

As noted above (s.v. את הכר), there is some
question whether utensils used to grow food
(rather than to process it) are included in this
prohibition (e.g., a plowshare). For this
reason, Rabbeinu Tam (Tos. 113a) rejects the
interpretation of Rashi that the yoke in
question was used in plowing and explains
that it was used for having the oxen stamp
the grain (prior to winnowing).

שֶׁנֶּאֱמַר: ,,כִּי נֶפֶשׁ הוּא חֹבֵל." — as it is said:
for he takes away a life as security.'

This concluding clause of the verse
includes other utensils used to prepare
food for human consumption (Gem.
116a).

Chapter 10

1.

הַבַּיִת וְהָעֲלִיָּה שֶׁל־שְׁנַיִם שֶׁנָּפְלוּ, — [If] a
ground floor [lit., house] and an upper
story belonging to two [different people]
collapsed,

i.e., the ground floor belonged to one,
and the upper story to another (Rav).
For example, two brothers divided their

father's house, one taking the ground
floor and the other taking the upper
story. The stones of the walls from the
ceiling of the ground floor and higher
belong to the one living upstairs, and
those below belong to the owner of the
lower floor (Rashi). Subsequent to the

They did not speak only of the lower millstone and the upper millstone, but [of] anything with which food for human consumption is prepared, as it is said (ibid.): *'for he takes away a life as security.'*

1. [If] a ground floor and an upper story belonging to two [different people] collapsed, the two of them divide the wood, the stones, and the earth; and they determine which stones are likely to have been broken. If one of them recognized some of his stones,

YAD AVRAHAM

collapse, however, it could not be determined which stones came from which part of the structure (*Rav*).

שְׁנֵיהֶם חוֹלְקִים בָּעֵצִים וּבָאֲבָנִים וּבֶעָפָר; — *the two of them divide the wood, the stones, and the earth;*

Since we cannot discern which building materials belong to each of the occupants, they divide (*Rav*).

Should the height of both stories be equal, they divide the materials equally. Should one story be higher than the other, they share proportionally (*Tosefta* 11:1).

This is the ruling of all authorities. *Rashi*, however, according to *Rashba*, *Maggid Mishneh* (*Hil. Shechenim* 4:1), and *Beis Yosef* (164), explains the mishnah to mean that, since we cannot discern which stones belong to each of the occupants, they share equally even if the two floors are of unequal height. *Rashba* questions this very strongly, and *Maharshal* in *Chochmas Shlomo* emends *Rashi* to agree with all other commentators (*Tos. Yom Tov*).

The *Gemara* (116b) explains that even if the stones fall into the property of one of the partners, the other is not considered the plaintiff to be required to bring proof that the stones are his. Since partners are not particular with each other, and allow each other to keep things in each other's property, the fact that they are lying in the property of one of them proves nothing regarding their ownership (*Tos. Yom Tov*).

In those days, earth was used to cement the stones together, as we find in *Lev. 14* (*Tos. Yom Tov* from *Rashi*).

וְרוֹאִים אֵלּוּ אֲבָנִים הָרְאוּיוֹת לְהִשְׁתַּבֵּר. —*and they determine which stones are likely to have been broken.*

If the building blocks were bricks, many of them are likely to have broken in the fall (*Tos. Yom Tov* from *Rashi*). If the foundation crumbled and the building caved in, the stones of the ground floor, upon which the entire structure fell, are likely to be the broken ones. Hence, the broken bricks are awarded to the owner of the ground floor and the whole ones to the owner of the upper story. If the building fell outward, the stones of the upper story, which fell from a height, are likely to be the broken ones. Accordingly, the broken bricks are awarded to the owner of the upper story and the whole ones to the owner of the ground floor.

The previous ruling of the mishnah, that they divide the stones, deals with a collapse that took place at night, in which passersby moved away the debris before dawn, so that the nature of the fall could no longer be determined (*Rav* from *Gem.* 116b).

אִם הָיָה אֶחָד מֵהֶן מַכִּיר מִקְצָת אֲבָנָיו, — *If one of them recognized some of his stones,*

I.e., he recognized some of the whole stones and claimed that they were from his part of the structure (*Rav*; *Rashi*).

[ב] **הַבַּיִת** וְהָעֲלִיָּה שֶׁל־שְׁנַיִם, נִפְחֲתָה הָעֲלִיָּה,
וְאֵין בַּעַל הַבַּיִת רוֹצֶה לְתַקֵּן, הֲרֵי
בַּעַל הָעֲלִיָּה יוֹרֵד וְדָר לְמַטָּה, עַד שֶׁיְּתַקֵּן לוֹ אֶת־
הָעֲלִיָּה. רַבִּי יוֹסֵי אוֹמֵר: הַתַּחְתּוֹן נוֹתֵן אֶת־
הַתִּקְרָה, וְהָעֶלְיוֹן אֶת־הַמַּעֲזִיבָה.

יד אברהם

נוֹטְלָן — *he takes them,*

[He may keep the stones he claims to recognize.] This ruling cannot be taken at face value, since without proof for his claim, why should he be believed? The *Gemara* (116b) therefore explains this part of the mishnah to refer to a case in which the other one admits that he recognizes some of the stones as belonging to his neighbor but he is uncertain concerning the remainder of the ones identified by the neighbor. This makes him liable for the Biblical oath for one who admits part of the claim and since he says he is uncertain concerning the remainder he is incapable of swearing an oath denying the remainder of the claim. He must therefore give all the stones in question to the one claiming them, as is the rule for anyone who is obligated to back his denial with a Biblical oath which he cannot swear (see above, 8:2 s.v. חייב).[1]

Should he not admit to recognize any of the stones his neighbor claims, but be uncertain of all of them, they divide all the stones equally (*Rav* from *Gem.* 116b).

וְעוֹלוֹת לוֹ מִן־הַחֶשְׁבּוֹן. — *and they are counted for him in the reckoning.*

I.e., they are counted for him in the reckoning of the whole bricks to be divided — and the other one receives a like number of whole bricks. Since this one claims a certain number of whole bricks, he apparently had no more. On the other hand, the one who made no claim also has a weak argument. Therefore, since the bricks are in the possession of both of them, they divide the whole bricks equally. The one who claims to recognize some of his bricks gains only insofar as these may be bigger and better than the other whole bricks (*Gem.* 116b; *Sma* 164:12).

2.

הַבַּיִת וְהָעֲלִיָּה שֶׁל־שְׁנַיִם, — [If] a ground floor [lit., house] and an upper story belonged to two [people],

In this case, the entire structure is owned by one person, but the upper story is rented out to someone. The lease specified that the unit being rented was 'this upper story which is above this

house' (*Rav* from *Gem.* 116a). [The significance of this will be explained below.]

Rashi deletes the words שֶׁל־שְׁנַיִם, *belonged to two,* since the occupant of the upstairs apartment is not an owner but a tenant. *Rabbeinu Tam* maintains that the terminology belonging to two is nevertheless

---

1. *Nimmukei Yosef* proves from this that, even if the defendant is not expected to know the truth of the claim he is asked to swear against, he must nevertheless pay if he is unable to swear. *Tos.* (Bava Kamma 46a), however, rule that one who cannot swear must pay only if he is expected to know and he does not. They maintain that even in our case, the defendant may be expected to recognize his stones (*Tos. Yom Tov*).

he takes them, and they are counted for him in the reckoning.

2. [If] a ground floor and an upper story belonged to two [people], [and] the upper story partially fell in, but the owner of the ground floor does not wish to make repairs, the occupant of the upper story may go and live downstairs, until he repairs the upper story for him. R' Yose says: The downstairs one supplies the ceiling, and the upstairs one the plaster.

YAD AVRAHAM

appropriate, since it is convenient for the Tanna to refer to the upstairs tenant as בַּעַל הָעֲלִיָּה, the occupant [lit., master] of the upper story (Tos. Yom Tov from Tos.).

נִפְחֲתָה הָעֲלִיָּה, — [and] the upper story partially fell in,

I.e., a portion of the floor of the upper floor, which also serves as the ceiling of the lower story, fell in. The hole measures at least four handbreadths by four handbreadths (Rav from Gem. 116b), a loss of space large enough to represent an appreciable decline in his usage of the rented upper story (Rashi). Although the owner of the house could replace this loss of space by allowing the tenant of the upper story the use of an equivalent amount of space in the lower floor, it is unreasonable to expect the tenant to live partially upstairs and partially downstairs (Rav from Gem.).

וְאֵין בַּעַל הַבַּיִת רוֹצֶה לְתַקֵּן, — but the owner of the ground floor does not wish to make repairs,

I.e., he does not wish to repair the floor of the upper story (Rav).

הֲרֵי בַעַל הָעֲלִיָּה יוֹרֵד וְדָר לְמַטָּה, עַד שֶׁיְּתַקֵּן לוֹ אֶת־הָעֲלִיָּה. — the occupant of the

upper story may go and live downstairs, until he repairs the upper story for him.

The tenant may move into the lower floor with all his belongings and live there until the owner of the house repairs his floor. By the terms of the lease, the ground floor is pledged to support the tenancy of the upper story (Rav from Gem. 116b). This is derived from the seemingly redundant phrasing of the rental agreement — 'this upper story which is above this house.' By saying 'this upper story,' the residence in question has been clearly identified. The additional phrase, 'which is above this house,' is therefore redundant unless it is understood to pledge the entire house to supporting the tenancy of the upper story (Tos. Yom Tov from Rashi). Consequently, as long as the upper story is not restored to its previous level of habitability, the tenant has the right to use the lower floor (Rav).[1]

רַבִּי יוֹסֵי אוֹמֵר: הַתַּחְתּוֹן נוֹתֵן אֶת־הַתִּקְרָה, וְהָעֶלְיוֹן אֶת־הַמַּעֲזִיבָה. — R' Yose says: The downstairs one supplies the ceiling, and the upstairs one the plaster.

[I.e., the owner of the house must

---

1. It is for this reason that the Gem. qualifies the mishnah as dealing with a landlord and a tenant rather than with a jointly owned house. In the latter case, the owner of the ground floor is not responsible to the owner of the upper story and he need therefore not repair the ceiling. In the case of a landlord and a tenant, however, since the landlord pledged the ground floor to support the tenancy of the upper story, he must either repair it or allow the tenant to live on

[ג] **הַבַּיִת** וְהָעֲלִיָּה שֶׁל־שְׁנַיִם שֶׁנָּפְלוּ, אָמַר
בַּעַל הָעֲלִיָּה לְבַעַל הַבַּיִת לִבְנוֹת,
וְהוּא אֵינוֹ רוֹצֶה לִבְנוֹת — הֲרֵי בַעַל הָעֲלִיָּה בּוֹנֶה
אֶת־הַבַּיִת וְדָר בְּתוֹכוֹ עַד שֶׁיִּתֵּן לוֹ אֶת־יְצִיאוֹתָיו.
רַבִּי יְהוּדָה אוֹמֵר: אַף־זֶה דָּר בְּתוֹךְ שֶׁל־חֲבֵרוֹ
צָרִיךְ לְהַעֲלוֹת לוֹ שָׂכָר; אֶלָּא בַעַל הָעֲלִיָּה בּוֹנֶה

יד אברהם

supply all that is necessary to rebuild the floor between the two stories (his ceiling) with the exception of the plaster which covers it. This must be supplied by the tenant himself, if he wishes to have his floor plastered.] R' Yose is of the opinion that the plaster spread over the floor dividing the upper story from the lower is primarily to level it. The landlord is, therefore, not responsible

for it, and if the tenant wants a level floor, he must pay for it himself. The *Tanna Kamma*, however, maintains that its purpose is to reinforce the ceiling. Consequently, the landlord, who is responsible to replace the ceiling, is responsible for the plaster as well (*Rav* from *Gem.* 117a).

The halachah is in accordance with the *Tanna Kamma* (*Rav*).

3.

הַבַּיִת וְהָעֲלִיָּה שֶׁל־שְׁנַיִם שֶׁנָּפְלוּ, — [If] a ground floor and an upper story belonging to two [people] collapsed,

As in mishnah 1, the ground floor belongs to one and the upper story to another (*Rav; Rashi*). The entire building collapsed and the owner of the upper story can consequently not rebuild his apartment until the owner of the ground floor rebuilds his (*Meiri*).

אָמַר בַּעַל הָעֲלִיָּה לְבַעַל הַבַּיִת לִבְנוֹת, — [and]

the owner of the upper story demanded of the owner of the ground floor that he rebuild,

I.e., he demanded that he rebuild the walls and the ceiling[1] of the ground floor, so that the owner of the upper story may build his apartment above it (*Rashi*).

וְהוּא אֵינוֹ רוֹצֶה לִבְנוֹת — but he refuses [lit., *he does not wish to rebuild*] —

the ground floor (*Tos. Yom Tov from Rosh*).

This holds true only if the tenant is deprived of the use of his apartment because of a defect in the lower story, such as in the case just discussed. Since it was the ceiling of the ground floor which was faulty, having broken through when the occupants of the upper story walked on it, the owner of the house is obligated to make good on the lease. Should the walls of the upper story cave in, however, the landlord is not responsible since the mishap did not occur because of the defect in the ground floor (*Tos. Yom Tov*, quoting *Maggid Mishneh, Hil. Sechirus* 5:8 from *Rashba*).

1. This comment appears inconsistent with the ruling of *Rosh* and *Rabbeinu Tam* cited in the footnote to mishnah 2 that in the case of partners, the owner of the ground floor is not obligated to repair the ceiling. Yet *Tur* (*Choshen Mishpat* 164) quotes *Rashi* as concurring with *Rosh* and *Rabbeinu Tam*. To reconcile this, *Sma* (164:4) distinguishes between our case and the case of the preceding mishnah. In our case, since the entire building collapsed, the owner of the ground floor is required to rebuild his ground-floor dwelling. Since a dwelling must have a ceiling, he is required to build the ceiling as well. In the case of the preceding mishnah, however, in which the ceiling alone broke, since the owner of the ground floor has the roof above the second floor to protect him, the ceiling between the two floors is not

3. [If] a ground floor and an upper story belonging to two [people] collapsed, [and] the owner of the upper story demanded of the owner of the ground floor that he rebuild, but he refuses — the owner of the upper story may rebuild the ground floor and live in it until he reimburses him. R' Yehudah says: Even this one [who] lives in his neighbor's property must pay him rent. Rather, the

YAD AVRAHAM

[The owner of the ground floor does not wish to rebuild his ground-floor dwelling.]

הֲרֵי בַּעַל הָעֲלִיָּה בּוֹנֶה אֶת־הַבַּיִת וְדָר בְּתוֹכוֹ עַד שֶׁיִּתֵּן לוֹ אֶת־יְצִיאוֹתָיו. — *the owner of the upper story may rebuild the ground floor and live in it until he reimburses him.*

The owner of the upper floor may rebuild the first floor in the manner it was originally built *(Meiri)*, and live in it until the owner of the ground floor reimburses him for the building expenses. He then leaves it and rebuilds his upper story *(Rav; Rashi).*

רַבִּי יְהוּדָה אוֹמֵר: אַף־זֶה הַדָּר בְּתוֹךְ שֶׁל־חֲבֵרוֹ צָרִיךְ לְהַעֲלוֹת לוֹ שָׂכָר; — *R' Yehudah says: Even this one [who] lives in his neighbor's property must pay him rent.*

R' Yehudah does not consider this solution advisable for the owner of the upper story, because once the owner of the ground floor will reimburse him for his expenses, the ground floor will revert [retroactively] to its original owner, and the owner of the upper floor will have to pay him rent for all the time he lived in the lower story. R' Yehudah subscribes to the general view that one

who derives benefit from another's property must pay for that use even though the owner of the property sustained no loss therefrom [זֶה נֶהֱנֶה וְזֶה לֹא חָסֵר חַיָּב] *(Rav).* Thus, even though the owner of the ground floor sustained no loss from the upper story's owner living in his rebuilt house — in view of the fact that he did not wish to rebuild it — he must nevertheless pay him rent for the time he lived there *(Rav).*

Rashi adds that if he does not pay him, it appears as though he is charging interest for waiting for him to reimburse him for his expenses. *Tosafos* object to this reasoning on the grounds that this reimbursement cannot be considered a loan in view of the fact that the owner of the ground floor would be exempt from paying anything if the new dwelling burns down.

The *Tanna Kamma*, however, holds that since the owner of the property sustained no loss, although the owner of the upper story derived benefit therefrom, he is exempt from paying for that benefit [זֶה נֶהֱנֶה וְזֶה לֹא חָסֵר פָּטוּר]. Alternatively, he is exempt since the owner of the ground floor is obligated to the owner of the upper story *(Bava Kamma* 20b).

necessary for his dwelling. Therefore, if they were partners the owner of the lower story would not be required to pay for the ceiling's repair and the previous mishnah which does obligate him to pay for its repair must refer to a landlord and a tenant, as explained above.

Tos. Yom Tov ventures to differ with *Tur* and maintains that *Rashi* indeed rules that even in the case of a ceiling between two floors which partially gives way (the case of mishnah 2), if the two stories were each owned by someone else, the owner of the ground floor would be obligated to rebuild the ceiling. The *Gemara* qualifies the above mishnah as referring to a landlord and tenant only because two mishnayos concerning jointly owned houses are unnecessary, not because the ruling would be any different.

אֶת־הַבַּיִת וְאֶת־הָעֲלִיָּה וּמְקָרֶה אֶת־הָעֲלִיָּה, וְיוֹשֵׁב
בַּבַּיִת עַד שֶׁיִּתֶּן לוֹ אֶת־יְצִיאוֹתָיו.

[ד] **וְכֵן בֵּית** הַבַּד, שֶׁהוּא בָּנוּי בַּסֶּלַע וְגִנָּה
אַחַת עַל־גַּבָּיו, וְנִפְחַת, הֲרֵי בַעַל
הַגִּנָּה יוֹרֵד וְזוֹרֵעַ לְמַטָּה עַד שֶׁיַּעֲשֶׂה לְבֵית בַּדּוֹ
כִּפִּין. הַכֹּתֶל וְהָאִילָן שֶׁנָּפְלוּ לִרְשׁוּת הָרַבִּים
וְהִזִּיקוּ, פָּטוּר מִלְשַׁלֵּם. נָתְנוּ לוֹ זְמַן לָקוּץ אֶת־

יד אברהם

אֶלָּא בַּעַל הָעֲלִיָּה בּוֹנֶה אֶת־הַבַּיִת וְאֶת־הָעֲלִיָּה
וּמְקָרֶה אֶת־הָעֲלִיָּה, וְיוֹשֵׁב בַּבַּיִת עַד שֶׁיִּתֶּן לוֹ
אֶת־יְצִיאוֹתָיו. — Rather, the owner of the
upper story rebuilds [both] the ground
floor and the upper story, and puts a
roof on the upper story, and lives in the
ground floor until he reimburses him.

In R' Yehudah's view, it is in the
upper-story owner's best interest to
complete the entire structure [and then
live in the ground floor until the owner
reimburses him]. In this arrangement he
will be exempt from paying rent for his
occupancy of the ground floor. Since
his upper story has also been rebuilt, he
does not really need to live in the lower
story and he is thus not considered to
have derived any monetary benefit from
his occupancy of the ground floor. At
the same time, the owner of the ground
floor, who had neither the interest in
rebuilding the lower floor nor the right
to live in it now until he pays for it,
suffers no loss by his neighbor's living
there. Therefore, we apply the general
rule that where one derives no monetary
benefit from the use of something and
the other suffers no loss from its use,
the user is exempt from paying for his

use [see *Bava Kamma* 20a,b] (*Rav*).

Others object to this explanation
because the owner of the lower floor
must inevitably suffer some loss as a
result of the occupant's blackening the
walls with his cooking. They therefore
explain that, although the owner of the
ground floor suffers a loss, since the
owner of the upper story derives no
monetary benefit, he is not liable (*Tos.
Yom Tov* from *Nimmukei Yosef*,
quoting *Rashba, Tos.,* and *Ran*).

Ramban, basing his view on *Yerushalmi*,
qualifies the mishnah as referring to a case in
which the owner of the ground floor is absent
and he can therefore not be compelled to
rebuild the house. Should he be present,
however, the *beis din* compels him to rebuild
the ground floor so that the owner of the
upper story can build his upper story.
Although *beis din* can collect even from the
assets of an absent debtor, they do so only in
the case of a borrower who leaves the
country, to prevent people from borrowing
money and then disappearing (*Tos. Yom
Tov*).

Rashba, however, rules that even if the
owner of the ground floor is present, he
cannot be compelled to rebuild (*Tos. Yom
Tov*).

4.

וְכֵן בֵּית הַבַּד, — Similarly, [if] an olive
press,

I.e., a structure in which olives are
pressed to extract oil (*Rav; Rash*).

שֶׁהוּא בָּנוּי בַּסֶּלַע וְגִנָּה אַחַת עַל־גַּבָּיו, — which
was built in a rock with a garden above
it,

A person hewed a chamber in a rock

owner of the upper story rebuilds [both] the ground floor and the upper story, and puts a roof on the upper story, and lives in the ground floor until he reimburses him.

4. Similarly, [if] an olive press, which was built in a rock with a garden above it, partially caved in, the owner of the garden may go down and sow [his seeds] below until [the other] makes a dome for his olive press.

[If] a wall or a tree fell into a public domain and damaged, he is exempt from paying. [If] they gave

YAD AVRAHAM

and built an olive press inside it. He then made a garden on top of the rock. When he died, one of his sons took the olive press and the other took the garden [thus leaving the press in the possession of one person and the garden in the possession of another] (Rashi).

וְנִפְחַת, — *partially caved in,*

Part of the roof of the chamber caved in, leaving a hole four handbreadths by four handbreadths. This made a corresponding hole in the garden above, appreciably reducing the space available for sowing in the garden (Rav). Although it would be possible for the owner of the press to make up this loss to the owner of the garden by allowing him to sow an equivalent area in the chamber below, a person cannot be expected to tend a garden on two levels (Gem. 118a).

הֲרֵי בַעַל הַגִּנָּה יוֹרֵד וְזוֹרֵעַ לְמַטָּה — *the owner of the garden may go down and sow [his seeds] below*

The apparent meaning is that he may sow all his seeds in the olive press. Although the entire olive press, with the exception of the area directly beneath the hole, is shaded from the sun, it is possible to plant crops which do not require sunlight, e.g. lettuce; see Avodah Zarah 3:8 (Tos. Yom Tov from Beis Yosef 165).

עַד שֶׁיַּעֲשֶׂה לְבֵית בַּדּוֹ כִּפִּין. — *until [the*

other] makes a dome for his olive press.

[He may keep his garden in the olive press until the owner of the olive press builds a dome to close the hole.] This is an arch-like ceiling over which the owner of the garden can place earth and sow his seeds (Rav; Rashi).

Although in the cases of the two-storied houses mentioned in the preceding two mishnayos the owner of the ground floor was not obligated to rebuild the broken ceiling for the owner of the upper floor (his obligation to do so is only for a tenant, not an owner — see footnote mishnah 2), in this case the owner of the olive press is required to roof over his press for the sake of the garden. Since he cannot conduct his olive press if there is a hole in the roof, because the rain will spoil his press, he too needs this roof. In the above cases above, however, since there is a roof over the upper story, the hole in the floor between the two apartments causes him no harm [and it is only the owner of the upper floor who needs it] (Tos. Yom Tov from Rosh).

הַכֹּתֶל וְהָאִילָן שֶׁנָּפְלוּ לִרְשׁוּת הָרַבִּים וְהִזִּיקוּ, פָּטוּר מִלְּשַׁלֵּם. — *[If] a wall or a tree fell into a public domain and damaged, he is exempt from paying.*

The owner of the downed tree or wall is exempt from paying for the damages since their collapse was an unavoidable accident (Rav; Rashi). Obviously, this is

הָאִילָן וְלִסְתֹּר אֶת־הַכֹּתֶל, וְנָפְלוּ בְּתוֹךְ הַזְּמַן,
פָּטוּר; לְאַחַר הַזְּמַן, חַיָּב.

[ה] מִי שֶׁהָיָה כָּתְלוֹ סָמוּךְ לְגִנַּת חֲבֵרוֹ וְנָפַל,
וְאָמַר לוֹ: ,,פַּנֵּה אֲבָנֶיךָ,"
וְאָמַר לוֹ: ,,הִגִּיעוּךָ," אֵין שׁוֹמְעִין לוֹ. מִשֶּׁקִּבֵּל
עָלָיו, אָמַר לוֹ: ,,הֵילָךְ אֶת־יְצִיאוֹתֶיךָ, וַאֲנִי אֶטֹּל

true only if the wall was properly built. Should the wall have been built inadequately, however, the owner would be liable for damages caused by it (*Nimmukei Yosef*). Indeed, *Tosefta* (11:5) states explicitly that he is exempt if the wall fell because of tremors, high winds, or rains only if it had been built properly; if not, he is liable (*Tos. Yom Tov*).

Where the collapse was not due to negligence, he is exempt from damages occurring at the time of the fall, since they constitute an unavoidable accident, as explained above. Should the damage occur after the fall [for example, by someone tripping over the fallen debris], as long as he had no time to clean up the debris, he is exempt, since that accident was similarly unavoidable. Should the accident occur after he had time to remove the debris, the accident was no longer unavoidable and he would thus be liable for any damages caused by it [under the category of damages known as *bor*, a pit, which includes any obstacle placed in the public domain; see *Bava Kamma* 3:1]. However, if he renounced ownership of the debris before any damage resulted, he is exempt from liability for any future damages. Since he is neither responsible for the obstacle's placement in the street nor is he any longer its owner, he cannot be held legally accountable for damages caused by it. [This is the rule of one who *abandons his obstacle after it has fallen*

accidentally; see *Bava Kamma* 3:18.] Should he retain ownership of the debris, he is responsible for any damages caused by it (*Tos. Yom Tov* from *Nimmukei Yosef*).

נָתְנוּ לוֹ זְמַן לָקוּץ אֶת־הָאִילָן וְלִסְתֹּר אֶת־הַכֹּתֶל,
— [If] *they gave him time to cut down the tree or to demolish the wall,*

The *beis din* noticed that the tree or wall was in danger of falling and they gave him the usual thirty-day period to remove it (*Rashi; Meiri* from *Gem.* 118a). This would happen only if the danger is not imminent; even then *beis din* does not grant a period longer than thirty days. Should it appear to them that the tree or the wall might fall in as little as fifteen days or the like, they would require him to cut down the tree or demolish the wall even sooner (*Rabbeinu Yehonasan*, quoted by *Shitah Mekubetzes*).

וְנָפְלוּ בְּתוֹךְ הַזְּמַן, פָּטוּר; — *and they fell within the time, he is exempt;*

Since the court allowed him thirty days to remove the hazards, if they fell before this period had elapsed and caused damage he is exempt from paying for the damages. Since they were not expected to fall so soon, their early collapse is considered an unavoidable accident (*Rabbeinu Yehonasan* ibid.)

לְאַחַר הַזְּמַן, חַיָּב. — *after the time, he is liable.*

If he delayed removing the wall or

him time to cut down the tree or to demolish the wall, and they fell within the time, he is exempt; after the time, he is liable.

5. [If] one's wall abutted another's garden, and it fell, and he said to him: 'Clear away your stones,' [to which] the other replied: 'They are yours,' we do not listen to him. [If] after he accepted, he said to him: 'Here, take your expenses, and I will

YAD AVRAHAM

tree past the deadline and it fell, he is liable both for damages occurring at the time of the fall and for damages occurring after the fall, since these came about through his negligence. In this case he is liable for damages occurring after the fall even if he immediately renounces ownership of the debris.

Since the obstacle came to be in the public domain through his negligence, he is accountable for its damages regardless of whether he owns it. [This is the rule of *one who abandons his obstacle after it has fallen through neglect;* see *Bava Kamma* 3:1] (*Nimmukei Yosef*).

5.

מִי שֶׁהָיָה כתלו סָמוּךְ לְגִנַּת חֲבֵרוֹ וְנָפַל, — [If] one's wall abutted another's garden, and it fell,

The wall fell into his neighbor's garden (*Rav; Rashi*).

The *Tanna* chose the case of a garden rather than courtyard, since the wall abutting a courtyard usually belongs to both neighbors, while a garden wall customarily belongs to one (see *Bava Basra* 1:1,2). Furthermore, in the case of a courtyard wall, it is not customary to clear the stones away, but to rebuild the wall immediately (*Tos. Yom Tov* from *Sma* 166:1).

וְאָמַר לוֹ: ,,פַּנֵּה אֲבָנֶיךָ", — and he said to him: 'Clear away your stones,'

I.e., the owner of the garden told the owner of the wall to clear away his stones because they were ruining his garden (*Meiri*).

וְאָמַר לוֹ: ,,הִגִּיעוּךָ", — [to which] the other replied: 'They are yours,'

The owner of the wall told the owner of the garden to keep the stones for

himself and take care of clearing them (*Rav; Rashi*).

אֵין שׁוֹמְעִין לוֹ. — we do not listen to him.

If the owner of the garden does not want them, he need not accept and the owner of the wall is still obligated to clear them away (*Rav; Rashi*).

Although it was taught above that in a case in which one's obstacle fell accidently, he may renounce ownership of it and thereby escape liability for it, it is assumed in this case that he does not really mean it, but is merely trying to evade the owner of the garden's pressure to clear away the stones (*Tos. Yom Tov* from *Tos.*).

מִשֶּׁקִּבֵּל עָלָיו, אָמַר לוֹ: ,,הֵילָךְ אֶת־יְצִיאוֹתֶיךָ, וַאֲנִי אֶטֹּל אֶת־שֶׁלִּי", — [If] after he accepted, he said to him: 'Here, take your expenses, and I will take what belongs to me,'

The owner of the garden accepted the offer to keep the stones and cleared them away at his own expense, and the owner of the wall then recanted and

אֶת־שֶׁלִּי,״ אֵין שׁוֹמְעִין לוֹ.

הַשּׂוֹכֵר אֶת־הַפּוֹעֵל לַעֲשׂוֹת עִמּוֹ בַּתֶּבֶן וּבַקַּשׁ,
וְאָמַר לוֹ: ,,תֶּן־לִי שְׂכָרִי,״ וְאָמַר לוֹ: ,,טֹל מַה־
שֶּׁעָשִׂיתָ בִּשְׂכָרְךָ,״ אֵין שׁוֹמְעִין לוֹ. מִשֶּׁקִּבֵּל עָלָיו,
וְאָמַר לוֹ: ,,הֵילָךְ שְׂכָרְךָ וַאֲנִי אֶטֹּל אֶת־שֶׁלִּי,״ אֵין
שׁוֹמְעִין לוֹ.

הַמּוֹצִיא זֶבֶל לִרְשׁוּת הָרַבִּים, הַמּוֹצִיא מוֹצִיא,
וְהַמְזַבֵּל מְזַבֵּל.

יד אברהם

sought to reclaim his stones by offering the owner of the garden to reimburse him for clearing away the stones (Meiri).

אֵין שׁוֹמְעִין לוֹ. — *we do not listen to him.*

[The owner of the wall cannot compel the garden's owner to accept his recantation.] This is so only if the owner of the garden already cleared away the stones. Should the owner of the wall recant before the stones were cleared away, he may do so (*Tos. Yom Tov* from *Gem.* 119a).[1]

According to *Rosh* and *Nimmukei Yosef* (as understood by *Beis Yosef* and *Darchei Moshe, Tur* 166), and *Rashba* (quoted by *Maggid Mishneh, Hil. Shecheinim* 3:8), the owner of the wall may recant unless the owner of the garden cleared away the stones in his presence. Then, since he did not protest, it is assumed that he was willing to give up the stones. Should the owner of the garden clear them away in his absence, however, he may still insist that he did not mean seriously to give him the stones.

Rambam and *Tur* do not make this distinction (according to *Derishah, Rosh* agrees with them). *Bach* therefore explains that when the mishnah previously assumed that the offer to

keep the stones was not serious, the intent was only that it is *doubtful* whether he meant to give them up. Therefore, as long as the garden owner did not take physical possession of the stones, he may still recant. However, once the owner of the garden actually clears them, the burden of proof lies on the owner of the wall, who cannot prove that he did not mean the offer seriously.

הַשּׂוֹכֵר אֶת־הַפּוֹעֵל לַעֲשׂוֹת עִמּוֹ בַּתֶּבֶן וּבַקַּשׁ, — [*If*] *one hires a laborer to work with him with stubble or with straw,*

I.e., he hires him to gather straw for him, either his own or ownerless straw (*Rav; Rashi*). If the laborer picks up ownerless straw as an agent for his employer, the employer acquires it through the act of acquisition performed by the laborer (*Gem.* 118a).

וְאָמַר לוֹ: ,,תֶּן־לִי שְׂכָרִי,״ וְאָמַר לוֹ: ,,טֹל מַה־שֶּׁעָשִׂיתָ בִּשְׂכָרְךָ,״ — *and he says to him:* 'Give me my wages,' *to which the other replies:* 'Take what you have done for your wages,'

After completing his task the laborer comes to his employer for his wages. Since there was little profit in this enterprise, the employer tells the laborer to keep the straw he collected in lieu of his wages (*Meiri*).

1. Although the stones were lying in the garden at the time the offer was made, the garden cannot acquire the stones on behalf of its owner because we assume that the owner of the wall did not really intend to give him the stones but sought only to evade his responsibility (*Tos. Yom Tov* from *Gem.* 119a).

10

5

what belongs to me,' we do not listen to him.

[If] one hires a laborer to work with him with stubble or with straw, and he says to him: 'Give me my wages,' to which the other replies: 'Take what you have done for your wages,' we do not listen to him. [If] after he accepted, he said to him: 'Here, take your wages, and I will take what belongs to me,' we do not listen to him.

One who puts manure out in the public domain [may do so only if] the one who puts it out, puts it out, and the one who fertilizes, fertilizes [immediately].

אֵין שׁוֹמְעִין לוֹ. — *we do not listen to him.*

[I.e., he can refuse to accept straw and insist on receiving cash instead.]

Although in general anything worth money is adjudged as money and can be used in payment (since it can be sold for cash), in this case the Torah decrees: *The wage of a worker shall not stay over with you until morning,* meaning that the employer must pay him what he stipulated *(Rav; Rashi).* If the employer has no money, the laborer may tell the employer to sell some valuable [rather than give it to the laborer to sell] and bring him the money *(Tos. to Bava Kamma 9a; Mordechai, Bava Kamma 1:1).*

Should he hire him to work with foodstuffs, e.g. wheat or barley, he can compel him to accept that in place of money *(Tos. Yom Tov from Mordechai, Bava Kamma 1:2, Hagahos Maimonios, Hil. Sechirus 9:40).* Interestingly, this ruling was revealed to R' Meir of Rothenburg in a dream, and he accepted it as a halachah. [The probable reason is that since the worker's most pressing need is food, and money is merely a medium of exchange with which to purchase food, he may surely give him food itself.]

Shach (Choshen Mishpat 336:4) differs, noting that even divinely inspired dreams can have no bearing on halachah. *Rashash* (118a), however, conjectures that *Shach* differs only in the matter of wheat or barley,

which require preparation. In the case of bread which is ready to eat, *Shach* concurs with *Mordechai* and *Hagahos Maimonios.* *Aruch HaShulchan,* however, rules that there is no difference what the material is. He points out that the *Shulchan Aruch* does not differentiate.

מְשֶׁקִּבֵּל עָלָיו, וְאָמַר לוֹ: ״הֵילָךְ שְׂכָרְךָ וַאֲנִי אֶטֹּל אֶת־שֶׁלִּי,״ אֵין שׁוֹמְעִין לוֹ. — *[If] after he accepted, he said to him: 'Here, take your wages, and I will take what belongs to me,' we do not listen to him.*

[If after the laborer agreed to accept the stubble and straw for his wages, the employer can no longer retract and pay the laborer his wages and take back the straw.] This is true only if the laborer performed a *kinyan,* act of acquisition — e.g., picking up the straw, or placing it in his field — thereby legally acquiring it. Once it belongs to him, he need not surrender it to his employer unless he so desires *(Tur, Choshen Mishpat 336, quoting Ramah).*

הַמּוֹצִיא זֶבֶל לִרְשׁוּת הָרַבִּים, הַמּוֹצִיא מוֹצִיא, וְהַמְזַבֵּל מְזַבֵּל. — *One who puts manure out in the public domain [may do so only if] the one who puts it out, puts it out, and the one who fertilizes, fertilizes [immediately].*

I.e., as soon as one person carries the manure out of the stall into the public domain, someone should be ready to

אֵין שׁוֹרִין טִיט בִּרְשׁוּת הָרַבִּים, וְאֵין לוֹבְנִין לְבֵנִים. אֲבָל גּוֹבְלִין טִיט בִּרְשׁוּת הָרַבִּים, אֲבָל לֹא לְבֵנִים.

הַבּוֹנֶה בִּרְשׁוּת הָרַבִּים, הַמֵּבִיא אֲבָנִים מֵבִיא, וְהַבּוֹנֶה בּוֹנֶה; וְאִם הִזִּיק, מְשַׁלֵּם מַה־שֶּׁהִזִּיק. רַבָּן שִׁמְעוֹן בֶּן־גַּמְלִיאֵל אוֹמֵר: אַף מְתַקֵּן הוּא אֶת־מְלַאכְתּוֹ לִפְנֵי שְׁלֹשִׁים יוֹם.

[ו] שְׁתֵּי גַנּוֹת זוֹ עַל־גַּב זוֹ, וְהַיֶּרֶק בֵּנְתַיִם — רַבִּי מֵאִיר אוֹמֵר: שֶׁל־עֶלְיוֹן. רַבִּי יְהוּדָה אוֹמֵר: שֶׁל־תַּחְתּוֹן. אָמַר רַבִּי מֵאִיר: אִם יִרְצֶה הָעֶלְיוֹן לִקַּח אֶת־עֲפָרוֹ, אֵין כָּאן יֶרֶק.

יד אברהם

carry it away from there to fertilize his field. He may not leave it in the public domain for any period of time (Rav; Rashi).

There is, however, a baraisa in Bava Kamma which (30a) states that during the season when it was customary for people to clear out manure, one may leave it in the public domain for up to thirty days, so that it should be trodden by the traffic. This is one of the conditions Joshua made Israel accept when he distributed the land after its conquest; see Bava Kamma 3:3.

אֵין שׁוֹרִין טִיט בִּרְשׁוּת הָרַבִּים, — One may not soak clay in a public domain,

In some places, they would gather clay in one place and soak it for a long time (Tos. Yom Tov from Rashi). They would first soak it in water, then knead it into a heap (Meiri). This clay was used for making bricks.

וְאֵין לוֹבְנִין לְבֵנִים. — nor may one make bricks.

One may not make bricks in the public domain since they must be kept in the street for a long time in order to dry (Tos. Yom Tov from Rashi).

אֲבָל גּוֹבְלִין טִיט בִּרְשׁוּת הָרַבִּים, — But one may knead clay in the public domain,

I.e., one may knead it to be placed immediately into a building (Rav; Rashi) [as a kind of mortar].

אֲבָל לֹא לְבֵנִים. — but not bricks.

Meiri reads: לְלְבֵנִים, but not for bricks. Kneading clay for bricks was a longer procedure than kneading clay for building. It was therefore prohibited (Tif. Yis.).

הַבּוֹנֶה בִּרְשׁוּת הָרַבִּים, — One who builds in a public domain

If one builds a building on private property but requires the public domain as a place to leave his materials while construction is under way (Meiri).

הַמֵּבִיא אֲבָנִים מֵבִיא, וְהַבּוֹנֶה בּוֹנֶה; — [may do so only if] the one who brings the stones brings, and the one who builds, builds [immediately];

I.e., it is only permitted if the builder takes them immediately from the one who brings them and puts them into the building (Rav; Rashi).

וְאִם הִזִּיק, מְשַׁלֵּם מַה־שֶּׁהִזִּיק. — and if it caused damage, he must pay for the damage.

10
6
One may not soak clay in a public domain, nor may one make bricks. But one may knead clay in the public domain, but not bricks.

One who builds in a public domain [may do so only if] the one who brings the stones brings, and the one who builds, builds [immediately]; and if it caused damage, he must pay for the damage. Rabban Shimon ben Gamliel says: He may even prepare his work thirty days before.

6. [I]f there were] two gardens one above the other, with vegetables between them — R' Meir says: They belong to the upper one. R' Yehudah says: They belong to the lower one. Said R' Meir: If the upper one should decide to remove his earth, there

YAD AVRAHAM

As stated in *Bava Kamma* (3:3), all those who commit nuisance in the public domain, although they do so with legal permission, are liable for damages.

רַבָּן שִׁמְעוֹן בֶּן־גַּמְלִיאֵל אוֹמֵר: אַף מְתַקֵּן הוּא אֶת־מְלַאכְתּוֹ לִפְנֵי שְׁלֹשִׁים יוֹם. — *Rabban Shimon ben Gamliel says: He may even prepare his work thirty days before.*

I.e. he may prepare his work in the public domain thirty days prior to his building, and he is not liable for damages (*Rav; Rashi*). The halachah, however, is not in accordance with Rabban Shimon ben Gamliel (*Rav; Rambam Comm.*).

6.

שְׁתֵּי גִנּוֹת זוֹ עַל־גַּב זוֹ, וְהַיָּרָק בֵּינְתַיִם — *[If there were] two gardens one above the other, with vegetables between them —*

Two gardens belonging to two people lay side by side with the soil of one at a higher level than the soil of the other. Vegetables grew out of the side of the upper garden, hanging over the lower garden (*Rav, Rashi*).

רַבִּי מֵאִיר אוֹמֵר: שֶׁל־עֶלְיוֹן. — *R' Meir says: They belong to the upper one.*

The vegetables belong to the owner of the upper garden since they are growing out of his soil and are nurtured by it (*Rav; Rashi*).

רַבִּי יְהוּדָה אוֹמֵר: שֶׁל־תַּחְתּוֹן. — *R' Yehudah says: They belong to the lower one.*

They belongs to the owner of the lower garden because they are growing in his air space (*Rav; Rashi*).

The *Gem.* (118b) explains that there is no dispute concerning the roots, and that even R' Yehudah concurs that the roots belong to the owner of the upper garden. The dispute is only in regard to the foliage. R' Meir rules that we count the foliage with the roots, and R' Yehudah rules that we do not count the foliage with the roots (*Tos. Yom Tov*).

אָמַר רַבִּי מֵאִיר: אִם יִרְצֶה הָעֶלְיוֹן לִקַּח אֶת־עֲפָרוֹ, אֵין כָּאן יָרָק. — *Said R' Meir: If the upper one should decide to remove his earth, there would be no vegetables.*

If the owner of the upper garden

אָמַר רַבִּי יְהוּדָה: אִם יִרְצֶה הַתַּחְתּוֹן לְמַלֹּאות
אֶת־גִּנָּתוֹ, אֵין כָּאן יָרָק. אָמַר רַבִּי מֵאִיר: מֵאַחַר
שֶׁשְּׁנֵיהֶן יְכוֹלִין לִמְחוֹת זֶה עַל־זֶה, רוֹאִין מֵהֵיכָן
יָרָק זֶה חָי. אָמַר רַבִּי שִׁמְעוֹן: כָּל־שֶׁהָעֶלְיוֹן יָכוֹל
לִפְשֹׁט אֶת־יָדוֹ וְלִטּוֹל, הֲרֵי הוּא שֶׁלּוֹ, וְהַשְּׁאָר
שֶׁל־תַּחְתּוֹן.

wishes, he may dig up all the earth of his garden and level it with his neighbor's garden, in which case there would be no vegetables growing out of the side of the elevated garden. Consequently, it is only fitting that everything growing on that earth belong to him (Meiri).

אָמַר רַבִּי יְהוּדָה: אִם יִרְצֶה הַתַּחְתּוֹן לְמַלֹּאות אֶת־גִּנָּתוֹ, אֵין כָּאן יָרָק. — Said R' Yehudah: If the lower one should decide to fill up his garden, there would be no vegetables.

R' Yehudah argues that by the same token the owner of the lower garden can fill it up with earth until the top of it is level with his neighbor's garden,

thereby crushing the plants growing out of the side of the elevation. Therefore, since this air space is his, all that grows in the air should belong to him (Meiri).

אָמַר רַבִּי מֵאִיר: מֵאַחַר שֶׁשְּׁנֵיהֶן יְכוֹלִין לִמְחוֹת זֶה עַל־זֶה, — Said R' Meir: Since both of them can stop one another,

I.e., since each one has the ability of preventing the vegetation from growing, either by digging away the earth or by filling it in ... (Meiri).

רוֹאִין מֵהֵיכָן יָרָק זֶה חָי. — we [should] see from where these vegetables sustain themselves.

Since they both have the legal right to destroy the plant, that factor cannot be used as the determinant of ownership.

would be no vegetables. Said R' Yehudah: If the lower one should decide to fill up his garden, there would be no vegetables. Said R' Meir: Since both of them can stop one another, we [should] see from where these vegetables sustain themselves. Said R' Shimon: Whatever the upper one can stretch out his hand and take is his, and the remainder belongs to the lower one.

YAD AVRAHAM

Consequently, the decisive point should be the fact that the vegetation grows from the earth belonging to the owner of the upper garden *(Meiri).*

אָמַר רַבִּי שִׁמְעוֹן: כָּל־שֶׁהָעֶלְיוֹן יָכוֹל לִפְשׁט אֶת־יָדוֹ וְלִטּוֹל, הֲרֵי הוּא שֶׁלּוֹ, — *Said R' Shimon: Whatever the upper one can stretch out his hand and take is his,*

I.e., whatever the owner of the upper garden can reach from his garden and take without endangering himself he may keep *(Tif. Yis.* from *Gem.* 119a). In principle, R' Shimon agrees with R'

Meir that the vegetation belongs to the owner of the upper garden since it grows from his soil *(Rav; Rashi).*

וְהַשְׁאָר שֶׁל־תַּחְתּוֹן. — *and the remainder belongs to the lower one.*

Since the owner of the upper garden is ashamed to request permission to go through the lower garden in order to pick the vegetables growing too far out to reach, he relinquishes them to the owner of the lower garden *(Rav; Rashi).*

The halachah is in accordance with R' Shimon *(Rav, Tos. Yom Tov* from *Gem.* 119a).

סליק מסכת בבא מציעא